MORE PRAISE FOR
One Man Tango

"There are wonderful vignettes of Marlon Brando pretending to speak Chinese; Marilyn Monroe visiting the set of *Viva Zapata!* in Brownsville, Texas; Gary Cooper romancing star Barbara Stanwyck on location in Mexico; and Laurence Olivier booming onstage with Quinn in *Becket*."

—*Chicago Tribune*

"Quinn has ego, appetite, and opinions; you may not like him, but he won't bore you."

—*Cosmopolitan*

"Fascinating . . . There are many wonderful stories throughout the book."

—*San Antonio Express News*

"[A] frank autobiography . . . There is something very compelling about this giant of a man whose career is still going strong after sixty years in the business."

—*Ocala Star Banner*

"With poignancy and poetry, Quinn reveals the consequences—both good and bad—of life lived in the extreme."

—*Women's News*

"Quinn follows up his first book, *The Original Sin*, with this deeper, more contemplative memoir recalling his varied careers before and beyond acting. . . . The eighty-year-old Quinn's life reads like a picaresque novel, its rogue hero of cinematic invention."

—*Publishers Weekly*

BOOKS BY ANTHONY QUINN

The Original Sin
One Man Tango

One
Man
Tango

ANTHONY QUINN

with Daniel Paisner

HarperPaperbacks
A Division of HarperCollinsPublishers

![] **HarperPaperbacks**
A Division of HarperCollins*Publishers*
10 East 53rd Street, New York, N.Y. 10022-5299

This title is also available on cassette from HarperAudio.

A hardcover edition of this book was published in 1995 by HarperCollins*Publishers*.

HarperCollins®, ![]®, and HarperPaperbacks™ are trademarks of HarperCollins*Publishers* Inc.

ISBN: 0-06-109491-9

Cover photograph copyright © 1995 by Eric Kahan

First HarperPaperbacks printing: November 1996

Printed in the United States of America

Visit HarperPaperbacks on the World Wide Web at
http://www.harpercollins.com/paperbacks

❖ 10 9 8 7 6 5 4 3 2 1

To my children
Know your father, to know yourselves.

Am I not a man? And, is not a man stupid? I'm a man, so I married. Wife, children, house, everything . . . the full catastrophe!

MICHAEL CACOYANNIS,
Zorba the Greek (screenplay),
based on the novel by Nikos Kazantzakis

ONE

Ride

I AM SOARING LIKE AN EAGLE. I have taken wing—my arms outstretched, my body slicing in a fine swath through a breeze of my own making—and as I soar among the clouds I am exhilarated, bathed in a euphoria unlike any I have ever known.

But, alas, I am no eagle. I am an old man on a white bicycle, coasting downhill, with no thought of putting a bullet to my head.

The year and I have reached the October of our lives, and I am pulled back to earth by what I am doing. I am coasting, wondering why failure is known as the long, downhill ride. Surely, this is something else. Ask screaming kids on a roller coaster where the great thrill comes, and they will tell you it is here, just before the next climb. I fill my lungs with the autumn air, my heart with an overwhelming sense of well-being. God, if this is how failure feels, make it last forever.

In the distance I see the bare Lepine Hills. To my right stretch six hundred square miles of the verdant Pontine Valley. Beyond the green valley is a bright, silver streak: the Mediterranean, reflecting the morning sun. When I left the farm, at dawn, I had no idea the weather could turn in such magnificent ways. A heavy mist hugged the countryside, underneath a gray wind. I am now over-dressed for such a lovely morning: two sweatshirts, plastic shell, dark blue windbreaker, ballet "longies" under my workout pants, and a pair of black, perforated cycling shoes—these last my only concession to the uniform of Italian bicyclists.

It is a glorious day, and God is putting on a show for His doubting angels. His handiwork calls to me, and I must listen. This day, this ride, this moment . . . all have something to tell me. I strain to hear it. I do not expect a blinding light, or a guiding voice, but I am ready for . . . something. Anything.

Perhaps I am here to embrace the bare essentials. If that is all, then that is enough. If there is more to my life, then that is fine too.

I peel away my clothing, to keep cool. I am down to a single sweatshirt, and soon I will consider shedding it as well. The marker on the side of the road announces the thirty-seventh kilometer south of Rome, and I glide past, imagining I look like Prince Valiant on a white steed. Of course, I probably look foolish, out of my element, but this does not keep me from dreaming.

The free ride is over. I approach a long, gentle incline that leads to Velletri. I resume pedaling, shift into low gear. The hill is steeper than it looks, but it will not break me or my bicycle—a white Kline mountain bike, eighteen gears. The grinding of the gears is like punctuation. My breath quickens. I break into a sweat. A truck passes, trailing the acrid smell of the grape on its way to the local *cantine*. Sadly, it has become impractical here for the small landowners to make their own wine, and the smells from the truck suggest progress, commerce, haste. Behind the truck is a long line of cars, anxious to pass. Their drivers are restless, and the bleat of their horns keeps me far to the shoulder. The trucker puffs on his cigarette as he goes by, and I ape his indifference. The horns of impatience will not shake me from my peace, from this splendor.

But they do. As I reach the Appian Way, I wonder

whether such shared anger has to do with the road's history. The Appian Way was built for war. For centuries, armies have traveled this path through these hills: Caesar and Napoleon, Goths and Visi-Goths, popes and antipopes. Most recently, the road bore the hobnailed boots of the German army, trailed by the Brooklyn and Texas accents of American GIs on their way to distribute chocolates and cigarettes in Rome. Lately, the history of this storied path has been smothered by asphalt, while those who have passed before me have been rendered ghosts. I can hear them, still, but I worry if I may be alone in this.

As I ride, I think of war, and Hemingway. He is one of those ghosts, for me. His life was about war, and his memory lives on war's path. Why Hemingway? Here? Now? I am considering playing him on stage, and I have lately been consumed by the ways he lived, and died. A bullet to my own head is probably beyond me, but I cannot discount a gentler suicide. Who knows what tomorrow has waiting? With Hemingway, there was nothing left. Without his memories, and his imagination, he was lost. With me, it would be the same.

These hills echo with blood and despair, but also with memory and wonder. I want to remember it all, always. I want to invest this place with more poetry than it perhaps deserves. That is how I know it, how I have imagined it.

I pedal on, bent only on good thoughts, on everlasting contentment, but my spirits are assailed soon enough. I crest around a corner to discover a dead dog, resting in a shallow ditch, its blood still damping its fur. A white Alsatian, dead not more than a few beats. I avert my eyes, but a car buzzes close and forces me toward the animal.

I am working to avoid all thoughts of death, and here I am, pushed to remember . . .

Sinbad

OF ALL THE DOGS I have had in my life, Sinbad was the one I loved most dearly—a splendid white Alsatian, from too long ago.

We lived in the Pacific Palisades, and Sinbad and I prowled the shale hills along the California coast as if they were our own. As we walked, I would frequently see the German expatriates Thomas Mann and Lion Feuchtwanger huddled in conversation. I cannot think of World War II without thinking also of this scene, of these two displaced writers, my friends and neighbors. Few had listened to their impassioned warnings about Hitler, and we were paying dearly for our neglect.

Sinbad loved these hills with a fury. He would race the steep banks that led to the Coast Highway and wait for me below. The traffic was heavy as we dashed across the road to the beach. He would run ahead, and soon his compact white form mixed with the foam of the waves until I had to struggle to make him out. I swear that animal laughed with joy as he rode the waves to shore.

When the weather was unkind, we hiked the mesquite-covered Malibu hills, or toughed it out along the sand. On these afternoons, I saw Sinbad as a fierce hunter, as he saw himself. This was his trouble. He saw everything as a potential threat to my children, to my wife, to me. I spent a fortune on torn pants and medical bills. In the end, the dog's disposition cost me the dog himself. I was in Utah making *Warlock*, a Western with Henry Fonda and Richard Widmark, when my wife called in a panic. Sinbad had bitten a neighborhood boy, who now required ten stitches in his leg. The boy's parents notified the police, and Sinbad had to be caged, and muzzled.

But the dog was accustomed to the freedom of the sea, and the mountains, and there was no confining him. He dug his way out of the fenced area and disappeared—perhaps to Utah, to look for his friend and master. He returned, but he was never happy in his cage.

I had my own troubles on the set, distracted from the dog. The picture was being directed by Edward Dmytryk, one of the targets of Senator Joseph McCarthy's war on communism, who eventually "sang" on his blacklisted Hollywood Ten colleagues in order to return to work. I did not know what to make of this man, and I passed many long nights with Fonda and Widmark, worrying what kind of signal we were sending by working with him.

It was a confusing time. Everyone was cutting his own deals, doing what he had to do. There was no separating the way we lived from the way we worked. Dmytryk was actually a nice man, or at least I had known him to be a nice man, and when I sounded him out, I came away thinking he still might be one. He told me what I already knew: blackballed writers like Dalton Trumbo and Ring Lardner Jr. were getting work, under pseudonyms, but directors who refused to testify before the House Un-American Activities Committee were getting squeezed.

After all he had been through, Dmytryk could not see that he had any other course, and I could not see that our condemnation would accomplish anything except to pacify ourselves. He had suffered enough. Too many of our friends had suffered enough.

And so, we worked.

While I tried to focus on the picture, my first wife, Katherine, handled the dog. She never cared for Sinbad, but she thought it cruel to keep him penned up. It was against his very being. In this, she was right, but her solution was enraging. She placed him with some friends who owned a farm in Mulholland Hills—the actor Harry Morgan, and his family—where she thought Sinbad could run and hunt to his heart's content.

When I returned home some weeks later, I was furious, and heartbroken. To give away a man's dog was, to me, unthinkable, unforgivable. It was like coming home and finding she had given away one of my children. By this time, though, the dog was part of his new family. There was nothing to do except leave it alone, but the beach and the hills were not the same without Sinbad. I missed him as much as any friend I had ever lost.

Finally, after four months, I drove up to the farm to see him. Just one look, from a distance, was all I wanted. I parked about a half-mile from Harry Morgan's house and took a trail to a knoll where I could possibly catch a glimpse of the dog. I heard him barking through the bramble. My heart filled.

"Sinbad," I called, but in the clearing I saw that his hair was standing on end. His bark warned me away.

I pleaded with the dog to forgive me. I spoke softly, and he seemed to listen. Then I fell to my knees and cried, but my tears meant nothing to him. I had betrayed him. I was his enemy now, an intruder. He had a new family to protect. I had come and gone, and he had moved on.

Ride

I CYCLE ON.

For all my thoughts on death, the ride is about life. I will it to be so. I thank God for another October—a lovely month, a transitional month. I too am in transition. I am always in transition, but now, as I picture my last kilometers, I must weigh where I have been against where I am going. I pay homage to God and rejoice in His work, but I cannot think of myself as merely His toy, His plaything. Do not tell me the purpose of life is not life. Do not tell me we are here to ponder the mystery of creation. It happened and it shall happen, and all I am concerned about are the parentheses. They are all I can control, and to do that I must survive, move on. I want to last it out. I want many more Octobers, many more downhill rides. I want to hear the voices of my children, see the sated smile on the face of my woman. I want it all—the aches and fears, as well—because this is what it means to be alive.

Yes, to me, today, life is the visible. I am free to taste, to touch. The rhythm of life is in my legs, pumping up these hills, moving through space. The bicycle is an extension of myself and I am like a long-distance runner, gliding mechanically over my days.

The hills pitch steeper, and I shift into a still lower gear. I do not know why, but the effort reminds me of a years-ago comment from Laurence Olivier, made in an offhand way during rehearsals for *Becket*, the Jean Anouilh play we did together on Broadway. It was 1960, and Olivier was trying to articulate what separated his work from mine. He was given to this sort of posturing, but sometimes he had a point. "You American actors wait to catch the truth before you start running," he said to me one afternoon. "I prefer to run first and let the truth find me."

Precisely, I think, as I press on. I am running. Let the truth catch up to me.

TWO

Ride

THERE ARE A great many forces at work on me today. I do not recognize all of them. I do not even understand them. All I know is that I must respond to them, and remain open to what they have to tell me.

First, there is this. Yesterday afternoon, after lunch, a packing crate arrived from the United States. It was from Katherine, and I suspected its contents: the detritus of the life we had built and shared for nearly thirty years. I am not entirely sure why she has sent it to me, now, but I have some idea. She is suffering from Alzheimer's, and our children are helping to sort through her things and bring some order, perhaps even some closure, to her life. Who knows, maybe they think that by sifting through her past their mother can better understand her present. Maybe they have been told there must be a clean slate on which she might build new memories, new impressions. Or maybe Katherine is simply tired of all my things lying around after all these years—mementos, notes, pictures, diaries.

A covering letter to the package confirmed my hunch: inside, it was promised (threatened?), I would find a student essay I had written almost sixty years ago, an adolescent fantasy speculating on the life I would lead, the people I would meet, the choices I would make. It was a daunting prospect, to be made to look over my shoulder in this way. I remember what I wrote and know what I have lived. What I do not know is how to weigh the two alongside each other. I do not know that I want to. What happens to a man when he faces the heaven he has prayed for? What does it mean when he realizes his hopes have been fulfilled? All of us who go to church, to pray, to ensure our entrance into that exclusive country club, what do we do when we recognize that next state?

Probably we run. Probably we are afraid, and hopelessly lost. We enter a valley where there is no evidence of humanity and we are cowed by it. There is no sound, not even the shuffling of our own feet against the earth. Our steps leave no footprints. It is as if we have not been here at all.

God knows what is in store for me, if I read my adolescent musings. God knows what else I will discover when I sift through this box. God knows why it is really here, now. Perhaps it is here for some confluence of reasons I have not yet contemplated, but it does not really matter. What counts is that I must deal with it.

But I could not. Not yesterday. Not yet. I had a cloying fear that if I opened the box, I would lose a part of myself, a part I would never reclaim. I have never believed that if you close one door another one opens. What nonsense. If you close a door, you close a door. Here, though, I wanted to keep this door open, or at least ajar. But why? I was never truly happy with Katherine, and if she was ever truly happy with me, I cannot imagine it was for very long. I have been married to my second wife, Iolanda, since 1966. We have three grown children of our own. Like my long-lost Sinbad, I have a new family to protect, but unlike the dog, I will never loose the bonds with my other children. They are as much a part of me as I am of myself. Even with Katherine, there is an enduring connection. We are forever linked—through our children, through our history, through whatever the hell it is she has thrown into that cursed box.

brogue. His father came from Ireland to work for the
Union Pacific railroad, laying tracks from New York to
Los Angeles. The only people the railroad could get to
work under such back-breaking conditions were the
Chinese and the Irish. The men were separated from their
families for months at a time; the pay was dirt; the working conditions horrendous. Before long, the rails were in
my grandfather's blood. He was eventually killed in a
train accident when my father was still a boy, and my
father wound up in Chihuahua with my grandmother,
Sabina, and a reputation. The neighbors all knew about
the pension being doled out by the railroad, and everyone
speculated about the aristocratic Mexican widow and her
strapping teenage son who lived in one of the better bar-
rios up by the cathedral and went by the exotic Irish name
of Quinn.

The Mexican boys did not accept my father as one of
their own. He was a loner. He hung out on a corner with
the various gangs, not feeling a part of any one group.
One day, he spotted my mother on this corner and fell in
love. My mother had bad skin, from the smallpox, but in
every other aspect she was a beauty. She had a lovely figure, and beautiful hair. My father would watch her from
across the street and follow her every move. When the
other boys spoke of her in lascivious terms, he flashed
them a menacing look. He could not find the courage to
talk to her, but in his heart she was his.

The revolution emboldened my father to act. He was
off to join Villa's army in the morning, firm in his belief
that the man who planted the lettuce should be allowed to
eat the salad. He was prepared to battle the wealthy
landowners, to fight for his people, but he knew he might
never get another chance to speak to his Manuela. He
crossed the street to where she was walking, knocking on
doors, collecting laundry. He had something important to
ask her.

"I want you to be my soldadera," he said. He was asking a lot. To be his soldadera was to be his woman, to fight by his side, to cook for him, and tend to his wounds.

She looked at him as if he were crazy. "I don't even know you," she said.

"You know who I am," my father said.

"Yes, I know who you are," my mother said, "but that's not enough."

"Just think about it," he pleaded. "The train leaves tomorrow morning, six o'clock. We are headed south, to Durango. If you're not there, you're not there."

She looked back at him, not knowing what to say.

"You'll think about it, then?" my father persisted. "Tell me."

"I'll think about it."

And she did. All that night, she could not get this curious young man out of her head. He was tall, and handsome, and paper-thin. How dare he ask such a thing of her, she thought, although a part of her was glad that he had. The idea of fighting by his side, and pledging her life to his, had an intoxicating pull. The life she had here, washing other people's clothes, feeling as if she did not belong, was nothing. She could not sleep.

In the morning, she went to the station, still not sure if she was going to be with him or to see him off. She had packed a roll, but she could have gone either way. When she saw my father, pacing the crowded platform, towering above the others, laden with his gun and his blankets, looking hopefully from underneath his big sombrero for some sign of her, she finally knew what she would do.

The train to Durango was just leaving when he reached her, and he lifted her up onto one of the freight cars without saying a word.

Ride

IT IS FIVE-THIRTY IN THE MORNING. This time of year, the sun sleeps in. The ground is wet. The air is still, and moist, and cold. A thick mist greets me like a bad shower. The sky is just turning. On the horizon, bounding over the silent Mediterranean, I can just now make out the ignition of sunlight.

I am dressed for the moment, bundled against the chill. I grab my bike from its hook in the shed and set it down. I kick my leg over the seat and straddle the frame. Then I pause for a beat to take in the morning.

This is the way I begin most of my days, when I am here in Italy. I am alone, silent among my trees and my garden, while the rest of the world sleeps off another rotten round. Iolanda is asleep inside, oblivious to the turmoil inside me. My children are scattered around the globe, running from their own demons, chasing their own dreams. They cannot know what I am going through.

I can see my breath, and in it there is hope, and life. Anything seems possible. For a moment, I have forgotten the terrors of the night before, the unease surrounding the box from Katherine, the bullet that will not claim me, the crossroads that have sneaked up ahead . . . but in the next moment it all comes back to me.

I climb aboard the bike and start pedaling. I have no course in mind, no agenda. I only wish myself away from these uncertainties, to be free. It is an uphill ride, at first. Vigna S. Antonio, which leads from my house to the main road, is on a steep incline. Perhaps there is justice in this. The street has been named in my honor, and I have never been able to begin a journey without being reminded of my past, without working to overcome it. Even in a car, it is an effort to get up the road. Either the legacy gets to me, or the fight of the climb. Today, on my bicycle, it is both. My lowest gear is not low enough, and I stand as I ride, to gain strength. I used to be able to take this hill like it was nothing at all, but now it takes me.

When I finally reach the rise at the main road I am weary, and gasping. I have not gone anywhere and already I am out of breath.

Viva Villa

THE MEXICAN REVOLUTION was an odd war, fought in odd ways. My father saw romance in it. My mother saw food, and dying men, and my father. In Pancho Villa, they both saw a man who would stand up to the rich Federales.

The country was divided. Fathers fought sons. Brothers fought brothers. Everyone saw the revolution through his own circumstance, and Villa's suggested a class struggle. That is how I came to see it too, filtered through the eyes of my father. By 1913, when Villa allied with Emiliano Zapata in Mexico City, he spoke with the voice of the working man, and my father listened.

I believe one of the things my father was fighting for was an identity. My mother, too. In a way, they were also fighting for each other, and to be a part of something bigger than themselves. They later told me they were married by a priest they met on the freight car to Durango, before their first night together. My father, a "gringo" in the eyes of his compatriots, wanted to be accepted as a Mexican. My mother, caught between two cultures, simply wanted to invest in one or the other. She chose Villa's cause because for most of her life she had been shunned by the wealthy landowners whose blood she carried, because she believed it was where she belonged, and because it was where my father was.

My parents fought at each other's side. My mother cleaned my father's gun, mended his uniform, cooked his meals. She fired covering rounds for him, when that was what he needed. At night, she lay with him under his blankets, under the stars. The fighting followed the clock, in an almost cultured way. With daylight, Villa's men marched over the hill and started shooting. Then they broke for lunch. After lunch, they fought some more, until dinner. When the shooting stopped, the women searched the hills for their men, if they had not returned for their meal.

What stayed with my mother most about these battles was the smell of gunpowder mixing with the dried mesquite from her cooking, the call of the bugle to signal a cease-fire or the breaking of camp to take another hill, the screams of the women who had found their men dead or bloodied, and the persistent fear that my father would not return for his next meal.

One afternoon, some months into this routine, a sergeant and some soldiers rode down to a riverbank, where the women were washing clothes. The sergeant asked all the pregnant women to raise their hands. There were about a hundred women in camp, and a few dozen were clearly with child; several more were expecting in silence. My mother raised her hand, reluctantly. Just a few nights before, in Zacatecas, she felt the first stirrings of life in her belly, and she had not yet had the chance to tell her husband in a way he could understand. Even she could not understand it, at first. She wanted to tell Francisco, but she could not find the words. Now she knew that if she raised her hand she would be sent away from her husband, but she could not go against authority. Also, she knew that she could not conceal her condition forever.

The women pleaded for a chance to say goodbye to their men, but the sergeant forbade it. He did not want his

soldiers to have to worry about such a scene. It would interfere with their fighting, he said, spoil their concentration.
Many women did not acquiesce. Some had to be carried
to the train for Chihuahua, where they were given their
few belongings and about twenty pesos' worth of bilin-
biques, the scrip of Villa's army.

When Manuela returned home, her mother's house
was empty. No one knew where she had gone. A neighbor
took my mother in, and offered her some sewing and
washing to pay for her keep. She became an object of pity
to some, sympathy to others. Soon, many were bringing
her their clothes, to mend and to clean, and she busied
herself with her work.

For the first time, she thought of herself as Francisco's
woman. She belonged to him. In the fields of battle, there
had been no time to consider if she loved him, or if he
loved her. It had not been important. Now she had plenty
of time, and nothing was more important. She slept in a
hut, on a small mat on a hard earthen floor, waiting for
their first child to be born. She prayed for a boy. She did
not want her child to suffer the way she had suffered, the
way she was suffering still.

She cried at night, thinking about her husband, wondering who was taking care of him, if she would ever see
him again, if he would ever lay eyes on their baby.

Throughout her term, my mother tended to a geranium plant given to her by a local woman. Some of the
neighbors thought this woman a witch, but my mother
thought she was kind, and understanding. The woman
said that if the plant flowered white, her baby would be a
girl. If it was red, it would be a boy.

My mother watered the plant every day, waiting for
the geranium to blossom.

When the bud finally opened, it was red.

Remember the Eggs

CUT ME AND I BLEED images from a lifetime ago. My earliest memories are so deeply ingrained that I do not have to remember them to bring them to mind. They are there, always—below the surface and right on top.

My earliest memories are among my most vivid. There is a picture of myself at eight months, sitting on my mother's knee at the railroad station in Chihuahua, looking for my father. We were always looking for my father. It was what we did. I remember the business and confusion when the trains pulled in, the soldiers and families, the comings and goings, but there was no sign of my father.

There is the suffocating stench, still, of the coal car we rode to Juarez, to look for my father there. A soldier let us board the train and covered us with coal so we would not be discovered. Normally, the trip from Chihuahua to Juarez took hours, but we traveled for days as the train moved slowly north through enemy lines. It was a tiring journey, but my mother was a tireless woman. The only food she had to eat was an occasional bite of a tortilla, offered by the engineer, and she was barely able to make enough milk to feed me. We pulled into town tired, and hungry, and black as the coals we rode in on.

There is the taste of a hot breakfast—eggs—made for us by a benevolent stranger, who put us up on our first night in Juarez. My mother did not know a soul in town, and she was grateful for the kindness, but those eggs almost cost me my career. The woman called my mother over forty years later, looking for help. She remembered our name, and tracked my accomplishments. Her grandson, a boy named Levas, was one of twenty-one kids charged with first-degree murder in a famous Los Angeles gang killing. It was in all the papers. The Sleepy Lagoon case. I was under contract to 20th Century–Fox at the time, and my mother looked to me for help.

"Mama," I said, "what the hell do you want me to do?"

"The eggs, Tony," she said. "Remember the eggs."

I remembered the eggs, so I agreed to raise money for the boy's defense. This was no easy decision, but as my mother reminded me, there was no other decision to make. I got my friends involved. Orson Welles helped us out, and George Raft. I even asked Eleanor Roosevelt to look into the matter, and tried to hire a former judge named Brandt, whose brother was one of the heads of 20th Century–Fox, to represent the boy. I was accused of being a communist, and a knee-jerk Mexican, back when it was not a smart thing for any actor to be accused of the former, or for this particular actor to be accused of either. I might have been blackballed from motion pictures, were it not for the empathy of Darryl F. Zanuck. He called me into his office, and I told him about the eggs. He understood what I had to do.

Everything is connected to who I am now, to who I have been. If it is not the eggs, it is something else. There is the fetid canal that ran behind our one-room shack, the first home my mother and I shared after crossing the border from Juarez to El Paso. We stayed in El Paso because that was where all the men passed through, and we stayed in the shack because it was what we could afford.

We left word in Chihuahua and Juarez, should my father ever look for us there, but simply leaving word was not enough for my mother. She later told me she could not rest, not knowing where he was. There were many days when we doubled back to Juarez, to look for him ourselves. On each pass, my mother felt sure we would find him. We crossed the bridge between El Paso and Juarez so many times that the bridgekeepers came to recognize us. Sometimes, they would not accept the two-cent crossing fee.

Our home in El Paso was more a box than a shack:

four rickety walls, a dirt floor, and a tin roof. Mother cooked over a small stove, fashioned from cans. It was all I knew. It was wonderful.

The canal was just a few feet from our door, and it was fouled with animal carcasses and human waste. The smell filled our shack to where we got used to it. The neighbors had rigged a communal toilet on a rise just above the water: two posts, supporting a twenty-foot plank. Everyone did his business there, side by side, as if it was the most natural thing in the world. From the front it looked like a park bench, with men and women happily lost in thought or conversation, sharing the day's news, but from the back it must have made a funny scene. What is also funny is how a memory as benign as this has touched me through the years. Today, I will use only the bathroom in my own home. What I was forced to accept as a child, I was lucky to reject as an adult.

These early memories resonate in different ways, for different reasons. One of my happiest recollections is of what I now consider my first job. Everyone in the poor part of El Paso had little stoves they needed to keep lit, especially in winter, and when I was two or three I helped my mother collect faggots to sell to our neighbors. We found a place past the canal where the sticks were dry and plentiful. How important I felt, tromping through the woods with my mother, doing a man's work, my father's work. These were joyous afternoons, and much of the joy was in the assumption of my father's role.

Years later, after I had become well-known as an actor, this memory was colored by a clash of old-fashioned phrasing with contemporary slang. I was a guest on *The Tonight Show*, talking about my childhood, when one of Johnny Carson's producers picked up on the language I used in telling this story about the sticks before the show. Often, these backstage conversations would find their way into the program.

"And what was it you and your mother were doing out there in the woods?" Carson asked, straight, leading me to what he knew would be a big laugh.

"Picking up faggots," I said, and the audience roared. With me, it sometimes took a laugh track for a joke to register, and when this one finally did, I laughed like I was in on it. Underneath, though, I had not lost the wistful feelings of pride, and joy, and innocence that this memory still evoked. I pray I never do.

That this scene was later reduced to a cheap laugh on a television talk show could not change what it meant to me at the time, what it still means. I will always be that small child, taking the sticks home, rolling them into bundles, selling them door to door for a few pennies apiece. I will always know what it meant that my father was not there, what it meant to take responsibility, to take care of my mother as he would have, to fill the spaces where he might have been.

The First Picture Show

MY FATHER'S MOTHER brought an abrupt change to our daily rituals, and sent our lives on a wonderful turn. My mother might have seen it differently, but that is how I remember it.

Dona Sabina was a grand lady who did things on a grand scale. That she sought us out was grand enough. That she chose to remain was grander still. She was a proud, sophisticated woman, and she and my mother did not get along. There had always been a tension between them, a sparring for the affections of my father—and now, perhaps, I was caught in the middle. But it was more than a mere play for the two men in their lives, I came to realize. In her late thirties, my grandmother was truly a young woman, but in contrast to my mother, at nineteen, she was wise, experienced, and far less troubled with her place in this world. She was the adult in the relationship, my mother the child.

My grandmother arrived, unannounced, when I was two. She was looking for Francisco, and wondering if we had any word from him. She remained in our midst for the rest of her life, and she has never strayed from my thoughts. I loved her tremendously, and right away. She doted on me in ways my mother never could, and told me endless stories about my father. For the first time, I began to understand about him, and to feel connected to him, through her.

"There's still a war going on," she said to my mother, on her arrival. "I can provide for you and the baby, until it is over."

My mother was a very proud woman. "No," she said. "We'll be all right until Frank comes."

Dona Sabina knew that my mother would not take a handout, but that she could not turn out her husband's mother. She could have afforded a much nicer place of her own, but she recognized a way to contribute to our household expenses without shaming my mother. "Then I'll stay with you," she announced. "Until Frank comes."

And she did. We just had the one room with the dirt floor, but that was enough, and when I consider how my grandmother chose to live, for our sake, I cannot help but think of what she was giving up. She slept on a dirt floor, with no privacy. She wanted to be with her son's family, and this was what it cost.

My grandmother might have come from money, but that was all behind her. She needed to work to eat, just like the rest of us. She took a job at the delicatessen in town, and filled our house with magnificent food. She contributed in other ways, but the food is what I remember. Whatever would go bad at the end of the day, she would bring home for us. Some days, she took me to the store with her. In the winter, she would carry me. The delicatessen was on the other side of town, and I did not have proper shoes. She always said the walk would be too much for me, and that she did not mind.

I can remember one day as bright as yesterday. It was snowing. My grandmother carried me in her arms, wrapped within her shawl. It was cold, but in her arms I was warm, and comfortable. As we walked, she filled my head with stories of my father, from when he was a boy.

A black man approached us from the delicatessen. I had never seen a black man before. He was darker than the darkest Mexican. "Por que negro, Mama?" I asked my grandmother.

"His skin has too much sun," she answered.

The man greeted my grandmother by name. "He is such a big boy, Sabina," he said, pointing at me. "He is big enough to walk. What are you doing carrying such a big boy?"

"He's outgrown his baby shoes," my grandmother said. "His feet would freeze in the snow."

"Then he should have shoes," the man declared. "Come, let us buy him some shoes."

Dona Sabina was as proud as her daughter-in-law, and she was not about to take this good man's chiding. "I don't need your shoes," she yelled. "I can carry him fine." She marched down the street. She was angry, but she was not angry. Something in her tone suggested she and the man were friends, that they spoke this way all the time.

"Ah, Sabina," he called after her, in an afterthought. "There's a new Antonio Moreno picture playing at the theater. We open at four. Will you come?"

"I will try," my grandmother called back.

Antonio Moreno was the greatest Latin star in Hollywood at that time. My grandmother never missed one of his pictures. She knew the storylines by heart, and could spin them into marvelous bedtime tales. There was only one movie house in El Paso, and it was run by the man we had met on the street. She was one of his best customers, and they had become friends.

All that day, in the delicatessen, she spoke of the magic of moving pictures, of the great Antonio Moreno, of the adventures we would share at the movie house. I can still remember the warmth of the delicatessen, the wonderful smells of the pickles, pastrami, and sauerkraut, and the long wait for four o'clock.

I had never been to a movie house before, and my grandmother's excitement was contagious. She hurried through her chores, so she could leave work early. Her boss, Mr. Herman, knew what she was up to. He made me a breakfast of corned beef and Delaware punch, and a lunch of the same. It was my favorite. He was in love with my grandmother, but I forgave him that for the food.

At four o'clock, he told my grandmother she could go, then he pointed at me. "And don't forget to take this little animal with you," he said, playfully.

Dona Sabina did not return Mr. Herman's affections, but she was grateful for his generosity. She smiled, and bundled me back up for the cold. Then she ran with me in her arms up the street to the theater. We were the only two people there. The snow had kept everyone else away.

To call it a theater was probably generous. It was little more than a large meeting room, raked, with folding bridge chairs set out in rows, but when the lights dimmed and the grainy picture flashed up on the screen, I was transported, just as my grandmother said I would be. There were horses and trains and strong-looking men. There was wild, bustling energy. I could not follow the story, but my grandmother tried to explain it.

As I stared at the screen, the only sounds I heard were the whir of the projector and the rambling enthusiasm of my grandmother. "That could be you," she said, pointing to the screen. She whispered, even though there was no dialogue and no one to disturb. "Someday, you'll be bigger than Antonio Moreno. That's gonna be you. That's gonna be you. That's gonna be you."

I had no idea what she was talking about.

Hello, Elephant

AT THE CENTER OF MY childhood memories there is only one.

I was about two and a half years old. It had just rained. I was outside, alone, playing in a puddle with a cast-iron train. The streets were nearly empty, save for one horse and wagon. The bread man, on his daily rounds. He waved as he passed, and I waved back. Mostly, I was staring at the bread man's horse, fixed on the impressive power of his legs, the majesty of his stride. I used to love to watch the horses move—oh, the immense hump and rumble of their behinds!—and my eyes tailed the bread man down the street until the animal was gone from clear view.

Then a man took up the horse's place in my sight line. He also walked with a confident gait. He was tall, and handsome, and sure of himself. As with the horse, I could not take my eyes off him. He approached me, from the direction of the bread wagon. He seemed to be looking at me. I pretended to play with my cast-iron train, but when I looked up, his eyes were still on mine.

He kept walking. I was not afraid of the man, but there was something strange about him, something familiar. As he drew closer, I began to feel I knew him. I had never seen him before, not even in a photograph, but I knew him. It was a curious thing. He stopped just short of my puddle and looked down at me. He did not say anything.

"Hello, Papa," I finally said.

"Hello, Elephant," he said. He made a joke about how big I was, and asked that I take him to my mother.

We walked down the street, holding hands, and I led him along the canal to our small shack. He tousled my hair, and marveled again at how big I was. I was big, I thought, but not as big as him.

Word of my father's return spread faster than we could walk. My mother had spent so much time looking for my father, and talking about him, that the entire neighborhood puzzled things together: Frank Quinn had come home.

I led him to our door and we went inside. It was the happiest moment of my little life. No one said a word. Then my father took my mother in his arms and I melted away.

That night, my grandmother helped me to do a very brave thing. She knew I shared a blanket with my mother, but she knew that would have to change. "You and I will sleep by the stove tonight," she said to me, as night fell. "It will be warmer there."

And it was. From that night forward, my mother belonged to my father. My grandmother belonged to me. She became my mother. We huddled under our blanket by the stove and she pledged her devotion. There had been only three men in her life, she confided. First she loved my grandfather. Then she loved my father. And now she loved me.

I slept the sleep of an angel.

Ride

THE RIDE INFORMS ME, defines me, and puts everything into doubt. Like my life, it has a beginning, a middle, and a foreseeable end. I set off knowing what I have done, but not what I am doing. Yesterday, before I saw Katherine's box, what I was doing made sense. Tomorrow, it might make sense again. Today, I do not have a clue.

I slide along the main rode into Genzano, the first significant stretch of town south of my village. The town, for the most part, is still asleep. All of Italy is still asleep. About the only movements, other than my own, are the comings and goings of double-parked deliverymen, dispensing their warm newspapers and fresh milk. The day must be fueled before it can start.

I hop my bike onto the curb and dismount in front of the elegant pink home of my great friend, Dr. Vitorio Barbalishia. I do this without thinking about it. The house sits on a small piazza in the center of town. Were it not for the color, it could pass for a bank, or a library. Were it not for the man who lives inside, it might suggest a brothel. The man inside is someone special—one of the dearest people in my long life. Barbalishia has been my friend, and doctor, since I moved to Italy twenty-five years ago. We see things in the same way, from the same place. Every morning, we have our espresso together. Either he waits for me, or I wait for him. He is up early, to make the rounds of his patients at the hospital. I am up early just to get out of the house, to explore. Together, we are up to see what each other's day might bring, what the days before have left.

"Barbalischia," I call up to him. Sometimes I am ahead of our routine. "Coffee's on."

He waves through his window, to let me know he has heard me. He will be down soon. I walk to the bench in front of the cafe next door. It is the only establishment open on this small square, at this early hour. Usually there are tables set out, but this morning there is only the bench. No matter. I stand, and pace. It has not been a moment, but I am impatient. I am anxious to know what I will discover on this ride, what I will learn about myself, if there is anything left to learn. I want to get on with it. Perhaps Barbalishia's perspective will help me to realize my own, and to rein in my doubts before they run away from me.

"Antonio!" he says, bounding from his front step with his usual brio. "Buon giorno!" He greets me with a clap on the back, as if it has been twenty-four months, instead of twenty-four hours.

"Barbalishia," I say, and I turn his clap into a small embrace.

Barbalishia. I love to say this man's name, especially at six in the morning, over espresso and croissant. It helps to get my tongue in shape for the day's flapping. Barbalishia. A fine shave. There is no saying it lightly.

"Something's troubling you," he says, as we sit down. He does not ask. He just knows.

I tell him about the box, about Katherine, and Iolanda, and the tangle of uncertainties that are looking to derail me. I tell him everything that kept me up the night before, and some things I had not thought of until just now. I tell him what has gone from my marriage, from my work. I tell him I am off on a voyage of self-discovery.

"What are you afraid of?" he asks.

"Who said I was afraid?"

"You're not afraid?"

There is no bullshitting Barbalishia. "No," I admit. "I'm afraid. I'm afraid of everything."

"Ah," he says. "Good. Now we have a place to start." He laughs, and his laughter fills the empty streets like a rolling thunder. I join him, and together we sound like a storm. It is one of those shared fits of laughter that sneak up on you, and take control. I do not want to see it pass.

"It is good to laugh," I say, laughing still. I had been wondering if I would ever laugh again.

His laughing winds down. "Yes, but there are all kinds of laughter."

"Meaning?"

"Meaning there is the laugh of a man who is truly delighted, and the laugh of a man who is merely trying to distract himself."

"From what?"

"From pain, or conflict."

"Like a salve?" I wonder, and alongside my wondering I find room to consider why, with Barbalishia, I often place my thoughts in medical terms. I do not do this with anyone else.

"Salve, release, whatever. It is all the same."

"And my laughter, to you, sounds hollow?" I ask. It had felt genuine.

"Not at all," he says, "but what matters is how you feel underneath it."

The waiter arrives with our espresso and croissant, and I pause to reflect on this. The bench is wet, still, with morning dew, and the wetness reaches me through my many layers of clothing. Barbalishia does not seem to notice, or to mind. I rest the saucer on my lap and mix a sugar substitute into the cup. As I sip, the steam from the coffee reaches me cool, wet lips like a change of heart. Until now, it has not occurred to me to do anything but act on my emotions. Perhaps I should think about them, as well.

"So," my friend begs, coaxing me to the same conclusion, "how do you feel?"

"I feel like shit," I say, setting the cup down. "I feel like absolute shit." There, that's better.

He lets this hang between us and dissipate into the chill morning with the steam from our espresso. For a long time, he does not say anything. Finally, he says this: "Where are you going, all bundled up like that?"

"I don't know," I say. "Around. Perhaps I will loop down into Anzio, maybe stop there for lunch and look at the boats." This sounds to me like a plan, but then I realize that to loop down into Anzio I will have to ride through Nettuno, and I do not want to go to Nettuno. "Or maybe I'll ride down to Latina," I add, "or up the hills to Cori." It is better to have some options.

"Good for you," he says. "You'd think you were a young man, the way you ride around on that thing." He looks over at my bicycle, leaned against a small tree, sleeping off this morning's climb.

"You'd think," I concede. It is just something to say, but as I say it, I realize where my friend has taken me. "So that's it, then?" I ask. "That's what this is all about? Me, getting old?"

"You tell me."

That is a part of it, I allow, but my troubles run deeper. I tell this to Barbalishia. I tell him that I have been getting old since the day I was born, that perhaps what is really troubling me is the way I have invested Katherine's box with the power to validate my life, or to void everything I have ever done or believed in. It could go either way.

"But Tony, that's ridiculous," Barbalishia tells. "You know what's in the box. There are no surprises there."

"Perhaps."

"Perhaps nothing. I've known you too long. You don't forget things. If you kept a journal, you'd remember it. If you wrote something down in the margins of one of your books, you'd remember it. If you saved someone's photograph, you'd remember it. If you predicted what your life would be like when you were a kid, you'd remember that too. I don't care how long ago it was. These things are all a part of you already."

Again, we sip. The silences between us are not awkward, or confusing, and neither makes to fill it right away.

"Maybe that's the trouble," I finally say. "Maybe I remember all of it. Maybe I'd rather forget." I know this must be foreign to Barbalishia, a man who revels in his work and his family, a man who lives free of the monsters who regularly visit my thoughts. I do not expect him to understand. I do not want him to understand.

"You're impossible, my friend," he says.

"I'm impossible," I agree. I stand and slap the wetness from the seat of my pants, from the back of my shell. I am cold, and tired, and I still have a long way to go. I step to my bicycle and lift it from its place against the tree. Then I walk with it to my friend on the bench.

"Until tomorrow," Barbalishia says, still working on his espresso.

"Until tomorrow," I say, and as I hop my bicycle back down from the curb, I think that if I push myself I might make it to Velletri before the morning traffic.

THREE

Pickings

THE PAST SHADOWS ME as I ride. With every rotation of my tires I spin another memory, and soon I am caught in a delicate balancing act: if I pedal any faster, I might race over something important; if I slow down, my life might just pass me by.

There, in the rustling of falling leaves, I see a flash of my family, making to leave El Paso, to start a new life. When my father returned to us, in 1917, he was disillusioned in more ways than one. The revolution had come to stand for so many things, for so many people, that he no longer believed in Villa's cause with the same fire. For him, it had died out a year or so into the fight, and now he needed to find a new place for himself. Always, my father needed to feel a part of something, and without the revolution to define him, he was momentarily without tether.

His disillusionment was also literal: he was shot during one of his battles, and the wound almost cost him his sight in one eye. The eye turned slowly gray, and soon his vision was so blurry he needed to wear extremely thick lenses to correct it. Over time, his good eye began to suffer, from compensating, while the bad eye got worse. The adults among us spoke in hushed tones, wondering how long it would be before Frank Quinn was legally blind, while I tried to sift through these eavesdroppings and weigh what they told me against the man I knew.

Nine months after my father's homecoming, we were

joined by my sister, Stella. Our family was complete, but our household was ever-changing. Dona Sabina was still with us, along with an assortment of aunts and uncles and cousins—my grandmother's sister, and her children. It was a glaring contrast to what had once just been my mother and me. I did not mind the company, and my Uncle Glafiro was a kindhearted man, but I could have done without his cruel son. My cousin was a few years older, and he used to humiliate me by sitting on my face and breaking wind. Once, out by our stinking canal, he rubbed his own excrement in my face. If I was big enough, I would have killed him, and when I became big enough he knew to stay clear. If I was to be Papa's Elephant, this was an indignity I could never forget.

I was thrilled with my baby sister. Poor Stella was a sickly infant. Virtually every childhood malady found its way to her in her first few years, and much of that period moved to her needs. I belonged to my grandmother now, and my mother belonged to my father, but Stella belonged to all of us, and we doted on her. Most afternoons, the shack was quiet, while the baby got her rest. In the evenings, we did our visiting outside, so as not to disturb her. At mealtime, we worried whether Stella had enough to eat. And at night, we dreamed great things for her.

Stella was our hope. There was a line from *A Streetcar Named Desire* that would echo throughout my career, but its specter was relevant to my childhood as well: Stella for star. In a thousand performances as Stanley Kowalski, on the road and on Broadway, I could not hear the line without thinking of my baby sister. Stella was our star, the light of our lives, the emblem of our future.

The real hardship of these first years was finding work. Once found, it was not easy to keep. My father was prepared to do anything, despite his failing eyesight. He was a strong man, and a conscientious worker. When there was no steady work, he took what he could find. When there was no work to be had, he despaired until his luck turned. Somehow, it always did.

One of his most lucrative jobs was with the railroad. The trains had been in his father's blood, and he saw no reason they should not also run through his. Besides, the money was good. My mother often worked at his side, just as she had fought there. She held down the stakes for him to drive into the ground. They worked this way for weeks, for the extra wages and for each other's company. We lived in a boxcar at the base camp, and each day my parents traveled to the end of the line to lay new tracks, while Dona Sabina stayed behind to look after the children. Before long, after laying so much rail, we had to move our boxcar farther down the line, to cut down on the commuting.

This arrangement came to an abrupt end. Late one afternoon, my mother was too tired to return to work after her siesta. She could not lift her arms. My father and uncle tried to cover for her, and collect her full day's wages. They were not out to cheat the railroad, but to keep the railroad from cheating them. Papa figured a way to hold the spike in the pincers with one hand, and swing the hammer with the other. It was difficult, but not impossible. He alternated swings with Uncle Glafiro, and after about an hour they had developed a nice rhythm, and a nice pace. My mother looked on and thought they might finish the day without any drop in production. Then my father's hand slipped and Glafiro could not stop the momentum of his swing. The hammer drove the stake through Papa's hand.

It was horrible. Luckily, my mother was there to wrap the wound with the hem of her dress, but it was not enough to stanch the blood. She made a tourniquet above my father's elbow, and carried him with Glafiro to the handcart. Next, they backtracked home and began an all-night vigil, soaking the hand in hot water and salt. Papa's fever shot dangerously high. Around midnight, his hand turned blue. My grandmother was worried about gangrene, and urged my mother to summon help. Just then, they heard a whistle, and my mother raced outside to flag the passing train. She stood on the tracks and waved her arms frantically. The train was not scheduled to stop, but my mother hoped the engineer would see her before running over her.

It took three men to help Glafiro lift my father onto the train. Papa was delirious from the fever, and unable to help himself. The engineer advised my mother to stay behind, and promised to get him to a good doctor. We all stood and watched the train disappear into the distance, my mother wondering if she had done the right thing by not accompanying her husband. My grandmother assured her she had no choice—after all, the engineer had said she would only be in the way—and there was nothing to do but wait for word. Anyway, her children needed her. Who knew where the train was headed, or how long my father would be away?

Three days later, we received the standard communication available to itinerant families along the line—a note, tied to a piece of coal and thrown from a passing train. Papa was fine, and resting in a hospital. The news was welcome, but incomplete. The note was not signed, and there was still no way to reach my father directly, but at least we knew he was okay.

We had become accustomed to waiting for my father, and now we waited for him again. This time the waiting was tempered by the certain knowledge that he would be home soon, and in one piece. When he returned a few weeks later, he naturally sought less hazardous work. The railroad would not take him back so soon after the accident. One day he went out to look for a job and came home all excited. They were sending men and women to San Jose, in northern California, to work in the fields. He reported the news as if it would change our lives. No one had ever heard of San Jose, but California sounded heavenly.

"Come on, Nellie," Papa said to my mother, trying to win support for his idea, "anything's better than this stinking canal."

He enlisted Glafiro and his family in his enthusiasm, and soon we were all headed north, in a cattle car filled with Mexicans, traveling for a time over the very tracks my family had labored into place, as if we had to work our own way out of town.

The journey took about four or five days, over mountains and deserts, in all kinds of weather, most of it bitter cold. The wind kicked through the slats in the siding as if there were no barrier at all. The only warmth we had was from too many bodies crammed into too small a place, but this was a mixed blessing. We were pressed so tightly together, there was barely any room to lie down. There were other cars on the train, but these were for paying passengers, and horses, and merchandise. It was so crowded in our car that some people could not make it to the doors to throw up, or go to the bathroom, and it was not long before the train was smelling far worse than the canal we had left behind. We staked out a spot in the corner and kept to ourselves. I spent the trip huddled with Stella, trying to keep warm.

When we stepped off the train in San Jose, we were pelted with rocks. At first, we could not see where they were coming from, but then we saw the men charging the station from over the hill. They were mostly Mexicans, just like us, and they called us scabs and strike-breakers. It was an ugly, ugly scene. These men were out to scare us, and to hurt us. I was just a child and could not understand it. All I knew were fists and tempers, stones and confusion. All I knew was the fear my family felt.

It was an ambush. The strikers all knew we were

coming, but we had no idea what was waiting for us. We had been shipped in to break a labor strike, and my father and the other men were outraged at the duplicity of the landowners. It was one thing to bring in outside workers at cheaper wages; it was another to cast them into a labor dispute without their knowledge, to place their families in danger. I could see the loathing on my father's face as he realized what had happened.

Most of us were able to scramble back into the cattle car for cover. My father was one of the men from El Paso who went out to speak to a delegation of the striking workers. These men had been picking walnuts for twenty cents a bag, while my father and the other men on the train had been promised only ten cents. It was no wonder they were angry. Soon, the two groups redirected their anger at the plantation owners. They reached an agreement. The men on the train would not press for the higher wage, but they would not sign on until after the twenty-cent pickers returned to work. In this way, the old workers would not be displaced, and the new workers would not be turned away. To Papa, ten cents a bag was better than nothing at all. Besides, we had come all this way, and with his family working with him, he figured to outearn everyone else by the end of the day, even at the lower rate.

We lived in a small hut on a knoll about a mile from the grove, and the secret was to reach the shade of the trees before the sun was too high. God, it was hot, but under the trees it was tolerable. I scrambled to keep pace with my father on the long walks to work each morning, trying to beat the sun. His strides were tremendous next to mine, but he did not slow to accommodate me. Either I kept up or fell back.

In the walnut grove, each man worked an area of ten or twenty trees, and it was my father's job to shake the nuts from our trees with a long hook. It was a tricky business. He had to drive the hook into the limb of the tree and shake with everything he had, or the nuts would not fall. When they did, we took cover, and then quickly collected the droppings. It was my job to separate the nuts from their peels and bag them. My hands were browned by the juice and blistered by the tugging. It was awful work, but I loved this time with my father. I was only five years old, but I imagined myself a young man, sharing the burdens of our family. I fashioned myself in his image and hoped he would notice. My mother and grandmother helped, when they were finished with the cleaning, and with Stella, but these long days were remarkable for the ways they let me see my father, and for the ways I let him see me.

My father liked the work, and the lifestyle, and soon he had us following the seasons. We moved from one plantation to the next, wherever there was work and a place to stay. In this, my father was nearly alone. Most migrant workers worked the same crop, one season to the next, but he had us moving everywhere, picking everything: tomatoes, nuts, lettuce. We picked grapes in the north, between Oxnard and the Napa Valley, and lemons and oranges in the citrus groves of Southern California.

After a while, we developed our preferences. A day in the cotton fields was the worst. We had to pull the flowers from the ground and rake them with our hands; whatever was left in our hands we put into the sack. We wore no gloves, and I was torn and bloodied by the drill. String beans were less painful, but just as bad. We stood behind a huge threshing machine, picking the beans with one hand and shielding our faces from the dirt and debris with the other.

The most pleasant jobs were among the fruit trees, out of the sun. We picked peaches, apricots, apples, pears, quinces. These jobs were harder to come by, but my father somehow managed to land us in the better fields before the positions were all taken. He made friends wherever we went, and people told him things. The plantation owners liked him because he looked whiter than most Mexicans, and because he spoke English. The other pickers liked him because he was a hard worker, and a great storyteller, and because his English helped them to stay one step ahead of everyone else.

It was a marvelous, rambling existence. Like gypsies, we vagabonded from one home to the next, but one stop was much like another. We carried our home on our backs and in our routine. I will never lose the feeling of waking before the sun, and tromping down to the fields with my father, of wanting to please him, and to help him provide for our family. It was a magical thing. It did not matter where we were, or what we were picking. What mattered was that we had a job to do, together, and that he needed me. What mattered was that we were finally making a life out of no life at all.

Black Panther

SOME TIME DURING OUR glorious vagabonding, my father decided that the life of a migrant worker was no way to raise a family, and we eventually moved to a small house on Daly Street, by the railroad yards in East Los Angeles.

It was less a house than a grander version of our old shack. Only the scenery had changed, and even this was obscured. To me, it was a palace, although in truth it was something less. Papa hated to look out on the rail yards and painted over our windows with the pastoral images from his childhood, or a Pacific Ocean scene, or a castled medieval horizon, but there was no avoiding the reality on either side of the panes. Instead of the rank canal we had the thunder of the trains. Instead of the mad scramble of El Paso we had the roar of Los Angeles. Instead of one small room we had one medium-sized room and a small kitchen. Until there was money for furniture, we slept on the floor and took our meals around a huge packing crate at the center of the room. The only running water was the creek behind our house.

My father found work at the Lincoln Park Zoo, feeding the animals for twenty-four dollars per week. It was not a lot of money, even then. Every morning, he hopped one of the trains outside our door and rode it the eight or ten miles to the zoo. He could not afford the fare, but it was too far to walk. The only difference between my father and the other well-dressed commuters on the train was that they were sitting comfortably inside, while he was standing uncomfortably outside, trying not to slip between the cars.

Most weekends, I hopped the same train, to help tend the animals. I was eight years old, and I loved the big cats. There was one panther, an elegant female with a shiny black coat, who had a strange pull over me. She was my first love. None of the keepers could tame this beast, but with me she was docile and calm. There was a connection between us. I used to dream about her. In the beginning, Papa warned me not to get too close, but I reached into her cage and stroked her fur. I was afraid, but drawn by the danger. She was soft and powerful, and her purring was like music from a deep, mysterious place.

I was mesmerized by this animal. I brought her food, and she took it hungrily. Soon, she would not take meat from anyone else. She sat still when I stroked her fur.

The attachment almost cost my father his job, and his life. Some months into this routine, I was taken to the county hospital for a tonsillectomy. It was an assembly-line operation, and what we could afford. I watched the boy in front of me take his turn under the ether, and the knife, and I knew what was in store. I tried to be brave. I hoped that at least they would change the bloody sheets before setting me down on the operating table.

When the anesthetic wore off, I was in a dormitory-style room with a dozen other boys. My father was sitting beside my bed. I had never known him to miss a day of work, but he wanted to be there when I woke up.

"How is my Elephant?" he said.

It hurt to talk so I just smiled.

I slipped in and out of sleep. He sat with me all day, and when visiting hours were over he refused to leave. When the nurses threatened to call a security officer, he wrapped me in a blanket, scooped me in his arms, and carried me down the fire escape. A doctor shouted from the window for him to bring me back, and warned that there might be problems from the anesthesia, but my father kept walking, all the way home. It was the only time he ever held me.

The next day, he returned from work early. Again, this was not like him, but he had something important to tell me. "Your friend, the cat, she's not eating," he said. "It's been over a week now."

The day after that, he was home early again, with the same story.

"Let me go with you, Papa," I pleaded. "She will eat for me."

He laughed. "Your mother is still mad at me for stealing you from the hospital," he said. "You hurry up and get well and then we will see about the cat."

I did not sleep that night. I was thinking about my poor friend. Had she thought I abandoned her? Did she worry about me, the way I worried about her? Was she grieving? Or angry? Or simply not hungry?

My father worried too. He tried to feed the panther again the next morning. It had been almost ten days since she had eaten. He talked to her gently, told her I was home sick, that I would be back soon, that she had to eat.

She seemed to listen, and understand. Finally, he thought he had won her confidence. He reached his hand into the cage, and she attacked. She nearly tore his arm off, and it was two weeks before we knew he would recover. He lay in the hospital all that time, not knowing if he would lose his arm, or if we would lose him. Once again, my mother and grandmother worried if my father would ever return.

I went to the zoo before I went to the hospital. The panther told me she was sorry for what she had done. Her growls were like low moans, asking for forgiveness. I fed her the thickest slab of meat I could find. I promised never to leave her again.

When I went to the hospital, I told my father where I had been. "I've been disloyal, Papa," I said. "I've been to see the cat."

He smiled. He was weak, from the loss of blood, and the medication. The look on his face told me I had done the right thing—in the telling and the going, both. "Good," he managed. "I'm glad."

"You're not angry?"

"Why should I be angry?" he said. "I would do the same. The cat loves you."

"But she almost killed you, Papa."

"She was right to attack me."

"No, Papa, it was an accident."

"It was no accident, Tony. Your panther is a woman. She belongs to you. I had no call to interfere with someone else's woman. That is the kind of woman I hope you find someday, one who will pledge herself to you no matter what. When you are ready, look for a woman like that cat."

To my father, my love for the panther, and hers for me, were like confirmations. He was a fiercely loyal man, and he saw in this devotion a purity he could not always bring to his own life. I could not recognize this, as a boy, but I came to understand it in time.

"Go to her," he said. "She needs you. I am fine here. The nurses will take care of me. Your friend, she has no one but you." In truth, he was not fine. He had lost a dreadful amount of blood, and was suffering from a related infection, but he was insistent. "Go to her," he said again.

And I did.

Through the Lens, Darkly

AS A BOY, I was charmed by the chance happenings of my father's life. I remain so. The circumstances that took my grandfather from Ireland to Mexico, to my grandmother, that pulled my father across the streets of Chihuahua to my mother, and from Villa's army to the canals of El Paso, were all factors in my own equation. They were what made me, as I was still taking shape.

I consider this now, as I consider the stuff of my life, and realize that my father's splendid struggle has touched me in a profound way. I do not mean this as a cliche, but as a learned truth. The way he lived and worked continues to move me. What he did, I would do, always. At least I would try.

Providence even took my father to the motion picture industry. Through his work at the zoo, he was introduced to a man named Selig, who specialized in animal pictures and supplied most of the exotic creatures to the fledgling movie studios in Hollywood. When a producer needed a giraffe or a camel for the next Rudolph Valentino picture, or a horse for Tom Mix, he looked to Selig, and to save money he often shot the required footage on Selig's property.

It was a neat arrangement, and Selig knew a good thing when he stepped in it. Soon, he set up a studio of his own, with an in-house menagerie, and for a time in the early

1920s ran one of the more successful operations in town. There was always something doing on the Selig lot.

In those days, it did not take much to get a movie studio going. Warner Bros. was just a couple of rickety buildings. Columbia was a few shacks on Gower Street. Charlie Chaplin ran his tiny operation out of an old warehouse. Until the development of sound technology, most of the pictures were filmed outdoors. There were very few lights or interior shots, and the studios themselves were used principally as offices for the writers and producers, so the start-up and overhead costs were not as significant as they would become.

Selig put my father to work as a grip, and eventually as a cameraman. Papa could not see, but he could work a camera. The irony was never mentioned in our house. Mostly, he just cranked the camera after someone else had set up the shot, but he had an instinct with the animals, which no doubt saved an enormous amount of film. If you could not get the animals to do what you wanted, you were likely to run over budget.

The job nearly led to my first acting role. Two trained grizzlies were to do a scene with a cub, but no one could find a trained cub in time for the shoot. To solve this dilemma, Selig created another. He decided he would dress a child in a bearskin to play the part of the cub, but then he could not find a parent willing to submit his child to such dangerous work. Finally, my father said he had a son who would not be afraid, and I was given the part.

That night, I put on the costume and rehearsed for my debut. I had never been more excited. The women worried about putting me at the mercy of two bears, but we men insisted I would be fine. My grandmother and I had been to the movies almost every week since El Paso, and the idea of seeing myself on the big screen was thrilling. I was eager to make a good showing. I practiced putting my shoulder to the ground and rolling over slowly, the way I had seen the cubs somersault at the zoo. I went to sleep on the floor by the stove, still wearing my bear suit, and dreamed of stardom.

In the morning, I woke in a sweat and a puddle of urine. I could not eat any breakfast. My mother sensed something was wrong and felt my forehead. I was burning up. Papa thought I was probably just afraid of the grizzlies, and made his disappointment known. I could not let his doubts stand. Me? Afraid? I pleaded with him to take me to the studio so I could show him the truth.

But my mother and grandmother would not let him take me. I promised them all I would be fine, that it was just a nothing virus, that I would rest tomorrow, but they were firm. Even Dona Sabina, the source of my fascination with pictures, would not bend to my pleading. Papa finally gave in to their concerns, and enlisted Glafiro's boy—the same rotten cousin who had shit all over me!—to take my place.

I was furious, and cried all morning. My only consolations were in knowing that my cousin would have to spend the entire day walking around in a bear suit drenched with my piss, and that my time would come, again.

Papa worked with some of the great two-legged stars of the day. Valentino adored him. Antonio Moreno, my grandmother's favorite, and Douglas Fairbanks both became friends. People were drawn to him, for reasons he could never understand. After all, who was he? A caretaker of animals? A cameraman? He was nothing, except as a man, and in this he was exceptional. He was unselfish and charming and gregarious. He was strong, with few soft spots. And he had magnificent stories to tell—about the revolution, about laying tracks, about picking fruit with his young family. He made wonderful friends, wherever he went, no matter his station, or theirs. He still hopped the train to go to work, but he could visit as equals with the men who paid their way. Intellectuals or laborers, artists or hacks, it did not matter. My father had something for everyone, and he took something from each in return.

One of Papa's great regrets, I think, was the way we lived. He was embarrassed to bring his friends to our dingy little house. Dona Sabina kept a wonderful garden out front, and there were beautiful flowers in the sills and beds, but there was no masking the poverty of the place. It was at this point, through my father's shame, that I finally recognized how poor we were. I was embarrassed for him, but not for myself. Papa had managed to add on a small bedroom, for him and my mother, but really it was more of a lean-to than a room. My grandmother still slept on an old army cot with Stella in the one main room, while I slept on the floor. We still had a packing crate for a table, and a two-seater outhouse by the creek in the backyard.

It was no place for Douglas Fairbanks, and I could not pretend otherwise. Neither could my father. One of his great ambitions was to provide indoor plumbing for his family. He did not have the money for a professional job, but he was handy, and he had friends who were willing to help. When he could afford the supplies, he began to rough in a small bathroom in the evenings. He put me to work as his helper, and after a few weeks we had a working toilet. What a moment it was when we were finished! Now, at last, we would live like Americans. Now Papa could bring his friends inside to go to the bathroom. We all stood around the toilet, pulling the chain, marveling at our good fortune. I must have flushed that thing a dozen times before I truly had to.

But, of course, even a working toilet could not cover for us. Papa's friends rarely came around, and they never stayed long, and I often wondered why. As an adult, I thought it might have had to do with the fact that my mother and grandmother spoke no English. Spanish was the language of our household, and in our part of Los Angeles it was also the language of indigence. My father spoke English beautifully—I heard him myself, sounding like all the other men, when I visited the studio—and I spoke it at school, but when we sat to dinner around our packing crate, we might as well have been in Juarez. Perhaps my father worried we would in some way disgrace him, by appearing too Mexican. Or perhaps he was just a private man who saw no reason to mix his friends with his family.

At the studio, though, he carried himself with dignity and standing. He belonged. I cherished the sight of him there, in the middle of all that enterprise and excitement, in a position of such importance. Every weekend, I would go to him. They were sometimes shooting on Saturdays, but on Sundays we had the place to ourselves. We were alone with the animals, and in these stolen moments I saw myself in my father, and him in me. He was a giant to my young eyes, and he moved about the place with a self-assurance I could only fashion in my dreams.

To him, I was like a piece of clay, to shape in his own image, and in each moment there was an opportunity for remaking. Even on Saturdays, when the lot was busy with a Western and a jungle picture, both at once, Papa would flit between the two sets with a purpose I believed was meant for me.

I used to sit off to the side and sketch the scene on a small pad. I do not recall when I had taken to drawing, or why, but I remember my father's encouragement. To create, to him, was a wonderful thing, even though my sketches were an occasional source of shame. Some of the actors would look over my shoulder and offer their loose change for the pictures. My father saw this as a handout, but I never saw it that way. Usually, the actors only tossed me a dime or a quarter, but sometimes it was more. Once, I did a drawing of Douglas Fairbanks while he was making

The Black Pirate, and the great man gave me twenty-five dollars for it.

"God," my father said, when I told him of the exchange, "you make more money than I do."

I did not think to place his reaction in competitive terms, but it must have rankled. Here he was, a man who was raised under the wary eyes of his neighbors, who had fought desperately in the revolution, who had never avoided an honest day's labor, who had struggled to feed and protect his young family, who was probably going blind, and his ten-year-old son was able to eclipse him with a pad and a pencil and few flicks of his tiny wrist.

I stopped drawing soon after.

Uncle Cleofus

AS EVER, OUR HOUSE OVERFLOWED with relatives whose luck was worse than ours. Glafiro and his family were with us, off and on, for much of our time on Daly Street (I still vowed revenge on his asshole son!), and we were sometimes joined by friends my father had made during the revolution, or in one of the migrant camps, or by one distant cousin or another. We had little, but what we had we shared.

Probably our most memorable visitor was Uncle Cleofus, my grandmother's brother. He stormed into our midst and turned the small house upside down. I do not think we ever laughed as much as when Cleofus was around. He was the funniest, most contented man, and at night he slept in such oblivious bliss that he filled the room with his snoring. Oh, what wonderful noises he made! I used to lie awake on the floor beside him, wondering if I would ever make the same noises, from the same place, if I would ever be so at peace with myself, or my surroundings.

Uncle Cleofus had a way with women. Or so he said. In the evenings, he tried to pass his ways to me. He had an unusual strut to his walk, and he claimed women found it irresistible. I could not see the appeal, but he soon had me thinking that the way I walked was key. Never mind that I could not talk to a girl without stammering, or that I was too big for my age or my own good. If I could copy his walk, he said, everything else would follow. So I copied his walk. He paraded me up and down, and back and forth, reminding me to hold myself straight. There was a bounce in his walk, and a subtle tap of his foot, and I tried to mimic this as well but I could never carry it off. When he did it, he looked regal. Me, I looked like a prancing dolt.

He coached me for a week, and when he finally pronounced me ready, I went off to school to try myself out. I was a terrible failure. The boys all laughed at me, and the girls looked away. I could have crawled into a hole and died, but Cleofus was undaunted and had me practice some more. "You have no style, Antonio!" he would shout, as he tutored me in our front yard. "Style, nephew. That's what these girls want from a young man."

Cleofus himself never lacked in style, but he had no money to put behind it. What he lacked in funds, he made up for with fair doses of chutzpah and folly. His famous adventure with our family surrounded one of his typical get-rich schemes. One night, over dinner, he laid out for my father his latest invention. "Francisco," he said, "do you realize how much a banana costs in New York?" Somehow, on his shoestring, Cleofus had been a world traveler, and he delighted in telling tales of his faraway jaunts.

"No," my father said. "Tell me."

"Twenty cents."

Twenty cents! We could not believe it. In Los Angeles, you could buy a dozen bananas for a dime. My father told him it was outrageous.

"Exactly," Cleofus agreed. "But that is what it costs and that is what people will pay. It is too expensive to ship them to New York before they rot." Then he let us in on his big discovery. "I have invented a vacuum technique to deliver fresh bananas anywhere in the world," he announced. "It is much more efficient than those refrigerated freight cars." He calculated that his invention would yield a profit of two dollars for every dozen bananas. We all did the math and grew rich in our heads.

All Cleofus needed was a place to work for a few weeks, and some start-up money. My father offered the use of our shed and fifty dollars—the extent of our storage space and our savings. For this, he was made a full partner in my uncle's venture.

Over the next weeks, Cleofus turned our shed into a junk-heap laboratory. He shut himself in and went to work. He would not let any of us see what he was doing. Even my father was forbidden. Soon, Cleofus started eating and sleeping out in the shed, either for inspiration or to keep us from sneaking a look, and on quiet nights I could hear his snores through our window.

When he was finished, he had built the most terrific contraption—a huge oil drum, with tubes and valves and gauges. We all gathered in the shed to see the thing put to the test. It was a Sunday morning. The whole neighborhood, it seemed, had heard of Cleofus's doings, and soon our yard was filled with people wanting to see what he had wrought.

My uncle loved a crowd, and played the moment grandly. He opened a hatch to the main cylinder of his contraption. It creaked loudly. Inside was a large, cast-iron box that looked as if it was built from an old stove.

Cleofus reached for the handle on the box and made to open it. "Stand back," he warned. "There's compressed air in here. I don't know what will happen."

We all stood back, expecting a big explosion.

Then he opened the box and there was nothing. No explosion. No sound. There was only the overwhelming stench of the single rotten banana Uncle Cleofus had been preserving inside. My God, the smells that came out of that thing!

Cleofus was thrown, but not discouraged. My father was furious. The neighbors did not know whether to laugh or to run from the shed to escape the smell. "This is nothing, Frank," Cleofus assured. "This was just an experiment. I think I know what went wrong."

Papa refused to invest another penny, or to let my uncle stay on in the shed. I learned how to keep a grudge from my father. He was never a man to forgive a transgression, and here he could not excuse the foolishness of this moment—Cleofus's, or his own.

The next morning, my uncle woke with the sun and walked down to the railroad tracks. Despite his joy and animation, he could not face my father another day. It would have been deflating, to such a spirit.

At the train yard, waiting to see him off, was a crowd of seventy or eighty people. For all his bluster, Uncle Cleofus was a beloved character. In his short time with us, he managed to touch all these people with his heart, and his laughter, and his dreams. (I would meet such a spirit again, in the pages of a Nikos Kazantzakis novel about a fiery Greek soul named Zorba.) Cleofus really was quite a colorful man, as his jubilant leave-taking suggested. It was six o'clock in the morning, and the entire neighborhood had turned out to wish him well. What should have been an everlasting degradation was for this man a moment of triumph. He shook hands with everyone, and thanked them for coming.

The train started to pull out of the yards and Cleofus raced for an open boxcar. He carried a knapsack, and he slipped and fell when he tried to climb aboard. The crowd was with him and cheered him on. On his second pass, he managed to hoist himself up on the ladder. When he was safely inside, he leaned back out for a final wave. The people clapped, and continued clapping, until the train finally disappeared around the bend.

It was the most beautiful exit I have ever seen a man make.

The Tarantella

THERE IS A WEATHERED OLD CAR parked at the edge of Genzano, about a kilometer from Barbalishia's. It might have been here a half-century, from the looks of it, but I know better. It was green once, probably, but its coat has been beaten and faded to a dim brown, its rusted-through shell only vaguely reminiscent of what it once was. It is a wonder the thing is still running, but it was not here yesterday. If it is no longer running, it has just recently run.

The heap reminds me of the first car we ever owned: a black Ford Model T. Of course, the two vehicles are nothing alike, but these days every old jalopy reminds me of the first car we ever owned. For this, I am grateful. The car was my father's first extravagance, purchased from one of the other hands at the studio for next to nothing. He had just gotten a small raise and was tired of riding the rails to work. He pulled up to our house one evening and astonished us with his purchase. We all heard the loud motor and raced outside to see what was happening.

This—a new car!—was the last thing anyone expected. No one even knew Papa could drive a car, or that he was considering buying one. There was a lot we never knew about my father.

My mother called the car the "tarantella," and refused to go near it. Mostly, she was terrified of my father's ability to operate it. The car, at rest, was a fascination to her, a joyous symbol of her family's place in this strange, new world, but the thought of it moving, with my father behind the wheel and her seated next to him, was anathema. She would no sooner let her husband drive her in an automobile than she would let him take her up in the air in a plane.

Papa tapped me to accompany him on his maiden voyage. He knew I was not afraid of anything—certainly not this. "The Elephant will be the first to ride," he said. Then he looked to my disappointed sister, and promised to come back for her later. Always, with my father, his son came first, and I cannot say I ever minded.

We made for the Lincoln Park hills, and as we drove, the wind slapped me silly with excitement. It was a crisp, autumn afternoon, and I was on top of the world. I had felt the same rush of air when leaning from an open train car, but it was nothing next to knowing that the wind was meant for me. I held my face to the breeze and closed my eyes, and in the blackness imagined I was flying.

"Someday," my father shouted over the motor, "when you are old enough, I will teach my Elephant to drive."

I was ten years old, winging through the clouds, and there was nothing I could not do. "It does not seem so hard," I said, back from my reverie. "I could drive this car now, if you'd let me."

Papa flashed me a look that could have spoiled milk. I had insulted him, and inflated myself, and I knew I was in for it. "You are talking nonsense," he said, trying to quell his anger.

"No, really," I persisted, "I've been watching. It does not look so hard. You just turn the car where you want it to go."

I should have left it alone. My father lifted me from the passenger seat onto his lap, with the car still moving. He did this before I could struggle against it. Then he slid out from under me to where I had been, leaving me at the wheel. We were speeding downhill, and I could not hold the car on the winding, bumpy road.

"Okay, Elephant," my father said, lighting a cigarette and looking calmly at the passing hillside. "You said you could drive, so drive."

He had switched our seats on the fly, and there was no time to protest. "But Papa," I protested just the same. "I can't. Please. I can't." I started crying. I thought we would die.

"Go on," he goaded. "You've been watching. It should not be so hard. Like you said, you just turn the car where you want it to go."

"Papa!" I pleaded. We were careening down a dirt road, the trees darting from our path at every last moment. I was gripped by panic. "Papa!"

At last, I had punctured his composure—or pushed his patience, I could not be sure. "Listen!" he yelled, turning to me. "You said you could drive this car, so goddamn it, you drive it!" Then, his anger passed, he turned back to his cigarette and scenery.

"But Papa! I'll kill us!"

"So you'll kill us," he said, still unruffled. "At least I won't have a son who goes around saying he can do something if he can't do it."

"Papa!"

"Drive, Elephant," he said. "You are a big man. Show me how easy it is."

I was hysterical, but somehow managed to keep from colliding into anything. Thank God there were no other cars on the road, else I would surely have found our way into them. I tried to think through my fear. Following the twists in the winding road was only putting off the inevitable. There had to be a way to stop the car. My little legs could not reach the brakes, but I had seen my father work the gas-line lever to kill the motor. I pushed the lever up, as he had done, but the car kept moving downhill.

"The brakes, Papa!" I screamed. "I can't reach the brakes."

My father just smoked, and pretended to be enjoying the ride.

By some miracle, I reached the bottom of the hill, and steered the car through its coasting until it ran out of momentum. The engine coughed, and the car stopped. I surveyed the scene, for damage. There were no other cars in sight. We had not crashed. We had not driven off the cliff at the side of the road. We were okay.

My father took one last puff of his cigarette and flicked the butt to the ground. "You drove well," he said. "I did not think you could do it. Do you want to drive us home?"

"No, Papa. I think I am through with driving for now."

"Good," he said. Then he stepped out and cranked the car. He sat back down behind the wheel and drove off as if nothing had happened.

Spin the Scissors

I THINK MY FATHER knew his time with us would be short. Perhaps we all knew this, on some level, and perhaps he even prepared us for knowing.

His final day was filled with such portent that I might have thought to say goodbye. It was January 10, 1926, and we were having a rare family party. My father had invited some friends from the neighborhood and some of the other Mexicans from the studio, and some of our extended family. There were maybe ten to twelve guests, mostly men, and there was more than enough to eat and drink. Papa made his own beer, to serve to his friends. I can still see the big washtub of ice, squatting on our front lawn, overflowing with bottles. One of his guests ran a grocery store down the street, and he provided some of the food. Someone else brought the Aguardiente, a fiery concoction made from pure alcohol.

For all the preparations, it was not much of a celebration. Papa was in a melancholy mood, and it rubbed off on the others. He was noted among his family and friends for his singing, and on this day he sang only the sad songs from his repertoire, the songs of farewell. He sang a Mexican ranch song: "La vida, em-piesa siempre llorando, por eso es quen este mundo, la vida no vale nada." Life is worth shit. You come into it crying and you leave it crying. That is why life isn't worth a shit.

Finally, the guests tired of his sad singing, and one of them suggested a round of Spin the Scissors, a traditional Mexican game of superstition.

Papa did not accept the mystic notions of his homeland, and shared his vexation. "Ah, that's nonsense," he said. "I don't know why anyone believes in that crap."

But the guests persisted, and someone produced a pair of scissors for the game. The object was to sit in a circle and take turns spinning the scissors to see who would live the longest. If the scissors stopped spinning and pointed at you, it was believed you would die next; if you were never chosen, you would die last.

"Come on, Frank," one of the guests coaxed. "You're the host. You spin first."

My father took the scissors reluctantly, and twirled them on the table. All the other guests had gathered round. When the scissors came to rest, they were pointing at Papa.

Everyone laughed.

"That's what you get for tempting the Devil," one of his friends said.

My father spun the scissors a second time, and again they pointed at him. This time, no one laughed. This time, Papa picked up the scissors and threw them to the ground in disgust. Then he picked up his guitar and returned to singing: "Yo ya me voy, al puerto donde se halla, La Barca de Oro. Solo vengo a despedirme. Adios, mujer, Adios. Para siempre, adios." I am now leaving for the port where I will find the Golden Barge. I have just come to say goodbye. Goodbye, woman, goodbye. Forever, goodbye.

Rain broke the party before my father's mood. There was no room in the house, so everyone went home. Papa took his guitar and came inside. There was an awful sadness about him. It was not like him. My mother and grandmother were already cooking dinner over our kerosene stove, and they knew right away that something was troubling their man. The house smelled of frijoles and mustard greens, but they smelled something else.

"Never mind about the rain, Francisco," my grandmother said, thinking this would help.

My father said nothing. He just sat on our packing crate, cradling his guitar.

Just then, we heard one of his friends calling from across the street. His car was stuck in the mud. It was the same car Papa once made me drive down the Lincoln Park hills. He had sold it just a few weeks before, after deciding that we did not need a car after all.

Papa grabbed his hat and went outside to help his friend. It was twilight. I stayed inside with the women, where it was warm and dry, waiting on dinner.

We heard a terrible thud, and in that instant I knew what had happened. My mother and grandmother looked up from their frijoles, and from the ashen looks on their faces, I guessed they knew the same. They ran out of the house to the street, but I stayed inside. I heard yelling and crying, but I went to my parents' bedroom and climbed on their bed. Whether I wanted to shut out what had happened, what was still happening, or whether I wanted to make my own peace with it, I am still not sure. My father's coat was hanging on a hook behind the door, and

I reached for it and hugged it close. Under the arms of the coat I imagined his strong arms. I knew he would never hold me again.

My sister walked into the bedroom. She had heard the noise, and the yelling, and wondered what was happening. I loved her, and felt her fear as if it were my own, but I resented her intrusion. I told her that everything would be all right and to wait for me in the other room. I wanted to be alone with my father. I felt his presence there with me. I felt he had come to say goodbye. Stella would have to make her own goodbyes, when she was ready.

What happened outside was this: Papa was helping to push the car out of the mud and up a small rise in the road, when another car came around the corner. The driver could not see my father in the fading light. When my mother and grandmother raced into the front yard, they could see the two cars down the street. It was not until they drew closer that they could see my father, prone, on the pavement. I heard their screams from around the block—"Francisco! Francisco!"—and it struck me that there was nothing worse than the anguished cries of Mexican women. Jesus Christ, what a ghastly sound.

Soon, our house was filled with the wives of the men who had been drinking on our front lawn that afternoon. I stayed in the bedroom, hugging Papa's coat, listening through the thin walls to the loose talk about my father, about his rotten mood, about his failing eyesight, about the possibility that maybe he wanted to die. That was why he was singing all those songs, the women said. He knew. He was only twenty-nine years old, and maybe he thought it was a far nobler thing to place himself in the path of an oncoming car than to live the life of a blind man. I never believed he killed himself, but I listened. They talked into the night about this, consoling my mother and grandmother and sister, while I clung to the coat. It carried my father's smells, and his secrets. It was here to tell me what my father could not.

The next morning I woke early and took a shovel out to the street where my father's body had been. The pavement was stained with his blood, and I covered it with dirt. Then I went down to the Los Angeles River and won a job as a water boy for the construction workers there. They were building a wall for the river and needed someone to run fluids and refreshments to the men on the line. I needed to provide for my family. I was not quite eleven, but I was the man of our house now. Already, my mother and grand-mother were talking about going out to look for work, but I would not stand for it, just as my father would not stand for it. I could support them just fine. I could shine shoes or pick fruit or bring water to the men in the hot sun.

Still, there was no money for a headstone, so I went to a man who ran a marble shop in town, the father of a friend of mine, and asked if he had any materials to spare. His name was Nardini, and he let me pick out whatever I needed. He helped me to carve a cross, with an etching of a beautiful winged creature. Then he told me to carve the letters myself. "He was your father, Tony," the man said. "It is your job, not mine."

I did not go to the funeral. My father was not the man in that box. My father was off on a golden barge, watching over me and my family, collecting stories of his next great adventure. I could not bury him until his journey was complete, until I could show him the man he taught me to be.

I visited the cemetery only once, on a Saturday after-noon a few weeks after his death, to replace the cheap brass plate marking his grave with my homemade tomb-stone. I knelt down as I planted the stone into the earth. Loose blades of grass had already sprung from the fresh dirt in clumps, and I was reminded that life—all life—goes on, even here, even now.

I tried to find my father at the cemetery that afternoon,

but he was not there. He was in his coat, in his room, watching over me at school or as I brought water to the workers along the river. He was at the zoo, or on the trains, or any place he and I had ever been together. He was everywhere for me but in the ground beneath my feet.

Ride

I HAVE NEVER LOST the boy I was when my father died. He visits me, from time to time, to challenge me, to question my darker impulses, to make me look at myself through the eyes of the man I wanted to be.

The boy is my judge, and I am in no mood for his appraisal. He is with me as I ride. I have ignored him since I first spotted him, cresting from Vigna S. Antonio onto the main road, but I cannot shake him. He has stayed with me these first kilometers. How he manages this, I do not know. He is on foot, but it is no effort for him to keep up.

There is a sanitarium outside Genzano, and we race past. Like me, the boy is an arrogant sonofabitch, but he is not crazy and·neither am I. Still, it strikes me curious that we reckon in the shadow of this institution. Perhaps there is a kind of madness in what I am doing, in my relationship with the boy. Other men exorcise their demons, while I externalize mine.

When my children were younger, we used to walk in the fields below the sanitarium and hear the mad moaning of the men inside, or see them staring out their windows as if at television. The joke in our family was that the madness was contagious, that in living so close to the crazy house we were exposing ourselves to the virus that eats at logic and reason, and that as the oldest I would be the first to succumb to it.

Let them call me mad, I think, as I streak past the crazy house. I do not need their approbation. Besides, they may be right.

The boy laughs, and I make to ignore him. "How you've stayed out of there is beyond me, old man," he says, looking over his shoulder at the sanitarium.

"I'm no crazier than anyone else," I finally answer, "no crazier than you."

"Ah, but you're wrong. You're the one talking to me."

He is right. I am. Out loud. But this is not craziness, I tell myself. This is metaphysics. This is me talking to myself. This is nothing.

"Oh, so I am nothing?" he challenges. He can read my thoughts.

"In a manner of speaking, yes."

"If I am nothing, what does that make you?"

He has me here, so I finesse it: "You are nothing I do not need you to be." This pleases me, this dodge.

"Ah," he dismisses. "That's a tired old man who can't face the truth." I do not remember where the boy developed his disdain for convention and propriety, but here it is.

"The truth about what?"

"You tell me."

"I have no idea. Tell me. The truth about what? I want to know." He is on to something, I can tell, but he will make me beat it out of him.

He does not say anything.

"About Papa?" I try.

Still, he says nothing.

"What?" I demand. "You think he killed himself? Is that it?"

"It's not important what I think."

"He wanted to leave us?"

"No," he mocks, "he wanted to go on living in that stinking little shack, cleaning the animal cages at the studio, scraping just to put food on the table. That was all he ever wanted."

"What about Mama?" I want to know. The kid has me thinking the worst.

"What about Mama?"

"He loved her," I say—asking? telling? "There was no question he loved her."

"If he loved her, then where was he all those years, when we were in El Paso?"

"He was with Villa, fighting for the cause."

"Maybe," says the boy. "Maybe not."

I pull over to the side of the rode and step off the bicycle. It is exhausting me, this talking and riding, and I do not like what the kid has got me thinking. "You know something, or you're just guessing?" I ask, trying to catch my breath.

"I have reason to guess."

"You have no right to question my father!" I yelled. "He was fighting! He was injured! He was looking for us! He came when he could!"

I am off the bike, but the boy still rides me. "You're pathetic," he says.

Perhaps I am. The kid has never approved of me, but I have inured myself to this. At eleven years old, or just about, he thinks he has me figured. Once he told me he did not pick all that fruit, choke on all that dust, for me to walk around in expensive Italian loafers. He hates me for the way I live, and he is too angry at my father to venerate him.

"He is one man to you and another to me," he remarks, meaning my father.

"No," I say. "He is the same. It is the two of us who are different."

He considers this. I look over at him, to see how this notion registers on his face, and it is like examining myself in a mirror, reflected over time. His features are crinkled in contemplation, but then he goes blank, with no aspect. He cannot change who he is or what he thinks. The idea of my father as a tragic, heroic, romantic figure is as foreign to him now as it was to me then. "No," he says. "We are the same, you and me. It's just that you have chosen to reject who you are."

"But what about Papa?" I want to know. I cannot let the boy leave without coming clean.

"What about him?"

"What is it that you know?"

"Same as you. He was here one minute and gone the next. Even when he was alive, that's how it was with him. Here and gone. Christ, for three years he didn't even want to know us!"

This is it? This is the big revelation? The kid may have loved my father, but he could never accept his leaving? "You bastard," I say.

"Be careful who you call a bastard, old man."

He slinks into the brush at the side of the road and disappears. He will be back.

FOUR

Ride

I HAVE WONDERFUL FRIENDS along this path. Some live only in memory, but they breathe life into me. Others will outlast me deep into the next century. And still others I have never known.

Here, at the thirty-seventh kilometer, south of Rome, I pass the home of my great friend, the legendary Italian actor Eduardo De Filippo, and slow for a look. I cannot pass the mouth of the drive without pause. It is one of my landmarks. Indeed, it is more than that. Eduardo's moving here, along the Via Appia, has marked the road in a personal way. I am connected, through his home and our friendship, to more than three thousand years of historical confrontation. It is a marvelous, sinuous thing, this link to the past, and I welcome it on this morning, of all mornings.

I have often wondered at Eduardo's good fortune, to have landed on such storied ground. To me, it seems like good fortune, although to Eduardo it could have been something else. The house itself is dank and uncomfortable and sits at the bottom of a canyon, but Eduardo was taken by the landscape, and the views. He knew what he was looking for when he bought this place. He used to visit me, on Vigna S. Antonio, and talk openly of wanting a house just like mine, somewhere nearby. He loved the peacefulness of the valley, and the plenty, and I loved his company. Eduardo was a man of tremendous gifts. As an actor, he was virtually without peer, but he was also an accomplished artist and director. He spoke with the soul of a poet, and the heart of a maestro. For years we had been friends, and now I could think of no man I would rather have as a neighbor, so I combed the valley to help him find the perfect home, and to keep him close.

When I discovered an impeccable villa a few weeks later, I went to Eduardo immediately with the news. The house was not far from my property, and it had everything my friend was looking for: privacy, splendor, charm. I took him to see it, hoping he would fall in love with it as I had, but when he arrived his anticipation fell to disappointment. He had the most expressive face, my friend Eduardo, and I could read his moods like my own. "I can't live here, Tony," he said sadly. "Look at the trees."

"Forget about the trees," I said. "You can plant new ones."

"That's just it," he said. "I don't have time to plant new ones, and these trees are too small. I will not live to see them grow."

Eduardo was older than I was and I could not argue, but he soon found a house with big trees a few kilometers down the road, and this made us both happy. Now, at least, the trees would not remind him of his own clock.

What rich history there is here! It is in the air and under foot and all around. It is in Eduardo's big trees. His house overlooks the Pontine Valley—made lush, by design, by Mussolini. On the horizon looms the ancient fortress of Circeo, and as I consider Homer's account of the Trojan War, I consider also my lousy attempt to recreate the bard's epic for Dino De Laurentiis and Carlo Ponti. It was 1953, and I was cast in *Ulysses*, my first Italian film, opposite Kirk Douglas in the title role, and Silvana Mangano as Penelope. It was a mess of a picture, but it signaled a marvelous transformation for me—my

Italian sojourn!—and for this it holds a permanent place in my fading memory.

I played an unscrupulous palace nobleman, attempting to deceive Penelope into choosing a new husband, but I could only wear the role like a costume. I had no appreciation for Italy or its heritage. Circeo was a place in my tourist guides, and not a grand old rock inching up from the sea and casting shadows in my path. It was nothing to me. I had no idea of its history, and no grasp of its place in the hearts of most Italians. I walked through the script as it was written, but it called for far more. I was ignorant, and naive, and as I now fix on that great rock, I find myself wishing the part was mine to play all over again.

But my regrets are nothing here. This region has known far greater conflict than mine, for centuries. The worst of it was perhaps the most recent, when these hills were laid bare in one of the greatest bombardments of World War II. The Americans thought the Germans were camped up here, and unleashed a great salvo into these hills, only to discover that the enemy had moved on. In the end, there was nothing but scorched earth and destruction.

The valley is now Mussolini's everlasting legacy, and I have only lately come to understand this. As an American, I thought Mussolini an evil dictator who had hypnotized his countrymen. My indoctrination was thoroughly against him. I refused to go to a Hollywood dinner given for him by my father-in-law, when it would have been nothing for me to attend. Today I am living with a woman who sees a different Mussolini. To my Italian wife, Mussolini was a hero, because Italy achieved dignity under his rule. She forgives what she rejects, and looks past everything else. Her father lost a leg in World War I, and she was raised to believe that it meant something.

But I am an Italian now as well, so I have come to modify my view. I need look no further than the valley beneath me. For sixty miles, stretching down to the Mediterranean and all along the coast, there is beauty, and life, where before there was nothing but desolation. Mussolini filled in kilometer after kilometer of swampland with top-grade soil, magically transforming the quagmire into one of Europe's most fertile valleys. He did not care about the cost, or the effort. He built canals and bridges, and brought in farmers to colonize the region. There was no political strategy here. The man simply had a vision for the land and its people, and was willing to move mountains to fulfill it.

Now the valley is ripe with olives and tomatoes, grapes and flowers. Poverty stands as possibility. The scent of Italian pine fills the air, and the trees dominate the lower landscape. My own farm is famous for its wonderful olive trees. Every two years, people come from all around to sample my olives, and were it not for Mussolini the olives would never have taken to the soil.

Knowing this, from this place, helps to balance my view of the man with the history of this region. It is my region now, and I can look at Mussolini from two perspectives. Somewhere in the middle I expect to find the truth: the soul of a poet who would not be around long enough to watch his own trees grow, struggling within a heartless man who could only cut the best deal for his people.

I too have struggled, in my own way. I have cut my own deals—for myself, and my family—and I know what these hills have seen. Like Ulysses, I have had an endless thirst for adventure, sometimes at great cost. Like Mussolini, I have tried to reach an accord with man and nature, to justify my concrete failings with aesthetic successes. And like my friend Eduardo De Filippo, I am determined to ignore time into submission. If I cannot live long enough to watch the trees grow tall, then I do not want to know about it.

Surround me with only finished business and I will die a contented man.

I let the bicycle upend me from my thoughts. I leave Eduardo's drive and I am soaring again, hurtling along the winding road. This is the last of my coasting. Soon I will reach the uphill climb to Velletri, and I am grateful for this final stretch. It is a gift, this coasting, an affirmation, a painfully physical reminder of the hills and valleys in my life as an actor, and as a man.

I kick my legs to the side—they are my wings!—and let gravity have its way.

Odd Jobs and Holy Rollers

IT WAS NO EASY RIDE from the death of my father into the arms of God. I took comfort there, but I had more questions than He could answer, so I kept riding. Even today, I am riding still.

Back then, I was in desperate need of guidance. It did not have to be divine, but that was where I knew to look. When I was not looking, I worked, and ditched school, and chased girls, and fought with the kids on the other side of town, and tried in my adolescent way to fill my father's role. In this, I failed in theory but succeeded in fact. I became my father—a son to my grandmother, a provider to my mother, a father to my sister—before I was ready for the part.

I floundered at first and for what seemed like a long time. No one day was like another, and I woke each morning not knowing how to fill the hours. I hustled for whatever jobs I could find. There was nothing I would not do. I worked in a factory one day, and in the fields the next. Sometimes, when there was no work, I wandered the streets for hours, ashamed to go home with empty pockets. My days had no shape, no meaning. Without my father, I felt I no longer belonged anywhere, that I was clocking time, waiting to be told what to do, or for something to happen. With his death, I had inherited his rootlessness, his uncertainty.

Eventually, I found firm footing. I can still recall the day that set me along my present course. It came to me but I was there to greet it. It was less than a year after my father died, and one of the hottest days on record. I should have been in school, but I was walking the street, looking for a job, trying to keep cool. It was so hot the tar was sticking to my shoes. I was almost dizzy from the heat, and from a terrible hunger in my stomach. It was mid-afternoon, and I had not eaten since the night before. I was weak, and wanting, and just shy of hopeless.

I steadied myself in the shade of a building and made a promise: I was going to be somebody. I had to be somebody. I could not go on prowling the streets just to bring home fifty cents or a dollar at the end of the day. I could not live with this want, this emptiness, and I swore on God that I would make something of myself, and my family. This was no way to be. Even if I had to take a machine gun and shoot down the whole world, even if I had to preach, to change the way of things, I would be somebody. I would do whatever it took to lift myself from this undignified place.

I was only moderately successful. I learned I could put food on our table—shining shoes, mixing cement, butchering, working as a foreman in a mattress factory, selling stones in a local rock shop. I could pay for medicine for my grandmother and dancing lessons for my sister. But I could not put hope in our hearts. I could not replace my father. My mother tried, and I hated her for it. She cleaned other people's homes, and brought back their throwaways for me and my sister to wear. It was a way of life for us, even as I determined to shed it for a new one.

What I could not accept was when my mother came home with another man. His name was Frank Bowles, and this was the killing touch. The idea of my mother calling out to this man with my father's name was an execration. Maybe if he had gone by another name I could have tolerated their relationship, but as it was, it was unthinkable. As it was, I could not look on this man—a fucking window-washer!—without contempt. I was fourteen when they married, and I refused to attend the ceremony. I would not accept the man's gifts, or grant him my approval. I would not live with them. Instead, I dragged my grandmother and sister into my contempt and moved with them into a small apartment. They were my family now, and we would take care of one another.

For a time, I found guidance with a Catholic priest named Anselmo. I thought he had what I needed. I was a devoted altar boy with a lot of questions. I studied with him after school, and he had me thinking I might someday follow him into the priesthood. This became my calling. If I was going to be somebody, I thought, I should start at the top. Father Anselmo cautioned me that his was not an easy life, but I was drawn to it. I thought I could cloak myself in the rituals of the church and escape the terrors of the real world. I thought I could forget what my father had left us, and what my mother was doing to his memory.

My convictions were tested soon enough. My grandmother was suffering terrible chest pains, and she called on a Protestant group from the Foursquare Gospel Church of Aimee Semple McPherson to help see her through her illness. She was not rooted to the Catholic church, as I was, and the Foursquare Gospel Church was well-known throughout the country for the commanding presence of its leader, and for the devotion of her Holy Roller disciples. These Protestants were among McPherson's most zealous followers. They came to pray

with my grandmother, and I looked on them as if they
were the Devil's children.

I did not want these people in our house, but my
grandmother insisted. "They're not doing anything
wrong, Tony," she said. "They just want to help."

I went to Father Anselmo. "There are many ways to
reach God," he told me. "If your grandmother believes
these people are the way, that is what's important. Let
them come."

And so they came. Most days they arrived in groups of
three or four, to sit with my grandmother. Her pains
eventually subsided, and I began to look on McPherson's
followers as benevolent souls. They did not smoke or
drink or swear. They did not go to the picture shows or
possess material things. They dressed simply. They called
one another brother and sister. They were like the loving
family I had never truly known, and with them I felt
acceptance.

My grandmother was suffering from cancer, but all we
knew was that she was in pain, and that somehow her pain
was eased by the prayers of these good people. She
believed this deeply, and I came to believe it too. I even
promised one of the young followers that if my grandmother got well I would go with him to McPherson's
Angelus Temple to hear his spiritual leader for myself. I
was skeptical, but curious. People were traveling clear
across the country to Hollywood to listen to this famous
woman preach, and I thought I could at least make it
across town to hear what she had to say. I saw it as a kind
of payback for the kindness her disciples were showing my
grandmother.

I was not prepared to renounce the Catholic church
just yet, but I was open to other ideas. Even Father
Anselmo encouraged me to explore them. I asked about
this one Sunday after Mass, as I was helping him with his
robes in the vestry. He said that if I followed my heart,

and tried on the different guises of religion, I would eventually return to the church a better Catholic.

When my grandmother was well enough, I took her to one of McPherson's revival meetings. She wanted to testify, to give thanks. I had no idea what to expect, and what I found was an epiphany. It was nothing like the staid Mass of the Catholic church. It was all bells and whistles, hoots and hollers. A preacher sounded the usual themes—sin, redemption, hellfire, and brimstone—but underneath his warm-up act of a sermon there was singing, and laughter, and joyous shouts of Amen! and Hallelujah! and Praise the Lord!

I had never seen so many people happy at the same time. There was but one soul in that temple, a collective soul, and it stood ready for the heavens to open up and thunder with the word of God. I knew my days as an altar boy were ended.

I sat and waited for the great Aimee Semple McPherson to make her appearance. The room fell silent. The stage was lit with a spotlight, aimed at a lone lectern. A Bible lay open on the stand. Two thousand people, many on crutches or in wheelchairs, held their breath. Finally, a distant figure with bright red hair and a diaphanous gown crossed to center stage. We were well back in the crowd, but I could sense a mesmerizing presence. Then the woman on stage spread her arms wide, to hold the silence. The light played off her flowing gown like magic. She riffled the pages of the Bible, and stopped to read where it fell open. When she finally spoke, it was in such a rich melody—"Glory! Glory! Glory!"—that I was lifted.

"Glory!" I shouted back, without thinking. "Glory!" For the first time in my life, I felt truly blessed.

This was a woman who could work a room. Certainly, there was more to Aimee Semple McPherson than mere presence, but there was no denying her strength. She had a magnetic personality, and a dramatic flair I had never seen in the service of religion. She was a wonderful, powerful performer. The audience was hers, completely. I have known most of the great actresses of my time—Greta Garbo, Ingrid Bergman, Katharine Hepburn, Anna Magnani—and not one of them could touch her. She was like a goddess to me, and I was in complete awe.

It is telling to me now that I invoke McPherson with the language of my profession. I talk about her on stage, and not at the pulpit. I compare her to great actresses, and not to other preachers. I talk about how she moved her audience, and not her congregation, and note what she was wearing and how she spoke but not what she actually said. I think of her as a performer and I am not sure why. Her words are lost to me now, with the years, but her delivery remains, and perhaps that is how others remember her as well.

McPherson had a fantastic influence on me. I wound up preaching for her in some of the Mexican neighborhoods on the East Side of Los Angeles, and playing saxophone in the orchestra of the Angelus Temple. Sometimes I played the sax on the streets, to help gather a crowd for one of our sermons. She spoke no Spanish, so I translated for her, or spoke directly on her behalf. When I preached, I did more than interpret her words. I also copied her style and inflection, and learned to hold my audience the same way she held hers. We often traveled together in her car, going over what I would say and how I would say it. It was a great honor to ride with her, a point of pride among the other Holy Rollers. She told me that one day I would be a great preacher, and lead my own congregation, and accomplish immense things, and her praise was like nectar.

We became friends, in a fashion. There were twenty years between us, but McPherson treated me as an equal. Plus, she saw something in me that I had not yet recognized. She believed in me, and helped me to believe in myself. It was one thing to vow to be somebody, as I had done on that hot, hot day, but quite another to see a way to it. Through Aimee Semple McPherson, I saw the way, and it would take me far from the dirt poverty of our tiny house and the stilted pomp of my Catholic upbringing.

Ultimately, McPherson's greatest influence on me was nondenominational. Did she lead me any closer to God or to my own peace? I do not think so. I was religious as a child, and I am religious as a man. It does not matter to me how I get to God, only that I reach for Him. As for my internal peace, I am apparently still looking for it. Did she awaken in me a desire to reinvent myself in God's image or in my father's? Again, probably not. I had already set this path for myself before we met.

But she rubbed off on me in other ways. She gave me hope, and confidence, and dignity. She also gave me a shortcut to the stage. In the end, that was what it was most of all. I could not see this at the time, but I know it now to be true. In the Catholic church, I would not conduct Mass for many years. I would stand behind good Father Anselmo until he dropped from the weight of his own piety.

In McPherson's temple, her congregation was mine, right away, and she gladly shared her spotlight. All I needed were the balls to get up on stage with her, and I had those. My, the view from her stage was magnificent! It filled me with enough energy to shake the walnuts from a thousand trees, to shine a thousand pairs of shoes. It was like nothing else, and the space between evangelist and actor was like nothing at all.

On the Ropes

THE ROAD SPRINGS To life. By now it is past breakfast, and my neighbors are spilling from their homes. The climb to

Velletri is congested with cars and trucks and the putt-putting Vespas that make a mockery of my pedaling. There is also a school bus, filled with singing, laughing children. Their day is just beginning, their lives are just beginning, and their cries take me back . . .

The truant officer struggled to keep up with me, and I rarely shrank from the chase. I was fired by the Holy Roller spirit, and there was no chaining me to a desk. I was hungry for knowledge, but I could not find it at Belvedere Junior High School in East Los Angeles. Or it could not find me. I was too much of a moving target. The truant officer always caught up to me, although sometimes it took longer than others. The longest was three months, until he tracked me to a spring factory where I was making twenty dollars per week as an assembly-line foreman, and when he did he dragged me back to school just like they did to the kids in the old Hal Roach movies. I wished like hell I could have made a more dignified exit.

My prospects were limited when I stayed in school. I could shine shoes or buff floors when there was work, but there was nothing to replace the steady income of my factory job. I drove a taxi some afternoons, or warmed up cars at Ascot Speedway. On Saturdays, I unloaded the trucks at the market on Central Avenue for a dollar a day; on weekend nights, I made the circuit of the local dance halls, entering dance contests I knew I could win, and pawning the trophy or selling it back to management for a few dollars. The money was something, but not enough.

Finally, I met a friend who told me he was making twenty-five dollars a night—boxing. This I could do. I was strong, and fearless. The same balls that put me on the stage with Aimee Semple McPherson could put me in the ring with another amateur. The next morning I sought out a man on Spring Street who booked smokers. He worked out of a seedy gym, and the walls behind his desk were covered with pictures of Gene Tunney, Jack Dempsey, Mushy Callahan, Dynamite Jackson. I looked on and imagined myself in fighting togs, chin tucked to my left shoulder, eyes cold and dead ahead, a slight sneer creasing my face. It was the classic pose, and I would be the classic fighter.

I lied about my age and gave my weight and took a slip of paper. On it was written my first assignment: a four-rounder in Gardena, welterweight, with five dollars to the winner and three to the loser. Either way, it would not be a bad payday. I did not count on all the roadwork and sparring, but I figured these would pay off in future fights.

I rode the streetcar to Gardena on the night of the fight. Mine was the third bout on the card. The place was filled with well-dressed businessmen. They were smoking, drinking, eating dinner, having a swell time. The room was so small that the men could tap you on the shoulder and tell you how much money they had bet on you, or yell it out from their seats. It was my first fight, and the shouts told me I was the favorite. I could not understand why. When I crossed to the dressing room, so many men told me they were counting on me that I began to feel uneasy. I did not want to look ridiculous, or cost these men their money. I worried I had not trained enough. I dressed for the fight in silence, while the other fighters all shuffled around inside their own fears, avoiding each other's stares. The room smelled like iodine and cheap soap and wet leather.

I had no idea how draining twelve minutes of fighting could actually be. For all my running and sparring, I was not prepared to go four full rounds. By the time it was over I was barely able to lift my hands, but I was in better shape than my opponent. I could not dent an aluminum can with my punches, but he could not even find one with his.

I was given the decision, and when I reemerged from

the dressing room the men who had bet on me were jumping all over each other to buy me dinner and drinks. I still smelled the iodine, but now I also smelled champagne. As I rode the streetcar home that evening, I fantasized about a great boxing career. This was easy, I thought. I would be a famous fighter.

After nine or ten smokers, all winners, I graduated to the real thing. A manager named Jim Foster agreed to take me on. He handled all the great local fighters. He paid me ten dollars a week, to train and stay out of trouble. I started living like a real boxer. I stopped shining shoes and driving cabs. I ran and shadowboxed, and ran some more. I ate huge meals, and napped during the day. I was one of Foster's boys.

My grandmother could not understand the transformation, but she accepted it. I was making good money, and I had not been scratched in the smokers. She may have fretted over what she must have seen as my shiftless work habits, and she may not have liked the fight game, but she could not talk me out of the ring. After a while, she stopped trying. My success had taken her argument. She even made a wonderful robe—a symbol of her resignation—for me to wear from my dressing room into the arena.

I worked out at the Main Street gym, with Mushy Callahan and Newsboy Brown. I sparred with Primo Carnera, when he came to train near Echo Park. I fought in semi-windups or preliminaries all around Los Angeles, from Anaheim to Watts. I was making twenty, thirty, sometimes fifty dollars a fight, and winning them all. I thought it would be no time before I was a star.

Then came my undoing. It was in Long Beach, in front of a packed house. The crowd was with me before we started. I was something of a showman by this point—a by-product of my preaching—and I liked to work the shouts to my advantage. I usually thrilled when the crowd booed my opponent in the introductions, and drew from it, but on this night it made me sad. I was fighting a black kid, in one of the featured bouts, and there was something lamentable about him. He was lanky and unassuming, and he did not shoulder the taunts as well as he might have. The people called him "Smokey," and "Boy," and I resented their arrogance. My corner man, Buddy, was one of my best friends, and he was also black, and I was distracted by all this hateful jeering.

My head was not in the fight, but we battled evenly for the first four rounds. In the fifth round, I caught my opponent with a hard left and sent him reeling. I followed with a right to the stomach, and another left hook. The crowd started chanting—"Kill the nigger! Kill the nigger!"—but I was unable to respond. The kid had left himself wide open, and I could not put him away.

By the sixth round, the crowd had turned for my opponent. They would sooner root for a tentative black kid than a yellow Mexican. The other fighter had the momentum now, and he hit me with a hammer blow to the right of my jaw. I was stunned, and dropped to the canvas. The pain split me in half. I thought my head would crack open and give blood. I could not move, but that did not keep me from trying. I made it to one knee, but dropped again before the ten count.

Everything went black.

Jim Foster came to see me in the dressing room after the fight. "What happened out there?" he asked. "The kid was wide open."

I had no answer. I did not know if I was ashamed, or secretly pleased. "Look," I said. "I could beat this kid. Get me another fight and I promise you I'll beat him."

But there would be no other fights. Foster said if he ever saw me in the ring again he would climb in and beat the crap out of me personally. "You're not a killer," he said. "You don't belong in the game unless you're a killer."

He was right. I loved the glamour, and the accolades, and the showmanship, but I hated the tawdriness, and the sweating bodies, and the scramble to earn a living from my fists. There was no sport in it, and no peace.

I was sixteen years old, fighting to stay alive and to make something of myself, but I could not fight to eat.

Sylvia

THE ROAD FORKS AT VELLETRI, and I must make a decision. Until these crossroads the ride has taken me, but now I must steer. If I turn left, I will head into the hills, away from the sea. The road to the right will leave me doubling back into the valley, hugging the fertile coastline on my way to Nettuno.

Either way, the views will be magnificent, but I am not sure what I am meant to see, whether I am running away from something or heading toward it. I let the bicycle decide. It leans with me to the right, to the downhill road away from town. It is no plan at all. I do not want to go to Nettuno, but that is where I am headed. At least I can coast over these next kilometers, until the road rises again at Campoverde.

This is what my life is like, I think, as I race past my indecision. Either I think things through until there is nothing left, or I let the moment wash over me and collect me in its tide. Today, I am being swept out to sea.

Talk to me about the roads I have not taken in my long life, the relationships I have thought through until there was nothing left, and I will always come back to Sylvia.

The back-story to our time together was a tale in itself. It started with her daughter, Evie, a sixteen-year-old redhead I met at a party. She was a pristine beauty from the inside of a fairy tale. I was nineteen, all bones and acne and nerves. Evie walked over to where I was sitting and introduced herself. She said she knew who I was and had wanted to meet me. There was an ease about her I instantly admired. She was so disarmingly sweet that at first I did not realize I was talking to her. I felt relaxed around her, as if I had known her for a long time, and when she spoke of her mother and sister and brothers, I felt a part of her family. I asked if I could meet them, and she took my hand in hers and said, "Would now be too soon?"

It was not. We left the party and walked to the corner of Mickeltorena and Sunset, still holding hands. It was less than an hour since we had met, and there was already a silence between us. It was a cool night, and as we walked her sweetness reached me in what there was of the wind.

She took me inside to meet her mother. Sylvia was Evie more fully realized, but underneath her refinements was the same clean sweetness, the same girl. We walked in on a peculiar scene. Sylvia was feeding the fireplace with broken mahogany toilet seats. "What else should I use them for?" she said, when her daughter questioned her behavior. Evie was embarrassed, but her mother was resolute. "The wood makes a lovely fire," Sylvia added, as if this alone should justify the act. She was as self-assured as her daughter.

Sylvia sent Evie to the kitchen to get me a glass of homemade beer and looked me over. It did not feel like she was judging me, only that she wanted to learn who I was and what was important to me. "Are you Spanish?" she asked, more curious than probing.

I knew it was more fashionable to be Spanish than Mexican, but I did not care. "Mexican," I said.

"What about your name? Surely, Quinn is not a Mexican name."

"My grandfather was Irish."

"What a mix! You must be in constant conflict."

I had not thought of it, but I supposed I was, and pondered if it had to do with my heritage or circumstance, or some aspect of each.

Evie returned with the beer, and with her sister and brothers, and soon the whole family was sitting down to a late supper, talking about art and literature and politics. Actually, they were talking and I was eating, and drinking. They talked of Walt Whitman and Edna St. Vincent Millay, about the Fauve period and the Renaissance. My ignorance was apparent. In my silence, I showed myself.

I became more and more self-conscious, as the night wore on and the beer seeped through me, until finally I could stand it no longer. I had eaten quite a lot, and contributed quite a little to the conversation, and I overheard her brother and sister giggling about the stray Evie had brought home for supper. I took this as my signal to leave.

Sylvia intercepted me on the way to the door. She could see that I was drunk, and ashamed. "Don't let them get to you, Tony," she said. "They've just read a lot of books. They're no better than you."

These were her children, and yet she was subverting their interests to mine. I was a stranger to her, and they were her blood, but she would not let them diminish me.

I was touched by her generosity, and emboldened. "Have they read the Bible?" I said. "I can quote the Bible." I recited from Ecclesiastes, to prove my point, and then I lapsed into a long sermon. I spoke for almost an hour, saying things that I believed deeply but had not articulated until just this moment. I did not know where it all came from, or what it all meant. The bottled-up dreams and anxieties of a lifetime tumbled from me of their own accord, and it was all I could do to keep up with them. When I was finished, I realized I had been crying.

Mother and daughter walked me out to the street, and I could not shake thinking what a fool I had made of myself. First I was ignorant and then I was childish, altogether too pathetic to be cast off into the night alone. Who knew what these people were thinking? But Evie and Sylvia seemed to understand. They waited with me for the streetcar, and tried to talk me down from my humiliation. "I can teach you to read, Tony," Sylvia said gently.

"I know how to read," I answered. She was trying to help, and I would not let her.

She laughed. "I know you can read, but I can teach you what to read, and why."

It was past midnight, and clear, and in the moonlight I could read the warmth on Sylvia's face. She was ravishing, and safe. I imagined what it would be like with her, what we would be like together. I did not notice the years between us. She was everything I thought a woman could be: exciting, nurturing, challenging. She would fight for me like my black panther from the Lincoln Park Zoo. Evie was also wonderful, but she was just a girl. Sylvia was a finished product. She was the one I wanted.

"Come by tomorrow," she said. "I'll give you some books."

When the streetcar came, Evie reached up and kissed me on the mouth, and as I pulled away, I wondered what her mother's lips would feel like against mine.

I returned the next morning, hoping to catch Sylvia alone. Evie was not due back until late afternoon, and her mother invited me in to wait. The whole day was spread out before us. We sat in the parlor and resumed our conversation from the night before. Sylvia did most of the talking, while I continued in my fantasy. It was a delicate illusion, being attached to the daughter while falling in love with the mother.

"What do you like to read, Tony?" she said.

"Like I said, I don't read much."

"But you read the Bible. You quoted beautifully from it last night."

"Well, I suppose I know a little bit about religion."

"So that's where we'll start. After all, that's the most important subject of all. God is at the core of everything."

We started in on Santayana, and Schopenhauer. I thought Santayana was too theoretical, but Schopenhauer spoke to me; I liked his notion that life was precious, that man should spend all his time advancing himself. For me, there had been nothing practical about Santayana's preaching, but Schopenhauer wrote of man's struggle in ways I could understand and apply.

Over the next weeks Sylvia had me read Nietzsche, Thoreau, Emerson. Her course was a total immersion in world literature and philosophy. She suggested that I pattern my life after the writers I was reading, and urged me to keep reading each as long as I could adapt his principles to my own. In this way, if something did not ring true, I would recognize it immediately.

I read constantly. Baudelaire, Dante, Smollett. Wolfe, Fitzgerald, Hemingway. There were not enough hours in the day. I started sleeping in Sylvia's study. I knew my grandmother and sister would get along fine without me. I could not afford my own apartment just yet, but Sylvia's study offered a nice transition. Her library was my nightstand, and it was filled with classics and contemporary works. When I was not reading I listened to Mozart, or Beethoven, or Bach, and came to recognize the styles of the master composers. We studied the great painters: Gauguin, Del Sarto, Van Gogh. Sometimes Sylvia made a game of it, tossing postcards of famous paintings on the floor and asking me to identify the artist.

I came to cherish our time together. I abandoned school in favor of these loftier pursuits, and the money I was able to make in my steadier jobs. I lived a kind of patrician existence, working as little as possible, devoting myself to my studies.

Evie was still in school, which left me free to explore the world with her mother. I loved Evie, but only as a boy. I wanted to hold Sylvia as a man. She was all I ever thought about. I built my days around our time together. I longed to kiss her, and to lift our study sessions onto a romantic plane. I felt deceitful when I was with Evie, but I was helpless against it.

One afternoon, with Evie in school, Sylvia and I went for a long walk through the Hollywood Hills. We stopped for a rest on an overlook atop the San Fernando Valley. Below us, I could see the orchards where I had worked as a boy. Above us, I could see the snow-capped mountains I hoped one day to conquer. Between us was the space between desperation and possibility.

I reached out to Sylvia and touched her shoulder. I could no longer keep my desire to myself. She stroked my hair, but her caresses were more motherly than I had wished. In an instant, I lost the resolve to tell her how I felt about her, but in that same instant, she knew.

"You are in love with Evie, Tony?" she said softly. It was a question and a declaration, both.

Evie and I were engaged soon after. Sylvia encouraged the relationship, and I allowed it. I did love Evie, but it was not the same. It was not a lie, but it was not the truth. When she gave herself to me, in a cheap hotel in downtown Los Angeles, I started to cry. Her blood on the sheets was a gift I could not accept. I was unworthy of her devotion. I was her first love, her only love, and all I could think about was being with her mother. It was the beginning of what was to become an endless struggle for me, the yearning to be the one and only with the women in my life, and yet here I was rejecting pure fidelity when it was first at hand.

I moved from the study into Evie's room. She cooked for me and mended my clothes. I began to contribute to the household expenses. She became my woman, even as we lived like children, even as I longed for her mother.

It could not last. I would not let it, and I have often

wondered why. Evie made me happy, but maybe happiness was not what I needed. She loved me unconditionally, but I needed conditions, even from this sweet, virginal girl. It would have been enough for her if I was a truck driver or a fruit picker, but it was not enough for me. And it would not be enough for her mother. Sylvia challenged me to reinvent myself, to move from my present place into another dimension. Evie was content to take me as I was.

Sylvia. Surely I would not be the first and only man in her life. She had four children, and she was married to a man even she did not respect. But I knew I could be first with her in other ways, and I thought the principal ways would not matter.

Finally, on the beach one summer evening, with Evie asleep in a tent only a few yards away, Sylvia and I lay by a fire and found each other's arms. We were off on a family vacation, camping at Playa del Rey, and Evie and her siblings had turned in early. Sylvia's husband was back in Los Angeles. We rested on the sand, staring up at the sky. Neither one of us said a word. My hand fell into Sylvia's and she held it for a long moment. Then she pulled a blanket over us and the rest of the world disappeared. We were alone, together. It happened before we could think of it.

She cried when it was over. I tried to say something, but she put her hand over my mouth. Then she stood and walked to Evie's tent, to sleep. I fell asleep on the beach, blanketed by the smells of our love.

Evie must have known. The two people she loved most in the world were killing her just a heartbeat away. How could she not have felt it? And yet the poor girl did not say a word.

What duplicity! I was selfish, and cruel, and blind to the rest of the world. I know it now and I knew it then. I loved Evie, but not enough to cut her loose. I needed the

fact that I was the first man in her life. I needed her innocence, her dependence. I craved these things like air and
water. But I also craved Sylvia's worldliness, her womanhood. She was hungry for life, and I was hungry for her.
For a while it took the both of them to make me feel
whole.

Evie took it well when I finally broke our engagement
and confessed my love for her mother. At least she
seemed to. I do not know what I wanted. A part of me
probably wanted Evie to tear her hair out and beat me on
the chest for ruining her life. Another part hoped she
would concede gracefully, and leave me a clean escape.
She said she knew it all along, and soon took up with
another man, and I learned that this was not the reaction I
was hoping for. I wanted her to fight for me, to drag me
back into our bed, to tell me her life had no meaning
without me. Instead she looked to someone else. I was
insanely jealous, even after what I had done to her, but
Sylvia helped me to understand.

Sylvia was my woman now. She left her husband to be
with me. She helped me fix up my apartment. She came
by to do the cleaning, after she had finished cleaning her
own home. We talked of marriage. I hated to be apart
from her. The long nights alone were a tremendous
ordeal, although sometimes the nights together were also
difficult. I could not lie in her arms without thinking of
the men who had lain there before me. I had thought it
would not matter, but I could not get past it. She told me
she had been with three men before me—Evie's father,
her estranged husband, and one other—and they began to
haunt our time together. Mostly, they haunted me, but I
brought Sylvia into my paranoid delusions. I made her sit
for hours to help me destroy these ghosts, and yet they
always returned. These men had stained my woman, and I
could not will them away.

Sylvia tried to understand my internal rivalry, but it

was a new ideal to her. She tried to guide me through it, as she had with my jealousy over Evie. "Tony, it was so long ago," she would say when I set one of her lovers up for dissection. "He is not important to me now. I can't even remember what he looked like. You are the first in my heart."

But I was not the first and it was killing me. I was so deeply in love with Sylvia that I could not abide the idea that these other men had touched her in the same places, had felt the same embrace in return. I began taking her to museums she had never been to before, to parks she had never visited. I wanted to be the first in what ways I could. In my darkest moments, I questioned what I had done in casting off Evie. With Evie, at least, I was number one.

When Sylvia's divorce became final, I drove her to Santa Monica to apply for our marriage license. We went to city hall the same day her papers came through. I thought that if we raced to the altar I could put the ghosts of these other men to rest. We would be married, and I would be first, at last.

But it did not quite work out this way. The clerk sent us for a blood test, and the bald-headed doctor did a double-take when he reviewed our application. I had put down my correct age, twenty, and he looked at Sylvia to clear his confusion.

"Are you the boy's mother?" the doctor asked.

I could have killed him.

"I'm to be his wife," Sylvia declared proudly, but I could see that underneath her pride was a shame she had never worn. She seemed deflated.

"I'm afraid the boy is underage," the doctor continued. "I can do the blood test now, but he'll need parental consent before he can be married."

He spoke about me as if I was in another room, and as I listened in I considered the implications of his discovery. I should have just lied about my age, but all was not lost.

My mother's approval would not be a problem, even if it would be a degradation to have to seek it. She and my grandmother were grateful to Sylvia for what she had given me. They had never seen me this happy since my father died.

But for Sylvia the doctor had pointed out more than just a problem of logistics. She tore out of his office, and I chased after her. We drove to my apartment in silence. I was afraid of what she would say, so I did not push her. I did not see that the doctor held any authority over us. He could not condemn us for the difference in our ages, even if he could get Sylvia to second-guess herself.

Inside the apartment, she finally spoke. "That man made me feel dirty," she said.

"Don't listen to him."

"But we have to listen to him, Tony. We have to get your mother's permission. I'm two years older than she is and I need her approval." She laughed, and then her laughter rolled into tears, and she shut herself in the bathroom. She was in there for a long time, and when she came out I could see she had reached a decision. I did not wait to hear it.

"No," I said, pulling her toward me. "No."

She pushed me away. "We were foolish, Tony," she said. "To think we could get married. In a few years we'll look ridiculous. Just think about it and you'll see I'm right. You'll be a young man. You won't want anything to do with me."

So that was it. She did not want me to reject her later so she would send me away now. Trade the big killing for the lesser hurt. I tried to talk her down from her decision. "I love you," I implored. "It does not matter how old we are."

"You love me now," she allowed. "Beyond that, you can't know."

She was right, but I would not concede the point for

many years. "There's a whole world out there," I said. "I can't face it alone."

"You must learn," she said. Then she touched me tenderly on the cheek and walked out the door.

I was devastated. Sylvia had opened up a new way of seeing for me, and now it was falling apart. I fell down on the bed and closed my eyes. I wanted to cry but the tears would not come. My mind danced around what might have been, what was gone forever. I thought about Evie, and what we had both put her through. God, that poor girl! And me? What was wrong with me that I could not accept the love of such an innocent creature, unadorned? Why did I have to go looking for trouble? I was first with Evie, and it was not enough. Nothing was enough next to Sylvia, and now I despaired I would never find a woman to match her. Perhaps I would not even bother to look.

In the short time we were together, Sylvia had become everything to me: my sweetheart, my mother, my only friend. I was her son, her lover, her work in progress. I wanted each of us to be the other's creation, but I had to settle for her remaking of me. She remained my teacher, my spirit guide, my advocate, and I pledged to never let her down. I wanted more, but I would take what I could get, and give what I could.

In the middle of all of this damning introspection, I found a small piece of lint on the bedcovers and started playing with it. I was completely lost in my thoughts, and when I looked up from what I was doing it was late. The street lights had come on outside my window, and I realized I was hungry. I shook myself alert and realized I had been fiddling with this same piece of lint for hours—rolling it between my fingers, flicking it across the bed—all the time thinking, This is what it is like to be in love. This is what happens when it all unravels. There is nothing left but the threads that once held me together.

I promised myself I would move on, and grow. If

Sylvia had given me anything—and she had given me everything!—it was a passion for knowledge, an intellectual curiosity. I rededicated myself to my studies. I had decided I would be an architect, and there was much to learn.

Frank Lloyd Wright

LOOK AT THE SIMPLE HOMES that dot this hillside! They are but mere boxes, set into the earth to shelter against the rain and the wind. They are all the same. Still, they are a part of this landscape, now and always, as vital to the region as the trees that offer its shade, the fields that serve up its harvest.

Some of these stone structures have stood for centuries, inhabited by generations of one family. It is no way to live, and yet it is the only way, around here. The buildings are plain, the air around them quiet, and the silence belies the lives inside. Smoke spills from the narrow stacks popping from every other home, and fades into the chill morning air: the breakfast fire, filling the valley with penury, and clearing the way for lunch.

When I dreamed of being an architect, I dreamed also of changing the ways mankind thought about hearth and home, and these buildings reinforce what I once knew: most people do not know how to live. We do not care. We live in boxes, in utter sameness, confined by four walls to keep the world away. Every home is like another and I do not understand it. What a perversion! We spend all eternity in a box, so why do we have to live our lives in one?

I learned early on that it was the job of an architect to build not to the physical size of a man but to the size of a man's spirit. I learned this from no less a spirit than Frank Lloyd Wright, a Michelangelo of his time and a guiding force in mine. Before I left high school, I won first prize in an architecture contest, and Wright had agreed to look over the drawings of the winner and offer some advice. In the end, he offered far more.

Throughout my life, I have been surrounded by marvelous teachers, great artists, and world-class writers. I have often thought there must be a fine magnet inside me, because this is the only way I know to explain the kindness and friendship of so many luminous souls. They were drawn to me, and I to them, and in the correlation I found the touchstones of a lifetime.

I am lonely now, but as a younger man I was alone in good company. There were always people looking after me. One of the first of my mentors, after Aimee Semple McPherson and my dear Sylvia, was Frank Lloyd Wright. The great architect walked like a movie star: ramrod-straight and eyes aglow. He was not a tall man, but he moved like a giant, well aware of his presence. The world seemed to clear a path for him. His eyes were probably his most impressive feature. They were lively, full of hope and energy, and they saw through me right away.

"Why do you want to be an architect, boy?" he asked me straight off. In all my years, he was the only man ever to call me "boy" without patronizing.

"I want to build cities, sir."

"Whole cities?" He had about a thousand matters competing for his attention—drawings to correct, appointments to confirm, measurements to refine—but despite his distractions he was completely focused.

"Yes, sir. Cities with room for a man to grow, and breathe. Cities that take from the land, and give something back. I don't think we were meant to live in boxes, on asphalt. I don't think we were meant to never see the sun or touch the dirt."

He considered this awhile, and then moved on. He glanced at my drawings, and then up at me. "What's the matter with your speech, boy?" he said.

I was startled. I had never noticed anything wrong with my speech, other than a slight stutter whenever my mind ran ahead of my mouth. But even then, no one had ever said anything. Here I was, in Frank Lloyd Wright's office, surrounded by drawings and mock-ups of projects in progress, spinning grand notions about cities, and the standardization of man, and how we should live, and all the great man could hear was a problem with my speech. "I don't know, sir," I said. "What seems to be the problem?"

"You're stammering," he said plainly. "That seems to be the problem. Why are you stammering?"

"I hadn't realized. I suppose I'm just a little nervous."

"There's no reason to be tongue-tied around me. Open your mouth."

I did as I was told, and Wright peered into my mouth as if he were a dentist. He asked me to lift my tongue.

"There's the problem," he said, while my tongue was held high. "Your frenum's too thick. You should have it cut."

My frenum? I did not know I even had one, and now I had to have it cut. Wright lifted his own tongue, to show me the piece of skin underneath, and explained that a thick frenum made it difficult to enunciate clearly. "Your drawings are fine," he said, "but it's not enough to be a good draftsman. If you want to be an architect you have to be able to communicate your ideas. Your clients won't listen to you if you stammer."

I nodded. He scribbled the name of a doctor on a piece of paper and told me to come back when I had taken care of the problem. I left thinking I could never afford such an operation, and that it probably was not necessary. Who was Frank Lloyd Wright to tell me that I had a speech problem? He may have been a pioneer in the world of architecture, but he was no vocal coach. I stood defiantly outside his office building and tore up the piece of paper with the doctor's name on it. Then I let the breeze take the scraps down the street.

One year later, Sylvia arranged for a second appointment. "Maybe you were just nervous that day," she said. "It was a long time ago. Maybe he won't remember about the stammering."

But Wright remembered. I never knew him to miss a thing. He took one look at me and started right in on my speech. "Peter Piper picked a peck of pickled peppers," he said, indicating that I was to repeat after him. He would not take the portfolio I had prepared, with all my new drawings, until I stammered my way through the tongue-twister.

"Damn it, boy," he said. "That frenum's still there. What kind of a student are you going to be if you can't follow simple instructions?"

"But I can't afford the operation, sir."

"Then you can't afford to be an architect. If you can't articulate, you'll be no good to anybody." Once again, he told me not to come back until I had followed his advice.

This time, I went to see a throat specialist. He confirmed that the operation was needed, and told me it would cost $150. I thanked him and said I would be back when I could afford it.

"When would that be?" he asked.

"When I make something of myself," I said. I explained about Frank Lloyd Wright and my need to enunciate clearly, to become a great architect.

The doctor was a kind man and offered to do the operation on speculation. "You'll pay me when you can," he said. "I wouldn't want you to miss out on being an architect, if that is what you are meant to be."

It was an easy procedure, but there was no immediate improvement in my speech. In fact, it got worse. My tongue was not used to flapping about unfastened, and I could not get it to do what I wanted. After a few weeks of struggling, I decided to take voice lessons. Frank Lloyd Wright would never take me on sounding like this, and I could not figure my tongue for myself. I rifled through the telephone book and found an ad for a drama school run by a former actress named Katherine Hamil. The ad said the school emphasized elocution and speech. It was located on the corner of Cahuenga and Hollywood Boulevard, which seemed as good a place as any. I went over without an appointment and noticed that the place could have used a good cleaning. Miss Hamil agreed to take me on as a janitor and student, and to waive the tuition for the labor.

It was to be the start of something else entirely.

FIVE

Ride

ARTISTS SEE PEOPLE as colors on the canvas; actors see them as characters; sculptors as forms; writers as words; doctors as intestines and tubes; lawyers as legal problems. Few of us see one another for what we really are, and I am as guilty of this as anyone else.

I have known a great many people in my long life, but I am astonished at how few of them I have known well, for any length of time. And the number that I have let know me is fewer still. I cannot explain my own failing, but it is reinforced in these hills.

Consider: I have walked almost every inch of this countryside. Some patches are as familiar to me as my own reflection. Here I know every tree, every stone wall, every church, every ridge and promontory. I sometimes think I know everything but the people. Oh, I know where they fit in my image of this place, I recognize certain faces, but that is all. Only lately have I learned that the landscape and monuments are simply dressing, that humanity is the true measure of this earth.

The people have begun to fascinate me—my neighbors, the true players in this drama—and I am playing catch-up. And yet I know I will never touch them. There is a leap I will not let myself make. The faces that I pass have their own worlds behind them, their own histories. I want to draw from them, to leave behind something of myself, but I cannot find a place to start.

For too many years, I have taken the people of this region for granted, and I do not know how to change. Today, on this bicycle ride, I do not know that I should. A cyclist must be able to accept his loneliness if he is to discover new things about himself on each trip. It seems an essential aspect of any voyage. I used to think I needed a man or a woman to share the long walks and rides with me, but thank God I never found the right companion. I came close, once or twice, with other men with the special gift of silence, but never with a woman. Now most of my friends are gone, or someplace else, and I am left to sort through my dilemmas for myself.

The wind is at my back as I continue to coast from Velletri, looking for someone to talk to. This gift of silence only works if you can share it. It is a contradiction, I know, but it is so. I need the validation of another voice, another set of ears. These days, I find myself listening to old men in coffee bars and trattorias, or sitting on the benches in the village piazzas. There is something beautiful and sad when old men start remembering. When I was younger, I found it pitiful, unless the old men were telling big lies about their big winnings. Back then, I only wanted to hear about the victories, but I no longer mind the failures. In fact, I now prefer them, and eavesdrop with kindred interest, hoping I will come upon some valuable piece of information, some expert advice on how to approach that last hill. I am listening still.

The road corkscrews on the way to Nettuno, and as I bend with the turns I remember the prostitutes: two enterprising women, backed to a wall and open for business on the bank of one of Mussolini's canals, looking to eke a living from the lonely truck drivers or dejected pickers who travel this road. They charge as little as two dollars a throw, whatever people can afford. They are sad, and beautiful. They are this region.

There, just ahead, I can see their small shack in the

tangle of bushes by the side of the road. Some men prefer the privacy of the rickety building, while others accept the prostitutes' wares in the ditch of the canal, or beneath the small footbridge that traverses the water, or brazenly out in the open.

I hop off my bicycle, but the prostitutes are not about. Or, if they are, they are otherwise engaged. They will emerge soon enough, and I do not mind the wait. Even their longest sessions, they once told me, run to no more than five or six minutes. I have collected this detail and worked it against the other math: the girls are good for eight or ten or twelve sessions a day; on the best days, they might take home as much as one hundred dollars; in winter, or in rain, they sometimes go hungry; they like to have at least a half-hour between appointments; they have been doing this since they were teenagers.

There is nothing lascivious about my fascination with these girls. Perhaps at one time there was, but I no longer recognize it. They are attractive enough, but I have replaced any carnal impulses with pure curiosity. I am a friend, not a customer. I have never paid for sex, and I do not intend to start now. Over the years, some women have undoubtedly tendered their favors with ulterior motivation, but direct compensation has never been one of them. This has been a constant source of arrogant pride, even if the distinction between loves won and loves settled has sometimes been uncertain.

It was Dona Sabina who taught me about prostitutes, and I spent the rest of my life trying to unbutton myself from her first impression. My lesson came at a Chinese restaurant on Spring Street, where we were enjoying one of our regular lunches after an afternoon movie. We could not afford such indulgence, but could not lose the routine of the movies—and Chinese food was cheaper than most. Besides, the waiters knew us and tended to go heavy on the helpings and soft on the bill.

One afternoon, at one of the back tables, we saw a woman with short flapper hair plastered down to her bloated cheeks. Her lips were like a bloody gash against her too-powdered face. She looked as if she smelled of urine and lavender.

We were sipping tea and cracking fortune cookies when my grandmother pointed her out. "Don't look now, Tony," she said in a hush, "but there's a woman over there you must never have anything to do with." She gestured with her head, to show me where I should not look.

I was fourteen years old, and dying to turn around. "Who is she?" I said. "Someone we know?"

"I should say not. She's a bad woman, someone who goes with men just for money. A puta." She said this last like a snake spitting venom, and then she warned that if I ever patronized such a woman I would get terrible sores on my body, that my "thing" would turn green and fall off, and that I would never be able to truly enjoy the love of a true woman. She explained about venereal disease, and advised me to drip lemon juice on the breast of the girls of my choosing to see if they were infected. (I no longer remember what the lemon juice was meant to signify, or how it was supposed to respond, but I never lost the image.)

I turned to look, against my grandmother's orders, but her warnings were not necessary. I found the poor woman revolting. She was like a bad Halloween mask, with all that makeup. What horror! Already I knew all I needed to know about sex, and in an instant I knew I would never be able to mount a prostitute, not if they all looked like that. It would have been like making love to death.

I realize now that my grandmother did me a disservice. She was wrong. All prostitutes do not wear false eyelashes and painted cheeks, or smell of rancid perfume. How comfortable it would be if they did. Some are actually quite lovely, and few are any worse than the rest of us.

What Dona Sabina could not know was that there was nothing these painted souls could do to me that a shot of penicillin would not cure. They could not hurt me, but there was no panacea for the hurts the others would leave.

As a younger man, I could not recognize a puta if I fell on one, and I fell on many. The most dangerous ones seemed almost innocent. They had skis on their feet, or tennis rackets in their hands. Some were even expert horseback riders, while others attended universities and spoke passionately about art and politics. Mostly, all danced well.

And yet I persist in my arrogant pride, championing my lifelong pledge to keep out of the whorehouse. To come to my age with such foolish notions is a delusion. I know now that I have been with hundreds of whores, and that I have paid through the nose. How much easier it would have been to have left the money on the dresser!

There is a rustling in the bushes to my left. It is one of my friends, apparently finished with her morning appointment, and making ready for the next. Her dark hair is kinked and matted as she emerges from the bramble, and there are some dried leaves at the back of her head. She looks about thirty-five, but I know her to be younger. She was pretty once. She seems to be concentrating, but not on any one thing. She is brushing distractedly at the dirt clinging to her loose garments when she finally notices me, straddling my bicycle, staring.

"Signor Quinn," she sings, her eyes filling with light. "You are like clockwork." She looks at the sun and points to her wrist, where there is no watch.

For the past week or so, I have begun most of my rides along this same path, and I look forward to resting here. I enjoy the strange comfort of this stretch of road, the company of these women, the glimpses into reality they provide. They are married, but their husbands do not mind their work. Or, they are willing to tolerate their minding.

Where else can they hope to earn the same money, under the same terms? Without land, or a trade, it is difficult to earn a living in this part of the country. The husbands are laborers who prefer to idle, so for them it is a good arrangement. For the women, it is not so good, but it is what they can manage. They have children to feed, rent to pay, and not too many options. Whoring is what they know, and they do it well. Through them, I will know the people of this region.

"Busy today?" I ask.

"My first," she says, meaning the trucker who emerged from the bushes a few beats behind her.

"Well, it's early." I have enough on my mind without her dejection.

"It's cold. The men, they don't think of fucking when it's cold. They are late for where they have to be, or they are all shriveled up."

I had not thought of this, but suspect it must be true. "And your children. They are well?"

"Well enough. The oldest has the stomach flu. My mother-in-law is looking in on him."

I take a long pull from my water bottle. The water has taken on the plastic, and I gulp once and gargle-spit the rest. I will need something else to drink, before long. Then I think of the girl's mother-in-law, at home, know-ing of this place. Again, I shift gears. "Your friend," I say, "she is working today?"

"She's got a shy one," she says, looking over at the shack. "Should be pretty quick."

"How can you tell?"

"After a while, you can just tell. It's like a trade secret."

"What about me? What can you tell about me?" I am too old and too familiar with this girl to be flirting, but here it is.

"Signor Quinn, a girl never gives away her secrets." I would have thought her too unassuming to tease back, but perhaps I have left her no other way to go. I try to see myself through her eyes and guess that I am no different from the other men who come around, except for the fact that I have never come through.

A spindly teenager steps from the shack, working his belt, straightening his shirt. I can count his pimples from these twenty paces. He squints against the harsh sun, acclimates, and races for the Vespa parked about a hundred meters up the road. He does not want to be seen, like this. The redheaded girl follows, and notices me by the footbridge, talking to her partner. "Tony!" she shouts, "Tony, wait! I have something for you."

She disappears into the shack and reemerges with a small bag. It swings at her side as she takes the twenty steps to where we are standing.

"Bread," she says, handing over the bag.

I look inside and see a small loaf, wrapped in aluminum foil. I bring the bag to my nose. The bread smells wonderful. It is still warm.

"What kind?"

"Banana. I made it this morning. I thought you'd be by."

Here I am, I think. By and by. God, what a sweet mystery this world continues to be, that a working mother such as this would take the time from her troubles to bake me a loaf of bread, to presume to know me and my habits, to look up from the doleful depths of her reality and see a kind of hope.

Ah, yes. Indeed.

My Los Angeles

I LIVED IN DIFFERENT CITIES, at the same time. The East Los Angeles of my growing up was nothing like the Hollywood of my young adulthood, and yet each was interwoven with who I would become.

Even after I left my sister and grandmother, I lived in two worlds. I wanted to be on my own, and closer to downtown, but my apartment was still five miles from any place I cared to visit. The rent was only eight dollars per month, so I learned not to mind the location, or the long walks home to start and end each day, or the protracted intervals during which I could not tell if I belonged in one place or the other.

I was like my father all over again, wanting to fit where I could not find room, where I could not afford to be, where I was not wanted.

As before, my days could not spot each other in a line-up. The one constant, for a time, was Miss Hamil's acting class, which I attended several times a week. It very quickly became the locus for everything else. When I was not studying I was sweeping the floors, or stalking the local bookshops for new plays to interpret.

I struggled through the first sessions with a cork in my mouth. Literally. The great lady said it would be easier to enunciate if I gave my tongue an obstacle, and in this way I hurdled through phrases like "Theophilis Thistle thrust three thousand thistles through the thick of his thumb" with the grace of a buffalo. Eventually, I shed the cork and graduated to lectures on the Stanislavski method, listening intently while the other students sat and wasted their parents' money. All but I were children of privilege, and the talk after class seemed always to surround what parties were being thrown that weekend, and at what cost.

I begrudged the other students their backgrounds. I resented them all, and reflected their stares as if nothing could hurt me. I leaned on my broom and listened in, not knowing whether to spend my last ten cents on a sandwich for lunch or a new book.

The students were preparing a production of Noel Coward's *Hay Fever*, of which I was not meant to be a part. I was just a freeloading janitor, and my efforts on stage were not taken seriously—that is, until one young man, a rangy fellow named Lang Hargrove, developed a real fever just a few days before opening night. He was cast in the role of Simon, and could not go on. The director, Max Pollock, had seen something in my toilings on stage, and after consulting with Miss Hamil decided to offer me the part.

I was thrilled, and unafraid. I have sometimes thought that I never again showed such courage as I had in taking the role, but I understand now that it was not courage at all. What I had in abundance was ignorance; what I lacked was something at stake. My agenda was still to learn to speak and return to Frank Lloyd Wright to apprentice as a brilliant architect. The acting was only a means, so I jumped to play a proper Englishman. I did not know any better, or have anything to lose.

Lang Hargrove, the boy who had disinherited the role, was my only friend in the group. Unlike the other kids, he carried his family's wealth like a burden. It was not a part of him. He was very encouraging, and helpful, running lines with me late into the evening, going over the complicated staging. He was sick, and unable to perform himself, but he was determined to help me.

I did not know enough to be nervous. I knew there would be Hollywood agents and producers in the audience, but they were not there for me. As it turned out, I got rather good notices in the play, and the director asked me if I would appear in another—a production of Gorki's *Lower Depths*. Again, I got good notices, and I started to think I had found my calling. Out there, on that stage, I was a different person. My disappointments fell away, and I was left to breathe, unencumbered by the normal constraints of my time on this earth. It was like nothing else, and like everything else. If I was not meant to be a preacher, or an architect, then perhaps I was meant to be an actor.

I was encouraged enough to join a small theater troupe called the Gateway Players, and my world changed yet again. I started to hang out in bookstores, and meet all manner of artists and intellectuals, just as my activities on the stage brought me into contact with a whole other batch of personalities. My Los Angeles beat with a new enthusiasm. Life was about literature and philosophy, ambition and promise. Anything was possible.

I began to run with a colorful crowd. Through my work with the Gateway Players, I met George Cukor, who had already made a name for himself as a young director, and was something of a legend among fledgling actors. I was delighted to have won his attention, and fantasized that our friendship would lead to my first movie role. What the hell did I know? Cukor fed me and my fantasy. He recognized a green kid when he saw one. He took me to fancy restaurants and poured me expensive wines, and underneath all the bounty I decided to ignore his scheme in favor of my own.

This was my plan, but it was not easily accomplished. One evening, after we had retired for a nightcap to his Beverly Hills home, the director started plying me with liquor and girlie magazines until I was fairly drunk and somewhat aroused. He negotiated me onto a comfortable chair and sat on the floor at my feet, using the ottoman to display the dirty pictures. He turned the pages, and filled my glass, and promised to make me a big star. I was drunk enough to believe him.

Before I fully processed what was happening, Cukor was rubbing my thigh. "I have a picture in mind," he said, rubbing. "I'm just now doing the casting. I think you'd be perfect for it."

I did not know whether to hit him or feel sorry for him. Then I thought, Well, this is not so bad, if this is all it is. Cukor continued with his rubbing and I pressed him for details.

"Is it a big role?" I asked.

"Oh," he cooed. "The biggest." He tried to part my knees, but there was no moving me. I had an erection, from the girlie magazines, and Cukor could probably see it through my trousers and take it the wrong way.

Still, I let him linger there, longer than I would have thought, all the time balancing what I was giving up against what I might receive in return. What was the harm? I wondered. Even if I let the man go down on me, that did not make me a queer. All it made me was a kid who let some pansy Hollywood type go down on him in order to get a part. There were worse ways to sell your soul.

"What sort of picture is it?" I asked, finishing the rest of my drink. If I was going to go through with this, I would need reinforcements.

"Perhaps you know the material? *Little Lord Fauntleroy*?"

Little Lord Fauntleroy! Jesus Christ. What was Cukor thinking? Forget about him—what was I thinking?

With this, any thoughts I might have had about acquiescing to this strange man's advances were gone as quickly as they had surfaced. I may have been prepared to suffer for my art, or to get ahead, but not for *Little Lord Fauntleroy*, not in this lifetime. I stood to leave.

"Where are you going?" Cukor asked.

"I have a girl," I said, thinking this would dissuade him. "I have to go."

"We all have girls, Tony. That is no reason to leave." He grabbed for me again. I pushed him away and made for the door, but Cukor screamed after me: "You'll never be an actor! You'll never be anything! You have no class!" When I reached the street, his shouts were waiting for me through an open window.

"Don't forget. Life is two mountains and there is no valley!"

I had no idea what he was talking about, and even

though we went on to make a wonderful picture together, it never occurred to me to ask.

One Smart Cookie

GEORGE CUKOR WAS NOT the only Hollywood legend out to seduce me, but he was certainly the first. Mae West soon followed, and once again I did not know how to steer clear, or that I should. Miss West was one of the reigning sex symbols of the day, but her bawdy demeanor did no more for my libido than Cukor's not-so-latent homosexuality.

We met during auditions for a new play she was producing. She had me up to her hotel suite to read for the part. When I arrived at the appointed time she was dressed in a flimsy, see-through chemise, leaving nothing to my imagination. There was something almost coarsely sensuous about her, but she was not for me. The paint on her face and the thick perfume reminded me of the putas I was supposed to avoid. True, she was the same age as my Sylvia, but she did not wear her years as well.

"Come closer, boy," she said. "Let me look you over."

I did as I was told. She ran her hands over my shoulders and through my hair. Then she took my hand and walked me over to the bed. I had no idea what to expect, but she offered instructions. "Here's the setup," she announced. "You're standing beside my bed. You are so close I can feel your breath down my neck."

I listened carefully, thinking I was preparing a scene. I did not know what to do.

Miss West noticed that I was standing where she had left me and told me to get closer, before continuing: "I gaze into your liquid brown eyes and open my mouth. I want you desperately. I am lying there with my mouth open, your hot breath on my neck, and I can feel you coming closer, closer."

I stood closer still, figuring this was what she wanted.

"Now you can't resist me," she went on, leaning back against her pillows. "You are bound to kiss me, and I know your mouth will taste so sweet. I know you are a boy, but you must have a woman like me before you can know what a woman can really be."

By now her seduction was transparent, but I played dumb. I stupidly tried to imagine myself in the scene she was describing, to remove myself from what was actually happening. I knew that if I did not sleep with this woman I might never again get a chance at such a good part, but I also knew that if I slept with her I could not stand it.

Either way, I was screwed.

"It sounds like a great scene," I said. It was a ridiculous comment, but the best I could manage.

There was a long, awkward silence, and the moment passed. Finally, Miss West reached to her nightstand for a wad of gum and starting chewing it fiercely, almost cow-like. "Boy," she said, "either you are one smart cookie or one stupid sonofabitch, I can't quite figure."

She could not get rid of me fast enough, but she did cast me in her play, which taught me to always trust my gut over my better judgment. The play was called *Clean Beds*, and I landed a part originally intended for John Barrymore. (It was loosely modeled after him, as well.)

Miss West stood at the back of the theater as I tried to sound like a sixty-five-year-old man in my audition. When I was finished, she applauded. She came down the aisle and motioned me to the edge of the stage. "You were very good," she whispered. "Maybe I passed up a good thing." Then she turned to the director and said, "If I were you, I'd give him the part."

And that was that.

Ride

WE ARE ALL BORN OF A DREAM. Our fathers dream of
worlds we are to conquer. We ourselves search beyond
our horizons, dreaming of the vastness we will pound to
our measure. But all dreams die a slow death. Soon we
limit our vision, giving up our dreams for practical plots
of six-by-six.

I do not want to go to Nettuno, for this is the way it
gets me thinking. It has become for me a place of death, a
portent of what remains in store. I know too well who is
buried here.

Already, as I approach the twenty-sixth kilometer, I
can see the stands of tall cyprus trees associated all over
Italy with cemeteries. The trees fill the area with their
fine scent and sweep, but they are deceptive in their
beauty. Their grace is tempered by what they represent.
Beneath the trees are acres of white markers, row upon
row, mostly crosses, set against fields of well-kept green.
There is an odd geometry to the broad canvas, and as I
draw closer I become a part of it. It envelops me, as I step
inside. There is not a flower in sight, save for those
already dead and left behind to honor one loved one or
another.

Nettuno was a special place, once. For many, I suspect
it remains so, but its charms are forever lost on me. For
centuries, it has been a thriving seaside village, first settled
by the Saracenes—Muslims from Syria, Egypt, and North
Africa, cast off during the Crusades. It is surrounded by
an ancient wall. A tremendous medieval fort dominates
the coastal landscape and sits majestically on the beach,
facing the sea. The village itself is thick with houses on
the high, massive walls of the old castle. The piazza at the
center of town is dotted with grand old statues and a lavish fountain—Fontana di Nettuno—and rimmed with

merchants peddling all manner of meats, fish, cheeses, and local produce.

It is the cemetery, though, that leaves its fingerprints all over this region. The regimented rows of markers extend as far as the eye can see, recalling the landing of the Third Division of the American army, at dawn on January 22, 1944, at nearby Lorincina Beach. The legend of the invasion has the locals all huddled in front of the church of S. Rocco for protection, but there was no protecting the soldiers. The imposing iron gates of the American cemetery, and the well-stocked goldfish pond within, are the only monuments to the fallen.

I roll to a stop and step my foot against the curb, for balance. I take in the setting. One sign warns drivers to lock their cars, in deference to a recent wave of vandalism. Another forbids bicycles or motorcycles to enter cemetery grounds. Cars are okay, but no two-wheelers. I wonder why. Perhaps it has to do with the sanctioned rituals of mourning: to arrive in small groups, in a sensible car, is the proper way to grieve; to arrive alone, and unburdened, is to insult the memory of the dead.

Ah, what nonsense, I think, as I leave my bicycle to lean against the stone wall rimming the parking lot. Who are they to tell me how to get to this place? I am managing well enough on my own.

It is no coincidence that the man who cleared a path for me is resting on these grounds. Lang Hargrove, the boy who was forced to abandon his part in the Noel Coward play, was one of hundreds of American soldiers who lost their lives on that January morning in World War II. He is buried here, with all the others, and I am pursued by the connection. It is what takes me back and brings me here.

We were friends for a time. Lang brought me home to meet his family, and helped me to realize that I was meant to be an actor. He was not suited to it, he always said, but he recognized something in me that was. He loaned me money when my luck was running particularly sour. It was only twenty-five dollars, but it was everything. Before long, we went our separate ways, but we kept tabs on each other until the war. He used to take credit for my successes, in a joking way, but he was more responsible than he knew. His mother contacted me to tell me what happened at Lorincina Beach, and I remember feeling as though an angel had left this earth.

I am returned to the present by a man and his two sons. They pass a few meters from where I am standing, kicking a football. They begin to play among the headstones, zigging and zagging, and I am reminded that even a monument such as this cannot beat down the spirit of man. Perhaps it should—football? here?—but it cannot. I start to think that perhaps when I am dead it would not be such a bad thing if my children and grandchildren came to play and kick the ball around on the earth above me.

I make for the regimented rows, looking for Lang's marker, and I am struck by the number of markers bearing stars. A caretaker misreads the bewilderment on my face and says, "Jews."

"I know," I say, "but so many?"

When I finally locate the grave of my friend, there is nothing to distinguish him from the other soldiers. My very presence, standing before him, is the only thing to set Lang Hargrove apart. Someone is here to remember him, and in this he is alone.

I try to pray for him, but today I am no good at praying. It wrestles with my memory, and sets me to thinking where my own roads would have taken me were it not for the intersection with my acting school companion. I was redirected by our time together, and so was he. Our entire lives turned on that moment, and yet now we are both here, at the same place, with the same things to look forward to.

I search for a stone to leave on the marker—to tell the world that I was here, reappraising the man who once reappraised me. It is the least I can do.

I return to my bicycle and walk with it down to the Piazza del Mercato. It is good to be on my feet. The sun has burned away the morning haze and the day has turned hot, unseasonably so. I need the tumult of the market-place to distract me from the solitude of the cemetery. Also, the water in my bottle has gone warm, and artificial. I want something cool to drink, to fuel the next leg of my ride.

The piazza is ripe with the smells of the huge cheeses and sausages hanging in the stalls. I am assaulted by the riot of color of the green pepperoni and the dark mauve eggplant, the huge phallic stalks of finocchio and celery. The smells and colors and shapes are like nothing else in nature, and I begin to feel as though I have stumbled onto some other plane. My senses are not used to this.

There are the fish stalls with the dripping octopi, the merluzzi, the huge muddy sea bass, their scaly-wet skins turned up to the sun. The stink collects itself under the plastic awnings meant to shelter the merchants from the elements. Also: the carcasses of the freshly slaughtered calves, the porchetta, the rabbits.

It is almost too much to take in on one pass, and the loud voices of the hawkers and buyers drown the sights and smells into afterthoughts:

"Due cento al chilo."

"Ma lei e' matto? Un pepperoni a due cento?"

"Signora, sa quanto costa la mano d'opera?"

In one stall, a man has erected a small fence around his chickens. It is set up so that the buyer makes his choice and watches the macabre choreography—the butcher, casually grabbing the bird by the throat, whirling it in a big arc, and breaking its neck. Then he throws it on the scale to determine the cost.

I consider the juxtaposition: life and death, so swiftly dealt, in the shadow of the American cemetery. Kill to live. Live to kill. There are no lofty sentiments, no big philosophical observations, no romantic garbage about how just a few hours ago these chickens and roosters crowed in the coming of the dawn and death seemed so far away. They will all dress some table this evening, garnished with olive oil and garlic. People will lick their lips and wash them down with chianti, or some homemade wine.

The dead feed the living and the cycle goes on.

Clean Beds

TO PLAY JOHN BARRYMORE was to place two left feet in the shoes of an immortal and somehow walk. It was a role written larger than life, to be interpreted by a young man of far smaller dimensions, and it would take everything I had to pull it off.

I was grateful for the part, even if I did not feel entirely qualified. The opportunity was just the gravy; I took the job because I needed the money. Who was I to question the producers' judgment? My grandmother was dying of cancer, and the bills for her medication were running well ahead of me. My sister, Stella, wanted to continue with her dance lessons—after all, she was to be the star of our family—and with my mother married off to her window-washer, I was the only source of income for my two girls. My custodial job earned me nothing but a waiver on my tuition, so I worked most nights parking cars, or waiting tables, or shining floors in some of the downtown showrooms. I was once known as one of the best floor polishers in all Los Angeles, for the way I left the cars reflecting in my sheen.

The Barrymore role promised to relieve me of some of this mad scrambling and polishing, at least for the run of the play, but I still had to make a success of it. Of course, it would not do simply to walk and talk like the fabled actor. I had to look like him as well, right down to the trademark profile, and for this I was fortunate to have befriended one of the most talented makeup artists in Hollywood. The road to that friendship was its own story, and illustrative of the rambling lifestyle I was leading at the time.

I was broke, and hungry. I had just finished another long day at Miss Hamil's drama school, acting and cleaning and shouldering the stares of my privileged class-mates, and facing my long walk home to my dreary apartment, when someone tipped me to a downtown nightclub offering free hors d'oeuvres to anyone who cared to audition.

"Can you sing, Tony?" the someone asked.

For something to eat, I could do anything.

I raced the few blocks down Hollywood Boulevard to claim my place in line at the nightclub, but when my turn finally came and the orchestra leader asked what song I had prepared, I drew a blank. The Russian woman who owned the place was very patient. Her name was Madame Sonja, and she could see that I was hungry, and out of breath, and plainly laden down with books. "Take your time," she said. "The orchestra can play anything you want. Russian songs, Hungarian songs, Mexican, anything you want."

The only song I could think of was "Shortenin' Bread," and I blurted out the title.

"That one we don't know," the band leader said, in a thick Russian accent.

I hummed a few bars, and a few of the musicians smiled. "You start," one of them said, "and we'll follow along."

So I did. "Mama's little baby loves shortenin', short-enin', Mama's little baby loves shortenin' bread." I was awful, but I did not care. At least I would eat. I could not remember the words, but I struggled through the song. "Put on the stew, put on the ra, ra ra ra ra, da da da da." Jesus Christ, what an embarrassment!

Somewhere in the middle of my effort, I heard an enormous laugh from a man in one of the back rooms. It sounded as if the poor fellow would choke on his own enthusiasm. His laughter was aimed at me, and from behind a closed door I heard a thundering voice: "What the fuck is going on out there?"

A huge man followed the voice into the main room. He seemed to be about six and a half feet tall, nearly as big as his laugh. The sight of me, backed by a full orchestra, gamely performing a silly American song, was apparently too much for him.

"You are terrible!" the man roared. He too spoke with a Russian accent. Then he let up on the guffawing and caught his breath. "You are terrible, but you are wonderful!" he said, stepping to the stage to introduce himself. "Feodor Chaliapin," he said, extending his meaty hand. "Pleased to make your acquaintance."

I shook his hand. At twenty, I stood six foot two inches tall and weighed 185 pounds, but I was nothing next to the famous Russian basso. "I have heard of you," I said, "but I have never heard you sing."

"Hah!" he said, "but I have heard you, my young man. Ironic, no?"

He sat with me as I ate and told me his stories. He said that when he traveled to perform he often received real estate in lieu of payment. He owned a paper factory in Italy, a block on Wilshire Boulevard in Los Angeles, and several valuable lots in Japan. "Money, I just spend," he said. "The land I have forever."

Like my features, my stories were small next to Chaliapin's, but he listened well. He could not understand how a strapping young man with an inquisitive mind could go hungry in America, but I explained that we were not that far removed from the Depression and that a lot of people were going hungry.

"You'll be cold," he said, looking me over when the night was through, "walking home like that. Let me give you my coat." He said he had so many coats, he would not notice one less. The thing fit me like a blanket, but I knew it would be warm, so I accepted it gladly.

I went back to see Chaliapin from time to time and we became friends. He introduced me to most of the Russian musicians, artists, and writers in Hollywood at that time—and they all passed through town eventually. I became immersed in a thriving Russian colony. Through Chaliapin, I met Michael Chekhov, the noted character actor, director, and teacher, who would have a profound impact on my acting career. Katherine Hamil may have taught me how to speak, and Max Pollock may have taught me how to stand on stage and deliver my lines, but Michael Chekhov taught me how to act. He had me redirecting my energy and inhabiting a role before I knew what I was doing. For this, I am forever in his debt—and, by extension, in Chaliapin's.

But the great singer's influence did not end here. He knew everyone, and soon so did I. Rachmaninoff, Horowitz, Heifetz . . . they all became my friends. A few years later, after I had some early success as an actor, I was sent by train from Los Angeles to New York to promote a picture, and found Heifetz in the compartment next to mine. By the time we reached Pennsylvania Station I was reminded that practice may have made perfect, but in the end it was still practice; scales were just scales, no matter the maestro. I was never so bored in my life, listening to Heifetz play his violin eight hours a day, all week long.

"Hey, Heifetz," I used to shout, slamming on the walls for emphasis, "shut the hell up!"

He never did.

Chaliapin also brought me into the talented hands of Akim Tamiroff, an Armenian actor who had been working in Hollywood since the middle 1920s, which returns me to the beginning of this story. Chaliapin himself was known as a genius in making himself up for his brilliant characterizations, and when I went to him seeking advice on how to transform my twenty-year-old body into a sixty-five-year-old man with a prominent profile, he recommended Tamiroff. If anybody could pass me off as John Barrymore, Chaliapin said, Tamiroff was my man.

Tamiroff arrived a half-hour before the opening night curtain and went to work. I did not see how he could pull off my transformation, but he told me that was not his job. He could age me with paint and putty, but the rest was up to me.

I knew I had Barrymore's voice down, and some of his mannerisms, but I did not know if that was enough to sustain a character. I took the stage with a confidence I did not deserve, but when the curtain came down it was still there. The seconds between curtain and applause were agonizingly long; for a beat, I could not be certain the applause would even come. I did not know if the audience would look past the obvious age difference, or my inexperience, until they stood in ovation.

There, underneath the roar of that opening night crowd, I became an actor. My heart was thumping like a jackhammer. For the first time on stage, I felt a meaningful success. I felt I belonged. During the two hours it took to run through the play, I had been lifted, high up among the clouds, and now the applause was pulling me back, grounding me in the center of a thing impeccably done.

God, how I swallowed that moment!

Backstage, I retreated to my tiny dressing cubby to decompress. The evening was still not real to me. Sylvia was there, rooting for me. She would not marry me, but she would always care for me, and she was the first to seek me out after the show to hail my performance. She was truly thrilled, and I sponged at her excitement. Mae West came by to hug me, and slip in a little opening night flirtation. The director, Vadim Uraneff, knocked on my door, and he was followed by assorted members of cast and crew.

Next, Akim Tamiroff stopped in to offer his congratulations, and to receive my thanks, cementing a fabulous friendship that would last until his death in 1972. Many of my new Russian friends had been in the audience, and they too checked in with their effusive praise. Even some of Barrymore's circle—strangers, until this evening—reached out to offer their admiration.

It was a heady moment that swelled with each embrace.

After my last well-wisher had gone, I could not shake the feeling that something immense was still about to happen. As if the evening had not already been enough! I heard a loud noise down the hall, and then a knock at the door. My makeup was half on, half off. I was dressed only in trousers and a T-shirt. There was another knock. My visitor was impatient. I went to open the door.

There, absolutely larger than life, was John Barrymore himself. He stepped in without being asked and filled the small room.

He took one look at me and said, "Where's your father?" After mimicking him on stage for so many weeks, I thought his voice seemed like my own.

"My father's dead, sir," I said. I could not understand what Papa had to do with all of this.

"Then whose dressing room is this?"

"Mine."

"And who played me out there tonight?"

"I did, sir." I could not tell if he wanted to rip into me or collect me in his arms. His glower could have meant anything.

He looked me over carefully. "Christ, you're just a kid," he said softly. There was a long pause. I was dying to learn what would happen next. Then a grin creased Barrymore's face, and his stare softened. "You cocksucker!" he bellowed in his grand blast of a voice. "You shit!"

This, I was to learn, coming from John Barrymore, was high praise indeed.

Barrymore & Co.

THE GREAT BARRYMORE took me out to dinner that night, and for many nights afterward. Soon he invited me up to his sprawling home on Tower Road, and I became a fixture there, passing many long, drunken evenings with his famous friends—Gene Fowler, John Decker, Roland Young, and W. C. Fields. Occasionally, Thomas Mitchell and Errol Flynn would sit in on our merrymaking, but they were less regular than the others.

I was delighted to be included among Barrymore's "shits," even as I tried to figure what it was that had swept me into their midst.

Barrymore's house was like a funhouse maze. The front door was guarded by a suit of armor he had worn in a London production of *Richard III*, but the interior was more ramshackle than stately. In all the years I visited, there was always some kind of construction going on, most of it haphazard and for its own sake. Barrymore worried that if he ever stopped building he would die, and he had put in so many different rooms he did not know what to do with them. He had a room for birds, a room for his stamp collection, a room for his books. For most of the time I knew him, he lived alone.

His favorite room was little more than a seedy closet, with peeling paint and no comfortable place to sit. The room gave the lie to the rest of the house, but this is where he spent most of his time. There was a sink in one corner, and he used it to relieve himself. "Rather like a dressing room, wouldn't you say?" he bellowed, pissing.

I loved him enormously, from the first. He was the most gregarious man, but there was more to him than even that. He had a quality about him that made me feel like the most important person in his life, at each moment. His other friends were made to feel the same way, but I only saw what was meant for me.

As we sat in his hovel of a dressing room that first afternoon, Barrymore drifted into a story about old bull-fighters passing on their swords to the young matadors, to perpetuate their legacy. "It's called an 'alternativa,' kid," he explained, and through this explanation I sensed what he had in mind for me. He would teach me everything he knew about acting—to prepare me for the battles ahead, and ensure his place in the pantheon of the theater.

Whatever his intentions, I gave myself over to this wild, generous spirit and relished the ride. One of the preferred pastimes of the Barrymore crowd was to dress up in smoking jackets and entertain a group of prostitutes in grand manner. This was terrific sport for these men, and they did it often. Before long, I was a coconspirator. I did not own a smoking jacket, but they let me come up to the house in my one sports jacket and tie.

The whores, presumably, did not have any fine evening wear of their own, but Barrymore had a room full of ladies' costumes, and they all went upstairs to pick out their dresses. When we sat down to dinner, it was like a soused comedy of errors, with the men lost in drink and song and the girls grappling with the tableware and trying to maintain their dignity.

"Always treat a whore like a lady and a lady like a whore," Barrymore would say on these evenings. Or, similarly: "Anyone can make shit out of beauty, but it takes courage to make beauty out of shit."

To declarations like these, we would raise our glasses and wail with laughter. With these women, we could be as boorish as we pleased, without consequence.

One night, in the middle of one of Barrymore's marvelous yarns, one of the girls let out a small belch. We men had been belching and scratching ourselves all evening, but this was not the sort of behavior Barrymore expected from his ladylike whores. The incongruity simply would not do. The poor girl excused herself, and Barrymore continued with his story. A few moments later, she belched again. "Mr. Barrymore," she finally said, "I'm terribly sorry."

"It's quite all right, my dear girl," Barrymore said dismissively. "The mere fact that you haven't farted yet proves conclusively that you are still a lady."

He had a saberlike wit, and a flair for storytelling. In these tales, Barrymore's stage triumphs were never as important to him as his backstage doings. There did not have to be a theme to his stories, or even a point, but there always had to be an enormous payoff. Christ, I thought I would die laughing!

And Barrymore was not the only one of his crowd with a sharp mind and a quick tongue. W. C. Fields, of course, was a splendid comedian and raconteur, and Mitchell, Young, and Flynn were endlessly entertaining, but Fowler and Decker were also terribly amusing characters. Each was an accomplished artist in his own right. Gene Fowler was a magnificent writer, who took his role as the scribe of the group rather seriously. He would go on to write two definitive books about our various friendships with Barrymore—*Good Night, Sweet Prince*, and *Minutes of the Last Meeting*—and I cannot revisit one of his bittersweet accounts without imagining myself in Jack's decrepit "dressing room," with the rest of the crew.

John Decker was a talented painter, with a special gift as a knock-off artist. Decker could do Picasso better than

Picasso. He turned everything he painted into a kind of joke, almost always at someone else's expense, and his talents were a particular delight to Barrymore's crowd. At one time, half of Hollywood was decorated with Decker's deft imitations, and most of the stuffed shirts who bought his paintings had no idea they were not the real thing.

How Decker loved selling forgeries to those snobs! He would bring the stories of his duping to Barrymore's table and leave us howling. Once, when Decker heard that New York impresario Billy Rose was coming to town, he quickly knocked off a half-dozen paintings with his customer in mind. Rose, who was married to the great vaudevillian Fanny Brice, was an avid collector who happened at the time to have a thing about Rouault, so Decker painted Rouaults.

Rose arrived in Los Angeles, and Decker invited him to his studio for a showing. He was still putting the finishing touches on his paintings when Rose knocked on the door. "Billy," Decker said, ushering Rose inside, "I've just acquired the greatest collection of Rouaults in the world."

"My God," Rose exclaimed, looking at the fresh paintings, "they're wonderful! Where on earth did you find them?"

Decker went on and on about a German woman who was forced to liquidate her collection because of Hitler. It was all gibberish, but Rose accepted it. He simply had to have the collection, he said, no matter the cost.

The men agreed on a price, but when Rose went to take the masterworks with him, some of the paint rubbed off on his hands.

"Why are they wet?" he asked, quite reasonably.

"Oh, that's nothing," Decker said, quick on his feet. "I just put some varnish on to preserve the work."

Rose bargained a few dollars off the price and bought them anyway—wet or not, they were a steal!—while Decker pocketed the cash and the story.

Anecdotes such as these were like hard currency among Barrymore's group, and I constantly worried I could not pay my way. These were older, more accomplished men. They had all led rich, colorful lives. They had something to contribute. I had been raised in poverty, and had yet to amount to anything, but for some reason they accepted me. I was their innocent mascot, their link to disappearing youth. I belonged because their dynamic leader had made a place for me.

Even then, I knew that my Jack Barrymore was but a shadow of what he once had been. To my young eyes, he was everything, but he had been so much more. He was in failing health, and Hollywood producers were reluctant to hire him. He was a man of once-enormous wealth, and spectacular fame, left to live on what remained of his reputation. By the time I met him, Jack was known to drink his way through a picture, or to behave impossibly to those he judged beneath him. In some circles, he was no longer taken seriously, his greatness a long-forgotten thing of the past.

And yet even in these waning moments, he rose to most occasions. He once dragged Decker, Fowler, and me to Earl Carroll's nightclub on Sunset Boulevard, to ogle the famously beautiful dancing girls there. The evening started poorly, and for a moment looked as though it would finish even worse. The manager would not let Jack in without a tie, even though he was John Barrymore. He had to borrow one from the captain, but he managed this with aplomb.

We sat at a table down in front, sipped champagne with the flourish of kings, and went about the easy business of enjoying ourselves immensely.

At some point, the master of ceremonies had a spotlight put on our table and asked Barrymore to the stage for a dance with the most beautiful Earl Carroll girl on the line. Jack was reluctant, but the audience egged him on. At this point in his life, Barrymore was suffering terribly from gout and could hardly walk, but he could not resist the challenge.

He stepped to the stage and waited for his dance partner to emerge from the wings. When she did, I was astonished. She had painted black teeth, hobo clothes, and a clown's wig, and she moved with a knock-kneed walk. The audience, expecting one of the nightclub's trademark beauties, laughed wildly. They were laughing at their own surprise, but also at Barrymore. He had become a drunken caricature, and this was confirmation.

I wanted to storm the stage and save my friend from making a fool of himself, but I held back. The Barrymore I knew would find some way to save himself, to turn shit into beauty, and I hoped the moment was not yet lost. He signaled the orchestra to play a waltz and collected the girl in his arms. Suddenly, nothing existed for her but John Barrymore. She was clowning one moment, and weak-kneed the next. As he twirled her around the stage, she was transformed, and so was the audience. The room fell silent, save for the music. Everyone seemed to sense that something remarkable was happening, something intensely personal, something that had nothing at all to do with the lampooning they had all anticipated.

When the music stopped, Jack kissed the girl's hand and thanked her for the waltz. Then he stepped to the microphone, and looked around the quiet room. He held the moment for a long time.

"And as for you, ladies and gentlemen," he finally said, "you can all go fuck yourselves."

The audience was stunned, but as Barrymore walked off the stage, several people began to applaud. By the time he reached our table, two thousand people were on their feet, cheering.

It was, I thought, one of Barrymore's finest moments. Sadly, it was also one of his last. As he lay dying of cirrhosis of the liver, we moved our regular bacchanals to his hospital room, or to his bedroom at home. Jack kept a little water bottle filled with whiskey at the side of his bed, and he was never sober for very long. The rest of us drank to keep up with him, and to drown out the thought of what was happening to our friend.

It was my blood that kept Barrymore alive at the very end. We all had ourselves tested, and I was the only good match. Jack would not take blood from just anyone. Every other day, I went down to the hospital and gave another pint of blood. I would have given more, but this was all the doctors would allow. I used to look on Jack during these waning moments, as he drifted in and out of consciousness, thinking that my blood was but a small token next to what he had given me. He had gifted me a kind of life—a front-row seat to the stage I hoped someday to command, a precious validation of the man I sought to be—and I was simply paying him back in the only way I could.

A few days after Jack died, Decker arrived at Tower Road with a deathbed sketch of our friend. There was a cuckoo clock in the room above Jack's bed that had not worked in years, and it found its way into the scene. Decker drew the hands of the clock where they had always been, awaiting repair. When he arrived with the sketch, which he had hurriedly framed, I was drawn to the hands on the clock. I had been meaning to go upstairs and set the hands to the moment of Jack's death, for posterity, but I realized I would not have to.

John Barrymore had died at the appointed hour.

Begin Again

THINGS HAPPENED QUICKLY after my professional debut—and almost of their own accord. I was on a predetermined course, careening headlong into my future.

During the run of *Clean Beds*, I was asked to read for a small part in a movie being directed by a man named Louis Friedlander, over at Universal. Friedlander, a veteran of the silent era who would go on to direct a string of "B" Westerns for RKO under the name of Lewis Landers, had seen me in the play and found something to like in my performance. He was shooting a gangster picture called *Parole!* and had me in mind for a thug.

I was enthralled by this new profession, and flattered at the attention, even if I was too dumb to know that most auditions went nowhere. To me, this call to Universal was everything, and at first my ignorance was fortuitous; I was given the job on the spot, but then I lost it to my means.

When I arrived at the studio to shoot my scene, Friedlander told me to put on my suit. Regrettably, I did not own a suit, and had not been told one was necessary. Again, I was too dumb to have thought to ask. I assumed the studio would supply whatever I needed for the part. As it was, I reported for work wearing the most presentable clothes in my closet—a pair of threadbare trousers and a decent sweater—but they would not do for a natty gangster.

One of Friedlander's assistants rushed me to wardrobe, but they could not fit me in time to do the scene. The director was a kind man, but he had a job to do. There were extras to pay, and overtime to consider. He could not afford to wait around for someone to find me a costume. He was apologetic, and so was I. "It's just a misunderstanding, kid," Friedlander said. "There'll be other parts." He gave the job to another young actor who happened to walk by wearing a handsome suit of his own.

I walked away with my hands in my pockets. For the first time as an actor, I was disappointed. By now I had shed most thoughts about becoming an architect, and fantasized instead about a career on stage and screen. That was the way things were for me back then. I changed my life as I changed my mind. I still did not know how to pursue an acting job, or a coveted studio contract, but I knew this was what I wanted, where I belonged. I knew this as well as I knew myself, which may or may not have been all that well.

To have come so close to such opportunity, only to lose the role to my miserable clothes, was a terrible blow. And the worst piece was that I had told everyone about the part—my grandmother, Barrymore's crew, and my *Clean Beds* costars—and now I would have to face them and tell them what happened. I hated the way it made me look, and wished like hell I had kept my mouth shut.

Friedlander must have seen the dejection in my gait, because he called me back before I left the set. "Tell you what, kid," he said, throwing me a bone. "This afternoon, we're doing a jail sequence. It's not much, there's no dialogue, but I can pay you seventy-five dollars."

The money was as important to me as the chance to save face. "Sounds great," I said. "Tell me what to do." At this point, I would have done anything.

Wardrobe outfitted me in prison garb, and I prepared for the small scene. I was to play a stool pigeon named Zingo Browning, who is knifed to death while watching a prison show. I had to laugh, get stabbed, crumple to the ground, and die in under forty-five seconds. It was not much, but it was enough to salvage the afternoon. There was hope for me yet.

It was just a walk-on bit, but I tried to imagine an entire life for my character, beyond what was written in the script. It was not necessary, but I did not want to leave anything to chance. I decided Zingo was not a very nice man, but not a bad man either. He believed everyone, no matter what they told him. He got caught on someone else's bank job, and was sentenced to a long stint in the penitentiary. The injustice of it was almost too much for him. He could not accept it. He was no innocent, but he was not guilty of this. Now, during the life of the picture, someone convinces him to rat on a fellow inmate, to ease his sentence, and he is in for it. The payback comes while he is watching a show with the other prisoners, laughing at the antics on stage. Someone plunges a knife into Zingo's back and his expression freezes. In the instant of his death, I wanted the look on Zingo's face to be a mixture of shock and stupefaction; I wanted him to wonder why anyone would kill a laughing man.

The seventy-five dollars went far, but not far enough, and I was back at my odd jobs before long. The picture was a long time in coming out—four to six weeks, which by today's standards is no time at all but back then seemed like forever. I filled some of the spaces at Miss Hamil's acting school, when I could find the time, and I had even enrolled in a writing class, thinking that if acting did not work out for me I could always be a playwright, or a novelist, or perhaps even a screenwriter.

I was encouraged in this by some of my bookstore friends—John Steinbeck, Bill Saroyan, Scott Fitzgerald, and William Faulkner. There was a regular group that used to hang out in the back room at Rose's bookstore, on Hollywood Boulevard, and I fell in with them like an old-timer. It was almost like an old boys' club for writers, and for some reason I belonged. As it was with Barrymore and his friends, I had no business being there, and yet there I was, no more or less a part of the group than the most acclaimed artist.

By now, Sylvia had succeeded in her transformation of me, and I was a voracious reader, desperate to soak in what had for too long eluded me, but this alone did not qualify me for acceptance among such exclusive company. And yet these men treated me as if I was one of them, when in truth I was nothing—at least not yet. Here was my miraculous magnet again, in full force, drawing me to these distinguished writers and colorful personalities and bringing them to me. I do not know what it was about me that attracted such giants, but I did not question it. Why mess with a good thing?

There, in the back room at Rose's, I told Steinbeck endless stories of my family's experiences in the migrant fields of California, some of which he filtered through his own lens and reimagined in his novels. I sat for hours with Fitzgerald, listening to his frustrations about whatever script was then occupying his time. Books did not come easily to Fitzgerald, but screenplays were a torture. Faulkner too struggled with motion pictures.

Saroyan took a special interest in me and sent me to see a woman who conducted a writing class downtown. He was a member of the class himself, and a friend of the instructor. He thought there was a hunger in me to be a writer, and I was in no position to argue. The instructor could not see this same hunger (neither could I, for that matter), but she would not go against her friend's recommendation.

"What have you written?" she asked, when I went to enroll in her class.

"Nothing."

"Nothing published, or nothing at all?"

"Nothing. I read a lot, though, and take a lot of notes."

She asked what I did with my time. "After all," she reasoned, "someone who spends all his time not writing must be doing something." Her tone was pleasant, but sarcastic, as if she could not understand what I was looking for but did not mind helping me to find out.

I told her about my acting, and my odd jobs. I said that when I was not reading I liked to draw, and paint, and sculpt, or go to a motion picture with my grandmother. "Sometimes I take long walks," I said.

"Well, then, you are clearly not a writer. If you were a writer, you would write, but you have left yourself no time." The teacher explained that part of the pain and pleasure of being a writer was the discipline of carving out the time to work.

Of course, she was right, but I was persistent. If my writing friends thought that I should write, then I would write, and I convinced the woman to take me on as a student. She did not have to—I could no more afford her tuition than the acting school's!—but I gave her a hard sell.

That she bought it was significant, for it is this ancient transaction that has hurled me from my house this October morning, looking to pull myself away from the visions of my past, or to escape the hidden truths of my present. It was for this woman that I wrote the damn essay that has left me so unsettled, the one that likely sits at the top of the box my Katherine has sent from the States. In one of our assignments, the teacher had us wax prophetic on the lives we would lead, and the labored result has haunted me for nearly sixty years. How was I to know how I would live? I was just a kid, asked to speculate on what my life would be like, what I would become.

Perhaps it was a useful exercise, but I did not recognize it as such. I still do not see the point. And I certainly do not think I was meant to keep the result at hand for all these years. I have not reread my innocent musings, and do not know that I will—whether or not they are in that box. I do not particularly need to know what I was thinking, hoping. These are things better left to the transfigurations of reflection.

And so I ride on, losing the place in my thoughts but not the time. Even heading downhill, with the wind at my back, I cannot pedal too far ahead of where I was. The rush of memory still surrounds my twentieth year, and my first role in pictures. There I was, waiting for the gangster picture to open, romping through Hollywood with Barrymore and Decker and Fowler, filling up on drink and splendor at places like the Garden of Allah, on

Sunset, at the mouth of the strip leading out to Beverly Hills. Now here was a place for the storybooks!—and a favorite haunt. It was a lush hotel, known for its pools and fountains and riotous all-night parties. I was but a lesser light among the luminaries—Dorothy Parker, Robert Benchley, Tallulah Bankhead, Charlie Chaplin, Sheilah Graham, Groucho and Harpo Marx—but in my mind I shone as bright.

There were no rules at the Garden of Allah, but there was a routine. The hotel was mainly occupied by transplanted novelists, brought to town to work on scripts. Fitzgerald stayed there, and Faulkner. Everyone. At night, around six, the writers would spill from their bungalows and start drinking, to be joined by actors, directors, gossip columnists, and various hangers-on. There were small tables set up around the pool, each lit with a single candle, and on any night you could see as many stars on the deck as in the heavens. I cannot imagine how many pictures were born, or still-born, around those tables.

Before long, most of the guests were swimming in the pool—naked or fully clothed, drunk or sober. It did not matter. There was always wild yelling and singing. Everybody slept with everybody else. It was like a star-studded orgy with an open bar, and I was the wide-eyed child, pacing the sidelines, waiting to get into the game. It was wonderful.

One of the glorious residues of my visits to the Garden of Allah was the chance once again to mingle with the legends of the day. Occasionally, these minglings led to loose friendships, on more proper grounds. Once, former tennis champion Bill Tilden spotted me playing tennis in a Los Angeles playground and invited me to Charlie Chaplin's place for a game of doubles, with Greta Garbo. I had met them all, at one time or another, at the hotel.

I was thrilled at the invitation, but I did not own any tennis togs. (Christ! was my wardrobe conspiring to keep me from everything?) Tilden offered to lend me some clothes, and I went along, feeling at least tenuously connected to these people because they had seen me with Barrymore.

Chaplin moved as gracefully on the court as he did on the screen. He was quite an exceptional athlete, with a playful rhythm to his game, but he was no match for Tilden. That is, he should have been no match, except that he paid Tilden to go easy on him. Tilden was like a human backboard, serving up gentle, waist-high returns, right at Chaplin's forehand. Charlie barely had to move to get to the ball. Garbo was his doubles partner, and she enjoyed the same treatment. Tilden made the two of them look like pros.

There I was, hustling on the other side of the net, doing what I could, but my partner would never put the ball away.

"Boy, Charlie," Tilden would say, failing to reach another shot, "you're too fast for me." His compliments were solicitous, and over the top.

When the game was over, I saw Chaplin slip Tilden fifty dollars, and I later learned that the former champion was a frequent guest on Chaplin's court, on similar terms. I did not mind the losing, but I could not shake feeling sorry for Tilden. It was pathetic, what he had let himself become: a man who accepted handouts in order to overstay his welcome among the rich and famous. He seemed to need the left-behind adulation as much as the money, and I could not decide which was worse. He had been a great tennis player, and now I wondered how he lived with himself.

For all of my desire to belong among this crowd, I vowed I would never degrade myself like this. I might degrade myself in other ways, but never like this.

Finally, the calendar fell on my big screen debut. I built the picture up in my head as a kind of turning point, from which everything in my life would then follow. The months spent gamboling about town would either continue or come to an abrupt end on the cutting room floor. In truth, the opening of *Parole!* would not make or break me any more than any other moment, but I vested it with a power beyond all reality. It would be remembered or forgotten.

There was to be a gala premiere, at the Pantages Theater, and my grandmother was dying to attend. Actually, she was not dying to attend. She was terribly sick, battling the cancer, hoping to last long enough to see me in pictures. It was everything to her. She would come to see me on stage, and these outings were her remission.

"You are no architect, Tony," she would say to me afterward. "You are an actor." It was the same line she had been feeding me since the movie house in El Paso, only now it was attached to possibility.

When the day came, I borrowed a car and drove my grandmother downtown to the theater. Her body was so weakened, I had to carry her upstairs to the balcony. She had once weighed 140 pounds, but she was like a sack of feathers in my hands. I thought the balcony would be quiet, and she would be more comfortable there. Plus, I was embarrassed. Everyone would be there—the director, the producers, the other actors—and I was ashamed to be seen with this great lady. I adored my grandmother, but I did not want some reviewer or columnist to make me out as a mama's boy. I was too stupid to realize that nobody knew who the hell I was, or cared. I was a bit player, with a walk-on.

But Dona Sabina was in her glory. If she noticed my unease, she did not let on. The moment, for her, was bigger than anything else. She gripped my arm throughout the picture. "Tony," she murmured, "you are my Ramon Novarro. You are my Antonio Moreno. You are going to be a big star." She spoke softly, but in her mind her voice was booming.

Louis Friedlander shot my scene as a close-up. He was a sweet man. He did not have to give me the camera's attention, but he did. My face filled the screen. It was everything, and in less than a minute it was over. I suddenly felt sheepish, to have driven halfway across town, to have carted my grandmother up the stairs, all for a lousy few seconds! I begged Dona Sabina to let me take her home after my one scene, before the lights came on, but she would not move. She wanted to see where I fit with the rest of the picture. She wanted to see my name in the credits. She wanted to taste the whole damn thing.

When it was over, she leaned into me and whispered, "Now I can die in peace."

Two weeks later, she was gone.

Ride

WHAT IS IT WITH ME AND CEMETERIES? I have not been to see my grandmother. I have not been to see my father, save for the one trip to place his headstone. I have not been to see my mother, or my son.

I avoid these formal lamentations because these dear spirits are not dead to me. They are alive in my heart, always, and in the air around me. They are everywhere. To imagine any one of them in a pine box, six feet under ground, is an execration. I would sooner die myself than consign my loves to such a fate. No, no, no. Death is not for them. No.

And yet here, in Nettuno, my legs take me to the American cemetery without objection. Lang Hargrove was a friend, for a short time, but he was a relative stranger next to these others. Why is it that I can mourn for him, in the ritual ways, and cannot bring myself to grieve for my own flesh? Is it that I am far enough removed from the Lang Hargroves buried here that their deaths will not touch me in a substantive way? Perhaps, but I think there is more to it than this. I think it probably has to do with the deals I have made with mortality, over the years. If I acknowledge death, where it counts, then death has won. If I let God claim my own blood, then He will next claim me. If I give in to the transience of this earthly place, then all is lost, forever. If I leave my loved ones to die, then they have not been here at all.

Even this, granting death a place in my thoughts, is too much for me. Today of all days, I do not need this. I am off in the busy marketplace, away from the cemetery, but I am still too close to it. The rows of markers are in my sightlines. The only way to lose them is to run, immediately. I cannot remain a moment longer.

I make for my bicycle with long strides. It is leaning where I left it, against the short stone wall encircling the cemetery parking lot, resting from the morning's work. I mount the thing like a cowboy, and kick it into gear, and as I pull away from these sacred and storied grounds, I remember about the drink. I had meant to refill my water bottle with something cool, but now the chance is lost. The sun is high and hot but there is no stopping, or doubling back. I can always stop for water later.

I pedal faster, willing myself away from this place and on to the next one.

SIX

The Breaks

THE CASTING OFFICE at Paramount Studios was filled with actors looking for work. The studio had placed an advertisement in the local newspapers—an open call for actors who could pass as Native American Indians—and the office was filled with swarthy, muscular types, banking on stardom. There were not enough pictures to go around, and we were like moths to a porch light.

To a struggling actor, Hollywood was the Holy Grail, the pot of gold at the end of the rainbow, and the pull of an open call was stronger than any force I knew. I was pulled all the way from Mexico, on this day in 1936, to claim a role in a Cecil B. De Mille picture called *The Plainsman*, starring Gary Cooper and Jean Arthur. I was in Ensenada when I saw the ad, about to sign on to a huge fishing boat on its way to Japan. My walk-on in *Parole!* had not been everything I had hoped, and despite Dona Sabina's predictions, a career in pictures did not look promising. There were a few uncredited bits, in forgettable "B" movies, but I worried I would never land a speaking role. I was either too dark, or too Mexican, or too unusual-looking, and the good parts always seemed to go to the actors who fit a more conventional mold. For me, the opportunities around every corner only led to dead ends.

My latest whim had me thinking of the life of a commercial fisherman, and I was about to change course yet again. I was just back from a stint in the Southwest—hoboing from one town to the next, digging ditches for a few cents a day, mending fences for room and board—and I was no more an actor than an itinerant laborer. I had even spent a short time in a Texas jail, after an ill-advised romance with a widowed landowner. I was rootless, and desperate.

I needed a plan. My only obligation was to my sister, Stella, but she had gone back to live with my mother after Dona Sabina died. She would be fine without me. The idea of setting sail, to exotic ports where I might reinvent myself yet again, had tremendous appeal. No one would know me. My only history would be that which I would build, day by day. If I came back at all, I would come back a new man—with stories to tell, money to spend, and a new set of terms. Maybe then I could make something of myself.

I hopped a freight train to Ensenada and waited for the next ship to pull out. I made all the arrangements, but then I found a discarded Los Angeles newspaper on one of the piers. Paramount's advertisement was a powerful lure—Hollywood's porch light was too damn bright!—and I decided to make one last pass at this acting thing before moving on to something else. I had not counted on this. According to the ad, I was the right height, and weight, and color. (Even an incompetent makeup man would not cost me this one!) I abandoned the fishing boat and hitchhiked back to Los Angeles. If I could not pass for a Native American, then no one could.

I walked into the Paramount offices as if I were expected. "Mr. De Mille wants to see me," I announced to Joe Egley, a bighearted man with a slight stutter who was slaving as the studio's casting director.

"What about?" he said.

"I hear he needs a young Indian for his new picture."

"And you're the young Indian?" Egley asked, skeptical.

He had seen me on stage in *Clean Beds* and allowed, quite accurately, that there was probably no more redskin blood in me than there was in him.

"Ksai ksakim eledski chumbolum," I said, refusing to be put off.

"What's that?" Egley wondered.

I had no idea. "Cheyenne," I said. "I speak fluently."

"No kidding," he said, suddenly impressed. "That's Cheyenne?"

"Of course it is," I insisted. "How could I make it up?"

Whatever I said, it was good enough to get me in to see De Mille. Egley passed me off as a full-blooded Cheyenne, and I had my first speaking part. The only hitch was I could not speak English around De Mille, to corroborate Egley's story about my native background. The job paid seventy-five dollars per day, with the promise of two or three days' work. The money was unbelievable; in just three days, I could make more than I had ever made in three months!

Of course, I did not consider my own time, spent in rehearsal, but it was still a rich deal. For a week, I studied five pages of gibberish dialogue and learned to ride a horse at a San Fernando Valley stable run by a former boxer named Ace Hudkins. I practiced my big speech on horseback, trying to associate certain images with the words, to help me remember. I did not know if my pronunciation was correct, but I did not know if this mattered. How many Cheyenne Indians would go and see the picture?

Finally, with my gibberish and riding skills committed to routine, I turned up for my scene. It was a Monday, and I was on the lot in time to see the stars arrive for work: Cary Grant, Bing Crosby, Maurice Chevalier. It was intoxicating, to share even a sliver of their limelight, even from such a lowly vantage point.

In wardrobe, I was given a ragged shirt, a loincloth,

and moccasins. I had been told I was playing a proud chief, and was expecting something more regal. The costume was humiliating enough, but there was no place for me to change on the set, so I had to march across the lot to the soundstage with my bare ass hanging out. There was a huge lawn in the center of the lot, and all the stars were gathered around an elaborate fountain there, waiting for their limousines to take them to their stages, while I was left to stand nearly naked in my loincloth.

I might have arrived, but surely I was not there yet.

Nothing inside Stage 7 was as I expected. I thought there would be other Indians in the scene with me. There were no other Indians. I thought my horse would have a saddle. There was no saddle. I thought the speech I had rehearsed into memory was to be delivered to my character's tribe, but there was no tribe.

There was me, and Gary Cooper.

It was a nightmare. I sat behind a fake rock, waiting for my cue, and I prayed: All right, God, this is a disaster, but please help me. Make me an Indian. Make me an Indian for the next two hours. I suddenly felt a peculiar peace, as if I could do anything. If anybody had spoken to me at that moment in Cheyenne, I would have answered.

The next moment was something else. The next moment, I got on my horse, took the reins of a second horse, and came out from behind the rock to a camp fire, as instructed, but then an agitated De Mille wondered why I wasn't singing my Cheyenne song.

"What in the world is going on?" De Mille screamed. "This kid doesn't even know the damn song!"

I tried the scene again, the same way, only this time I sang an Indian-sounding song. I had no clue what I was singing, but I did not think it mattered.

"Get me Joe Egley," De Mille yelled, stopping the scene again. "Tell him to get me somebody else."

There was a big commotion, with secretaries and

assistants scrambling to do the director's bidding. Just then, Gary Cooper asked De Mille to go easy on me. "The boy is going to be all right," he said.

"I don't want to waste your time, Gary," De Mille said. "We've got a busy day today."

"He seems like a nice kid," Cooper said. "Give him a break."

De Mille naturally consented to his leading man's request, and told my interpreter to have me sing again. "Nobody's going to know the difference," he said, "just so it's in Cheyenne."

All right, I told myself, climbing back on my horse. I am a Cheyenne. I will sing a Cheyenne song. And I did. I do not know how, but I heard my voice, singing. There was an Indian in me! I sang defiantly. In my head, I gave my words meaning: To hell with you, white men. You will not embarrass me. You will not take away my dignity. We are the Cheyenne people. We will win.

As I sang I thought, Well, if De Mille is going to fire me, at least I can tell him to go to hell. I might lose the job, but I will keep my dignity.

When it came time for our first take, something came over me. I sat on my horse, waiting for the light above me to signal the start of the scene, thinking, Okay, when that light goes on, either I will fail or my life will start. Then the light flashed on and I was an Indian. I forgot everything except that I was a young Cheyenne.

I got off my horse and noticed the fire, but then I did a strange thing. As I approached the fire, I suddenly turned and darted behind a tree.

"Cut!" De Mille yelled. "What the hell is that kid doing?"

There followed another scurrying commotion. No one could believe a young actor would deliberately screw up such a beautiful take—even a young Indian actor. Along came my interpreter, who seemed as comfortable with his

Cheyenne tongue as I was with mine, and he spoke to me in Spanish. "They've got another actor ready to do the part," he said, gesturing across the stage to a man dressed in the same outfit, with the same makeup: another spare part, just like me.

I knew that if I tried to explain why the scene was all wrong, or if I messed up again, my bare ass would be tossed right into that fountain out on the lot. So I held back, took my horses around behind the rock, and waited for my cue. While I was waiting, I caught the eye of a stunning young girl, talking to De Mille. She had jet-dark hair, beautiful skin, and the most piercing eyes I had ever seen. She almost looked Indian, and I took her native appearance as a good luck charm. Perhaps it was an omen she was there. Then it hit me who she was—the great man's daughter, Katherine De Mille. Of course. She had been in a number of pictures (*Viva Villa*, *The Call of the Wild*), and I felt an immediate kinship. It was as if she understood about me. A slight smile appeared on her face, and I felt sure she was willing me to get through this next take.

The light flashed on and I was ready. This time, I had a pretty girl to play to and I was nearly chanting, transforming the song of victory into a kind of clarion call, championing the cause of young actors everywhere. I would do the scene their way, but the song was mine. Then I rode into the scene, looked around, got off my horse, and walked very tentatively toward the fire. I stood for just a second—and bolted again for the safety of the tree!

De Mille positively erupted this time, and there was yet another ruckus. The director was cursing wildly, ranting, calling me an idiot sonofabitch and a bastard Indian and whatever else raced into his fuming head. "Forget about it," he screamed, "forget about it! Pay him and send him home."

I looked over at Katherine De Mille, but she looked away. She seemed embarrassed for me, and I felt as if I had let her down. All was lost, but for some reason I was particularly saddened at the opportunity I appeared to have squandered with this beautiful creature. "Mr. De Mille," I said, emboldened by his daughter's presence and what I took to be her sympathetic manner, "let me explain."

He turned as if someone had cracked him with a whip. The room fell silent. "So," he managed, "you speak English?"

One hundred sets of eyes were on me. "Look," I said, "you fired me, and it's all right, but I am not an idiot and I am not a stupid Indian. I'm an actor. I know what I'm doing. I don't care about your fucking seventy-five dollars. You can shove the money up your ass. But I can't walk out of here without telling you that I think you've got the scene all wrong."

"Is that so?" he demanded, walking over to me slowly, and with great authority. I could not tell if he was about to hit me, or launch into another one of his tirades.

Either way, I would not let him make the next move. "That fire," I continued, "the one I'm to stand in front of for five fucking minutes, is that a white man's fire or a red man's fire."

"Gary Cooper built the fire," one of the assistants offered.

"Gary Cooper built the fire," De Mille confirmed.

"Exactly," I said. "You think an Indian doesn't know the difference between a white man's fire and an Indian's fire? The fire's still burning, someone's around, somewhere, and you want me to stand there all that time? What kind of Indian would just stand there, waiting, without hiding to protect himself?"

De Mille stared at me for what seemed an awfully long time. Everyone—the crew, Gary Cooper, Katherine—

held their breath. No one had ever heard an actor speak to the great De Mille in this way, particularly a green kid on his first real job in pictures. The director's hard features gradually softened. "The boy's right," he announced. "We'll change the setup."

Later, De Mille came over and shook my hand. He said he loved the new scene, and he was very understanding about the earlier confusion. He paid me for three days, and had Joe Egley put me up for a contract at the studio. Before I left the lot I had an offer for a $250 weekly contract. It was a tremendous amount of money, but for some reason I told Joe I would have to think about it.

I was already beginning to think in their terms.

My first thought, though, was not for the promising future I had suddenly bought, but for the gorgeous young woman who held my gaze and fed me silent encouragement during those tense moments on the set. I wanted to meet her, to thank her for helping me with the scene, to see if there might be anything between us. I did not care that she was De Mille's adopted daughter. She was someone I had to know, but when I started to ask questions, I learned I would never have the chance. Katherine was leaving for South America in just a few days, to be married.

My heart was broken. In my moment of victory, I lost the one girl I felt sure I could love.

"What Studio Is He At?"

KATHERINE DE MILLE'S hold on me lasted until later that afternoon. It might have lasted longer but something came up. Since my disappointment with Sylvia, my fancy was never fixed on the same point for too long. I was young, and it did not take much for me to move from one lovely young lady to the next.

There was also the matter of my career to think about—and right away. The entire studio was buzzing about what happened on Stage 7 that day, and it was quite easy to be charmed by the attention.

I was even flagged by the glorious Carole Lombard, as I stepped from the talent department bungalow after my unassuming contract negotiation. "So you're the young boy who told C.B. to go fuck himself," she cooed. She had a way of saying the vilest things in the most enchanting manner.

Lombard wound up finagling me a part in the picture she was shooting, *Swing High, Swing Low*. The director, Mitch Leisen, had once worked as De Mille's designer, and he had already heard of our clash on the set. He was amused enough to hire me on the spot—for one hundred dollars a day!—but not before warning me against the wiles of Miss Lombard. "You're just her type," he cautioned, although I could not see why this might be a problem.

I had allowed myself to imagine all these wild, erotic scenarios unfolding between us, but by the time I showed up for work, I had developed such an intimidating crush on this goddess that I did not know how to behave. When I was near her, I felt lost. I did not know what to talk to her about. I was naive enough to assume that all movie stars were incredibly cultured individuals, so I thought to engage her in a discussion of literature. "I'm just reading *Tom Jones*, by Henry Fielding," I said, thinking this would impress her.

"Henry Fielding?"

"Yes. I like him, don't you?"

"What studio is he at?" she asked, and I thought, Well, so much for literature. From that moment, I let Lombard determine the size of our small talk.

Much to my amazement, she invited me to her dressing room for a drink, and when we relaxed a bit she told me she was in love with a famous actor and was waiting for him to get a divorce and marry her. She declined to identify her lover, but it was well-known that she had taken up with Clark Gable. "I sit at home nights because we can't be seen in public," she confided. "Would you take me out?"

"Of course," I said. "Sure."

I smiled inanely. She was so incredibly beautiful, with lovely skin, long blond hair, and penetrating eyes. . . . What in the world did she want with me?

We made a date for that night, but when I rushed home to change clothes, I realized I had nothing to wear. (Again, my clothes were killing me!) All the money I made had gone to pay debts, and all I had were a few pairs of patched pants and some old sweaters. This was hardly appropriate for a night on the town with the fabulous Carole Lombard. Worse, I had only seven dollars in my pocket. I could not see myself taking this magnificent lady to a cafeteria, in patched clothes, so I stood her up.

I did not run into Miss Lombard again for several days, until I was back at the studio shooting my third picture in as many weeks—this time as a Hawaiian in *Waikiki Wedding*, directed by Frank Tuttle.

"You little shit!" someone shouted from across the Paramount courtyard. "You bastard! You fucking little prick!" Carole Lombard really did have the worst tongue in the world, and when I realized it was being directed at me, I felt ashamed. People were stopping to look.

"Miss Lombard," I said, racing over to her, trying to beat the next blast of obscenities, "please, I can explain."

"Fuck you! You no-good little shit! No one's ever stood me up before. You just wanted the goddamn job!"

I had wanted the job, but my designs on working had nothing to do with my designs on Carole Lombard. As far as motion pictures were concerned, I had more work than I ever dreamed—and a standing offer of a studio contract.

I was at least two weeks past the point of needing some-one like Carole Lombard to help me get a leg up.

But she would not stop to listen. She stormed off to her dressing room. I followed and knocked on the door. I had a whole story cooked up to explain my behavior, but when she finally opened the door, the truth just melted from me.

When I finished, she had tears in her eyes. "Is that the truth," she said, "or is that just a line?"

"It's not a line. I didn't have any money. Now I have money. I just cashed my check. If you still want to go out, I'll take you anywhere you want to go."

We went out that night, and many nights afterward. For a period of time, she was one of my closest friends, in nearly every sense. She became a kind of career counselor, introducing me to her agent, Charlie Feldman, who took me on as a client. She advised me on what contract terms to consider, what stars to emulate, what roles to pursue. She taught me who the players were in town, and who was just pretending. We were romantically involved but there was no romance between us—a liberated distinction with which I would become all too familiar.

Alas, my relationship with Carole Lombard never progressed beyond healthy indiscretion and youthful infatuation. The more time I spent on the Paramount lot (now as a full-fledged contract player, at four hundred dollars per week!), the more I set my heart on the boss's daughter.

It mattered little that she was about to be married to someone else.

Love . . .

KATHERINE.
Oh, how disturbing it is to weigh what has become of

her against what she once was. The last time I saw Katherine, her eyes told nothing of the life we once shared.

Alzheimer's is a terrible disease, slowly killing my first wife as it kills her family. My heart aches for what it has done to Katherine's spirit and memory, but it is also empty. In some ways, I love her more now than during our time together; in others, I struggle to see her as the same person. My love for her today is real—not the Hollywood love I felt as a young man, long before Alzheimer's staked its claim. Back then, I do not know that I ever even embraced her fully. I did not give either one of us a chance. All that survives between us are our children, and the vexing box she has sent to condemn me. Today, she resembles herself in name only, but I learned early that Katherine De Mille was rarely as she appeared. There was a hidden girl: frightened, insecure, timorous.

When she returned from South America, in 1936, she was happily unattached. I seized the opportunity to be with her, without considering the cost. She had gone off to marry a Colombian, but the relationship did not work out. I never knew why, and did not think to ask. Who was I to question Katherine's Colombian dream?

Fate was about to cast me in another Cecil B. De Mille production—the swashbuckling epic *The Buccaneer*—when Katherine reappeared. I had been up for the leading role of Jean Lafitte, but the great man was talked down from his impulse to hire me by friends and family. Like most producers who could no longer formulate their own opinions, De Mille was in the habit of inviting people to his private projection room to view screen tests of actors under consideration. Katherine, I later learned, was one of my detractors, and suggested Clark Gable for the part. She thought I was too young to play such a seasoned pirate, and perhaps she was right.

De Mille took his family's casting notes to heart, but

Gable was unavailable. Instead, he gave the lead to
Fredric March, and offered me a supporting turn as one
of Lafitte's lieutenants. I was happy for the consolation.
After a good-sized role in James Hogan's *The Last Train
From Madrid*, and a handful of stock character parts, this
would be my first chance to work in a big picture.

March must have known he was not the consensus first
choice for Lafitte, and that De Mille had briefly considered me for the role. "You're either going to be one of the
best actors around," he said to me, after rehearsing our
first scene, "or you're going to be the biggest flop." Then
he walked away, leaving me to think that most of the
actors I was meeting were a curious bunch indeed.

(Years later, when I was appearing in *Becket* on Broadway,
March came backstage and reminded me of his pre-
science. "You see," he said, "I was right." I did not know
whether he meant I was one of the best actors around, or
one of the biggest flops, and I could not bring myself to
ask.)

I do not know why, but I was blinded by the thought of
Katherine. I did not care that she had gone against me in
my audition, or that she was nearly married to someone
else. It did not matter that the only things we shared were
a few meaningful looks that day on the *Plainsman* set.

There was no courtship, really. From the first, it was
clear where our relationship was headed, although the
reasons for its course were unclear. I have no idea what
we were each looking for. Perhaps I knew at the time, but
today it is a whole other muddle. I think now I was looking to get back at Sylvia for not marrying me, even if I did
not recognize it. Maybe I was looking for a family, for
that sense of belonging that had always eluded me. And
for all I know Katherine was trying to defy her father,
bringing home a hungry Mexican from the wrong side of
town, even if she thought all she was doing was falling in
love.

Whatever our motives, we pursued each other with a purpose. We both loved to read, and literature became our common ground. In the beginning, there was not much else to share. I was uncomfortable with the differences in our station, but determined to set them aside. This was sometimes difficult. Once, early on, Katherine invited me on her father's boat for a weekend cruise. It was just the two of us, and the crew. The yacht stretched on forever, and at night we would sit on the deck under blankets and look at the moon. Jesus, I have never felt so pained and pampered at the same time! It was a magnificent vessel, but I hated the opulence of it. With Barrymore, at least, I had been a welcome guest in his home, but here I felt like an interloper. I half-expected the Coast Guard to pull alongside and charge me with trespassing. I had nothing against wealth or poverty, but I believed strongly that each should reflect a man's true spirit. I was not meant to have a crew. I was a peasant chasing a princess, too young to know where my true spirit would take me.

Katherine was untouchable to me, under the blankets, under the stars. Lord knows what she wanted from me that night, or on any of the nights before we were married. I made no move to be disrespectful and I cannot understand why. Maybe I thought my advances would be unwelcome, or that I would set her off in some way. Maybe I thought the long arm of Cecil B. De Mille would somehow reach down, grab me around the throat, and toss me out of town for messing with his daughter. Maybe I thought she was not that kind of girl. Most likely, I had put Katherine on a kind of pedestal, and could not sully her virtue before we reached the sanctity of our marriage bed.

The yacht was nothing next to her father's estate. My, what a palace! It was out in Los Feliz, where De Mille owned a lot of land, and the mansion sat on top of a special hill overlooking the property. It was simply enormous, with rooms upon rooms upon rooms. The grand entry hall was like something out of a museum. The road leading up to the house was christened De Mille Drive, and there were maids and butlers and valets. I was overwhelmed by the prosperity.

De Mille and I had a reasonable working relationship on the set, and he knew I had been running around with his daughter, so he was not surprised to see me in his home, under these terms. He may not have been happy, but at least he was not surprised. Surely, De Mille would have preferred a man of better means, and more pretentious beginnings, for his lovely daughter, but he never said anything. I could read his disappointment in his grudging acknowledgment and patronizing tone, but he respected his daughter too much to openly oppose her.

I used to joke that De Mille must have truly thought I was an Indian from some nearby reservation, and that he was terrified I would gather my tribesmen on his sprawling front lawn for a war dance, but the line rankled every time. I laughed about it, but I also knew it to be true, on some level, and a part of him could never look past it.

I was asked to dinner the first time I visited, and it stands as one of the most awkward evenings of my life. I did not know what forks or spoons to use at the table. What did I know from cutlery? In my house, growing up, we ate with a spoon and a tortilla. Here it seemed there was a different utensil for every bite of food. I had to follow Katherine and the others, to make sure I did not lose my place.

Katherine was seated to my right, and her mother, Constance, was on my left. Next to Mrs. De Mille was Mrs. Grismar, a lovely old family friend who was a fixture in the household. The two older women were actually very accepting of my relationship with Katherine. De Mille himself sat at the head of the table, unaccepting, staring me down throughout the meal. When I spoke, I was careful to choose my words as precisely as possible, and to enunciate clearly. I would not make a fool of myself in front of this man and his family.

On the table in front of me was a little blue dish with a tiny spoon in it. When coffee was served, I figured it for the sugar bowl. I rarely took coffee after dinner, but it was presented so grandly, in wonderful demitasse cups, that I decided to try some. I wanted to be a good guest, and try everything. I reached for the blue dish and sank two rounded spoons of what I thought was sugar into my cup. Everyone was watching me, aghast, but no one said anything, not even my Katherine.

One sip was enough to tell me what the stares of the others could not. I had filled my half-cup of coffee with two heaping mounds of salt! It was like a cliche from an old silent picture, but I could not laugh it off. I was mortified, and too proud to admit I had made a mistake. I was the dumb fool I vowed not to be. I swallowed hard and drank the whole thing.

After the shine had rubbed from our marriage, I asked Katherine why she agreed to marry me, and she said it was because of that first time she took me to see her family. "The coffee, Tony," she said, "the way you drank it down, it told me you had character, that you could live with a mistake, that the negatives in your life would somehow turn positive."

What Katherine saw as character, I saw as something else. Mostly, it was stubborn pride and secret shame, with a dash of fear thrown in for the hell of it. I did not know how to act around such grandeur. I did not belong in that house. I was afraid of what it would do to me. The cavernous rooms, the brocaded furniture, the Persian rugs . . . these things were not a part of any equation I knew.

As I pedal past the stuff of my life, I realize it is difficult to describe what I was thinking on that first visit to the De Mille mansion. I cannot do my feelings justice. The words do not come, I think, because my perspective has changed. Oh, I can remember what I was thinking, but I no longer feel things in quite the same way. Understand, I consider this now from a completely different vantage point, and the raw emotions are forever lost to the years. I have since known such luxury on my own. I have been a rich man far longer than I was a poor boy, and I can remember no transition. Back then, I had no reference points for a lifestyle like De Mille's. Even Barrymore lived simply next to this. As I sat there that first evening, I thought back to the one-room shack I shared with my mother in El Paso, sleeping on the floor; or the shitty two-seater outhouse I used to marvel at with my grandmother; or the lousy lean-to Papa built to pass for a master bedroom.

In my twenty-two years, I had survived on the bare essentials, just; I had walked through the snow in bare feet; I had done back-breaking work for next to nothing in wages; I had gone without eating to save money for a new book; and I had never left a scrap of food on my plate. Against all of this, I had more in common with De Mille's servants than with anyone sitting around the dinner table, but even the servants lived like royalty next to me.

It was as if I had come from another planet and landed in the world of Cecil B. De Mille.

I wanted no part of it, but one.

. . . and Marriage

MY MOTHER WAS NOT INVITED to the wedding. My sister was not invited to the wedding. Even dear Sylvia—my soulmate, still—was not invited to the wedding. Not a single one of my friends was invited to the wedding. It was a wonder they found room at the reception for me.

I was swallowed up by the storm of excitement and did not think to question the plans. In my cowardice, I probably encouraged them. I was ashamed of my past and wanted to wash it all away. If my family came, and my friends, there would be no hiding who I was: a poor kid from the East Side. This way, underrepresented, I could masquerade as a prince. I could belong.

Katherine should have looked out for me and my family's interests, but I cannot really blame her for my own weakness. Jesus, I was a sorry little ass! My mother was ten times the person that De Mille was. She did not deserve to be shunted aside by her own son. She deserved a position of honor, at the head table, but I could not even get her an invitation. I hated myself for the way I behaved. I like to think that I would have done things differently if my grandmother had been alive, but I cannot say for certain. I think I loved Dona Sabina too much to humiliate her. And my father? Well, I could never have put him through such indignation. He would have punched me in the face. For some reason, my mother was a different story. I loved her dearly, but her marriage to Frank Bowles had been at great cost to our relationship. We would make repairs after her husband's death, but I could not see that far into the future. I let myself be talked down from what was right because I no longer trusted her, or needed her, as I once had. I respected her, but it was not the same. Christ, I was her only son, and it did not even matter if she attended my wedding! Her own son!

The affair was not as lavish as it might have been, given the size of De Mille's wallet and his affinity for big-scale productions. Perhaps he too wanted to play it down. Katherine and I were married on a weekday evening in October 1937. We were both under contract to Paramount, and we each put in a full day at the studio before racing off to All Saints Episcopal Church in Hollywood for the ceremony. I supposed it would not have done for De Mille's daughter and soon-to-be son-in-law to have skipped out of work early, even for such a fine occasion. Appearances counted for everything in Hollywood, even to Cecil B. De Mille. There were limousines and a police escort to take us across town, and a row of photographers poised at the steps to the church. Inside, the pews were occupied by Katherine's friends and family, but mostly they were filled by studio and industry executives, putting in an appearance for the old man.

It was not exactly the wedding of my dreams, but the honeymoon was a nightmare. It almost ended on our wedding night. God, I was an idiot!—to have thought that Katherine, a woman of twenty-six, had never been with another man! She had nearly married that Colombian. What did I expect? And yet lying with my new bride, on our first marriage bed, I could not accept anything less. She was my woman. She belonged to no one else.

We had driven up to a hotel in Carmel. The white sheets after our lovemaking were like a dagger to my throat. My mind raced. What, no blood? I thought you were supposed to be a virgin! What the fuck is going on? I was overcome by a raging jealousy. I could not control my own emotions. I had no idea what I would do next, if I would do anything at all. In an instant, I thought, our marriage was over.

With Sylvia, at least I knew about the others. The Katherine I imagined for myself was pure, undefiled, and mine alone. She had no history but the one we would build together. I slapped her, hard, once the madness told me what it all meant. How the hell could she have deceived me in this way? But even in my fury I realized the deception was mine. How could I not have known? What the fuck was I thinking? I slapped her again. I was crazy, confused. Poor Katherine must have been terrified! She packed her few things and made to leave. I told her to take the train to Reno, where we would get a divorce. I gave her some money. She closed the door behind her, and I thought myself a fool.

I sat in the room, alone, wondering what a broken piece of tissue in a woman's vagina had to do with my strange concept of love and devotion. We lived in a time of changing values. Who was I to set such an impossible double standard? I had been with several women—a handful even since I began seeing Katherine. I had been with a virgin or two (dear, sweet Evie among them), and what the hell did that get me? One shot and even that was gone.

And yet, my transgressions did not mean I was any less committed to our marriage, so why should Katherine's mean anything different? I had no more right to a past than she did. But there was every difference, and I could not look away from it. I was married now, and no longer a boy. I knew that if I did not chase after Katherine, I would never be a man. Besides, I loved Katherine—enough, maybe, to take her as she was. I kept seeing the terror in her sad, beautiful eyes. She had no idea she had done anything wrong. She could not understand what had set me off. Her life had not been easy, I knew. She was orphaned as a small child, and it was years before the De Milles' adoption came through. She too wanted desperately to belong, and now I had cast her off.

I could not accept the way my behavior made me look, so I jumped into the car and gave chase, driving frantically over winding mountain roads, trying to beat Katherine's train. I caught up with her at a siding, fifty miles outside Reno. I boarded the train and found her compartment. She was sitting by herself, sobbing. I collected her bags and told her to follow me.

She did not speak until we were back in the car, watching the train pull away. "Are you sure, Tony?" she said. "Are you sure you can live with it?" Even after what I had put her through, her concern was for me.

"I can try," I said. "You are my woman now. I must learn to be your man."

And I did try. We took a small apartment in Westwood and set up housekeeping. We lived within my means, and not her father's. I insisted that Katherine give up her acting, and this was what we could afford on my salary. It was more than enough for me. All I had were my books and my few clothes. The books had been stacked eye-high on the floor of my old apartment, crowding me out of the room, so I built some proper shelves in the Westwood place. I was a man now, with a wife and a career, and I would have a library. When I was finished, the walls of the apartment were lined with books. There was barely room for any of Katherine's things.

We entertained her friends, but her friends were vacuous. They did not know what to make of me. Once, at a cocktail party, I overheard two of them wondering about all my books. They must be hers, they said. He's just a dumb Mexican. I doubt he can even read.

I listened until I could not stand it. "Fuck you!" I screamed. "Fuck all of you! Get out of my house!" I tore into Katherine's guests with a fierceness I could not place, and I did not let up until they were cowering by the door.

Katherine was disgraced, and her other friends were dumbstruck, but I did not care. I would not be judged by these ass-kissing society types. Who were they, to question me?

"These are my books!" I shouted after her friends as they hurried down the stairwell. "I've read every goddamn one of them!"

The other guests left soon after, and Katherine stopped crying soon after that, but it was my house and I would not be diminished by such insignificant creatures. How dare they speak of me in such a way! In my own home! It was bad enough, having to carry the dubious stares on the Paramount lot, where I was soon consigned to playing third-rate gangsters, Mexican bandits, and poor Indians. I walked past the fountain and heard the whispers. There goes De Mille's son-in-law. That's his son-in-law? Really? Jesus, and all he gets are those lousy parts? He must be sleeping with the wrong girl.

Eventually, the cocktail parties and the dinners fell away, and it was just the two of us. I did not want anything to do with Katherine's friends, and my friends were not good enough to invite to the wedding, so I would see them on my own. Slowly, our home began to move to my rhythms. I set the tone, and Katherine followed. That was the way it was in my father's home, and that was how it would be for me. She would not work. She would not take money from her father. She would not follow anyone's orders but mine. In this, I was hopelessly old-fashioned, but it was the only way I knew.

Our decisions were mine to make, and I made some foolish ones. When I had saved enough money, I bought a small house not far from the De Mille estate. If I had to compete with the old man at the studio, then I would tackle him on his home turf as well. The kid in me rejected such extravagance, but the rest of me had something to prove. I do not know what I was hoping for when we moved out there, but I am almost certain that I did not find it.

Underneath these domestic struttings, I still could not put Katherine's past to rest. Her lovers haunted me, and I could not defeat them. She had been with several men, before our wedding night, and I had her dissect them all. What about this one? What about that one? And that other sonofabitch? What was the story with him?

The worst part about it was that I knew some of these men, at least by reputation. Shit, she had been with Clark Gable! It was no wonder she had recommended him for the part of Jean Lafitte, over me. I was just starting out in pictures; the ink on my contract had barely dried, and my future was anything but certain. How could I compete with someone like Gable? Or the director Victor Fleming, another of my predecessors? In my lunatic paranoia, I imagined Gable and Fleming on the set of *Gone With the Wind*, comparing notes on Katherine, and laughing at me. Oh, how I hated that movie! I would not see it for more than forty years, until I had beaten back the ghosts, but even then it was a torture.

I kept Katherine up late into the night, going over the same terrain. It took us nowhere except around and around. These were not men, they were giants, and I struggled to knock them down and leave a place for myself, alone, where they once stood. In Hollywood terms, I was nothing next to these stars, and yet I measured myself against them every night, in my own bedroom. It was a constant battle, and more than I could take.

I made her tell me everything. She wanted to save me from the pain, but I would not let her leave anything out. I could not let it go unsaid. When she told me that Fleming had taken her to a ski lodge in Aspen, and asked that she lie around naked with him when they were not on the slopes, I wanted to kill the bastard.

(Some time later, when Ingrid Bergman confessed that a famous director had taken her to Aspen and preferred her in the nude, she was shocked when I identified the culprit, even if I was too ashamed to mention the source of my information.)

I was insane with jealousy, and poor Katherine could not quell my fears. I know now that she would never have been unfaithful to me, but this was unimportant then. This was not the point. She was sincere in her love and devotion, but this was not enough. What I wanted was to erase her past, to defeat the ghosts, to leave it so that I was number one with her, for all time.

We started staying home. I was deathly afraid of going

to a restaurant and having to make small talk with one of these assholes. Worse, I did not want to be somewhere with Katherine if she had been there with someone else. It did not matter if it was one of her lovers or just one of her girlfriends. I could not reduce myself to ask. If she had been there before, we would never go again.

It was a terrible way to live, but Katherine put up with it. How she put up with it, or why, I will never know. I kept her from her family, and now I was keeping her from her friends. Anything else, or less, was beyond me. She could speak to them on the phone, or see them at lunch while I was at work, but I did not want to know about it. And, God help us both, if she even looked at another man, I would be left to wonder, and make a scene.

I started to think that the only way to ease my troubled mind was to level the playing field. Katherine had gone to bed with some pretty big names, so I would go to bed with some pretty big names, and this would do the trick. Maybe then I would feel whole. It was a childish response, but I did not know what else to do, and I did not have to look far to act on it. The actress Estelle Taylor lived in the house behind ours, and I set my sights on her. She would be the first of many. She was married at the time to Jack Dempsey, the fighter, and she was alone as often as not. Mostly, she was convenient, living right next door, and our trysts continued for a few weeks. It was not a bad way to get back at Katherine, I thought at the time. Miss Taylor had about fifteen years on me, but she was still beautiful. Plus, she was a big girl, and planning to divorce Dempsey anyway, so I felt like a philandering homewrecker. She knew what she was doing.

Me, I had no clue. One of the main points of my infidelity had been to rub Katherine's nose in it, to even the score, and I thought the best way to do this was to bed Jack Dempsey's wife in our own backyard. When this did not work, I found someone else's wife, and someone else's. Someday, perhaps, I would reach the point where it would not matter anymore.

I had no idea what I was doing, and there was no stopping me.

Ride

I SHOULD HAVE WORN GLOVES.

My hands are blistered at the tops of my palms, from the handlebars. It is not the gripping as much as it is the working of the brakes, the way my hands are made to support my entire upper body weight as I lean into the road. Usually, for long rides, I keep a pair of leather biking gloves in the zippered pouch at the back of my seat, but today the pouch is empty. Mine are a finer version of the tattered wool numbers favored by the merchants in the piazza at Nettuno: leather, with a stitched escape for each finger, and perforations at the knuckles.

I can picture where I left them—on a crate in the shed at the house—and as I think of the house I think of the ghosts who haunt me there. Gable, for one. It was his house once. Audrey Hepburn lived there too, as did Gregory Peck, Mel Ferrer, Jennifer Jones, Darryl F. Zanuck, David Selznick, and a host of others. For a while, the house was owned by Dino De Laurentiis, and used to accommodate stars on location in Europe.

All of transplanted Hollywood, it seemed, passed through the house at one time or another. The cook and the gardener talk about them, and the scenes they left behind: the slamming doors, the flying pots and pans, the frantic long-distance telephone calls, the endless story conferences, the loves and rivalries. I hear it all, still. It is in the walls, and all around. The house exhales its history like hot air on a cold day.

Gable is the one who counts. He haunted me throughout his life, and now he haunts me in death. His spirit permeates the house. He comes to me late at night, an apparition, when he cannot find peace. He is a drunken old fool. He knows what he has put me through. "Look at me," he says. "What is there to hate?"

"I hate you for what you were," I answer, "not for what you are."

"And what was I? I was a pathetic actor, a burlesque. I had false teeth and big ears."

"You were the king of Hollywood. You were a giant. You had it all."

"Ah, that was just the columnists. I never thought of myself as the king of anything."

"You were a king to Katherine. You were first with Katherine."

He weeps, and I feel sorry for him. I sleep in his old bedroom, and the paradox is not lost on me. Once I would not be in the same restaurant with him, and now we visit on such intimate terms.

I could not beat Gable when he was alive, but in death he is not worth the trouble. Today he is just another ghost, filled with doubt and pain, just like the rest of us. He is no better than me.

SEVEN

Studio Days

WORK WAS NOT THE ESCAPE it might have been.

I learned quickly that the making of motion pictures is a strange dance indeed. It was strange at the very beginning, and it has remained so. It is seductive and intoxicating, yes, but ultimately it is just another way to make a living. I have picked fruit, and polished floors, and dug ditches, and making pictures is little different. It is unconventional, and the rewards can be quite rich, but it is mostly the same. It is what we do.

What differences there are come in the illusion, and the spectacle. Hollywood tempts its denizens into thinking that what we do is unreal, that what it offers is more than life itself. This is comfortable foolishness. True, if we are lucky, we might produce something that earns a life of its own, or changes the way we see the world, or fixes us in the cultural firmament, but even our greatest accomplishments are assembled from human elements. We are nothing but the sum of each other's efforts. It is sometimes easy to lose sight of this, but after hundreds of pictures it is burned into me. I know how low the percentages truly are. We are like baseball players, but we are no Ruth or Aaron. The best of us stroke only a dozen home runs in the course of a career, and most of these depend on luck for their carry. Most times we step to the plate and are lucky to make contact.

The baseball analogy ends here. Motion pictures do

not depend on the home run hitter. Perhaps this is less so today than it has been since Valentino, but big stars will always be more of a safety net than a guarantee. In my early days at Paramount, it was the material that mattered, and the confluence of actors, writers, directors, and technicians. Every time out, there was a new mix, and only rarely did we gel on a winner.

Making pictures under the vise of Hollywood's studio system was a crazy-making process, and it pushed its players to extremes. For years I searched desperately for that winning combination, and when I could not find it at Paramount, I looked all over town. People were afraid to work with me, because I was Cecil B. De Mille's son-in-law; some would not even sit with me in the commissary, they were so afraid the old man would find some reason to hold it against them! Casting directors would only put me to work as a gangster, or a bandit, or a thug. (No one wanted to be the first to give the son-in-law a decent part!)

I bounced from picture to picture, hoping to ride out the bad times and land on a hit. I needed to carve out a place for myself, an identity, and the only way to do this was through the extra efforts of others. I needed their faith, and their fortune, to build on my own. I could not do it alone.

When the hits did not come, I looked to shake up the combinations in my personal life—as if people were rabbit's feet or lucky charms and all I needed were the right pieces. I thought maybe having children would do it, and so we started a family, underneath my silent prayers that this might cement Katherine's devotion and help me to blot the ghosts of her past loves. Maybe romance was what I needed, and since I could not find pure romance in the arms of my wife, I continued on my interminable quest, seeking comfort in the arms of ready starlets. Maybe a bigger house would solve the puzzle, or a fancier car. Always, there was some new way to monkey with the equation.

My life became a series of false starts. Each new house was no more a home than the last. Each relationship duped me into thinking I had met my match, and that my world would begin anew. Each script arrived at my door with the promise of better days ahead. But eventually the houses fell apart, along with the relationships. As for the scripts . . . well, the best ones never came, the good ones rarely panned out, and the passable ones were invariably turned into passable pictures. Consider the string of "B" picture productions with which I began my career: *Dangerous to Know, Tip-Off Girls, Hunted Men, King of Alcatraz, King of Chinatown, Island of Lost Men, Emergency Squad.*

Paramount's renowned "B" unit was long on efficiency and short on almost everything else. We were a capable bunch, but with no real stories to tell. The emphasis was on production, and not the product, leaving one melodrama smelling much like the next. Even the component parts were largely the same—with myself, Anna May Wong, J. Carrol Naish, Lloyd Nolan, Lynn Overmann, Robert Preston, and my old friend Akim Tamiroff out in front of the cameras, and directors like Louis King and Edward Dmytryk on the other side.

With each new picture, the studio simply shuffled the deck and dealt out a new cast and crew. It hardly mattered where the cards fell, as long as we were all working. Naturally, some of the pictures made under these conditions were better than others, but none was great and most were variations on familiar themes. Some I would not recognize if I stumbled across them on late-night television. Some I have never even seen.

It was an assembly-line operation—a throwback, really, to Adolph Zukor's Famous Players unit—and we moved from one picture to the next without pause. Sometimes, I had a new picture in theaters, another already in the can, and still another ready to begin shooting. With such a hasty production schedule, some of the particulars occasionally fell away.

The editing room was usually the best place for a director to cut corners, with a deadline approaching. Sometimes, the cutting room floor offered an inadvertent source of material, or inspiration. In those days, the editing rooms were right next to each other. Outside each door was one barrel for the excess film, and another for the salvageable footage. On hot afternoons the cutters would sit out in the alley, cutting their pictures. They hated the solitude of their jobs, being cramped inside their dark cubicles.

With so many pictures being cut at the same time, under such loose conditions, mistakes were inevitable. If an editor was lucky, the mistakes would go unnoticed, or at least be found out before a picture was released. Once, while a cutter was working on an Edward Dmytryk gangster picture called *Television Spy*, he absentmindedly grabbed a length of film from the discard barrel of a "B" jungle picture, which was being cut in the adjacent room, and spliced it onto his working spool. For the longest time, the mistake went unnoticed. Somehow, when the gangster picture was finally screened, it contained about forty seconds of jungle footage. There I was, shooting it up on screen, when out of nowhere there came a parade of elephants, and tigers, and giraffes. It was the most incongruous thing.

The next day, the trade newspapers checked in with their approval. What an act of genius, they hailed, for Dmytryk to break from convention to show the jungle that is New York. With reviews like that, no one bothered to recut the picture.

That was the chaotic way pictures were made. There was never any time to prepare for a role, although in my case this was not usually a problem. My characters were all cut from the same sinister cloth, and yet I had studied enough under Akim Tamiroff and Michael Chekhov to try to bring something new to each role. All but one (the heroic Chinese undercover agent Chang Tai, in *Island of Lost Men*) were low-level henchmen or two-bit goons. I was the bad guy's bad guy, and I rarely made it to the final reel without being dispatched by a gun or a knife or a length of twine, typically administered by a rival hood.

I died more deaths than I cared to count. In 1986, when I saw an item in the trade newspapers announcing a Hal Ashby picture called *8 Million Ways to Die*, I thought someone had collected my stock death scenes for rerelease. Really, it would not have been such a doomed enterprise. Lord knows, studio vaults were filled with enough of my last breaths to fill a feature—going back, even, to my very first walk-on (drop-down? drag-off?), in Universal's *Parole!* when I died laughing.

But by now the joke was lost on me.

Christopher

SURELY, CHRISTOPHER'S PICTURE is buried somewhere in Katherine's box. Surely, she has emptied one of her gold-leaf frames and pressed the boy's snapshot inside the hard covers of a cherished book, like a delicate flower gone dry. Surely, his image is in that blasted packing crate, enveloped between bits of cardboard, or stuffed haphazardly in a shoe-box, or slipped into an album.

I will return from my ride—spent, anxious, resigned—and sift through what remains of my past, unaware, and I will come upon his face. I will break down. I know this as I know myself, as I know Katherine. Even in her illness, she wills me to confront the truth, to pierce my fantasy and drop me to my knees.

This is what I dread most of all.

He came to us early in our marriage, to hold us together, and in this he momentarily succeeded. God, how I worshipped that boy! He was like a fantastic fulcrum, around which our uncertain world could tilt and turn. It was incredible to me, and quite wonderful, the way our entire household pulsed to his doings, the way he could fill a room even in his sleep. He was everything— my flesh, my love, my hope for the future. He loved unconditionally. He was all we talked about, and all that mattered. He was, truly, a delightful child. Most proud fathers could toss off the same line without thinking about it, but I have thought about it. Often. For years, it was all I thought about. I think about it still, and I do not say it lightly. Christopher was a sunny slice of magic, gifted to us when we needed him the most and taken from us long before we were through.

Christ, he was just a child!

I will not offer a detailed account of what happened. I cannot. Some of the details I do not even remember. Others are etched into my every waking moment. It is not something I have ever spoken about, not even with a years-long string of therapists. Not even with Katherine. This, the not speaking about it, is probably what drove us apart, even if it took more than twenty years.

And yet I am afraid that if I do not face this today— here, on this ride—I will deny a part of myself. This journey is about absolutes, about the vein of truth that defines me, about the troubling compound of faith and fate that has marked my time on this earth. Christopher is a fundamental part of this, as much a part of me as I am of myself, so I must face what happened.

It is mostly a blur. It was March 15, 1941—the Ides of March—and we were spending an afternoon at the De Mille estate. I no longer recall who else was there, or what we were doing. Christopher wandered across the street and fell into W. C. Fields's pool. He was just three years old.

When they came to get me I thought it a cruel hoax. No! How could such a thing have happened? No! To my own son? No! I lashed out, vowing to kill the fucking nanny we had hired to look after him. I would kill her with my own hands. I would see her deported, or fired, or left to suffer the way she had left us to suffer, the way she had left Christopher to suffer. I screamed for revenge.

Ultimately, I could not move. Everything stopped moving. My entire world was frozen. All around me was commotion, and grieving, but I could not notice. Perhaps I thought that if I let the moment pass, uninterrupted, it would go away. It would be as if nothing had happened, and everything would go on as it was. I would not accept the truth, or even acknowledge it. I could not cry, because there was nothing to cry about. Nothing had happened.

I did not go to the funeral. I did not accept the grief or condolences of others. I have never been to the cemetery. I will not concede the point. Poor Katherine was devastated, and never the same (how could anyone be the same?), but I offered no support. I hated knowing I was not able to help her, but I hated more what helping her would have done to me. It would have been like death itself.

It was different with my father, and grandmother, and for the longest time I could not understand the place I had made in my heart for Christopher. Years later, I made an unusual picture called *The Savage Innocents*, written and directed by Nicholas Ray, in which I played an Eskimo named Inuk, and in preparing for the role I read all that I could on Eskimo lore and culture. I learned that when an Eskimo dies, his friends and family gather for five days to honor his life. They tell stories about the deceased—rude stories, spectacular stories, personal stories, apocryphal stories. They talk about the size of his "thing," the smell of his sweat, the way he chewed his food. They leave nothing to memory, for in memory a man can be forgotten. There is a great feast, with singing and dancing and laughing. It is a grand, aching celebration, and after the fifth day the deceased is never mentioned again. To talk of the dead, the Eskimos believe, is to summon the spirit back from its resting place, far across time: do so and the dead will never know eternal peace.

I talk of my father all the time. He is with me, always, and if I accept the Eskimo notion, then it is my talking about my father that has returned him to me, back from his resting place. My grandmother, too, is often at my side. To an Eskimo, this is an unpardonable sin, but I can find no guilt. They are comfortable here, a mother and her son, even if they are not at peace. They live with my successes, and my failures, and help to sort through my problems, but they are lost in today's world, suspended in time. I have been selfish, I know, in bringing them here, but I would be lost without them. Papa is my tie to the man I wish to be, and Dona Sabina the paragon of womanhood I will never know for myself.

And yet I talk of Christopher not at all. In this I suppose I am more Eskimo than one picture would suggest. The restless fate I handed my father and grandmother would not be the fate for my son. I would not disturb his spirit. I would let him be. A part of me felt that he left because I was not worthy of him, that he disapproved of Katherine and me, of the ways we lived.

When I think of Christopher—daily—he is alive, and smiling, and someplace else. It goes no deeper than this. He has gone from us, but he is still here. Somewhere. I have spun an entire life for him, and he is living it gloriously. He looks like his mother, still, but he has my eyes and my soul. Good for him. He is an architect, living in San Francisco. He is married, with children of his own. He drives a red Buick. He has worked in Chicago, and

Iran, and Rome, and points between. New York he finds too confining, with all of that oppressive vertical space, all of those zoning restrictions. He needs room for his imagination to flex, and breathe. He phones to tell me of his latest assignments, and the thrill in his voice tells me he has found his calling. Just now, he is consulting on an important new project in the Orient, working to marry elements of Western architecture to centuries-old Eastern traditions.

The buildings he leaves behind are monuments to his having been here. He has graced this place, and that one, and left each more beautiful in his wake. Sometimes, in my travels, I will happen upon a marvelous structure and find myself admiring the lines, wondering if they are Christopher's. Or I will catch myself staring at a child with his smiling eyes—my eyes!—marveling at the connection.

I see Christopher's hand in beautiful buildings and children all over the world. I see my hand in his, and we are at peace.

Goodbye to All That

TWO INCIDENTS DROVE ME from my Paramount contract, and each pointed to Cecil B. De Mille.

For a long time, my few acting friends had been riding me about my relationship with the old man, questioning how it was that De Mille's son-in-law could not get a good part. My God, how embarrassing! What my friends did not know, what I could not tell them, was that there was no relationship at all, and that the good parts were probably not finding me for reasons of their own.

It gnawed at me, to suffer the stares of my colleagues, or to hear the contempt beneath their mocking taunts: Jesus, Tony, you must be one helluva lousy actor . . .

Can't you get your wife to put in a good word for ya with the old man? . . . Say, Quinn, maybe I can come up to the house with you for Sunday dinner, get myself one of them hoodlum roles you're so fonda playing . . . Come on, tell me, who d'ya have to sleep with to get a second-rate role like that?

Carole Lombard, for one, used to counsel me late into the evening on the various ways my marriage was short-changing my career. "You'll never be an actor here," she told me one night, meaning at Paramount. "These ass-holes will never take you seriously."

"What do you mean? I'm doing good work."

"You're a goddamn Indian, Tony. That's what these people see. You're an Indian, or a Mexican, or a sleazy racketeer. You're not a leading man. You're a fucking kid. All you are is married to C.B.'s daughter."

I was beginning to think she was right.

My first epiphany came on the set of my third De Mille picture—*Union Pacific*, a rambling steamroller of an epic surrounding the building of the Union Pacific railroad. Like every other De Mille production, the picture was chock full of stars, with Barbara Stanwyck and Joel McCrea at the top of the bill, and most of Paramount's "B" unit at the middle and bottom rungs. I was cast in a small role as a gambler's hatchet man, and set to die another untimely death, this time at the hands of Joel McCrea.

It was another in a series of nothing parts, but I was made to play it just the same. We contract players had no voice in our own careers; we were slaves to Paramount. For all but the biggest stars, the studio system was a kind of indentured servitude. This was the unspoken truth behind the studio fantasy. If an actor declined to do a picture, the studio could suspend his pay and extend his contract. In other words, if a picture took two months to shoot, another two months would be added to the end of term. Sometimes, as a kindness, a casting director could place an actor in a second picture during production of the first, in which case the actor's pay would be restored, but it was usually in the studio's interest to let the actor sit idle.

The *Union Pacific* shoot slowed production on the rest of the lot. Most of Paramount's resources were at De Mille's disposal, and there was no other picture on which I could land. I could not afford to forgo my salary for such a stretch, or abide the thought of continuing in my commitment for any longer than I had to. I would not be warehoused by my own father-in-law. A more compassionate De Mille might have released me from my obligation, quietly offering the part to another contract player after I told him of my objections, but this was not about to happen. At the very least, he might have cast me in one of the picture's meatier roles, but this was not about to happen either. I could take it or leave it.

And so I took it. The picture itself was harmless enough, but it set me up for a fall. Perhaps I should have seen it coming. One afternoon, on location, De Mille asked me to join him at his special table for lunch. It was just a lousy picnic lunch, set up in a makeshift outdoor commissary, but the great man had his own private dining area, with linen and silverware and fine china. He did everything in grand style, even picnic. At every break, he would huddle in his exclusive area with his associates, while the rest of the crew snickered at the excessive show. They thought they were better than us, but we knew.

Like an idiot, I accepted my father-in-law's invitation, and sat down with him to lunch. He had no pressing agenda, and neither did I. Probably all he was doing was reaching out to his daughter's husband, to bridge the growing rift between us, and probably I had thought it was worth a try. We had already been all over and around my disappointments regarding my role, and there was no profit in continuing those drumbeats. We talked pleasantly about the picture, and my few scenes, and that was all there was to it.

A couple days later, one of the columnists ran a related item suggesting that I was now refusing to break bread with the "common" people on location, pointing to this one high-style lunch to validate the assertion. I was livid, but there was no one to blame. The gossips were just doing their rotten jobs, the studio hacks were just blowing smoke up De Mille's ass, and De Mille himself was just attempting a kind of peace with his distant son-in-law. I was the only one at fault, because I was the only one to have trespassed. After all, I was an ordinary laborer, born of ordinary stock. I had no business dining in such grand manner, removed from my own kind. Who the hell was I? I was a fruit picker's son. I was no better than anyone else. De Mille and his minions were above everyone, everything, but I should have known better.

Right then, I vowed never again to make a picture with De Mille. To hell with my contract, I thought. This was too much. Joel McCrea could not bump me off soon enough. I wanted done with the whole maddening business. I put in a call to my agent, to see if he could find me an early escape from my Paramount contract. He could not, but I kept pushing to leave. At nights, with Katherine, I talked of nothing but what I would do next, where we would go. I was by no means established, but I thought perhaps I could hook on with another studio, or work in the theater, or go back to studying architecture. If this was the way I was seen on the Paramount lot—as a blatant prima donna! milking my family ties and lording them over my peers!—then I wanted no part of it. My acting career would live or die on my own terms.

An even greater indignity awaited me a short time later, on the set of *Road to Singapore*, the first in the successful series of *Road* pictures starring Bob Hope, Bing

Crosby, and Dorothy Lamour. Here, again, the long odds against a hit were much in evidence: with a routine script and a journeyman cast, no one was expecting a run at the box office. And yet (well, what do you know?), the Hope-Crosby formula gifted the studio another long-running franchise. Something clicked. Lord knows what it was.

My role in this blueprint success was negligible (I played Lamour's jealous Latin lover), but some of the keen minds in Paramount's promotion office thought to trumpet my involvement as if it mattered. The way they chose to do this was particularly galling, and pushed me even further off the lot: referring to me in a preproduction press release as "Cecil B. De Mille's son-in-law."

It was the final humiliation, although I did not discover the slight until a few weeks later, when the resulting newspaper clippings began to pile up around on the set. By then it was too late. Papers all over the country had picked up on the item, and I was reduced by each report. Despite my two dozen pictures, this was the one credit the studio hacks thought worth mentioning.

In the hands of these people, there would soon be nothing left of me.

Ride

IF IT WAS UP TO ME, I would put everyone on a bicycle. I would strip the world bare and leave each man to his own devices. Imagine: a place where a man's progress is measured by the strength in his legs and the fire in his soul, a place without status, a place where the ride is as precious as the destination.

Ah, what a world it would be!

Here I am, working against traffic, straining for some final destination I have not yet determined. It is the getting there that matters most, because in the end we will all arrive at the same place. Am I the only one who sees this? I look around at all the tight-lipped faces on this stretch of road and cannot find another soul working the same puzzle. The people sit behind the wheels of their tiny sports cars, looking for shortcuts, willing themselves faster. Everyone is late, or wishing the moment to pass. To them, the getting there is drudgery. Behind the tinted glass of their windows, I envision an emptiness like no other.

I have reached the top of the afternoon, and the streets are filled with business, with overbearing people racing to meet their next appointments. They are all in such an orchestrated hurry. They know where they are going, but they will not reach their destinations without being somehow changed by the journey. The congestion and commotion cannot be good for their spirits, but this is what they know.

I am alone on my bicycle. Spread before me are all these other people, all these vehicles, but they cannot touch me. I am surrounded by movement, but I am not moving. I am attacked by impatience, but I am in no rush. If this is a sickness, I pray it is contagious. Let the world catch whatever ails me and perhaps we can finally get somewhere. Perhaps we can rediscover our purpose on this planet. Let the bicycle stand as our only means of transportation, and then see what happens. How fast our economy and our health would recover! What changes we would see!

But, alas, perhaps these changes would not be for the better. Perhaps people would merely kill each other in different ways. Knowing human nature, it would probably just be a matter of time before some countries cornered the world's rubber market, and tires became as scarce as oil. We would find ourselves fighting whole new wars, with whole new global powers, whole new enemies.

Here are those demons, war and hate, creeping back

into view. I am doing everything in my power to avoid such dark thoughts, but they are around every corner. The more I try to shut them out, the louder they assault me. I wish to pass this hatred through my pores—a spiritual detoxification!—but the bright noon sun and the effort of the ride are not enough to sweat it out of me.

I search for a distraction. There, up in the hills, I see a horse silhouetted against the sun, but even such a sight as this will not do the trick. The animal's coat is probably a fine gray, but in the distance it appears white. I find myself thinking that if it had not been for a beast like Montezuma the Aztecs might not have been overwhelmed by the Spaniards. (What is it about these hills that assails me with thoughts of death and destruction?) But then I shake this line of thought, as quickly as it latched on to me. What good does it do to go back five hundred years in speculation? To hell with the Aztecs and the Spaniards! Their battle is over. Their battle is not mine.

I refuse to dwell here. To consider my own battles, I need only look inward. The strong iodine scent of the sea reaches me like smelling salts, lifting my spirits from the canvas where they lie. I am alive, pedaling faster than any thoughts of death. There will be no stopping me until I am through. I am ahead of it all, and soon I am lifted, soaring once again, with only the whir of my rear wheel sprocket to signal that I am not truly airborne. The bicycle must sense it too, gliding along of its own accord, with nothing at all to do with me.

If we can keep up this charade, the ride down to the port of Anzio will be a breeze.

Eves of Destruction

TWO OR THREE DAYS BEFORE AN EARTHQUAKE, there is a peculiar electricity in the air. It permeates everything, but

I cannot place it. It is heavy in the atmosphere, and heavy in my bones. I can feel it coming.

After a lifetime along the San Andreas fault line, I have come to recognize the warnings. I feel it first in the mornings. I wake to an odd sensation. Something has changed from the night before. Perhaps it is my conscience, burdened with some matter or other. Perhaps it is my stomach, burdened with last night's dinner. I check myself, but there are no new neuroses, no new ulcers. The changes are external, and they are not mine alone.

Soon I find that others have the same uneasy feeling. We know what it is, but we do not give it voice. We fool ourselves into thinking the weird textures are here for some other reason, this time. We want to believe it can never happen again.

The next morning, the feeling is still with me. By now it has invaded each of my senses. Food tastes flat. Smells reach me as if for the first time. Pretty women look strangely . . . inanimate. Even the sky has taken on the color of ruin. And yet the day passes as before, all of us conspiring to ignore the obvious, to forestall the inevitable. At dinner, we set our fears temporarily aside, and turn our talk to the days to come. This thing, this feeling, has no place in our tomorrows. We are full of hope, and full of shit.

That night, in the distance, there is a rumble. It is a sound I cannot identify, and yet totally familiar. For a beat, I think it comes from the airport, but it is bigger than any plane. The clamoring is not on the face of the earth: it is in its very bowels.

Then it begins. It might start with a swinging chandelier, or a dish falling off the cupboard. A picture on the wall goes askew. It is like every cliche in pictures, played out in slow motion. Suddenly, it is as though a huge hand has grabbed the house and started shaking it. Somewhere a woman screams, or a child begins to cry.

There was always a quake, to jolt us from our dreams. Katherine and I rode out several together, of varying magnitudes. Each time—at 5.0 on the Richter scale, or 5.3, or 5.8—it was the same. We collected the children and headed for cover. The door jambs were our haven. There we stood, with prayers on our lips and the face of an angry God all around us, waiting for nature to finish its rampage.

In the waiting, I discovered that everything I knew was false. This earth, this solid earth, was transformed into a wild, raging sea, and we were being swept along on a tidal wave. It was beyond imagining. The streets filled with a helpless panic. There were no strong men to save us from this calamity, no heavenly acts to restore order and remake our world as it was. The ground below was undulating like an insatiable whore and there was nothing to do but ride it out. We were, each of us, on our own.

In these moments, I sometimes thought that God had turned His back on the world.

Slowly, slowly, the rolling thunder died out. Like a huge monster who has vomited his poison, the earth finished with its convulsive retching. It was over, but it never ended. The reality gave way to the fear that the beast would wake us once more.

We emerged from our hiding places to look at the damage, to answer the questions of our children. How do you explain a thing like this? Where is the justice in an act of nature? Outside, people prayed in the streets. Atheists were on their knees. The reconstruction was begun anew. We had all made our own deals with our own gods, and now faced living up to our own ends of the bargain.

None of us would be the same.

Sangra y Arena

IT WAS ON LOAN TO 20th Century–Fox that I made my first important picture—Rouben Mamoulian's powerful bullfighting drama, *Blood and Sand*. I had signed on with Warner Bros., at three times my Paramount salary, but could not land a significant role to save my career. The Mamoulian picture offered a fresh start. I was once again cast in a supporting role, but at least now I had something to support, and some hope of moving my career onto another level.

Blood and Sand was a breakthrough mostly in that it released me from the dark-skinned gangster characters that had become my routine. I played an upstart matador out to win the crown, the crowd, and the girl (played by Rita Hayworth) from Tyrone Power. The picture itself was a Technicolor wonder (it won an Oscar for its dazzling color photography), although my role within it was without much shading. My character may have triumphed, but the story was less about the rise of my Manolo de Palma than it was about the fall of Power's Juan Gallardo.

As the rival matador, I was left to wait in the wings for the bulk of the picture, and my first and best chance to show what I could do came in a memorable dance scene with Rita Hayworth. I had always been able to maneuver around a dance floor, and Miss Hayworth was a facile partner. She rode my hip like it was an extension of her own body. Together we moved like lovers—which, in fact, we were, by the time we wrapped the picture.

She was an incredible beauty, with fiery red hair and Irish and Latin bloodlines to match my own. I was cast as her young Spanish lover, and looked on our mutual attraction as inevitable. There was no avoiding each other.

Ah, what a delightful creature my Miss Hayworth appeared to be! Of course, I had been around enough to know that appearances could be deceiving, especially in Hollywood, but I allowed myself to be taken in. In truth, I did more than give myself to the deception; I probably solicited it as well. My diffidence took one look at this tempestuous redhead and hid under the covers.

I was deeply committed to beating Katherine's past into the ground with my own present, and each new picture promised an enjoyable entanglement to weigh against my wife's earlier sins. Someday, perhaps, I would balance the scales. Someday, I would hold my big names to Katherine's big names, and slay the Leviathans that stalked our marriage bed. However, I was still terribly shy around women. Unless a woman's interest was plain, I would never make the first move. For all my apparent experience, I was hopelessly lost.

Blood and Sand happened to suggest two such opportunities, but I could only recognize one of them. Miss Hayworth was hard to miss. We took to each other from the start, and began a romance that lasted throughout the shoot, although to call it a romance is perhaps overstating things. It was a simple affair. (It is a despicable term, but that is what it was.) The only true feelings that passed between us were sensory. It was almost a continuation of our roles in the picture, the way we were pulled together. We never found much to talk about, but talk was not important. There was enough heat in our scenes together to make up for everything else, and we passed an amusing few weeks in each other's company.

Hayworth's husband, though, was not amused, which I suppose was to be expected. She was married at the time to an oil man, and he did not approve of our affair, but it was the measure of his disapproval that I found surprising. "What's the matter with you?" he berated his wife, after he discovered us together. "Fucking a supporting actor? If you're gonna have an affair, you could have at least fucked Tyrone Power!"

Such were the values and vagaries of the motion picture industry.

The missed opportunity was with Mamoulian's other leading lady, Linda Darnell. I had always thought of Miss Darnell as the virginal sort, perhaps because she tended to play innocents in her pictures. (She was once cast as the Virgin Mary!) Even in life, there was something chaste about her. She was a pretty girl, but she seemed more sisterly than womanly. I wanted to protect her, but she had something else in mind. One afternoon, on location, she asked what I did on my days off. I told her that I liked to hike up into the hills, to draw and read. She asked if she could join me. I was flattered at her interest, but reluctant to invite her along. With a woman like Linda Darnell, I never knew what was expected of me. Always, I struggled to find the right things to say, the right clothes to wear. I was completely unsure of myself, like a pubescent schoolboy.

This was the last thing I wanted. On my days off, I liked to lose myself in my books, and not have to worry about making conversation, or making a false assumption with a woman I would have to see on the set the next morning. Nevertheless, a part of me was anxious for Miss Darnell's company, so I agreed. On the next Saturday, I went to collect her just after sun-up, and we made for the hills. I had a bag filled with books and art supplies, and an umbrella under which I hoped to escape the heat of the day.

We walked for a long time without talking. I did not mind the silence, but she seemed determined to catch my attention. "Oh, Tony," she said, rather demurely, when we reached a tiny river. "I don't want to ruin my shoes. Will you be a dear and carry me?"

So, of course, I carried her.

A few moments later, the picnic basket she was toting suddenly became too heavy—so, of course, I took it from her. Also, it had rained the night before, and now and then we would reach a patch of mud, so I lifted her around these as well. Every few moments there was some little thing she needed help with, and I always complied.

At the top of the hill, we sat under a tree and shared a bottle of wine and a nice picnic lunch, after which Miss Darnell lay back on the grass and breathed a deep sigh. It was an actor's sigh, I thought, more for my benefit than hers, but I could not be sure.

"Tony," she said, "I'm so tired. Do you mind if I close my eyes for a bit?"

"Not at all," I said. I had my books, and was hoping to get in some reading.

She pretended to sleep for about an hour, all the time purring and spreading her legs and touching herself in the most sensuous ways. Jesus, she was ravishing—and she had my full attention!—but I could not move. Her low moans might have roused another man into action, but I was terrified of doing the wrong thing. In my ignorance, I actually thought she was a fitful sleeper, nothing more. I tried to look past her suggestive posturing and concentrate on my books, but all I could think about was this horny little virgin lying at my side.

She opened her eyes. "Read to me, Tony," she said. "You have such a wonderful voice."

What a fool I was! She did everything but pull me toward her, or don a neon sign, and all I could do was open one of my poetry books and start reciting. After a while she tired of this and asked if we could leave. (What the hell was I expecting?) So, of course, we left.

We went back to work Monday morning as if nothing had happened, which in fact was so—nothing *had* happened. Despite the mixed signals, I dismissed it as an innocent afternoon in the hills with a friend. Really, the whole thing had been rather pleasant, if I ignored the uncomfortable emotions that hung between us.

But Linda Darnell had a different take, and it was some time before I learned what it was. We were working together again at 20th Century–Fox—on William Wellman's *Buffalo Bill*—when Maureen O'Hara pulled me aside to ask if anything had ever happened between Linda and me.

"Why?" I wondered.

"Just tell me," Maureen said. "I'm curious."

I told her about our long walk, and the wine, and the books. "She's a lovely girl," I said.

Maureen said she knew all about the long walk and the books and the pleasant afternoon. She laughed at my recounting, and let me in on her girl talk. "She thinks you're a fairy," she said, and then she laughed her full Irish laughter.

Apparently, I was the only actor who never tried to have sex with Linda Darnell, and the only one to have resisted her advances, and while another man might have been honored at the distinction, I was not sure I could live with myself. This pretty young virgin had been mine for the taking, and all I could do was read to her.

I was back playing Indians, no closer to top billing, and I still had a lot to learn.

Rejection

THE BIGGEST ACTORS IN THE WORLD have been turned down for the smallest of roles. It is a part of the business we cannot avoid. Most of us collect our rejections like stones, and toss them back when the tides have turned. My pockets are still bulging with them.

For instance: I had just signed with Warner Bros., and Jack Warner was looking to put me to work. He was also looking to cast a difficult property, and thought he might accomplish the two things with one act.

Warner had bought the rights to a play about a traveling jazz band called *Hot Nocturne*, by Edwin Gilbert, which he then had translated into a script by Robert Rossen. He was calling the picture *Blues in the Night*, and he was having all kinds of trouble casting the lead role. He sent the script to George Raft, but he turned it down. He sent it to Humphrey Bogart, but he turned it down. He sent it to John Garfield, but he turned it down too.

Finally, he sent it to me. I knew the history of the picture—we were all under contract at the studio—but I was in no position to care. It was a lead role and I should have jumped at it, but I thought the script was a disaster. There was no justification for my character. (That was a big thing, even then—looking to "justify" a part. What a lot of bunk!)

I read the script and made some notes. I would take the job, I thought, but there were some things I wanted to work out beforehand. When I was finished, I called Warner and arranged for a meeting.

"Did you read the script?" he asked, when I went up to see him.

"Yes," I said, "that's why I'm here."

"And what did you think?"

I did not know where to begin. "Well, Jack." I hesitated, but he cut me off before I could get going.

"Stop right there, Tony," he said. "I don't like the way you started that. 'Well, Jack.' No, kid, I don't like it at all."

"But let me finish . . . "

He cut me off again. "No chance, kid," he said, in his coldest tone, "and I'll tell you why. George Raft turned me down. Bogie turned me down. Garfield turned me down. You, *I'm* turning down!"

Then he stood and showed me the door.

I consider this now and break out laughing—it is, for my money, one of the classic rejection stories, made richer for the fact that it happened to me. But at the time, naturally, I did not fully appreciate it.

The part ultimately went to Richard Whorf; the picture opened to decent business and good notices; and I continued in bit parts for a number of years, wondering what the hell kind of career I had gotten myself into.

One Man Tango

RITA HAYWORTH TOOK HER husband's advice and moved on to leading men soon enough. The last I heard, she had divorced her husband and taken up with Victor Mature. He had joined the Coast Guard, and been sent overseas, and they planned to marry after the war.

This did not stop Miss Hayworth's many admirers from giving chase. She was such an intoxicating beauty, with such uncommon warmth and vulnerability, that men were drawn to her. We could not help ourselves. I may have had my fill, but there were others in line, and it sometimes fell to me to run interference.

If I had a dollar for every inquiry I received regarding Miss Hayworth, I might have bought out my Warner Bros. contract and moved on to better things. But I would not give out her number—until I heard from Orson Welles. He called me up one afternoon to sound me out on our relationship, and to press for an introduction.

"I'm going to marry her," he said, with great conviction.

"Orson, you don't even know her."

"Doesn't matter. I'm going to marry her."

He was just like every other man in America. I told him he was crazy, that she was about to marry Victor Mature, that a relationship with Rita Hayworth could never last. I told him he would only be sorry.

"Why me?" I wondered, after I realized I was getting nowhere with my admonitions. "Why do you need to hear this kind of thing from me?"

"You?" he answered. "You're a one man tango. You're the only man I know who's lived to tell about her."

I had no idea what he meant by this, but I refused to give him her number. "You'll thank me for it," I insisted. "Believe me. Now go away and fall in love with someone else."

But he would not go away. He called for weeks, looking for an introduction. He called everyone he knew. He was famous in his pursuit. Of course, he might have tried Miss Hayworth on his own—he was, after all, the toast of Hollywood, fresh from the triumph of *Citizen Kane*—but he would not settle for anything less than a proper introduction.

"You're not just looking for a fling?" I asked. "Because if that's all it is, you're on your own."

"No," he swore. "I'm going to marry this woman. I can't sleep at night thinking about her."

There was no sense trying to talk him out of it, so I gave him her private telephone number and wished him luck.

Even with her private number, it took Orson weeks to get Miss Hayworth on the phone. When he did, they began a whirlwind courtship that very evening. There was, he said, an instant, passionate rapport.

They were married in just a few months, and divorced less than three years afterward. At the other end of the failed relationship, he called me up to commiserate. We went out for a drink, to toast our shared disappointment over the most desirable woman either one of us had known.

"I should have listened to you," he said.

"Next time you will."

"To hell with next time. It's now that I'm screwed."

I tried to cheer him up. "So she took your money," I said. "So she took your heart. Tell me it wasn't a helluva ride. Tell me it wasn't worth it."

He took a long pull on his drink and lost himself to one of his trademark belly laughs. "Tony," he said, "you really are a one man tango."

Transgression

SOME OF THE MOST onerous aspects of the motion picture business were the endless promotional appearances we actors were made to endure.

Throughout the 1930s and 1940s, before the availability of wide radio or television exposure, we were often sent to far-flung posts on a kind of Hollywood caravan. We pulled into town, put on a show, and urged the locals to head on down to the Rialto to catch our latest picture. It was, we were told, great for box office, and who were we to argue?

Sometimes, the studio sent a train full of stars on a national tour, promoting several different pictures all at once, and these made for some amusing combinations, and interesting implications. I once found myself traveling with a young actress named Peggy Ryan, and she led me to one of the weirdest encounters in the annals of pictures. My, she was a beautiful child. I never made a play for her—she was accompanied by her mother, for one thing—but she was certainly lovely.

One night, Peggy asked me to join her for a drink. Her mother had gone to sleep, and she wanted some company. She was a bit more forward than I was expecting, but we wound up spending the most wonderful two weeks together. She really was a lovely girl. We went to Seattle, Portland, all over the Pacific Northwest. She had more energy than a dozen women.

In Vancouver, she started to cry. "Do you know Howard?" she asked me, from underneath her tears, from out of nowhere.

It took me a beat to place the name. "Howard?" I tried.

"Hughes," she said, and then she smiled. "Our boss. Dummy." (We were both promoting his pictures.)

Oh, I thought. That Howard. "No," I said, "not personally."

"He's a nice man, but very strange."

Her crying kicked up a notch—whether it was genuine or staged, I could not tell—and I realized she was his girl. Or, at least, one of his girls. Hughes was known to keep as many as a dozen actresses under contract, and was said to take a romantic interest in some of them. I looked at this sweet child and wondered at the mess she was in. Then I wondered at the mess I was now in.

"I know about the other girls," she said.

I tried to comfort her, and offer some counsel, but I did not know where to start. All I could think was that this whistle-stop romance had not been one of my better ideas, and that I should find a way to end it. I was not interested in doing any kind of battle with a powerful eccentric like Howard Hughes. When she calmed down, I told Peggy my concerns, and she agreed that we should stop seeing each other.

A few weeks later, back in Hollywood, I took a call from a friend named Johnny Meyers. We had grown up together, in East Los Angeles, and it was now Johnny's job to get girls for Howard Hughes. He dug up some of the great beauties for his billionaire boss, and it fell to him to occasionally manage the man's complicated affairs. "Hey, Tony," he said, "listen, Mr. Hughes wants to meet with you. Whaddya say?"

"I say if Mr. Hughes wants to meet with me, then I suppose he should meet with me."

"Tomorrow okay?"

"Fine. Sure. Tell me when." I could not imagine that the meeting held any great promise for my future in pictures.

"The thing is," Johnny explained, "he's not an office kind of guy. He doesn't go to the studio all that much."

"Any place is fine," I said. If I was about to have my head handed to me I could at least be accommodating.

"Do you know where Mulholland Drive meets Laurel Canyon?"

"Yeah."

"There's a hill on the right side. Pull over by the shoulder, and wait in your car."

"What time?"

"Mr. Hughes is not too good about times. Sometime between two and three. Just wait in your car and he'll be by."

"Johnny," I said, "let me get this straight. You want me to pull over by the side of Mulholland Drive at two o'clock in the afternoon and wait for Howard Hughes to happen by for a meeting?"

"Did I say two in the afternoon?" Johnny laughed. "Because if I did you'll have to excuse me. No, sir, Mr. Hughes is not an afternoon person. He wants it for two o'clock in the morning. Sometime between two and three in the morning. I'm assuming you're free at that time?"

I was scared to death. Howard Hughes wanted to meet me on the side of a road at two o'clock in the morning. I knew he was eccentric, but this was ridiculous. What could he want with me, in the middle of the night, out by Laurel Canyon?

The next night, I pulled up at the designated spot and waited. And waited. Time passed at an agonizing pace, and my anxiety grew with each moment. Finally, at about two-thirty, a car pulled up and turned around. Then another. There were three cars in all, and the drivers cut their engines. One of them got out, crossed to my car, peered inside, then returned to his own vehicle.

Then, one of the passenger doors opened and out stepped a tall, slim man. In the small beam of streetlight, I could make him for Hughes. He was not a good-looking man, even in this light. He crossed to my car, opened the passenger door, and sat down.

He spoke in a strange, droning voice. (I had been told he could not hear very well, and it affected his speech.) "I want to talk to you about Peggy Ryan," he began.

Jesus, I thought. This guy cuts right to it.

"How was the road trip you two did together?" he asked.

"Fine," I said. "No problem. She was a lovely girl. She did a bit where she sang a song, and I came out and we did a little skit." I was rambling, not knowing what he wanted to hear.

"How is she as an actress?"

"I think she's got potential."

He smiled as he thought about this. "Good," he said at last. "Good. You know, I have a lot of people under contract, and I never know if I should pick up their options."

"Oh, she's worth keeping. She's gonna be a real good one."

"And are you in love with her?"

Here it came. "What?" I said, buying myself some time.

"Are you in love with her?"

I knew right then that either Peggy would be fired or I would be killed. I tried to save us both. "I don't know, Mr. Hughes," I lied. "I'm a married man. I thought you knew that about me."

"Well, I just wondered." Then he looked me over carefully and opened the door.

I had the sense that Hughes was not well-versed in the social pleasantries, so I waited for him to make his good-byes. The meeting had gone well enough—I was still alive!—and I did not want to end it on a sour note. But he said nothing. He just stepped out of the car, shut the door behind him, and crossed the street back to his driver.

I watched the three cars pull away, one by one, and I sat underneath the streetlight for a long time, wondering if it had all been a dream. Or a nightmare. Or something else entirely.

Ride

ANOTHER HILL.

Thank God this one is going down, and taking me with it. It has just been about twenty kilometers, and already I am killing myself with this constant climbing. The ups and downs are far more than I had counted on, far more than I can take. Where will it all take me, that I have never been before? The better part of the ride is behind me; here on in, it will be an ordeal. Now and then I must stand on the pedals to stretch my legs and relieve my aching back, and I hate the way the gesture makes me look: hurt, tired, finished.

Ah shit, I am getting old! If there was any question it is long gone. Only yesterday, these hills were like nothing. Even this morning, I took them with something to spare. But this afternoon they are everything, and I am the thing left wanting. As I stand—to cheat!—I map the balance of my route in my head. I am thinking to avoid the steepest rises, but there is no way home to Vigna S. Antonio without leaving the flats. Some ways will be flatter than others, but I can think of no steady course.

Well, so be it. It is a bicycle ride, not a walk in the park. Whatever the road lays out for me, I will deal with it, although at this point even the downhills leave me despairing. Why? Just a short while ago, I relished the thrill of the downhill chase and now the free ride has turned melancholy. Funny how a few hours can change everything.

Perhaps the body will not tolerate the lies of the mind over such rigorous terrain, over such long stretches.

Or perhaps it just has to do with my friend Raoul Walsh, the wildly exciting character who first directed me in *They Died With Their Boots On*, an elaborate retelling of Custer's last stand, with Errol Flynn as the general. Yes, now that I think of it, I prefer to blame it on Walsh—a man who more than once compared his physical decline to a long downhill ride. The analogy returns to me here, over these last paces. If I was not in physical decline when I set out this morning, I most assuredly am by now.

He was a crazy bastard, my friend Raoul Walsh. He appeared in my life at a time when I was still looking to find myself, and the truths that had made me. He was no help in the search, but he made the looking tolerable. I was bouncing from picture to picture, studio to studio, bed to bed. Nothing could hold my interest for very long. Even our young family could not rein me in. Christina was born in 1941, Catalina in 1942, and Duncan in 1945. (Our third daughter, Valentina, rounded things out in 1952.) With each child, I thought I could commit myself to Katherine, to forgive her past, to nail myself down to this elusive animal, responsibility. But the kids were no answer. Each new arrival offered no more of a tie than the one before. Each new arrival offered a painful reminder that Christopher had gone, that I was somehow unworthy. I loved my children dearly, but they could not soothe the uncertainty that brewed inside me. It was a disappointment, but I should not have expected as much. Katherine too was a disappointment. I loved a great many things about her, but I did not love the ways we were together, the ways her history had made a monster out of me.

For all these reasons, and a litany of others, Raoul Walsh found a lost soul when I reported for work on his Custer picture. I had been cast as Crazy Horse—another

Indian, but for a change a legendary Sioux chief of histori-cal consequence—and I turned up in my braids and my native garb, ready to do what I was told. I looked like a natural but I felt like crap, and the director saw through me right away.

In all my years in the business, Raoul Walsh was prob-ably the most inspired lunatic I ever encountered. He was the least technical director I knew, but he relished the process with such a fire that I could almost taste it with him. He was absolutely marvelous at putting his actors at ease, and creating a rich environment for them to inhabit. There is more to directing than setting up shots and advancing the story, and Raoul was one of the first to have embraced the spirit of the job. To him, the process was everything, and no picture was worth making as a chore. His pictures were fun to make, and they delivered miser-able young actors like myself from the tedium of their marriages and careers. Throughout most of this period, I hated going to work in the mornings *and* going home in the evenings, but here I just hated going home.

Walsh was not only a great director, but also a fine actor. He might have been the Marlon Brando of his day were it not for a freak accident. While he was riding to work one morning, a frightened rabbit jumped through the windshield of his car. A small piece of glass pierced Walsh's eye, and he knew immediately that even the most forgiving camera could not forgive a one-eyed actor, so he stepped to the other side of the lens. There, with one eye, he saw more of human nature than most directors could see with four. There was nothing phony or cerebral about his work, nothing overly stylized. His direction and his dialogue were succinct and to the point, and in this he was virtually without peer.

He told me a story. As a younger man chronicling the waning moments of the Mexican Revolution, Walsh claimed to have asked Pancho Villa to postpone an attack on the town of Zacatecas when victory was in sight. His reasons for doing so were at first unclear.

"What are you saying, you crazy gringo?" responded Villa, who had agreed to let Walsh film the battle from his perspective, for posterity. "My army will march triumphantly into town tomorrow."

"With all respect, my general," Walsh said, "do so and it will be an empty victory. I will not be able to record it for history."

"And why is that?" Villa demanded. "You are busy? What could be more important?"

"Nothing is more important," the director explained, "but my camera is out of film."

Villa considered this for a long moment before speaking. "And how long will it take for new film to arrive?" he finally asked.

"It will be here by Friday," Walsh said.

"Then I will wait until Friday," Villa said, marking perhaps the only time in the history of human conflict that a leader let a motion picture director call the shots.

But Raoul Walsh is in my thoughts, now, for a more pressing reason. In our second picture together, *The World in His Arms*, with Gregory Peck, he complained constantly of an aching back, and turned his ailments into a metaphor on aging. I went over to him one afternoon, during a break in shooting, and asked how he was faring. "I'm sixty-five years old, kid," he said, "and at my age it's downhill and shady all the way."

I am older still, protected from the midday sun by stands of tall poplars on either side of the road. I am sore where I sit, where I grip, where I breathe. I am speeding downhill, toward death, and there is no place in the world I would rather be.

EIGHT

Running the Fuck

I QUIT HOLLYWOOD IN 1947 for a try at the Broadway
stage, and a last attempt to discover myself as an actor and
as a man. It was, for me, a package deal: I could not be
one without the other, and yet I was still searching for a
way to be both. As it was, I worried I was neither. If all I
was meant to be was a second-class movie star (in second-
rate pictures), and a second-string lover to Katherine,
then I would be something else. Or someone else. And
soon.

I have since realized that I am rather like a snake in
that I need to shed my skin to survive. I have not lived any
one life for very long. There is an almost primal force at
work, driving me to measure what I am doing against
what I will do next, who I am against who I will become.
Every decade has marked a period of reassessment and
reinvention, at the end of which I have reemerged a
changed man. It is an odd contract. Nothing good lasts
forever—ten years seems about right—and I have had to
move to keep up.

I know this now, riding through these hills, but I did
not know it as a younger man. If I did, it was soaked with
intuition, and tied to a clock whose ticking I could not
hear. If I did, things might have been so much simpler,
and easier to understand. Back then, all I really knew was
that I was unhappy, and unfulfilled. There was an emptiness my physical presence could not displace. My work

lacked direction, my marriage lacked foundation, and I lacked the focus to fill in the blanks. I was nowhere, no one. I needed to light a fire under myself, and ride the sparks to something wonderfully new, else I would die among the embers.

The decision to set the motion picture business aside was not a difficult one to make. Indeed, it was almost made for me, both on camera and off. A short stint at 20th Century–Fox yielded only a handful of meaningful roles, but the sum of my work still fell far short of the parts. There was a fortunate turn as a Mexican cowboy in William Wellman's classic look at the power of public opinion, *The Ox-Bow Incident*, and a respectable pirate picture called *The Black Swan* (which introduced me to Maureen O'Hara), but most of my pictures were forgettable contrivances. Some, like the ill-advised musical *Where Do We Go From Here?* in which I played an Indian chief who sold Manhattan island to Fred MacMurray, probably did more damage to my reputation than it could easily afford.

When my 20th Century–Fox contract expired, I did not sign another. After fifty years, I can no longer recall if there were any bona fide contract offers for me to even consider, but the result was the same either way. I was left to vagabond from one studio to the next, and my telephone did not exactly ring off the hook. Oh, I was busy enough, but I was busy with piecework, only here and there. I was called on by old friends to round out the cast of a World War II picture, or to play the foil in another Hope-Crosby *Road* comedy, or to swashbuckle through one adventure or another, but there was nothing steady, nothing sure. A few of these pictures continue to find an audience on late-night television, or on videotape (such as *Back to Bataan*, *Buffalo Bill*, and *Sinbad the Sailor*), but most have been gathering dust in vaults all over Hollywood.

I could not rely on my agent, so when I was not working I was hustling my next project, cutting my own deals. In this, I suppose I was ahead of my time, or at least apart from the norm. Most of my colleagues were content to feed their indulgent lifestyles with whatever pictures came their way, but I was out for more than just money. The money was important, certainly, but I recognized early on that what it bought you in pictures was the chance to stay in the game.

True success, for a motion picture actor, came in the quality of the work, in helping to capture the ephemeral and transposing it for all eternity onto the big screen. It was, as ever, a group effort, but the odds were stacked to favor the stars. Top-dollar actors had their choice of pictures, whether or not they were right for the part, while bottom-fishing free agents like myself had to balance the size of the role against the size of the paycheck. If I sold myself short just to work with a particular actor or director, then I would never get my price on the next picture.

One exchange, with director John Farrow, was fairly typical. These days, John is perhaps better known as the father (with Maureen O'Sullivan) of actress Mia Farrow, but at the time he was a hardworking director, famous for his facility with action yarns. Farrow's leading lady, Barbara Stanwyck, had recommended me for a role in *California*, a Western they were scheduled to shoot over at Paramount, with Ray Milland.

I was open to almost anything—on the right terms— and Farrow called me one afternoon to offer me the job. "It's a small role, Tony," he said, "just three or four days on the set, but it pays three thousand dollars."

Three thousand dollars! Jesus, I needed the money, and there was no shame in a quick payday. Plus, there was no denying the talents of the principals; without even reading the script, I could smell the ingredients for a hit, and I needed a hit like an infusion. And finally, it put me

in the earnings ballpark with some of the marquee contract players (who pulled about five thousand dollars per
week), even if it only put me there for the time being.

Still, like an ass, I held out for more.

"Look, John," I said, going into what had become a
standard response. (I hated to negotiate my own salary,
but I knew the drill.) "I'd love to work with you, and I
love Barbara, but I can't work for three thousand. In this
town, if I quote a figure like three thousand dollars, that's
where I'll be for two years."

"But it's just a few days," John countered.

He was right, but that was not the point. "It doesn't
matter," I said. "Next picture they'll want me for a few
months, on the same salary."

"I can go to five."

"Five thousand?" Sometimes, this negotiating dance
went better than expected. Here I had balked and Farrow
nearly doubled his first offer. Maybe if I held out he
would better the stakes, so I swallowed hard and turned
him down.

But Farrow would not be put off. I do not know what
Stanwyck told him, but he must have really wanted me for
the picture.

"What'll it take?" he wanted to know.

"Forgive me, John, but I can't do it for less than fifteen
thousand."

There was silence on the other end, which I might
have expected, and Farrow begged off, promising to get
back to me later in the day. I hung up thinking I had
blown the deal. Even Gable had never made fifteen thousand for a week's work! What was I thinking? I could have
lived off five thousand for months.

Later that day, Farrow called back to tell me I had the
part. "Barbara said to give the kid what he wants," he
reported.

My God, I was thrilled! It was more money than I had

ever made, and a fleeting validation of my standing. It was a minor role, but for major dollars—enough to see me through the year if it had to—and I jumped into the part with everything I had. If the producers had agreed to such an outrageous salary, then I would give them their money's worth. I would be the best damn supporting player in the company.

I had no idea what Barbara Stanwyck had told John Farrow about me, and I did not care. To tell the truth, I never liked Barbara all that much, and was surprised to learn that the feeling was not mutual. She was a powerful, realistic actress, and a rugged beauty, but she had too many opinions for my taste. I could never figure her out. She was abrasive one moment, and warm as hell the next. Mostly, she struck me as a shrewd, calculating girl. She knew what she wanted and did what she had to do to get it. She made a point of knowing every little thing about every technician, every prop guy, every stuntman. Hey, Frank! she would say, arriving on the set for work in the morning. How's the wife? She had the baby yet? Charlie, your kid get into that college? The crew loved her like one of their own, but her entreaties seemed false to me, almost staged. I had the sense she was lining up these guys in her corner, in case she needed them.

One of the best lines I ever heard about Barbara Stanwyck came from her husband, the actor Robert Taylor, who confirmed some of my hunches about his estranged wife's controlling behavior. Taylor and I worked together some years later on another John Farrow Western—*Ride, Vaquero!* for MGM, with the stunning Ava Gardner—and became friendly. One night, over drinks, I asked Taylor why he and Stanwyck had divorced. I was still chasing the ghosts of Katherine's past from our marriage bed, and the booze and the late hour had left me curious about the marital problems of others.

"Ah, Tony," he said, "that woman, she always wants to run the fuck!"

It was a phrase for all time—and a perfect description of an enterprising lady.

But I digress. The war years may have been a boon for the motion picture industry, but they were a bust for me. And the dry period could not have come at a worse time. I had bought into the Hollywood illusion in such grand manner—big house, fancy cars, the best schools for the kids—that I was soon desperate for cash, just to keep up appearances. Lord knows I did not have to live like that, certainly not after a lifetime of such poverty and want. But I was a foolish, competitive young man, trying to beat back the specter of Katherine's history. If it was not her laundry list of old loves, it was her childhood, her friends, her father. I rejected my father-in-law, and everything he stood for, and yet I ran up enormous bills to impress him. I was too stubborn to allow that Cecil B. De Mille would never fully accept a Mexican bandit like me, no matter how much money I made, or how extravagantly I spent it. To him, I would always be the Indian who had come to claim his daughter, or the arrogant young actor who had walked out on Paramount for no good reason. To him, I would never amount to anything.

It should not have mattered, but it did.

I do not mean to suggest that De Mille was completely uncharitable in relation to me, because he had his moments. Over the years, he softened his hard edges enough to suggest a fellowship between us. There were even times when he made an effort to include me in his world. One such occasion comes to mind. I was in St. Louis, selling war bonds over the radio with Errol Flynn and Gene Tierney, when my father-in-law consented to work his clout in an elaborate charade at my expense.

I will backpedal, and explain. Errol Flynn was a delightful man, and an outstanding friend. I met him first through John Barrymore, whom he greatly admired, but he stood much taller on his own. When he was around Barrymore, Flynn was like a little boy. He wanted so badly to be like Jack that he was almost cartoonish in his emulation. (He even went on to play Barrymore in a 1958 Warner Bros. picture called *Too Much Too Soon*, based on the memoirs of Jack's daughter Diana.)

Still, I loved Flynn and cherished our friendship. He was a sweet, troubled man, and a wonderful athlete. (There was such grace to his movement!) He was also a famous practical joker. We made several pictures together, and when we found ourselves on shared patriotic duty in St. Louis, he took the opportunity to dupe me in high style. The night before our scheduled appearance, Flynn kept me out late, drinking. In those days, it did not take much to keep me out late, drinking, especially when I was on the road for one of these promotional appearances. I hated these godawful publicity tours! There was nothing more distasteful than having to sell myself to the public every time a picture came out, and these war bond pitches struck me merely as more of the same. A night on the town with an old friend like Errol Flynn made it bearable.

We were due to appear live on national radio at about eleven o'clock the following morning, and Flynn roused me from my bed in my hotel room at seven. I had just fallen asleep, and now he wanted me to go to work. He said the time of the broadcast had been changed, and we were needed down at the studio earlier than planned.

"Christ, Errol," I said, trying to rediscover the powers of speech, "we were out till four in the morning. I must look like shit."

"Up, up, up," he said, bouncing about the room like it was nothing at all. (Even at seven o'clock in the morning, after a drunken evening, he moved like a dancer.) "It's just radio. No one will see you."

He called Gene Tierney, who was also a bit hung over from the night before, and told her of the change in schedule. The three of us gulped down some coffee and raced for the studio. When we got there, Flynn began to panic. He had been reasonably composed on the ride over, but now he unreasonably fell apart. There was no script, he railed. There was no coffee. There was no one from the war office to tell us what to do. It did not seem such a big deal—we had done the same thing a dozen times—but Flynn made such a flowery show of frustration that he soon had us all frantic. We hurriedly went over who would say what, and when, and developed a rough format to see us through the allotted time.

I went on first. I had a splitting headache, and wanted to be anywhere else but in that studio, but I tried to tough it out. It was for a good cause, and I had given my word. I introduced myself, made a little speech about my friends Gene and Errol, spoke about the importance of the American effort overseas, and turned the microphone over to Gene. She made her appeal, told a few jokes, and sent it back to me. Then I made another pitch, said a few kind words about Errol, and called on him to join me.

All of this took about five minutes, and we still had the balance of a half-hour to fill. We were counting on Errol to carry the day, but he stepped to the microphone and announced to all of America that he was so hung over he could not believe he had gotten out of bed at such a ridiculous hour. His speech was loud, and slurred, and colorful. "And this fucking Indian," he said, looking at me, "my friend . . . He's the son-in-law of that son-ofabitch, C. B. De Mille. Christ, I wish I could remember his name. He played with me in that Custer picture, maybe you've seen it. Ah, but what the hell, right? They're all the same."

I was furious. I did not know whether to beat the crap

out of Errol or pull him from the microphone to save all of us from any further embarrassment. In my indecision, I did nothing.

"And the lovely Miss Gene Tierney," he rambled on. "What a gorgeous thing. I want to just state for the record that I am not having an affair with her, that I have never had an affair with her, and that I have no immediate plans to have an affair with her. She's a real fucking sweetheart, but that's all. Of course, if she would like to try to change my plans, I would be open to suggestions."

He sounded more intoxicated than he had the night before, and it was a wonder Gene did not sock him right in the mouth, but he kept on, each sentence more inappropriate than the last. He must have gone on in this way for four or five minutes, but it seemed as if he filled the entire half-hour. Finally, the studio director shot out of his booth, screaming and waving his arms. He cut the mike and lit into Flynn: This is live radio! You're supposed to be selling war bonds! What the hell are you doing? Then he admonished me for my complicity, and told Gene that by not responding to Flynn's lecherous remarks she had come across as a fool.

Errol grabbed the poor bastard by the collar and started wrestling with him on the ground. It was an ugly, offensive scene, and I watched it play out as if in slow motion, all the time thinking of the damage it would do to my already tentative career.

By the time I got back to my hotel room, there were messages from Hedda Hopper and Louella Parsons. Louella and I were friends (we played poker once a week with Howard Hawks and assorted others), so I returned her call first. She told me that the broadcast was already the talk of the town, and wondered with me at the fallout. "Jesus, Tony," she sympathized. "It's a terrible thing, for you to be caught up in something like this."

As soon as I hung up, the phone rang again. It was

De Mille. In all the time I had been married to Katherine, he had never picked up the telephone and called me himself. We spoke only at family occasions, and at the studio. For him to call—now, over such as this—was something indeed. "Tony," he said, "about this mess our Mr. Flynn seems to have gotten us into . . ."

"Mr. De Mille," I said, cutting him off. "Let's not blame Errol. We were all out a bit late last night, and I'm afraid some of us had a bit too much to drink. He didn't know what he was saying." I do not know why, but I went out of my way to cover for Flynn.

De Mille blustered on about how my unprofessional behavior reflected badly on him, and on Katherine. He said he expected more of me, and worried that I would never be serious enough to sustain my career. I hung up the phone thinking I had let the great man down, even though I could not think of a thing I had done wrong.

Next it was Katherine on the line, and then my agent, and each call reinforced the urgency of the moment. God, this thing was turning out to be far more than I had counted on. I lay back down on the bed thinking my career was lost, the phone to my ear telling me I had stepped feet first into the latest Hollywood scandal.

And then came the punch line. The last call I took was from Errol Flynn, sounding sober as the day he was born. His was the last voice I wanted to hear. "Gotcha, Tony!" he said, and then he laughed like a madman.

When he calmed down enough to explain himself, my mischievous friend told me he had orchestrated the whole fine mess. He had slipped the studio hands a few bucks to let us in early to a dormant sound room, and asked the director to play along. Then he arranged for De Mille and the gossips to check in with their distress calls. No one outside the studio had heard Errol's rude commentary. The fight, the name calling, the loose talk . . . everything was staged.

(We went back to the radio station, at eleven, for the real broadcast.)

I did not know what to think. I was relieved, of course, but beyond that I was not sure. In the end, what I was left to think was that if icons like Errol Flynn, Gene Tierney, Louella Parsons, and C. B. De Mille would go out of their way to lure me into a practical joke, then maybe things were not as bad as they seemed. Maybe there was a place for me in this business after all.

But it was one thing to feel a personal connection to the motion picture industry, and quite another to forge a lasting professional link. I remained a free agent, with nothing lined up beyond my next gig, and I soon found myself with so much time between pictures that I started thinking seriously about going back to architecture. The Hollywood lifestyle was fast becoming prohibitively expensive. By the end of 1946, money was so tight that I even pressed Katherine back into service. At the time, I did not see any alternative.

Katherine had given up her acting career when we married, at my insistence, but when the chance came to play my wife in a Phil Karlson picture called *Black Gold*, for Allied Artists' Monogram Pictures, I encouraged her to take it. The decision was mostly financial, but there were other factors. We had never worked together on a picture, and I thought perhaps our time on the set would rekindle the passion that had died on our wedding night. After all, if I had found false love in the arms of endless starlets during the making of nearly fifty pictures to this point, then perhaps I might find the real thing in the arms of my wife during the making of this one.

I figured wrong. Katherine was so tentative on the set that she seemed out of place. In fairness, she had not acted in pictures in ten years, so it was only natural for her to want to ease back into it, but I could not look past her uncertainty. The experience brought us no closer together, and did nothing to rewrite our history—even if it did help to pay the bills for the next while, and leave us with a little extra besides.

But money was not my only worry. There were my other pressures to consider. For me as an actor, *Black Gold* was an important breakthrough—or at least it might have been, in a more perfect world. For the first time, I was cast as the male lead, and my career was riding on whether I could carry the picture. Trouble was, there was either too much picture to carry, or not enough. I played an illiterate Indian horse farmer named Charley Eagle, who adopted a Chinese boy and raised thoroughbreds and eventually struck oil on his ranch. The picture was all about hope and redemption, but it was hung on such an implausible storyline that Allied Artists could not drag audiences in for a look.

Katherine did a fine job with her role, and I received some of my best notices to date, but these were no help at the box office, which more accurately meant they were no help at all. When a picture sank, it took its stars down with it, and I was marked guilty by association.

The off-camera conspiracy to keep me from working was somewhat more complicated, but no less circumstantial. Throughout the middle 1940s, the House Un-American Activities Committee had set its sights on Hollywood as a virtual breeding ground for communist thinking. In a way, it was, but I could see this only peripherally. I was either too close to it, or not close enough. What I could clearly recognize was that the artistic community was indeed a breeding ground for all kinds of thinking, on all kinds of issues. From my vantage point, I was simply surrounded by a group of curious intellectuals. I never thought of my friends as communists or socialists, leftists or liberals. I never thought of myself as any one thing or another. To me, we were all just caring, thinking people, looking for deeper truths, trying to make sense of the world. (Hell, I did not even become a United States citizen until 1947, so what did I know?)

Actors were, and remain, an unconventional bunch. All artists—painters, writers, directors, sculptors—step to their own beat, and in times of crises we tend to step out in front. I do not know what it is, precisely, that leaves us to dwell in places where most people dare not tread. Perhaps it is that we are not afraid. Perhaps it is that nothing surprises an artist. Or, if something does astonish, we must steel ourselves against it. We must be open to everything, at all times, if we are to do our jobs well. After all, we do not just deal in the realities of life. We look for the surreal, or the ideal, and it is in the constant searching that we find a way to live with ourselves, and to make ourselves something else.

I was no political animal, but I ran with a crowd that challenged the standards of the day. If there were questions to ask, they asked them. In time, almost all my friends from the Russian theater were tabbed as "Reds," and a great many of my writer friends were considered socialists. I used to pass long hours discussing Marxist theories with the screenwriter John Howard Lawson—a passionate man whose beliefs eventually earned him a spot on the studios' infamous blacklist, as one of the Hollywood Ten—and I was often swayed by his arguments.

Once again I was guilty by association. I was never called to Washington to testify (either on my own behalf, or on behalf of my cohorts), but it would not have mattered. If someone called me a communist, I would not have denied it. If someone called me a Jew, I would not have denied it either. In fact, I was neither, but that was not the issue. My politics and my religion belonged to no one but me.

So there I was, surrounded by these marvelous thinkers—men and women who had really stretched me as an artist—having to face down the Red scare that was gripping the entire Hollywood community. Darryl Zanuck himself called me into his office at 20th Century–Fox one afternoon to tell me that I was on the gray list of actors tabbed as communist sympathizers. He told me not as an accuser but as a friend, hopeful that I might give him some reason to stand in my defense. "Tony, is it so?" he asked, with great concern.

"Mr. Zanuck," I said, "you've put me in a difficult spot."

"I haven't put you anywhere, Tony. I'm just telling you how it is."

"Are you asking me if these people are my friends? Yes, they are my friends. Are you asking me if I share their beliefs? Yes, I share their beliefs. Are you asking me if I am a member of the Communist Party? Yes, the answer might as well be yes, because I will not say any different."

"Tony, don't be a fool," Zanuck implored. "It's not as though you've got a contract to fall back on. You're the last person who should be taking a stand on something like this. You're on your own. If there's any doubt about your activities, for an actor like you, then no one will hire you."

"Then no one will hire me."

I stood to leave, and reached for Zanuck's hand, in good will. I had nothing against him—he was just trying to help—but I hated what he represented. He was a symptom of a dangerous disease, and I wanted out before it could claim me. I had been screwed around long enough by these studio powers. I would not be made to defend myself over such a profoundly personal issue. I would not roll over and do as I was told. And I would not wait around for the choice roles that always seemed to go to someone else. I made my decision in an afternoon. I went home to Katherine and told her to pack. "We're moving to New York," I said. "I'll never be anything but an Indian in this town."

To pinch from my friend Robert Taylor, it was time for me to run the fuck.

New York, New York

WHEN HOLLYWOOD would not have me, I gave Broadway a crack. I packed up our family and settled into a modest house in suburban Connecticut, thinking to make our lives over yet again. It was an agonizing upheaval for everyone but me. For Katherine and the kids, it was the first of many displacements; for me, it was a wondrous period of reinvention.

A less stubborn actor might have looked to hone his craft on a lesser stage, or in some repertory group or acting class, but I did not have time for all that. I was thirty-two years old, with more than fifty pictures to my credit, and I would start at the top. The theater would have all of me—right away, like it or not—or it would not have me at all.

We drove east on a vehicle called *The Gentleman from Athens*, a pedestrian comedy about a Greek-American gangster from Athens, California, who somehow wins election to the United States Senate. It was not the strongest play on which to pin my hopes, but it was the only one offered to me—and a starring role, to boot. And it was written by Emmet Lavery, one of New York's brightest playwrights, and staged by the talented Sam Wanamaker, so its pedigree was promising enough. In fact, I was so confident of the play's chances that I even sank twenty-five thousand dollars of my *Black Gold* salary into the production, in what may have been one of the more dubious investments in Broadway history.

The real problem with the play, we discovered in out-of-town rehearsals, was that it did not have an ending. This was not a good thing for an actor looking to make his Broadway debut—or for an investor looking to make back his twenty-five thousand dollars. I played a hood from the Napa Valley named Stephen Socrates Christopher who maneuvers his way to Washington and digs up dirt on his Senate colleagues to advance his agenda. The burning issue to Socrates is preserving American control of the atom bomb, and he openly challenges anyone who opposes him in this. He resorts to such unscrupulous tactics that he is eventually impeached, and at the closing curtain stands in his office and bemoans his fate.

The play might have carried an important ideological message (especially in this time of postwar euphoria), were it not left to unravel in its final scenes, but without a defining moment at the curtain, the audience was left to wonder at the complicated doings on stage. There was nothing to hold the pieces together.

At the end of our Boston tryout, I accidentally hit on a possible ending. Or, to be precise, the ending hit on me. There was a statue of my character's namesake at the edge of the senator's desk, and when I stepped downstage one evening, I somehow managed to knock my head against the thing. My Socrates had just received the news of his ouster, and I was deeply despairing on his behalf, and when I cracked my head against this bust of Socrates, it brought the audience to applause. I do not know why. (Perhaps because the play was billed as a comedy, theatergoers were conditioned to laugh at anything resembling a pratfall.) I tried it again the next night and got the same response. Sam Wanamaker and the producers were thrilled, and they had me repeat the beaning throughout the Boston run.

I could not be certain whether it was the business with the bust at the end, or the play itself, but the Boston critics had kind words to say about my performance. One— Elliot Norton of the *Boston Post*—compared me to Paul

Douglas and Humphrey Bogart, and predicted that if the play was a success I would take my place "among the stars."

(I carried that clipping around in my wallet until it yellowed, and fell to gossamer from the constant unfolding.)

Finally, when we returned to New York, I went up to Sam to see if we might change the staging with the statue. "I've got a fucking headache like you wouldn't believe," I said. "If that's our ending, and the play's a hit, I'll have scrambled eggs for brains."

"So what do you want to do?" Sam asked.

"How the hell do I know?" I said. "You're the director!"

The best we could come up with was a variation on our original ending, which in fact was no ending at all, and the play closed after just six performances. Once I realized that I would never see my twenty-five thousand dollars, or the salary I had been counting on for the run of the play, I offered to bang my head silly against any inanimate objects the producers could place in my path, but it was too late. By this point, and despite our individual efforts, we were all stamped as failures.

Our brief New York run followed by less than a week the premiere of Elia Kazan's original production of Tennessee Williams's *A Streetcar Named Desire*, with Marlon Brando as Stanley Kowalski, and the coincidental openings were not lost on me. Indeed, the dovetailing of the two plays would impact on my career in ways I could not have imagined. At the time, I was an overly ambitious creature, and had it in my head that Brando and I were battling for critical attention. In truth, we were not even on the same field. He was appearing in a landmark American play, while I was toiling in a mere trifle, and yet this did not stop me from weighing his notices against mine.

But for all its sweep and scope, the New York stage could only accommodate one breakthrough performance at a time, and it would not be mine, not this time. I was too young, and too proud to concede the point. I took Brando's triumph as a personal affront. It had to come from somewhere, I decided, and it came out of my hide. His success should have been mine.

This may have been Brando's moment, but mine was soon to come. In its limited run, *The Gentleman from Athens* made enough of a splash (and me within it) to capture the attention of Brando's director, Elia Kazan, a controversial figure in his own right and one of the theater's most respected craftsmen. Gadge, so called for his love of gizmos and gadgets, had his own problems with the House Un-American Activities Committee, but there was no denying his strengths as a teacher, or his gifts at staging contemporary American drama. He found enough to like in my performance to invite me to join his fledgling Actors' Studio (which would soon reach enormous prominence under the direction of Lee Strasberg), and to consider me for the role of Stanley Kowalski in a touring production of *Streetcar*. It was, in retrospect, far more than I should have expected.

All of a sudden, I was pulled into an arena of invention and possibility. My days pulsed with the drama of the theater, and the thrill of the stage. I immersed myself once again in the great plays of the period, and in the classics. I argued the merits of one production over another. I dissected the craft of an actor into its component parts and found viable performances in the reconstruction.

Evenings in Connecticut with my family, or weekends, seemed almost mundane by comparison. I was occupying two separate worlds—one charged by emotion and power, and the other dulled by routine—and I lived for my moments on the stage. Katherine could not understand it, or if she did, she resented it. She was an actress herself, and yet my passion for my work was as foreign to her as if I had been an electrical engineer. The change in me was basic, and all-encompassing; for the first time in a long while, acting was exhilarating, and tinged with hope. In Hollywood, all I could play were gangsters and Mexican bandits, but here in New York I could be anything at all. My God, what freedom! What abundance!

Brando was an instant legend among our group. He flouted convention in *Streetcar* and in acting class—and from what I could gather, in the rest of his life as well. His improvisations in our Actors' Studio sessions were prominent for the way he managed to mock the process and still do provocative work. Once, when we were asked to do a dance and freeze our poses at the clap of the instructor's hands, Marlon wound up locked in a headstand. We were then supposed to do a bit based on our frozen postures, and when Marlon's turn came he delivered his premise with deadpan seriousness.

"I have a stomachache," he announced to the rest of the class, "and I'm standing on my head hoping I can pass it out of my mouth."

The others pretended at shock, but I thought the insult was marvelous. We were all so full of shit we deserved to be called on it.

I longed to be as free as Marlon, but I was not sure he even knew who I was. One afternoon, I showed up to class wearing a snazzy brown sports coat. The coat was an important symbol for me—a real Hollywood number. I had seen one just like it in a magazine, and allowed myself the indulgence while I was still flush with cash from my *Black Gold* earnings. Kazan took one look at me and declared with grand superiority that sports coats do not make actors, that the trappings of success do not mark a successful man. "It's not what you wear," he said dismissively, in front of all the others, "it's how you wear it."

It was not clear whether Kazan's tirade was directed at me personally, or delivered to me on behalf of actors in general, but I was embarrassed to be dressed down in front of a free spirit like Marlon, of all people.

I vowed to find a way to show Marlon that I was not like all the others, that I was not like my Hollywood coat. My chance came later that same day. Marlon was assigned an improvisation along with two other students. He was to play a tenant in a rooming house, asked to stop playing the piccolo or vacate his room. One student played the landlady, and the other played the complaining tenant, and the three of them set off on a remarkable little scene. Marlon was clearly the strongest performer in the group, and the others followed his lead. He played the belligerent artist to perfection, refusing to give up his music for the sake of the others. "What the hell's the difference," he inveighed, "if I talk or sing or play an instrument? It's all just noise. We all make noise. What are you gonna do about that?"

The choices he made, the way he delivered his lines, the way he collected the other performers into his world . . . it was all so spontaneous and right that we might have been set down to observe a true boardinghouse conflict.

When Marlon was finished, the class erupted in applause, but Gadge quickly silenced the clapping. "Save it for the theater," he reminded. "This is not a competition."

And yet somehow, in my head, it was.

When my turn came, I was ready. Gadge gave me the premise. My family was down on its luck. I was to go down to the pawnshop with a vase from my grandmother's apartment; we needed to make the rent, but I was reluctant to sell a family heirloom; still, these were my grandmother's instructions, so off I went, hoping to find some other way to earn the money. Whatever happened, I was to leave the shop with the vase in hand, no matter how much cash I was offered.

Meanwhile, Gadge cornered the other student to play the piece with me and assigned him the role of the pawn-

Me at four and a half with my sister, two and a half.

(Used by permission, courtesy of the Anthony Quinn Collection)

Imagine my mother asking for a fan picture—with that face! Hollywood, 1933.

(Used by permission, courtesy of the Anthony Quinn Collection)

Posing with Frank Sinatra's "Swooners," back when
we were both still skinny. Hollywood, 1940.

*(Used by permission, courtesy of the Anthony Quinn Collection,
photo by Leo Kanter)*

When Katherine and I were happy.

*(Used by permission, courtesy of the
Anthony Quinn Collection)*

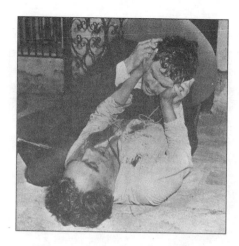

Brother against brother in *Viva Zapata!* Marlon Brando's Emiliano is hating to see me die. My Eufemio is hating to leave.

(Used by permission, courtesy of the Anthony Quinn Collection)

Doing a Mexican dance, with the Spanish actress Margo, for *Viva Zapata!*, 1952. She knows what she is doing; I can only follow.

(Used by permission, courtesy of the Anthony Quinn Collection)

The Paramount executives turn out to watch me direct *The Buccaneer*, Hollywood, 1958. The man with the unpleasant look, standing beneath me on the ladder, is my father-in-law, Cecil B. De Mille.

(Used by permission, courtesy of the Anthony Quinn Collection)

With Frederico Fellini on the set of *La Strada*, 1954. He was always asking me who the hell I thought I was. I was always trying to find out.

(Used by permission, courtesy of the Anthony Quinn Collection)

As Auda Abu Tavi in *Lawrence of Arabia*, a picture—and a moment—I will never forget, 1961.

(Used by permission, courtesy of the Anthony Quinn Collection)

Irresistible to young women, in *Zorba the Greek*, 1963.

(Used by permission, courtesy of the Anthony Quinn Collection)

With my beautiful son Frankie, on the set of *Lost Command*, 1966.

(Used by permission, courtesy of the Anthony Quinn Collection, photo by A. Ortas)

Playing a priest in Mexico, in *Guns for San Sebastian*, 1968.

(Used by permission, courtesy of the Anthony Quinn Collection)

I made nine pictures with Irene Papas. Ours was a love-hate relationship, but I think love will win.

(Used by permission, courtesy of the Anthony Quinn Collection, photo by Anita)

Working for the first time with my son Duncan, in *The Children of Sanchez*, 1978. I don't know who was more nervous.

(Used by permission, courtesy of the Anthony Quinn Collection)

On Broadway as Zorba, 1984. I loved every performance.

(Used by permission, courtesy of the Anthony Quinn Collection, photo by Anita)

Painting in Tunisia, during the filming of Franco Zeffirelli's *The Life of Christ*, 1988. Notice that the sheep are giving me their best side.

(Used by permission, courtesy of the Anthony Quinn Collection)

With my son Francesco, who played me as a young man in a television adaptation of Hemingway's *The Old Man and the Sea*, 1990.

(Used by permission, courtesy of the Anthony Quinn Collection)

As Don Pedro, the patriarch in *A Walk in the Clouds*, 1994. I wish I were as understanding as he.

(Used by permission, courtesy of the Anthony Quinn Collection)

Iolanda and me, on the town with Dean Martin and
George Jessel—a man who gave great eulogies.

(Used by permission, courtesy of the Anthony Quinn Collection)

A wonderful kiss
from my daughter
Valentina, with my
first wife, Katherine.

*(Used by permission,
courtesy of the Anthony
Quinn Collection, photo by
Metropolitan Photo Services)*

With Catalina and Christina.

(Used by permission, courtesy of the Anthony Quinn Collection)

Entertaining my children, on the road with the national company of *Streetcar,* Chicago, 1948. *Clockwise, from left:* Duncan, Katherine, Catalina, and Christina.

(Used by permission, courtesy of the Anthony Quinn Collection)

A man and his dogs. In Italy with Diana and Sinbad II. This is real love.

(Used by permission, courtesy of the Anthony Quinn Collection, photo by Sam Shaw)

In Durango, Mexico, celebrating my daughter Cati's wedding, 1967. We Quinns (*left to right:* Valentina, Christina, Frankie, Iolanda, and Danny) are flanked by two of my sons-in-law. The one on the left . . . left.

(Used by permission, courtesy of the Anthony Quinn Collection, photo by John R. Hamilton)

All's right with the world.

(Used by permission, courtesy of the Anthony Quinn Collection, photo by Herbert Fried)

When we were all happy. Probably Frankie had us laughing.

(Used by permission, courtesy of the Anthony Quinn Collection)

With my beautiful
Antonia. Together
we will ride into
the next century.

*(Used by permission,
courtesy of the Anthony
Quinn Collection)*

Relaxing in my New York studio, with all my friends.

(Photo courtesy Center Art Galleries— Hawaii)

shop owner; the vase, he said, was priceless, and the shop-keeper was to buy it at any cost. Whatever happened, he was not to let me leave the shop with the vase.

It was an inherently dramatic situation, made more so by my ignorance of the shopkeeper's agenda. I no longer remember how the scene played out, but I do recall an unflagging sense of wonder and purpose. I belonged on that stage that afternoon, in that role, as surely as I belonged anywhere else on this planet. I was that boy, sent to safeguard the family legacy and win the day. The vase (which in reality was an old coffeepot found lying about the stage) carried more value than anything I had ever held. I lost myself so completely in the improvisation that it took the backslaps of my classmates to bring me out of it. By my dispassionate gauge, my applause was just as great as Marlon's. But my applause was like music.

What a child I was! To reduce such a refined process to a base competition! I hate the petty contests actors wage with one another, and I absolutely despise the way I present myself in this account. But to color my behavior with shades of self-interest would be an even greater offense. The stage, to me, was a proving ground, and I would not let myself fail. I would show myself worthy, at all costs.

In my head, I developed an internal competition with Marlon Brando that was never reciprocated. I suppose it was envy that kept it going. God, how I craved his talent! His autonomy! These days, I measure the size of my fame against his, the size of my book advance against his, and I still fall short. As colleagues, on location in Texas, we even stood peeing across the Rio Grande, measuring the arc and reach of our stream.

But as an actor I no longer fear him. I look at the imp he has become and know that I would choose my life over his. We have become friends, and I have found much to love about the man, but a part of me will always place us on the dueling stages of our Broadway debuts. A part of me will never lose those early stakes, even if they seem ridiculous to me now.

At first, I tried to avoid Marlon's Stanley Kowalski. I knew I would follow him in the role, but his pull was too strong. Everybody was talking about what he was doing on stage, and I simply had to see him. I would be lost without his performance as a reference point, because he had changed everything. Plus, after I was asked to fill in for Marlon during the summer hiatus of the original company, I had to study the staging. That was one thing that never changed, once a production was up and running; the movements remained the same; it was what each actor did with them, and through them, that set one performance apart from another.

I watched Marlon with one eye closed, careful to soak up what I needed and not let it infect my approach. It was a tough charade. Gadge was directing the hiatus company, so he naturally looked to mirror the original in as many ways as possible (if only in the interest of economy), and I found myself lapsing into Marlon's mannerisms as if they were my own. Just as I once mimicked the great Barrymore, my instincts (and my director!) told me to parrot Brando, and I struggled against them.

It was not until we began our road tour, under the direction of Harold Clurman, that I was able to put my own stamp on the role—and received perhaps the most glowing review of my entire career. It came from Tennessee Williams himself, who sidled up to me backstage one evening and declared my Stanley Kowalski the best he had ever seen. His speech was slurred, and his breath rank with liquor, but that did not diminish his appraisal. For all I knew, Williams paid the same tribute to every actor he ever saw in the role, but it was enough for me. Hell, I wanted him to put it in writing!

I wound up playing *Streetcar* for almost two years, and

I never missed a performance. (Jack Palance was my understudy, and I sometimes thought he wanted to kill me—literally!—just for the chance to go on.) Marlon only lasted a few months in the part, but it never left him. He used to visit backstage, after we had brought the show back to New York, and ask me how I got a certain laugh, or what I was thinking when I said a particular line. He sat through our production a few dozen times, and he always found something to talk about in my performance. The play had defined him in such a way that he could not leave it alone, and it is only now that I realize how difficult it must have been for him to see it sustained without him. It must have been like discovering someone out with your ex-wife, or moving in on your daughter. I must have seemed like a poacher.

But he had moved on and I had moved in and neither one of us would ever be the same.

Mama Borgia

MY TIME IN NEW YORK was enriched by a curious friendship with an extraordinary woman. The circumstances of her life were like something out of a wonderfully drawn, multigenerational novel; the circumstances of our meeting were like a passage within.

I was at a party at a posh brownstone on Sixty-fourth Street. It was two o'clock in the morning, and the house was bulging with drunken theater people, gangsters, writers, and hangers-on. Katherine and the children were asleep in Connecticut, and I was alone among the crowd.

I set off in search of a bathroom, and stumbled into a small chamber lined with books. A large mahogany table dominated the room. I stepped inside and was overcome by the quiet and the darkness. It was an unlikely sanctuary, next to the bedlam of the rest of the house. The room was lit by a single lamp. I shut the door behind me, thinking I would catch my breath, and find my bearings, before heading back out. The din of the party fell deep into the background. The hour was late, and the drink was telling me to slow down, so I listened.

When my eyes adjusted to the light, I realized I was not alone. At the head of the table sat an attractive, middle-aged woman. She sat in silence, unaffected by the commotion that surrounded her. She was not reading, or writing, or talking on the telephone. She was, I surmised, the lady of the house, and she was sitting, just. I must have startled her, but I could not tell from her demeanor. She calmly looked me over and gestured for me to sit down.

I did.

"When were you born?" she asked.

It struck me as an unusual question to ask a stranger, straight off, but I could think of no reason not to answer.

"Nineteen fifteen," I said.

"No," she said. "I know. I mean what date?"

She knew? Now what the hell did that mean? "April twenty-first," I said.

A slight smile creased her face. She had once been a great beauty, I could see. "I thought so," she said. "That was the day my grandfather died, back in Italy. I had to be sure." Then she told me that I was her grandfather, reincarnated. "You have his eyes," she said. "And his manner. You are the same."

Well, I had read enough to remain open to such thinking, especially when proffered by such a formidable woman in such impressive surroundings. Who was I to question her? In her own house? If she saw her grandfather in me, then I would be her grandfather.

The woman proceeded to tell me her story, and my fortune. Her name, she said, was Rosa Urgitano Borgia. She was born in 1888 in Monteforte, Italy, the granddaughter of a prominent don who controlled the roads in and out of the Campagna, near Naples, and ran the produce for the entire region. Don Carlino Urgitano was said to have financed the voyages to America of thousands of emigrants by the turn of the century, such was the reach of his wealth and power.

For the first years of her life, Rosa lived like a princess—a child of means and muscle, both—but when her father killed her grandfather's mistress, he was banished to America with his young family. It was, to Don Carlino, an unforgivable deed (he had loved the woman dearly), but others saw it as an act of heroism; the boy was only trying to protect his mother's name, and her honor, they said; perhaps he should not be judged so harshly.

Once in America, Rosa missed her grandfather terribly. Don Carlino could not breathe without the child, but her place was with her parents. She no longer lived like a princess. Her father took whatever factory work he could find, in Boston or New York. Rosa herself was sent to work when she was just a small child. The don was a man of enormous influence, but there was nothing he could do for his precious granddaughter. He would send her gifts and letters, and dispatch his minions to look after her, but he ached that he could not be with her himself, that he could not do for her as he had always done.

The years passed, and Don Carlino's power shifted beneath him. He was still a widely respected leader, but he no longer wielded the same authority. He controlled the same roads, but now there were new and better roads for the farmers to travel, and these he could not control. He was an old man, and time was passing him by. He decided to travel to America, to consolidate his business interests and perhaps set eyes on his cherished granddaughter one more time before he died.

He sent a message to Rosa, telling her where to meet him, and when. She was by now a grown woman, with a sick husband and four children of her own, but she never lost the special bond she had with her grandfather. Her days were filled with work and chores, but she dropped everything to be at the harbor to meet Don Carlino's ship, never once imagining that his passage would be barred by the authorities. That it was, she thought, was a remarkable injustice. In her view, her grandfather had championed the farmers and workers of the Campagna for his entire life, and yet the law regarded him as a criminal. She could not understand how a man's life could stand for one thing to one group of people, and for something else to another.

She watched her grandfather step from the ship onto the dock, and her heart filled. Don Carlino was an old man, and he moved slowly, but he was the same. Her eyes caught his, and held them, and in this moment she was a princess again. But the don quickly noticed that the harbor was surrounded, and he was forced to double-back onto the ship. At his age, he could not face the prospect of incarceration. It would not be his fate. His eyes found Rosa and told her he was sorry. He had traveled all this way, and all they had was this one glimpse.

It was, for him, the darkest moment of his life. For Rosa, it was the day she stopped believing in her childhood dreams, the day she started to grow old.

Don Carlino returned to Italy to live out his days, and Rosa returned to her children and her ailing husband. Soon she opened a dress factory, to much success. She became known as a woman of virtue and discretion. She treated her workers fairly, almost like family. Her own family she treated with the devotion that had been lavished on her by her grandfather. When her husband passed on, she carried her widowhood like a badge. She would not remarry. She devoted herself to her business and her family. She was no longer a princess, but to some of her workers, and her neighbors, and her children, she was like a queen.

Rosa had nothing to do with her grandfather's associates, but they knew who she was, what kind of woman she had become. During Prohibition, when the warring mobs could not agree on a course for their shared interests, they sought independent counsel for guidance. The Italians controlled the wine and the speakeasies. The Germans had the monopoly on the beer industry. The Irish ran the politicians, and the Jews managed the numbers and the muscle. There was an ugly fight for supremacy; leaders were gunned down eating fried polypi at their favorite restaurant, or sliced at the barbershop while getting a shave; everyone lived in constant fear.

Finally, the rulers of the diverging factions agreed to meet, to settle their differences. It was to be the greatest gathering of gangsters ever: Capone, Torrio, Guzzie, Anastasia, Castellani, Wexler, Tommaselli, Prandela. The meeting was set for March 22, 1922, in a remote restaurant in New Jersey. Everyone arrived at staggered hours, to avoid suspicion. The men were to park at various locations and walk the rest of the way. The restaurant was not the hottest number in town. The police would not know what to make of so many fancy cars parked outside a dump.

There were no weapons allowed.

Capone opened the meeting with a joke. "A guy with a gun could take the whole caboodle," he said. Everyone laughed nervously, because they knew it was the truth. Of the eighty men in attendance, only two had tried to smuggle in a piece, but they were apprehended at the door.

Wexler spoke first. He was a skinny Jew with a head for numbers and faces. His clothes were rumpled, and he cut a nothing figure next to the others, but they all respected him. He was the brains of the outfit. He spoke softly, in a wheezing voice. Everyone strained to listen.

"We all function in the same way," he began. "We buy the judges, the politicians, the city councils, and then we kill each other over the small percentage that remains. I'm sick that so many good men have died out of avarice. Once a man claims his kingdom and shows he has the means, he holds it. But think of all the trouble it takes, fighting the cops, the politicians, every idiot who wants a cut. How many soldiers, how many lieutenants, how many 'capos' have been killed? I say it's time to stop it. Now. There's enough for all of us."

Capone and Torrio started clapping, and soon everybody joined the big chiefs. They determined that what was needed was a judge, someone outside the law and outside the mob, someone with no axe to grind, but no one knew where to find such a person. Finally, Castellani stepped forward to make a nomination. "I have a candidate for the job," he said. "She comes from a family that every Italian respects. Her grandfather was one of the fairest, smartest men in Naples. He ran the southeastern part of Italy single-handed. The only stain on the family is no stain at all, just a son wanting to protect his mother. It is just a matter of perspective. His granddaughter is an exemplary lady. We all know the ladies from the broads. I for one would listen to her and take her advice."

There was silence in the room. Castellani thought the men would not accept a women in such a critical position.

"Do you know this woman, Frank?" Torrio asked.

"I've seen her. I've never met her."

His answer seemed to satisfy everyone. There was some discussion about Rosa's brother, Charlie Cheesecake, who was in the rackets under Castellani, but there was no feeling that this would interfere with her ability to do the job. Besides, Frank was quick to note, Rosa would not have anything to do with the boy.

Finally, Capone had heard enough. It hardly mattered whom they chose to fill the role, as long as it was not one of Moustache Pete's men. "Thanks for the invite, boys," he said, standing to leave. "I've heard of Rosie. She's an angel. Take her."

The meeting was over, the decision made.

Rosa agreed to help out—on a trial basis, with no pay—but she soon realized she was born to the job. She ruled on petty disputes and major feuds. She decided who would run each corner, or who might profit from each distillery. She meted out fines and punishments, and arbitrated settlements. She helped people get jobs, get married, stay out of court. Her word was law, and she kept a tentative peace for a great many years.

The gangsters came to know her by Capone's early description—as an angel.

In time, Rosa Borgia won a high measure of notoriety in Manhattan. She was visited by leading artists and politicians, mobsters and legitimate businessmen. Her home became a gathering place for the luminaries of the day. She never received a cent for her counsel, but her business soon prospered beyond her wildest imaginings. Orders came in for more dresses than she could make, and she knew the work flowed from the bosses who now submitted to her rule. She accepted the rewards as her due. After all, she reasoned, she had to fill the orders to make a profit. If this was the only way she had left the gangsters to show their appreciation, then this would be fine.

It was almost dawn when Rosa Borgia finished telling me her story, but she was not tired. The party was still raging, and she wanted to talk. She wanted to hear my story, to learn what happened to her grandfather. She firmly believed that his spirit had passed into me on the day of my birth, and at this point so did I. Already, I was looking for pieces of Don Carlino's strength and passion in my own comportment.

"So," she said, when I had brought my own tale to the present, "you are an actor?"

"Yes."

"You shall have great success in the movies," she predicted. Then she reached for my hand and looked into my eyes. There was more to tell. "This woman," she said, "your Katherine, you will not remain married to her forever. She loves you, but it is not enough. You will meet a beautiful blond woman in Italy, and you will marry her."

I liked her first prophecy better than the second, but I could not embrace the one without the other. If this woman had been a charlatan, it would not have mattered, but she knew exactly what she was talking about.

I stayed for breakfast, and met her children. Her oldest boy, Carlo, was about the same age as me, and we became inseparable friends. He was like a brother, and Mama Borgia encouraged the relationship. We were good for each other, she said, and indeed we were. He was my ally, my confederate, my release. He was an unassuming man, of modest dreams. When the gangsters approached Mama Borgia with their plans for Las Vegas, she suggested Carlo to front the operation. All agreed they needed a mouthpiece to grease the local politicians and meet the press, and Carlo was an excellent choice. If he was Rosa's boy, they could trust him implicitly. The only problem was that Carlo did not want the job. He did not want the attention, or the responsibility, so they tapped Benny Siegel instead. They thought they could trust him too, but it was not the same.

(I knew Benny Siegel as well, but that is another story. In the end, I came to know him well enough to never call him by his famous nickname, which he hated, but we did not start off so well. I had taken up with Siegel's girlfriend, Virginia Hill, not knowing she was involved with another man. She did not think to tell me and I did not think to ask. I soon learned the truth, but I kept on seeing her. When Siegel found out, he put out the word that he wanted to kill me, and I could not blame him. Mama Borgia could not intercede. This was beyond her jurisdiction. Siegel confronted me—late one night, in an alley behind a restaurant—and I pleaded innocent. I would have fought him, gladly, but I thought it more prudent to talk him down from his task. I was good with my fists; I did not know from guns and chicanery. I told Siegel I had no idea that Virginia Hill was his girl. This had been true, at one time, so I merely stretched the truth. Either Siegel did not really want to kill me, or I was a better actor than I thought. I agreed to break things off with Virginia Hill—which I did, eventually—and Siegel and I parted friends.)

I became a fixture in the Borgia household. These good people could not get rid of me, for the next forty years. They became my second family. Sunday afternoons in Mama's parlor were filled with love and laughter, and all manner of celebrity. Once, in the early 1950s, she was visited by Krishna Menon, and he was charmed enough to return for dinner whenever he was in town at the United Nations. He even wanted to bring along a friend, Nikita Khrushchev, but Mama would not submit to the KGB security regulations. Her refusal was characteristically to the point. "Look," she said, "I got bookies I gotta talk to. I can't have the KGB or the FBI listenin' in. It'd be lousy for business."

So Khrushchev stayed away. He never knew what he was missing.

Mama Borgia counseled me on every aspect of my unpredictable life and career. She was certain that my marriage to Katherine would not last, but thought that our move to Connecticut, away from Hollywood, had been a good one. She told me that I could never be a good father to my children unless I accepted their mother and made a firm place for myself in our household. She thought that my continued affairs would only lead to ruin, even if I might someday encounter an Italian beauty offering salvation. She thought that I would never be satisfied as a man until I stood on my own in De Mille's domain.

Mama offered hard truths, and I struggled to make

sense of them. And she did not limit her counsel to affairs of the heart. She urged me to take the part in the touring company of *Streetcar*, as well as subsequent roles in *Borned in Texas*, staged by Sam Wanamaker, and *Let Me Hear the Melody*, staged by Burgess Meredith, opposite Melvyn Douglas and Cloris Leachman. The other two plays closed in just a few weeks, but Mama Borgia was right about the work; each part helped to round me as an actor, and brought me closer to fully realizing my next role.

She even encouraged my return to pictures, in a Robert Rossen bullfighting effort called *The Brave Bulls*. Mama did not know from scripts, but felt this was important because it would be shot in my native Mexico, and offered a chance for me to rediscover myself. In this, as in most everything else, she was right. Apart from costars Mel Ferrer and the Czechoslovakian ingenue Miroslava (who committed suicide soon after), the cast was entirely Mexican, and I thrilled to be in such company. After so many years as the token Latin on the set, I found tremendous security in numbers. For the first time, I belonged.

The picture itself was a small classic (it remains one of my favorites), although it failed to do any business; this, I suspect, had to do with Rossen being tabbed a communist in the months between production and release, and Columbia Pictures wanting to submarine the latest effort by the latest victim of the Red scare. It did not do to aggressively market a picture made by a man who might be in bed with the Russians.

Still, for me—another Red menace on the outs with the studio heads—it was a significant showcase, and a forceful reintroduction to the Hollywood community, and I owed it all to Mama.

If it had been up to me, I do not know that I would have ever returned; I would have meant to, perhaps, but I might never have gotten around to it. I might have been too afraid to retrace my steps and start all over again.

Ride

I DO NOT KNOW which is more wearying, the pedaling or the reminiscing. It is early afternoon, and I have run myself to extremes. I think back to the start of my journey—this morning, before the sun—and I have a new picture of myself in my head. I am no longer a prince on a white horse, galloping over the hills and valleys of my long life; I am the horse itself, lathered to exhaustion. I am desperate for a rest, and something to eat.

Lunch. Now that it occurs to me, I wonder what has taken so long. I have not eaten since I sat with Barbalishia over morning coffee, and then it was just a few bites of croissant. (There was also a slice of my fresh-baked bread, but it was too heavy to do any good.) My stomach has begun to talk back, and I must listen. I know a place in Anzio that serves the best calamari outside of Rome. It is run by a woman with gray-blue hair, which she always wears in a net. I have known her for years. The restaurant has been in her family since 1927. Perhaps I will pull in there for refueling, and further reflection. All of this thinking, on the fly, has got me reeling. It as if I have placed my life on fast forward, when what I need is to put it on pause.

(Listen to me! An old man, able to reduce our high technology to metaphor!)

Perhaps if I let myself sit, still, the truth will know where to find me. Perhaps then I will know what to do with it. I have lost sight of what I am running from, or toward, and I must rediscover my perspective before continuing. It does no good to keep moving, just for moving's sake.

I pull into Anzio not knowing what to make of the sleepy coastal village, site of one of the bloodiest dramas of the war. The Anzio landing—in January 1944—came smack in the middle of the worst Italian winter in memory. American soldiers were beaten back by mud, rain, and cold, but they pressed on. God, it must have been a scene! The locals now tell of the Germans who pried the doors from their hinges, to use as barricades, and I have seen the pictures in testimony. On the walls of Ristorante Garda, where I am headed, are framed photographs of the invasion—a woman looking for her child amid the rubble, boats sunk in the harbor—and in the landscape there is truth. The windows remain but the doors are gone.

These days, during summer months, the Anzio square is crowded with boaters and tourists. It is a seaside town like any other. But today, off-season, it is practically deserted. The harbor itself is busy with the getting and sending of Rome's seafood—Anzio remains the region's most viable coastal port—but many of the shops are boarded up for the winter, and many of the smaller boats have already been pulled from the water. Most of the restaurants have stopped serving lunch; the few that remain open cater mostly to local fishermen, and people like myself, who are just passing through.

I step from my bicycle and look about. The cobblestone streets are slick in spots, from the surf. It has not rained, but the sea walls cannot do much with the tides. I rest the bicycle against a post and step into the restaurant. I am the only customer.

"Signor Quinn," the headwaiter says, intercepting me at the entrance. "Your bicycle, you should not leave it there. Someone will steal it."

I look out the doorway with him and cannot spot another soul. "There's no one about," I say. "I can sit by the window and keep an eye on it."

"Better I should bring it in," the headwaiter says, and with this he steps outside and wheels the bicycle into the dining room. It strikes me like something from the Old West, when man and horse were given room and board.

"This way," he continues, now out of breath from the burst of exertion, "you can sit by the water."

He leans the bicycle against a dessert cart, and then brings a big *fiasco* of chilled white wine to my table by the window. The cold wine tastes good after the long ride in the hot sun. I gulp down a glass, and refill another for sipping. As I drink, I look out at the glistening bay, trying to forget the boys lying in the cemetery who had sailed into this harbor almost fifty years before. It will not do, to think of them, at a time like this. Now all I want is to rest, and replenish my spirits. There will be plenty of time for loss.

I search for a distraction. Below me, I spy an old man on his multicolored fishing boat, working his nets. Ah, what a thing to see! The man moves with absolute concentration, and I am taken by his aloneness, his purpose. He belongs out there, on that boat, and no place else. His fingers are gnarled and weathered, but they flit across the nets like a pianist working his keys. They know what they are supposed to do. The old man is completely absorbed in his task, and I marvel at it. He appears to have lost all sense of self; for him, the self and the it are one.

How every actor strives for such a state! How few of us ever reach it, even once! I drink down my wine and know that I am watching a moment of pure artistry. Nothing can touch this fisherman, or shake him from his end. When was the last time I worked like that? I wonder. Indeed, when did I ever work like that? Has the chance to work in such total immersion eluded me forever?

Jesus, the ride has left me a sorry bastard. I reduce spectacle to disappointment, admiration to envy. What is it about me that seeks to translate such as this into something I can never taste for myself? Why can I not just look at the fisherman and his nets and leave them alone? Why must I try to define everything, or put it into context? Look at me! If I do not check myself, I will go home to paint a bad postcard version of the scene, or scribble a sentimental note in my journal for eventual "use." The purity in a moment like this has evaded artists far more talented than myself, for centuries. Who the hell am I to think I might find a way to capture it, at long last? Who the hell am I to judge such a simple act, or the man who lives it?

Zapata

ELIA KAZAN FOUND ENOUGH to like in my portrayal of Stanley Kowalski to offer me the role of Marlon Brando's brother in *Viva Zapata!* The script, written by my old friend John Steinbeck, was a powerful dramatization of the Mexican revolution, and after reading it, I thought it was a story I had to help tell.

I had lived this piece of history, through my father and mother. It was a part of me. If ever an actor was born to a role, it was I to Eufemio Zapata, brother to the famed peasant revolutionary. True, I might have preferred the part of Emiliano Zapata himself, a true Mexican hero, but even then I recognized that Marlon's star shone brighter than mine, and convinced myself that the transformation of Eufemio, from swaggering sidekick to power-mad drunk, made for a more interesting characterization.

Gadge was my only hesitation. He might have been a wonderful acting coach, but he was also a pain in the ass. He would go on to become an even greater pain, singing before the Un-American Activities Committee in such a loud, willing voice that I wondered how I ever had worked with him. And this was a man who truly was a card-carrying communist. I did not begrudge him his politics, but his cowardice was tough to ignore. Jesus, the man was Red *and* yellow!

Production began in Los Angeles, with two weeks of

rehearsals, and right away Gadge showed himself to be one of the most egotistical directors I had known. He was a thorough workman, I will give him that, but he had no clue how to behave around people. He treated his cast and crew like chattel, and carried his reputation as if it mattered. The act did not work on me, but he conned most everyone else. At the time, the feeling was that he would shoulder the allegations from Washington with grace and dignity, although that turned out not to be the case.

One of the big concerns to Kazan, early on, was that Marlon and I get along like brothers. This, for him, was the key to the picture. He wanted us to love like brothers and to fight like brothers. When we shipped out to Brownsville and Del Rio, Texas, to begin shooting, he made sure the two of us shared a sleeping compartment on the train. He was a Method man to the core. The entire cast and crew were on board, but he wanted us to keep to ourselves, together, to forge an intimacy we might call upon in our shared scenes. It was not the worst idea in the world, but it was not the best one either. Marlon showed up with this peculiar little possum he used to travel with, and a brown paper bag stuffed with clothes. That was all he had. He was, even then, an unusual human being, and as the train pulled out, I thought the picture would be a disaster. What might have been the role of a lifetime was turning out to be a dubious undertaking.

I claimed the top bunk for myself—I had visions of that damn possum taking a dump during the night!—and vowed to make the best of a bad situation.

In Texas, Gadge was disheartened that the long train ride had not brought Marlon and me any closer together. I liked Marlon well enough, but he kept to himself, and I saw no reason to make any more of an effort than he did. Undaunted, Gadge asked the two of us to drive to work together each morning, to see if this might help. Once again, we agreed, yet all Marlon wanted to do on these rides was improvise. That was fine with me—I loved to improvise, and Marlon was a world-class sparring partner. He showed up one morning as a cop, one morning as a sailor, but never as a Mexican revolutionary. After two weeks, we were no closer, but we were having a hell of a time improvising. He did not offer a clue about himself, and neither did I.

This drove Gadge crazy. Steinbeck's version of events had Emiliano and Eufemio Zapata grow apart from each other, and Gadge wanted these scenes to be thick with emotion and tension. "It has to be like brother against brother," he used to say of the looming power struggle. "Brother against brother!" It was like a rallying cry.

As competent actors, Marlon and I could have played the scenes whether we were best friends or no friends at all, but Kazan wanted to force the issue. He would not leave it alone. Before long, he tried to turn each of us against the other, and in this he finally succeeded. It was years before Marlon and I could recognize the wedge that Gadge had placed between us, but his manipulations were transparent from a distance. He pulled me aside and confided that Marlon thought I was terrible in a scene, and then cornered Marlon and delivered the same message from me. Kazan went back and forth like this for the run of the picture. "Marlon said this about you." "Tony said that about you." The man spent so much time rubbing the two of us against each other, trying to work up enough friction for his precious scenes, he had nothing left for his other actors.

At one point, I even suspected Kazan of stooping to negotiate a bizarre little love triangle, to add further heat to the situation, although in this I could not be certain. Gadge was visited on the Brownsville set by one of his Actors' Studio disciples—an empty-headed blond with a fat rear who would soon reign as the leading sex symbol of her time. Marilyn Monroe had surfaced in a handful of pictures, but had yet to make her mark, and she arrived on the scene to soak up the director's insights on acting.

Oh, Monroe was pretty enough to look at, but there were hundreds of better-looking actresses poking around Hollywood. Even after she hit the big time, with *Gentlemen Prefer Blondes*, I never could see what all the fuss was about, but what the hell did I know? All I knew was that she walked around our dusty Texas set in a slinky dress that showed the crack of her ass, apparently unaware that her clothes could not hold her. All I knew was that there seemed to be precious little going on beneath her glorious blond mane.

At first, Monroe appeared to have a tremendous crush on Gadge, and she threw herself at him at every opportunity. Gadge, in turn, threw her right back at Brando. Gadge was a jealous man, and normally very protective of his relationships, but he seemed to want to cross swords with Marlon over his protégée. It was a strange piece of theater, but Marlon was quite adept at improvising.

The work itself was splendid. For the first time in pictures, I achieved that elusive alignment of head and heart that has left me mesmerized here, as I gaze down to the Anzio harbor at the old fisherman and his nets. It was only mine for a flash, but it was mine just the same. The moment came in a clash between Brando's character and mine, when Emiliano tries to turn his lecherous brother around. Steinbeck's dialogue was untouchable, but Marlon and I improvised most of the staging, and before the cameras rolled I tried to set things up to my advantage. I glued a cigarette to hang precariously from my lower lip, knowing that when the camera pulled in for a close-up of my dear brother, the smoke would curl up and annoy the hell out of Marlon. I would be out of the shot, but the smoke would take my place. Marlon tried to flick the butt from my lip but had not counted on the glue, and then he grabbed me by the hair and tried to shake some sense into me. We tussled, as all the tensions Gadge had placed between us rose to the surface, in what turned out to be one of the picture's most powerful scenes.

Kazan was a very particular craftsman. He wanted his pictures to be as authentic as possible, and I discovered quickly that if I wanted to sell him on an idea for a scene, I would have to cloak it with authority. I had a lot of ideas, but he would only listen to the ones that had something to do with my father's experiences in the revolution. So I lied. What did I care about authenticity? That was Gadge's problem. All I cared about was presenting the best possible scene, and giving myself a chance to do good work. I made up a story about how my father and the other revolutionaries used to take two stones, to rub and bang together in a kind of Morse code, to send messages to each other. It never happened, but I knew it would make a strong scene.

From there, it was just a small leap to suggesting that the soldiers should whistle to each other, across the hills, as another means of communication.

"Really?" Gadge said. "They used to whistle?"

"Oh, sure," I bullshitted. "All the time. They whistled all the time."

And so we whistled, supplying the picture with one of its more memorable moments. Kazan was so gullible he even had me show the other actors the "special" way my father used to trill!

Returning to Brando, it was thirty years before he and I could repair the damage Gadge had done to our budding friendship. We were in Hawaii together, around 1982. I was there to exhibit some of my paintings, and Marlon turned up at the gallery one afternoon, unannounced, to take in the show. He had been there for some time when he finally saw me.

"Tony!" he shouted, approaching me from across the

room. "Tony, these paintings, they're marvelous! Who knew you had any talent!"

We collected each other in a warm embrace, and it was like meeting an old lover. All of the pains and conflicts had disappeared with the years, and we were left to make up for lost time. We had never been close, but *Viva Zapata!* had become such a classic that we were forever linked. The celluloid bond between us had eclipsed our true relationship, and who was I to question it?

I was married to Iolanda at the time, and we had been invited to a private home that evening for dinner. I asked Marlon if he would like to join us. There was an exotic Chinese girl on his arm, and he mumbled something to her, and she mumbled something back. Then he looked to me and accepted the invitation.

Marlon and I spoke only to each other, all night long. I suppose we were rude to our hosts, and to the other guests, but we had a lot of catching up to do. Occasionally, he whispered something to his girlfriend in Chinese, or translated on her behalf, but mostly the conversation just went back and forth, between us.

We talked about our careers, about Kazan, about the people we had met along the way. He was very impressed with some of the pictures I had made, and I returned the compliment about his best work. At one point, deep into the evening, he confessed that acting, for him, had become a joyless burden. "It's such a load of shit, Tony," he despaired. "I don't know how much longer I can stand it."

One of Marlon's famous tricks had been to tape tiny cue cards on his costars' foreheads, or write his dialogue out on loose sheets of paper and paste them around the set, and his explanation had always been that in this way he might deliver his lines fresh, as if they were occurring to his character at precisely the moment of expression.

"Do you believe that shit?" he said, when the conversation turned to his technique. He laughed like the imp he had become, trapped in a prank, and then he caught enough of his breath to explain the real reason for his method: he could not be bothered to learn his lines.

We both let out such a roar that the rest of the guests looked at us in shock. Marlon relayed the conversation to his Chinese girlfriend, and she laughed politely.

At the end of the evening, Iolanda and I drove Marlon and his girlfriend back to their hotel. As the driver pulled up to the curb, and Marlon stepped out of the car, the girl leaned over to Iolanda and made a confession. "Mrs. Quinn," she said, in perfect English, "forgive me for not speaking to you all evening, but Marlon said I was to play the Chinese girl. Really, my Chinese is not all that good."

I could not help overhearing. "But all night long," I wondered, "back and forth, you seemed to have no trouble with what Marlon was saying?"

"Marlon?" she laughed. "Marlon can't speak Chinese either."

Ah, what a colorful bastard he was! And what a pair of dupes we had been!

Just then, Marlon reached to the other side, to collect the girl, and he opened the car door and leaned back inside. I could not think of a thing to say. A part of me wanted to call him on his deception, but a bigger part told me to leave it alone. Let him have his fun, I thought. There was no reason to spoil it.

Marlon kissed Iolanda on the hand, and clapped me on the back in farewell. Then he said something to his girlfriend in the gibberish he had been passing off as authentic, and the two of them disappeared into the night.

We have been friends ever since.

NINE

Ride

THE BUZZ OF THE MOTORBOAT reaches me through the plate glass and pulls me from reflection. My ears tell the story before my eyes can confirm it. My ears are sometimes wrong, but not usually.

There, no doubt, in the harbor beyond my window table, is young Rome at play. The slick engine noise does not belong here in Anzio, but it punctuates the seascape like a radio at the beach. For as long as I have known it, this harbor has been a playground for the Roman nobles, and I am heartened to hear it has remained so. I kept my own boat here, for many years, and I was always struck by the run-down dinghies moored against the yachts. I can take the inequality, the clash of the working man against the leisure class. I can take the discord with the harmony. Today especially, I can take it for what it represents.

What it represents—I am guessing, hoping—is first love, in full flower. It is autumn, I know, and long past the season for it, but I look up from my plate expecting to see a boy with dark sunglasses, a cigarette dangling dangerously from his lips, a scarved girl at his side, their bodies balanced against the tilt of the Mediterranean. They are stealing an afternoon on his father's speedboat, making love among the waves, pulling into port for a plate of calamari and a chilled bottle of Vino de il Posto, pulling back out to resume their passion. They have not a care in the world.

God, I am a pitiful old fool, to long for such a scene as this, but it is something I must see for myself, something I must remember.

Ah, there it is!—not quite as I pictured it, but close enough. I look up from my musings, out the window, and take it all in. The lovers do not come from money, I see at first glance. The boat is a hand-me-down job, reclaimed probably from a toothless uncle who once used it to ferry friends and relatives to distant sands; it is built for economy, not for speed. The boy is not handsome or muscled or particularly well-groomed; the girl is pretty, but queerly dressed in a ski parka, black baseball cap, and heels. (Who steps on a boat in heels?) But they are in love, and this is what counts.

I think back to the many loves I have known and I come away empty, and wanting. Yes, there has been passion in my long life, and boundless pleasure, but I wonder if I have ever loved without provisions, if I have ever been loved—truly loved!—in return. Perhaps, I consider. Yes, yes, of course. Surely, a man cannot reach his final sunset without knowing pure devotion. Surely, somewhere along the way, there has been a woman to take me as I was, forsaking all others. Federico Garcia Lorca put it beautifully: "One man and a wall three foot wide for the rest of the world."

There was my dear mother, first, but she truly belonged to my father. I kept her warm, blanketed from her worries, while she waited for Papa to return. There was Dona Sabina, but her love was like a consolation, and it was not enough. Sylvia might have been everything to me, were it not for the fiends who had beaten me to her. She tried gamely to talk me down from my jealousies, and she nearly succeeded, but in the end she would not have me. I was too young, she said. Her resolve nearly destroyed me, but I pressed on.

For a time, I thought Katherine would be the answer.

She was my literate princess, a knowing beauty, but those dreams came unraveled on our wedding night. Jesus, what an imbecile I was! To think that I was first! To think that it mattered! But it did matter—at the very core of my being, it mattered—and I spent the rest of our time together struggling against it. If I could not have one woman, I determined, I would have many, and I set off on a path of reckless adventure, looking for salvation in the arms of any woman who would hold me.

In some ways, I have never returned.

Once, I thought Maureen O'Hara would be my future. Now that would have been something! She was already a big star when we met, and I was bouncing from picture to picture. We landed together on the set of *Sinbad the Sailor*, and I fell hopelessly in love. She was dazzling, and the most understanding woman on this earth. She knew the situation between me and Katherine, and accepted it, but after a while we both tired of the deceit. It was one thing to bed around on our spouses, but quite another to settle into a serious relationship.

Maureen brought out the Gaelic in me, and it was a side I had never seen. I cherished what I looked like through her eyes, the ways she made me feel, and she in turn could touch a part of me that no woman had ever known. She counted the days until her husband returned from overseas, so she could divorce him and marry me, and the thought gave me pause. I was already disentangled from Katherine in all but the material sense, so it would have been nothing to pick up and start all over again. It would have been nothing and everything, both.

But Maureen and I were not meant to be married. Something always came up to keep us apart—usually a picture, or another affair, or some problem in the timing—and yet there was a connection between us that even our indecision could not shake. We stayed together, not knowing where our love would take us, not knowing that it mattered. Every once in a while, we landed on the same picture—*Against All Flags, The Magnificent Matador*—and resumed our affair. It was a wonderfully uncertain relationship, and in it we both found a lifelong friendship, but I was still left to search for the one woman who was meant for me.

Suzan

I CANNOT DWELL on matters of the heart without returning to Suzan—the one true love of my life. Ah, what a vacuum she has left in me! What loneliness! What wanting! To tell the story of our relationship is to mine the deepest recesses of my soul, to revisit the damning confluence of pain and wonder that defined our time together.

Suzan Ball was an absolutely breathtaking young actress, one of the fabulous beauties of her day. She would have been one of the great ones, no question. There was a radiance about her, a magic. She was only nineteen years old when we met, and yet she was already the answer to every question I had ever thought to ask. She was my promise, my virgin, my redemption. She had never been with another man, and I received her like manna from heaven.

"I will never know another man," she vowed, the first time we made love.

"How can you say that?" I wondered. "How can you know?" I was delighted, but conditioned against such a promise.

"I know," she said.

"Yes, but . . ."

She silenced me, her finger to my lips, and we never spoke of it again.

We met on a picture called *City Beneath the Sea*, directed by Budd Boetticher for Universal. Suzan played a singer in a Jamaican club who fell for my character, a deep sea diver in port to search for gold in the wreckage of an old ship. I was drawn to her immediately. She had the softest skin, and a smile like no other. When she spoke, the rest of the world fell silent. She was everything to me, and right away. What she saw in me I could not say, but I did not think it mattered. She loved me, and that was enough. That was everything. She chose me. She accepted me. I thought we would spend the rest of our lives together.

Suzan could make me laugh. It seemed we laughed all the time, and it was what got us started. At first, I could not get past our ages. At thirty-eight, I felt older than sixty, but I needed to laugh. (Oh, how I needed to laugh!) Most of my life had not been funny, but now I could afford a smile or two, so I gave myself over to this glorious creature with the downy skin. We laughed and laughed, and when I looked up, there was nothing else in the world.

I set up an apartment for the two of us, so we could behave decently. It would not do to run around with a girl like Suzan. She was not like any of the girls I had been with. She deserved better. I even started building a house, in the hills above Universal Studios, where she was under contract, thinking we would marry and settle there. I built it with my own hands: I designed it; laid the foundation, the pipes for the plumbing; everything. There was joy in the work, knowing that it was for Suzan.

It was a wonderful house, but a terrible house. Suzan never lived in it. Less than a year after we met, she developed cancer of the bone, and her decline was swift. The laughter stopped. We made another Universal picture together—*East of Sumatra*, again under Budd Boetticher's direction—and she accompanied me on

some of my location shoots, but we both knew our time
was short. She was incredibly strong, for both of us. I do
not know that I was any help at all. I looked at Suzan and
longed for the years we would not have.

When my career called me to Europe, I wanted desperately to take Suzan with me, but she was too weak to
travel. Plus, she thought American doctors offered better
treatment. In this, she was probably right. I wanted to
stay with her, to hold her hand through the horrible
ordeal, but she would not have me. She insisted that I go
on with my work, with my life. I wanted to divorce
Katherine and marry her, but she would not allow it. The
last thing she wanted, she said, was for me to tear my
family apart and for her to die before she had a chance to
make repairs.

I was crushed! To have known such tenderness, such
belonging, and to have it pulled from underneath me,
was a pain I had never imagined. And to hell with me!
My heart ached for Suzan most of all. She suffered
tremendously. In the beginning, neither one of us knew
what was happening. Back then, people did not hear the
sirens of cancer at the first sign of trouble. We had a
diagnosis quite by accident. Suzan was driving a car I had
given her and jammed her knee against the dash in a fender-
bender. The doctor who examined her was concerned. He
said he wanted to keep an eye on her. It was then that we
knew.

One day soon after, Suzan complained to me about a
tooth, and when she opened her mouth, it came loose
between her fingers. Another time, she blacked out in the
bathroom of our apartment, and I cleaned up after her. I
carried her to bed and washed her off and wept. I was
plainly in love with this girl—to share such an intimacy!
without a thought!—and I nursed her as if she were my
own child.

The prognosis was not good. Slowly, month after

month, Suzan lost all of her teeth. She started taking all kinds of strange medications. One doctor had her on gunpowder pills, mixed with gold, copper, and iron. She tried everything, but nothing worked. She kept the truth from me, while I was away. Indeed, she put up such a brave front that I had Dino De Laurentiis call her from Rome, to offer her a part in a picture we were shooting. Suzan had said she was feeling better, stronger, and I thought a few weeks on a motion picture set would be just the thing for her spirits, and mine.

But she told De Laurentiis what she would not tell me. She was in no condition to work. She could hardly sit up in bed, or walk across the room. How could she think about acting? Dino would not tell me the reasons she rejected the role, only that she rejected it. He was afraid that if I knew the truth, I would have been on the next flight to Los Angeles.

Suzan knew the same, but she kept the truth of her decline from me for her own reasons. She wanted to protect me from her suffering, and from some of the hard choices she had to make. She was to have one leg amputated, and did not want me to see her in such a state. She hated what the disease was doing to her appearance, but I did not care. It was her heart that mattered, her soul. It was that she loved me. I would have married her in a flash, but she resolved that I stay with Katherine. "You'll probably leave her one day," she once said, "but not for me."

And yet she wanted to marry before she died. She felt her life would have been for nothing without a husband. "What kind of way is that to go out, Tony?" she said, in explanation. "Alone?"

"But you're not alone. I'm here. I'll drop everything. I won't leave your side."

"No," she said, "that would be the worst, to see it on your face."

She would not put me through these paces. For Suzan, this was the hardest decision of all, and she would not let me be a part of it. She was introduced to a young actor and they married in haste. She presented the situation to me as if she were powerless against it. She asked for my forgiveness.

I understood, but I never accepted it. Underneath the pain of her illness there was now an even deeper hurt: I would not be the only man she would ever know—and I left her bedside knowing I would never again know such true love. I would never believe in miracles.

It is, alas, a miserable world. God tempts us with a winning hand, and we draw someone else's cards. The life we live is never the life we imagine. It takes an old man to recognize this. It takes knowing that life always turns us around, that dreams never come to pass, that the space between the elusive and the tangible is the grandest of canyons, even as lightning shoots from your fingers while reaching for the other side.

It takes never once knowing a simple happiness for any longer than a heartbeat.

"You are pathetic, aren't you?"

The voice reaches me like a pinprick. It is that lousy kid again, my younger self, come to sink me further in my own despair. His timing is reproachable. "Go away," I say. I do not want to hear my trials filtered through the jury of my adolescence, not now. "Please go away," I tell the boy. "I am in no mood for you."

"I'm not going anywhere, old man. There's no getting off easy, today of all days."

"What the hell does that mean?"

"Listen to you, feeling all sorry for yourself. No one's ever loved you, so now you're all misty? That what it all comes down to?"

"Could be," I say. "I don't know."

"Damn right, you don't know. You don't know shit.

Mama never loved you? Sylvia never loved you? Katherine? Suzan? The poor girl loved you with her life, and you're still crying like a baby."

I let the boy's invective hang like a cloud. Perhaps if I ignore him, he will go away, and his words will disappear with him.

"You wouldn't recognize love if you stepped in it," he continues. "You wouldn't recognize love if it sat in your lap and planted a wet one on your mouth."

"You don't understand." I want to tell him that it was not the same with Suzan, that for a short time I knew the boundless devotion of a brave woman, that what passed between us was like nothing else.

I want to shout it out—I was loved! I *am* loved!—but the words do not come.

"I understand plenty," the boy says. "You've had it all, over and over, and you throw it away on a technicality, every time. You're like a blind man."

"It's more than that."

He laughs like a stuck devil. "It's less than that, is what it is," he says. "It's nothing."

"It's the way I was raised."

"And I was raised different?"

I had not thought of that. "No," I try, "but I am no longer as forgiving as you. I am not the same. There are some things I can never accept."

"And because of that there are some things you will never have."

"Maybe."

"Maybe? What maybe? You're an old man. You can't even finish a lousy bicycle ride without stopping for a rest. Your time has passed."

"Look, I'm tired. I've tried my best."

"Want to know what I think?" he challenges.

"Not particularly, no."

He tells me anyway: "I think you're just another

motion picture actor with the hot wants. That's all. All of this, the despair, the longing, the wanting to be first, the one and only, it's all just you running away. It's an excuse to keep screwing around. It's all bullshit."

I consider this a moment, and turn away. I down the last of my wine and signal the headwaiter for another bottle. Where the first one has gone, I am not sure. I look down to the harbor at the young lovers, but they have had a change of plan. The badly groomed boy has untied his boat from the dock. The girl sits on a weathered cushion, facing the other way. The window keeps me from what has passed between them. The boy steps back on board and turns the engine, and it churns at the waters below.

I return my gaze to the table, but the kid is gone.

Oscar

IT WAS MARCH 19, 1953—a night made resonant by victory, but memorable on its own. I was on location in Mexico, shooting an otherwise forgettable picture for Warner Bros. called *Blowing Wild*, with Gary Cooper, Barbara Stanwyck, and Ruth Roman. We were holed up in a spectacular hotel, perched on a volcanic lake, in a place called Tequesquitengo, waiting out the Academy Awards with our Argentinian director, Hugh Fregonese.

In those days, producers rarely shut down a location shoot to allow a star to attend an awards ceremony. The statue was yours, whether or not you were there to pick it up. And you would hear about it soon enough. On this night, we might have even looked in on the proceedings. For the first time, the Oscars were broadcast live on national television, from New York and Los Angeles, so most of displaced Hollywood would not have to miss a thing.

And yet for all of the advances in technology, we could not pick up the signal at our hotel, but I do not know that I would have watched it anyway. I was up for supporting honors in *Viva Zapata!* and the nomination was enough. The previous year had been heady with rich parts in quality pictures, and I owed it all to the wonderful notices I was receiving as Eufemio Zapata. I worked constantly. There was another Raoul Walsh picture, *The World in His Arms*, with Gregory Peck; another Phil Karlson picture, *The Brigand*, with Anthony Dexter; *Against All Flags*, with Errol Flynn and Maureen O'Hara; *City Beneath the Sea*, with Robert Ryan; *Seminole*, with Rock Hudson; *Ride, Vaquero!* with Robert Taylor and Ava Gardner; and Budd Boetticher's *East of Sumatra*. I do not think I ever had a busier year, before or since. I would make better pictures, but never so many, in principal roles, back to back to back.

Chance placed Coop and me together on this night, but fate capped the evening. Coop was also nominated that year—in the lead actor category, for *High Noon*—so we passed the time in each other's company. Indeed, we passed most of our time in each other's company, while we were doing this picture. We had become good friends in the fifteen or so years since he talked Cecil B. De Mille out of firing a loudmouthed Indian on the set of *The Plainsman*. We had even taken acting classes together. I no longer called him Mr. Cooper, although my respect for him had only grown.

We began the evening with dinner. Suzan was with me on this shoot (her health was still good), and Coop was keeping company with his current leading lady, Barbara Stanwyck. Actually, he had another girl waiting for him up in his room, but he thought Stanwyck was a lot more fun to be around, so he asked her to join us for dinner. Coop was like that; he had different girls for different moods. I was never entirely comfortable around Barbara, but I could tolerate her well enough. To Coop, she was a ball of fire, and I did not want to argue.

After dinner, we went for a stroll on the lovely grounds around the hotel, and the four of us wound up lying on the grass, on a hill overlooking the lake, gazing up at the heavens. It was a spectacular night—the air crisp, the sky clear enough to make out the constellations. Coop did the talking, while the girls dozed. We had all been drinking, and they were quickly lulled by the deep melody of Coop's voice to where sleep could find them.

We did not talk about the Academy Awards at all. We had bigger subjects in mind. Coop talked of his Montana roots, and his disdain for Hollywood, but mostly he talked about the women in his life. This was one of his favorite subjects, and tonight he had a pressing reason to explore his familiar themes. There was a scene in the picture that was giving him trouble. He had to make a long, expository speech about women—how they made his character feel, what they had to teach him—but he never could get it right. Out here on the grass, though, he held forth without effort. He talked about the women he had known in Montana, and Hollywood, from Patricia Neal to Lupe Velez, how they taught him to dress, to carry himself, to show his emotions.

He was not known as a great thinker, my friend, but he felt things deeply. Carl Sandburg once called him one of the most beloved illiterates this country had ever known. But I always knew Coop to be a probing, caring soul, a shrewd judge of himself and of others.

At one point, I looked over and noticed that Coop's left arm appeared to be missing. It was a very strange thing. The moonlight had left him silhouetted in an unusual way, but as my eyes adjusted to the shadows I could place his hand underneath Barbara Stanwyck's skirt. Suzan was soundly asleep on my arm, and Barbara had her eyes closed and was feigning sleep. Coop was working his hand quite diligently between her thighs, and she moved with him. He kept up with his talking, going on and on about women, all the while diddling the famous lady who lay at his side.

A waiter came out to tell me I had a phone call from New York, and I took Suzan inside with me to hear the news. She was delighted for me that I had won, and we had a drink to celebrate, but it was clear that she was tired and wanted to call it a night. I was too excited to sleep, so I kissed Suzan and went back outside to sit with Coop. I knew he would want to share this moment, even if he had his hands full with Barbara Stanwyck.

They were right where I had left them. Coop was truly thrilled, and stood to congratulate me. Barbara too pulled herself together and offered her good wishes. Someone had thought to send out a bottle of champagne, and we passed it back and forth, drinking in the moment. After a while, Barbara went up to bed. Coop did not think he had a chance in hell of winning (among others, he was up against Marlon Brando, as Zapata himself), and she apparently did not want to offer false encouragement by waiting it out, so she wished him luck and retired to her room. I stuck it out with him, though, and we were soon back to our old subject. He just loved to talk about women, and I loved to listen.

Finally, a waiter came out with another bottle of champagne to tell Coop he had just won the Academy Award for *High Noon*, and we whooped it up all over again. We hugged each other, and did a little dance.

The waiter also announced that Paramount's *The Greatest Show on Earth*, a Cecil B. De Mille production, had been awarded best picture honors, and I realized this meant a first-ever Oscar for my father-in-law. How do you like that? I thought. My competitive juices pumped through me like never before: I had beaten the great man to the podium by a couple of hours, and it felt fantastic. I

thought of poor Katherine, back at the awards ceremonies, having to accept the statue on my behalf and
return to her seat underneath her father's jealous gaze.

I did another little dance, and helped Coop to drain
the bottle. Then we lay back down on the grass and again
looked up at the stars.

It was one of the richest nights I ever had in pictures,
although in almost every significant way it had nothing to
do with Hollywood. I was in the company of a lovely,
gentle man, a friend I truly adored and admired, and I had
a great deal to celebrate. I had nudged the legendary Cecil
B. De Mille from the spotlight, and stolen his moment
with one of my own. The love of my life was in my room,
sleeping peacefully, just a few hundred yards away. And
one of my dearest friends was riding along with me, on
the same cloud.

We had our Oscars, and our women, and the whole
night ahead of us.

Neo-realist Cowboys

IT IS A FUNNY THING, that I am here, now, in this restaurant. I have been returning to this place for years, but I
have come today for a reason. It is only now that I puzzle
together the realization.

This, after all, is the same place an exciting young
director took me to discuss a script, back in 1953, over
lunch. He wore a quizzical smile and an outlandish cowboy hat, each of which he refused to take off during the
meal. It was not much of a script—only a few pages—and
yet it held the rough edges of a masterpiece. The director
had sent it to me the night before, but it was in Italian,
and I pushed it back across the table, unread, asking my
host to tell me the story instead.

The story he told would change my life completely,

and immediately, and it is a wonder that I have returned to the very spot of its unfolding. How is it that in a moment of impulsive rediscovery a man manages to retrace his steps so precisely? Is there some path that has been predetermined for me? Is God pulling my strings and moving me along by design? I had no idea where I was headed, when I set out from Vigna S. Antonio this morning, and yet at every turn I stumble across a telling reminder of my past. Either I have lived too much of a life to avoid such coincidence, or I have entrusted myself so thoroughly to the whims of memory that coincidence cannot help but find me.

Indeed, as the headwaiter returns with my second bottle of wine, I realize that even he fits in the correlation. He is the same man who served that fateful lunch, all those years ago. What are the odds of this? It is not his restaurant—he is just a hired hand—and yet he is still here. He approaches, and seems to make the same connection. The director has become our mutual acquaintance, our secret. We talk of him often. He is the one thing we share.

"Our friend," the waiter says, filling my glass, "he was something, no?"

He was something, yes. Federico Fellini had only made two full-length pictures at the time of our first meeting—*The White Sheik* and *I Vitelloni*—and I had not seen either one, but his reputation was already enormous. He was one of the leading neo-realists, and the talk of the Italian cinema. I did not know what a neo-realist was, but figured I would find out. The ridiculous cowboy hat did nothing to diminish his standing, and he held forth underneath its wide brim as if he had worn one all his life.

I had gone to Rome earlier that year, as the axis of the motion picture industry tilted toward Europe. Italian pictures such as *Open City*, *Shoeshine*, *Paisan*, and *The Bicycle Thief* were having a tremendous impact in Hollywood, and signaled a renaissance in movie making. In contrast,

American pictures seemed locked in an industrial and creative crisis, and hopelessly stale. Now that I was enjoying some sudden success, I wanted to act on the richest possible stage, surrounded by the biggest talents. The only audience I craved was an audience of my peers. I needed to be where it mattered most, so I packed up my family and followed the wave.

It was an enchanted time. I fell in love with Rome the moment I set foot in the city. Six hours later, I was in hospital with food poisoning—it might have been the fava, the pecuno, or the wine—but that was part of Rome's charm. It gave as good as it took. Right away I felt the inventive energy that Hemingway, Fitzgerald, Picasso, and Joyce had created in Montparnasse. Rome had its own Gertrude Steins, but its literary explosion was fueled by images. The artists of this renaissance were not producing paintings for churches, or manuscripts for the ages, but pictures for movie houses. What the hell did I care? To me, one artist was much like another. All expression is the same. What difference did it make if we worked in a modern medium, as long as we worked well and remained true to our calling?

The city was seething with moviemakers from all over the world. It was like Hollywood, New York, and Cannes, all rolled into one. Most deals were made on Via Veneto, over Campari or espresso. Every player had to make an appearance. On Sunday mornings, sidewalk cafes on both sides of the street were filled to overflowing. An actor's popularity was measured by how many scripts he was offered as he traversed the street. Kirk Douglas, with whom I worked in *Ulysses*, my first Italian picture (produced by Dino De Laurentiis and Carlo Ponti), used to engage me in a singular game of one-upmanship. One Sunday, he ran the gauntlet from the Excelsior Hotel to the Porta Pinciana and back again, returning with nineteen legitimate offers.

He topped my best by two.

I had no frame of reference for such a spectacle. In Hollywood, the stars would only assemble at premieres or awards ceremonies, but along the Via Veneto it was common to see Greg Peck, Ingrid Bergman, Bill Holden, Anna Magnani, Gene Kelly, Silvana Mangano, Clark Gable, Audrey Hepburn, Gary Cooper, Jennifer Jones, or Errol Flynn turn out for the sidewalk show, often on the same afternoon. The six blocks between the Excelsior and the Porta Pinciana were the center of the motion picture industry, and we were drawn to it as if by suction.

To walk those six blocks with aplomb became quite an accomplishment, and a test of confidence. Ingrid Bergman strolled with a stately Nordic gait, like a conquering Viking. Coop refused to run the obstacle course; he saved his showmanship for the screen, but his refraining was itself a powerful statement. Kirk Douglas was probably the most successful at it—he overwhelmed everyone with his infectious enthusiasm—but I preferred Anna Magnani's majestic style. She paraded down the street with her two black German shepherds, while all other activity came to a halt. She walked that road just as Calpurnia must have walked through ancient Rome, the empress of all she surveyed.

I arrived during springtime and felt a part of things from the first. Rome is like that, I have come to realize, and in this it is like no other city in the world. All the great places sneak up on you—Paris has to be discovered; Athens takes its time—but only Rome grabs you at the outset, and never lets go. I was immediately drunk with its beauty, and felt the city had something to say to me, just. We shared a secret, Rome and I, and for the longest time I was not telling a soul.

The steps of the Piazza di Spagna were awash in color, limned by huge potted azaleas advertising the change in season. The entire city seemed to be on a festive kick. It was just eight years since the end of the war, and the energy that had been capped during the German occupation was still in release. And no people are more eager to release their energy, I learned, than the Italians. There was a famous line about Italians—"Forty million great actors, and only the bad ones make movies!"—and its root was on every face, on every corner. It was a place that breathed life, and gave life in return.

It was wonderful.

I ran the Via Veneto gauntlet immediately, and went to work. From *Ulysses*, I moved to a dramatic version of *Cavelleria Rusticana* (in 3-D, no less!), and a convoluted Giuseppe Amato picture called *Donne Proibite*, with Linda Darnell, who no longer thought I was a fairy. When one picture wrapped, I went straight to another.

Katherine and I lived in the city, in a house rented from Eduardo De Filippo's brother, and I took to the lifestyle right away. My wife was less sure of the change, and less sure of me. She was beginning to think I was crazy—talking to myself, and my father; stalking the demons that still prowled our bed—and I was beginning to think she might be right. I could find no happiness in our marriage, no peace. I walked around looking for answers to questions that had not yet occurred to me. Katherine was also searching. She had become a deeply religious person, and was by now extremely active in the Moral Rearmament movement, dedicated to the moral awakening of mankind, through faith and purity. (These evangelists had a hold on her I could never understand!) Our daughter Valentina was born just the year before, and I think we both recognized the child's birth as the beginning of our last act. We might stay together for the rest of our lives—for the sake of the children, for appearances, perhaps even for ourselves—but the marriage was dying. After more than fifteen years, it was clear that neither one of us had the power (or the inclination) to revive it.

Work was my release, my escape. I took a part in
another Ponti–De Laurentiis production, *Attila, Flagello di
Dio*—as Attila the Hun, opposite Sophia Loren and Irene
Papas. It was to mark the beginning of a long association
with the fiery Greek actress, who at the time preferred to
be called "Ereenee." She had an intensity about her that
was difficult to ignore, but her frailty was what I found
most appealing. We were too much alike to ever truly get
along. She seemed to be of my blood. She could have
been my sister or my grandmother. My feelings for her
were mixed with incestuous guilt, but I could not look
away from them.

Irene was the kind of girl who walked into your room
and held up her hand. She would not talk to you until she
looked under your bed, through your bookcases and your
collection of records and photographs. Then she would
know who you were. I remarked that her cataloging
would be useless with me—I was living with rented fur-
nishings!—but she was determined. I had no idea what
the bad hotel paintings told her about me, but she did not
go away.

The *Attila* production was notable for a comic disaster
that might have shut down the entire picture. If it was up
to me, it would have.

We shot a great many scenes on Monte Cavo, in Rocca
di Papa, just south of Rome. One afternoon, at the beginning of a rare snowstorm, the director left to shoot a few
scenes that did not involve Irene or me. He took the
entire crew with him, and left the two of us in a hotel up
on a hill. We welcomed the short break. There was a bar
and a restaurant. It would just be a few hours. We would
be fine.

I had spent hours in makeup and wardrobe that morning, and it made no sense to take everything off just to
put it back on again in the afternoon, so I walked around
the hotel in a suit of armor. My eyes were pinched back

with a powerful glue, to leave me looking properly Asian and barbaric. I was preparing to attack Rome in my next scene, and this was what you looked like when you attacked Rome. Irene too was dressed in a wild outfit, and we lounged around like two beasts from another century.

Actually, for a while, it was rather fun, noodling around the old hotel with Irene in period costume, but the novelty wore off soon enough when we noticed the snowstorm getting worse. There were no wristwatches in the Dark Ages, and we lost all track of time. Irene walked over to the window and gasped. "Tony, look," she said. "The snow. It's blocking the door."

I went over to see for myself. The snow was about three feet deep. There were drifts reaching up to the windows. The wind and fog made it difficult to see for more than a few feet.

"What the hell time is it?" I wondered.

Irene had no idea. We went down to the front desk to use the hotel telephone. It was four o'clock. Four o'clock! Jesus, where the hell did everybody go? We could not get an outside line at first, but eventually we reached the studio in Rome. I got one of De Laurentiis's assistants on the other end. "Where the fuck are you people?" I railed. "Are you gonna use us today or what?"

"You're still up there?" the kid said. He explained that shooting broke several hours ago, when the snows threatened the roads. Everyone had been sent home.

"Yes, we're still up here. Where are we gonna go?"

The kid was scared for his job, but it was not his fault. "Mr. Quinn," he said, "I'm terribly sorry. Would you mind staying in the hotel tonight?"

"You're fuckin' right, I mind. I can't stay with Irene in the hotel. Jesus, all of Rome will be talking about it. You get a car up here."

"We can't get a car," the kid tried to reason. "The

roads are closed. And that hill, leading up to the hotel, that hill must be treacherous."

The manager could not help but overhear my tirade, and he offered one of the hotel trucks to take us back down Monte Cavo and into Rome. "It's just a bread truck, Mr. Quinn," he cautioned, "and there's no room in the cab, but you should make it down the hill. The driver needs to get back down to the bakery, so he's going anyway."

So Irene and I piled into the back of the truck, dressed like barbarians and surrounded by sacks filled with fresh-baked bread. Jesus, we must have been a sight! We slipped down that hill like it was an amusement park ride. I was certain we would fly off the side of the road and tumble to our deaths in the valley below.

What a way to go!—crushed by a bakery truck, smelling of blood and flour, dressed as Attila the Hun. I imagined the headlines.

By this time, the snow had stopped and the skies cleared. The countryside was absolutely magnificent, like a winter wonderland, but I did not care about the scenery. I was cold, and tired, and hungry. I wanted to go home.

The driver made to let us out at the bottom of the hill, but I was not moving. "We can't get out here," I shouted. "Look how we're dressed! We're in costume, goddamn it!" Outside I could see children playing in the streets. It was like a mid-afternoon holiday. The entire town was out to romp in the snow. The last thing I needed was to step from the truck as Attila the Hun, into the middle of that scene.

I ripped the glue-mask from my temples in anger—I still have the scars!—and then I gave the driver about two hundred dollars in U.S. money to take us back to Rome.

The next day, I refused to go to work. I was furious at the director. What kind of asshole maroons his two stars in the middle of one of the worst storms in memory? What was he thinking?

"Fuck you," I said, when someone at the studio called to see where I was. "I'm not coming in."

The day after that, it was the same. I stayed home for a week. Every day they called, and every day I told them to go to hell. Finally, I thought I had punished them enough. A week was enough time for a proper tantrum. Anything more would have been unprofessional. I had wanted to shut down the picture, but I thought it was enough that I crippled it.

I got into my car and drove to the studio, but they were no longer expecting me. "What the fuck are you doing here?" De Laurentiis said, when I reported for work.

"I'm here to finish the picture," I said. "I was too mad to come back to work, but I'm not mad anymore. I've held out long enough. I know I've been costing you a lot of money."

Dino flashed a villainous smile. "Not exactly," he said. "We're collecting insurance. Your little protest is actually making us a profit."

"You bastard." I laughed. "I'm stewing at home, teaching you a lesson, and you're making money?" It was a fitting irony.

"Go back home," Dino said, conspiratorially. "Go back to bed. The insurance company is sending someone to check you out. You must tell them you've had a horrible experience. Tell them you don't know when you'll be able to come back to work." He hurried me back to my car, giggling like a boy caught with his hand in the cookie jar.

The making of *Attila* was also notable as counterpoint, for it was in the middle of my self-imposed exile that I first met Fellini. I had played opposite his wife, the actress Giulietta Masina, and she was forever touting her brilliant husband. It seemed that everyone was singing the man's praises. For all its grandeur, the Italian film community was rather intimate; it did not take long to recognize the players, and to know everybody's business. Fellini's name was all over the place. He was like an exciting storm on the horizon, and all we could do was secure ourselves against him.

Giulietta tried to arrange a meeting while we were shooting *Donne Proibite*, but for some reason we did not get together until I had begun work on *Attila*. She was anxious for me to work with her husband, she said, because it was meant to be. I was the man Fellini was looking for to make his next picture.

Well, I did not know about that, but I did want to meet him. My friends Ingrid Bergman and Roberto Rossellini told me to take absolutely any part he offered me, at any price. "You must work with him," urged Rossellini, who had given Fellini his first break as a screenwriter. "It will mean everything."

I liked Fellini immediately, even with the silly cowboy hat. He gave me the most marvelous piece of advice. He had seen me interviewed by some Italian journalists, and thought that I had been too forthcoming in my response. "Why do you tell these people the truth?" he wondered from behind his crooked smile. "I do not understand it. Are you psychoanalyzing yourself? Are you using your confessions so that you may fight your way out of them? Is that why you do it?"

He did not wait for a reply, but continued talking. "Me," he said, "I never tell the truth to a journalist. I always lie. It is like an exercise to me, because when I lie I have to use my imagination, I have to think. Tell them whatever you want and they will believe you. Tell them you are making a million dollars a picture. Tell them you have an identical twin who works in a fish hatchery. Tell them and you will read it in the papers the next day."

I looked at him with deep admiration. It had never

occurred to me to bullshit my way through the trappings of celebrity. "It is a remarkable philosophy," I allowed.

"What philosophy?" he dismissed. "It is just a game. I make up stories, then I make a picture out of it. You, you tell the truth and you're stuck with it. You don't move anywhere. Creatively, you don't move."

Perhaps he was right. The story he had made up and had now come to tell me was about a miserable minstrel who travels the back roads of Italy, staging cheesy road-side attractions for the locals. He is part showman, part strongman, part no man at all. He lives in a tiny shack of a trailer, hitched to the back of a beat-up motorcycle. He collects a simple girl from a small village and works her into his act. He treats her like a slave. They set off together on separate missions; to the girl, it is an adventure, and the chance to serve the man who has come to claim her; to the man, it is another leg of his long escape, and the chance to squeeze a few extra pennies from the townspeople along the way.

Fellini was calling his picture *La Strada*—The Road— and to him it was all about one man's bitter loneliness, and his rejection of the love and devotion of the one woman who would have him. I listened to Fellini's tale and for a moment thought he was talking about me.

I still did not know from neo-realism, but I liked the story well enough, and I was anxious to learn what all the fuss was about surrounding this looming giant of the Italian cinema. Fellini did not look like any giant, but he was an interesting fellow and he seemed to care about pictures. I told him I would gladly play the part of Zampano, the wandering strongman.

He asked me what my salary was and I told him.

"That's the budget for the whole picture!" he choked.

He was in no position to haggle, and neither was I. *Viva Zapata!* had made me a star, and my stock was rising. Who knew how long I would be in demand? The trick, in pictures, was to get your price while you could, and take whatever you could get after that. It would be some time before I could make a picture just for the hell of it.

"Tell you what," he finally said. "I'll give you twenty-five percent of the picture."

I looked across the table at Fellini and smiled. He must have really wanted me for the role. No one had ever wanted me enough to give me a piece of the picture. Plus, I liked him, and I liked the story.

"Fine," I said, extending my hand. "Let's make a picture."

We very nearly had a deal, but for Dino De Laurentiis. I had not counted on him, but he surfaced soon enough. I was under contract to Dino at the time, and smack in the middle of the *Attila* shoot. Fellini wanted to begin production right away. The only way around the conflict, I thought, was to get De Laurentiis to bend a bit on his exclusivity clause, and to break my ass in the bargain.

I had it all figured out. In those days, Italian studios functioned under so-called French hours, which meant we worked from noon to seven o'clock in the evening, without breaking for lunch. Of course, the hours were sometimes shifted to accommodate an exterior shot requiring morning light, or a tight deadline, but the producers were usually good about sticking to the later schedule. It was quite a civil change for the American actors accustomed to arriving on the set by seven or eight in the morning, but the Europeans—bless them all!—preferred to work later in the evening in exchange for a good night's rest.

What the French hours meant for me, and Fellini, was that I would be able to play the part of Zampano if he could arrange to shoot *La Strada* in the mornings. It was not an ideal situation for him—the picture was to be shot almost entirely outdoors, and he hated to give up all those daylight hours—but it was better than nothing. And it would not be ideal for me, working virtually around the clock for a stretch of several weeks, but I wanted to see if I was up to it.

It fell to me to extract De Laurentiis's approval.

"Dino," I explained, visiting him in his office the next morning. "I met a guy named Fellini, and he wants to make a picture with me."

"Fellini?" he said. "That no-talent? He's so full of shit I can't understand what he's saying. He wanted me to finance a picture of his, some nonsense about a circus, or a strongman."

"That's it," I said. "That's the picture. That's the one he wants me to make."

"Don't be an idiot, Tony. The man likes to put his wife in his pictures."

I chose not to remind Dino that his own wife, Silvana Mangano, was a fixture in several De Laurentiis productions. "What's wrong with that?" I asked instead. "I've worked with Giulietta before. She's quite good."

"She's wrong for the part. I'd rather use Gina Lollobrigida in that part."

He was talking like a producer. Gina Lollobrigida was wrong for Fellini's picture. "Look, Dino," I said, "I want to make the picture. I'll shoot that picture in the mornings and come to work for you in the afternoons."

"You can't do that!" he blustered. "We have a contract!"

"We do. That's why I'm here. I was hoping we could work something out."

What we worked out was that De Laurentiis and Ponti would finance Fellini's picture, in order to keep a tight rein on my schedule. It cost them $250,000, which was nothing next to the money they had already dropped on *Attila*. Plus, I convinced them it was a good investment. And it was. Dino and Carlo made millions on *La Strada*, and the picture established them as two of the most powerful producers on the international scene. Hell, it won them an Academy Award, as best foreign language film, when it was finally released in the United States in 1956, and as far as I know they never once thanked the director for his vision, or any of the actors for their performances—or me, for persuading them to invest in the picture in the first place.

But all of that was unimportant next to everything else. *La Strada* placed Federico Fellini at the vanguard of the motion picture industry, and laid the groundwork for his extraordinary career. I squired him around Hollywood, after the American release, helping him to shop for a studio deal. The studio heads were leapfrogging each other to sign up the Italian auteur, offering him as much as a million dollars for his next picture—a phenomenal sum in those days. I translated for my friend.

"A million dollars," Fellini said, incredulous. "What for?"

"For a picture. Just to direct a picture."

"No," he finally said. "I can't. I can't direct an American picture. I would not know how to tell an American actor how to hold his cigarette."

La Strada vaulted me from respect as a supporting player to international recognition. It might have made me a rich man too—if I had held on to my piece of the picture. I had no idea the movie would have such an impact, even after it was in the can. I arranged a special showing for my agent and several friends, and when the lights came on in the screening room, everyone was scratching his head. No one could understand it, and I was so convinced the picture would be a flop that I let my agent sell my twenty-five percent stake for a lousy twelve thousand dollars, turning one of the best deals of my life into one of the worst.

Even when the dice rolled my way, I crapped out.

Ride

THE DAY HAS TURNED, during my late lunch.

I step from the restaurant and into a biting cold. My clothes, damp from the morning ride, are no protection. I shiver against the wind as it kicks up off the water; it cuts through me, where my perspiration has cooled.

The wine too has left me unprepared for the chill. It has also left me drunk, a little, although this should not be a problem. I reach into my pack to see how I am fixed for the weather. I strip away my damp shirt and replace it with the dry top I peeled away this morning—thank God for layers!—and in the few beats it takes to accomplish this, I am like one of those polar bear fools, out for a swim. The steam rises from my naked chest as if from a fresh turd in the snow. Jesus, what an image! It must be the wine, I determine, leaving me to think in these terms. No matter. I will sweat out the alcohol in just a few kilometers, and adjust to the temperature as I ride. The raw chill is just a momentary discomfort, a nuisance. I ball up my wet shirt and stuff it into my pack. Then I hurry into dry clothing.

October is like this, I think, as the waiter steps outside to say goodbye. Turn away and it goes from hot to cold, sunny to gray. It is how I sometimes feel. Consider: I have always been a passionate person, but lately I have become moody as well. Only now, in my autumn, is it possible for me to find the short path from joy to sorrow, to downshift from hope to despair in the time it takes to change my clothes.

I have become as hard to figure as the space between seasons. The years have left me a different person. Each day, I am someone else, and I do not know that I will ever again make my full acquaintance.

I thank my waiter friend for taking such good care of

my bicycle, and climb aboard. Where to next? I wonder. Home, perhaps, but I am not ready to face that damn box, or Iolanda, or the life I am now living. Maybe that is it, I think. Maybe it is not the life I have lived that has sent me reeling, but the one I am living, still. (They are separate things, yes?) Maybe I do not like what I have become, the way things are with Iolanda, the relationships I have built with my adult children, the turns my career has taken.

Maybe the arrival of Katherine's box has merely awakened me to a simmering gloom. Or maybe it is just the contrast—between what? my two wives? my two lives? life and death?—that leaves me so uncertain. No. No, it is more than that, I tell myself. I have lived far more than two lives. When one no longer suits me, I try on another. I am a snake, remember. I must keep moving.

But where? Ah, I know. I will double back to Latina, about twenty kilometers to the east, along the coast, to trade what I have become for what I was. I will revisit one of my great successes. Yes, this is what I will do. It is a marvelous idea. These thoughts of Fellini have left *La Strada* very much on my mind, and Latina is a lovely memory of our collaboration. Goodness, it was glorious, working with that man, all those years ago! What better day to return to the scene of our shared distinction? And what better setting than Latina?

Always, as I tool about the countryside, the signs leading to Latina are a touchstone. They call to me, returning me to that special time and place. How could I have ignored them, this morning, on the way into Nettuno? What was I thinking? But it is not too late to turn things around, so I beat back a retreat. With luck, I will reach Latina by four o'clock, and from there it is only another twenty kilometers back to Vigna S. Antonio—mostly north and west, mostly uphill. If I do not dawdle, and the hills are not too terribly unkind, the sun should still see me home.

Latina is a fairly populous village, crowded with the faces of Fellini's pictures. He has made everyone familiar. He might have been a painter, my friend, were he born in a different time, to a different medium, such were the truths he could find in a simple human expression. Indeed, he might have been the most prolific painter the region has ever known. For *La Strada*, he would set up his cameras in one town square or another, and wait for the piazza to fill. He did not believe in casting extras for his crowd scenes. The backdrops to his pictures were always real, the faces those of Italy itself. No doubt many of them can still be found in Latina—a little weathered, perhaps, and wrinkled, but mostly the same.

I recall one early Latina shoot like it was just this morning. We waited for the sun to crest over the Alban hills, preparing a signature scene. Zampano, the strongman, is trying out a new show. His simple routine had been to break the chains strapped tight around his chest, to demonstrate his might, but now that he has recruited the waif Gelsomina (played by Giulietta Masina) he is looking to broaden his act. He wants there to be music and comedy and pathos. He wants the girl to expand his horizons.

Fellini kept us off to the side while the piazza filled. He did not want the people to see Zampano or Gelsomina until it was time. When the sun was sufficiently high to offer proper light, and enough people had gathered for us to shoot the scene, we marched out our characters and went into our routine.

It was sensational! On the very first take, we had these good people laughing and applauding like mad. I had never heard such clapping, such joy. We were all high with the performance, the reception we received. Fellini could not contain himself, he was so thrilled. It was, we all thought, the perfect scene.

There was no way to improve on it, so Fellini gave us

the rest of the day off. It was barely nine o'clock in the morning, and there was an entire day to fill. It was a marvelous treat. We had already wrapped *Attila*, so I was through with my double-time schedule, and free to enjoy the vacation. I took Katherine out shopping, to celebrate. We had a delightful afternoon, free of all tension and bickering. She did not talk about God, and I did not talk about her old lovers. Mostly, I talked about the scene we had shot that morning, how good it felt to be acting well and true, to be working with such wonderfully talented people. It was a special day, and I would not let anything spoil it.

And I would not let it end. That evening, we invited the cast and crew for an old-fashioned bake-out. I dug a big hole in the ground outside our rented house and cooked Mexican-style for Fellini and his wife, and for about thirty of our new friends. It was a wonderful party, and a fitting end to the day. I went to bed drunk and happy.

Life was good.

The phone woke me up at three o'clock in the morning. It was Fellini. He had no compunction about the late hour; when there was something on his mind, he had to find someplace to put it.

"Antonio," he said, "I am curious, what did you think about this morning?"

"God, Federico, I was so high! I am high still." It had been a great morning, and I could still feel its adrenaline.

"But it was all wrong," Fellini said, his voice thick with regret. "We can't use what we shot. We have to shoot it again."

"But why?"

He told me what I should have already known. Zampano and Gelsomina were pitiful road show performers. Their story was one of tragedy, not triumph. They were not supposed to be talented enough to bring a crowd

to applause. In fact, we should have played them slightly
off, and enough over the top to pull boos and jeers and
nervous tears. They needed to be bad, not good.

What a cruel bastard he was, that Fellini! He was absolutely right, and the high of the day fell to the reality of
tomorrow.

"It does not serve our story, Antonio," he said. "We
must try again."

And so we did, and as I struggled the next morning to
make Zampano as pathetic as he needed to be, to act
badly, I wondered what other directors would have been
courageous enough to admit such a blinding mistake, to
have to topple his performers from such a dizzying height,
drop them to the hard earth and send them off in the
opposite direction. A lesser artist—indeed, a lesser man!—
might have written around the scene, or made some
inconspicuous repairs in the editing room, but Fellini was
above that.

It was, to me, a remarkable thing.

I make to leave Anzio the way I came in, but as I
pedal away from town, I think better of it. I stop and
straddle the bicycle, setting my foot against the curb to
steady myself. To retreat to Latina would mean another
pass through Nettuno, and it was difficult enough deal-
ing with all that death and destruction on the way here.
What did I need to put myself through that again? And
the timing seems all wrong. I have no plan, no map in
my head, but to splinter off to Latina suddenly makes
no sense. It will take me nowhere but away, and back. I
have lifted what I need from Latina, just from the memory of it; to see it again will only reinforce what I already
know.

No, I will keep to my original arc. I do not need to suffer those hills after such a long ride. I step my foot from
the curb and turn around. I will go where the bicycle
wants to take me. I will circle out of Anzio and head north,

toward Aprilia. I will follow the path of the American soldiers, inching their way through occupied territory.

I will keep on.

The Reluctant Matador

MY WORLD MAY HAVE CHANGED with the release of *La Strada*, but it took a few years for American audiences to catch on to the transformation. In the meantime, I returned to the States to make a few pictures—including, most memorably, *The Magnificent Matador*, directed by Budd Boetticher for 20th Century–Fox.

We shot the picture in Mexico, but it was an American production in every respect, and it came with a story. I was cast opposite my old flame Maureen O'Hara, but the time between us had passed and I was not prepared to reignite those embers. Instead, I took up with a blond, blue-eyed society woman who was hanging around our set. Always, on location, prominent local women attached themselves to our various productions, looking for a piece of the glamour to rub off on them. And always, on location, my raging faithlessness attached me to at least one of these women, to quell my excess energy and see me through the lonely nights. If there was not a young starlet, or a companionable makeup girl, there was always a lovely local lady to take her place beside me in bed. I do not set this out to boast, and I am not proud of what my promiscuity says about me, yet that is how it was. The score would never be settled between Katherine and me, but at least I could run up the tally.

So there I was, with my society dame in tow, preparing to shoot the climactic bullfighting scene. *The Magnificent Matador* was my third bullfighting picture, and I thought I knew my way around the ring. At the time, in pictures, we were not allowed to depict an actual bullfight, so I had never

made a true pass at one of these beasts. For this picture,
though, we were planning an authentic ring demonstration
to cap the story, and Budd Boetticher needed considerable
footage of me, in a crowded stadium, tempting the bulls.
Naturally, there would be a stunt double—a ranchero, an
accomplished bullfighter—to stand in for me during the
long shots, but I would be there for the close-ups.

Finally, the day came for us to shoot the scene. The
producers had plastered posters all over town, advertising
the picture, and the chance to see me and Carlos Aruza—
known as El Citano—and Antonio Ordonez, the great
bullfighters who were serving as consultants. They also
offered lunch to anyone wishing to sit through our
demonstration. We needed to fill twenty-five thousand
seats, and this was all it took. Even the appearance of a
bullfight was enough to get these people going; they
poured in through the stadium tunnels as if we were giving something away.

I arranged for my society lady to sit in the front row,
along with forty of her closest friends, and waited in the
tunnels for my cue. I put on the mantilla. I was ready.
When the doors opened, I swaggered out into the ring
like the flamboyant matador I was playing. I did the
walk—that wonderful walk!—and then I paraded myself
to the judge's viewing stand, to receive his permission to
fight the bulls. The sport is rich with ritual and ceremony,
and we were careful to present it accurately. Then I
stopped in front of my society girl and bowed. She lapped
it up. This woman said she was in love with me, but
mostly what she loved was the way our affair had elevated
her in the eyes of her friends. This was her day, in her
mind, and I was her matador.

Once in character, I presented my mantilla to Maureen
O'Hara, who was also sitting in front. There was still a
closeness between us, and we were playing lovers in the
picture, so the meaningful glances we exchanged for the

cameras were easy to come by. I dedicated the bull to her, and made to begin.

Then, according to custom, I disappeared into the tunnel to prepare for my entrance. There, hidden from view, I quickly switched places with the ranchero, who was dressed exactly like me. He stepped into the ring and called out the bull, and he was met by a derisive chant from the crowd.

There was no fooling the aficionados in the stands. They knew the ranchero was not me, and they would not accept a substitute. The cameras, from a distance, would not have told the difference, but to these people, it was everything. To these people, I was a coward. I had assumed everyone was aware that I would not actually fight the bulls—that I was just an actor, playing a part—but I was wrong.

My fucking girlfriend led the chorus against me. "Tony!" she shouted. "Tony, where are you!" She was embarrassed, in front of all her friends, that her boyfriend had abandoned the ring.

The crowd turned ugly. People started throwing fruit into the ring, along with the box lunches prepared by our catering crew and whatever else they could find. They were yelling, "Ese media hombre, el chinqado de Chihuahua!" Tony Quinn's a whore! His mother should stuff him up her womb!

I wanted to crawl somewhere and die.

Budd Boetticher was directing the scene from his booth, and he had me hooked up to a tiny earpiece, so he could talk to me during the scene. "Goddamn it, Tony!" he said. "Where are you?"

I signaled to him so he could see me, and held my hands up as if to ask for direction.

"We're losing the scene," he said, "we're losing the picture. This fucking crowd is out of control."

Just then, the ranchero came back into the tunnel.

"The bull won't pay attention to me," he said, in a panic. "There's too much going on."

With the ranchero gone, the people in the stadium accelerated their protest. They started yelling the ugliest, most obscene things they could think of: "Didn't your father give you balls?"

My God, we were all so ashamed. After what seemed like the longest moment, Antonio Ordonez, one of the greatest bullfighters to ever live, approached me in the tunnel. He had a look of resignation on his face. "Antonio," he said, "I know what this means, to these people. You are billed as the head matador. You must fight the first bull. If you don't, none of us will be able to fight."

"But Tocayo—" I protested. ("Tocayo" is used to address someone with your own first name.)

Ordonez cut me off. "These people," he said, "they will lynch us if we don't fight. Or they will just leave, and you will lose your crowd. You must come out and face the bull."

"Are you out of your fucking mind?" I said. "I am an actor, not a bullfighter." I told Ordonez that if he could find me a cow to act the part of the bull, then perhaps we could work something out.

"Look," he tried. "All you need is to make one or two passes. That's all these people want, to know that you have balls. Show them that and they'll forgive any fucking thing."

"That's all?" I said, making sure.

"That's all. Carlos and I will be on either side of you. We know the bull. We'll never let him near you."

In truth, I was more indignant than afraid—and pissed that the audience had been misled at my expense. "What the hell," I finally said.

I stepped out into the ring to meet my fate. Most of the crowd was silent, but there were still some hecklers. My society girlfriend was one of the holdouts. "You're a fucking coward, Antonio!" she shouted, "a lousy, fucking coward!" It was scandalous, the things that were coming out of this woman's mouth.

I looked around the stadium and imagined the moment to come. I was no longer here as an actor, but as a man, and yet I approached the drama like any other scene. I was a bullfighter, and I would live or die by my instincts. I dropped to my knees and faced the bull. I had learned enough to want to goad the animal into passing me, and suddenly there he was, coming at me, head on, like a runaway train, and—Jesus Christ!—he buzzed me so close I almost ejaculated. It was, without exaggeration, one of the most thrilling passes in the history of the ring, and I was not through. I was hard with excitement. I had never done anything like this before, could not imagine anything more exhilarating. My God, I was hooked!

The bull retreated to the far end of the ring. I found his eyes and willed him to return. Carlos Aruza was a few feet away from me, reminding me to give the bull the cape. I did not need to be told what to do. In my head, I had done this a thousand times. In my head, I was the bravest matador ever to step in the ring. I locked on to the bull. For all his strength and majesty, his eyes were incredibly sad. For a moment, I thought he was trying to tell me something, although whether it was that he would not hurt me, or that he would tear my fucking guts out, I could not be certain. Then the bull began his thunderous approach. My world fell to slow motion. He came at me in a riot of dust and poetry. I gave him the cape, and pulled it back at the last possible instant.

This second pass was even more thrilling than the first! The crowd erupted in applause. I dropped again to my knees. Carlos and Antonio corralled the bull and led him out of the ring. Flowers were thrown at my feet. At first I could not move, but my friends lifted me up and set me right. The crowd lifted me the rest of the way.

There followed, I believe, the greatest ovation in the annals of bullfighting, and it was meant for me, alone. What power! What elation! It was better than winning ten Academy Awards.

The crowd would not quiet down for the afternoon card, so I took the microphone and made a little speech. I spoke in Spanish. I thanked everyone for their patience, and blamed the earlier confusion on a misunderstanding with the studio's lawyers. They did not want me to get into the ring because of insurance concerns, I lied. If something happened to me, they could not finish the picture. I did not care for myself, I explained, but I did not want to put the other actors at risk, or the crew.

It was a load of crap but the people bought it. Just a few moments earlier, they were willing to string me up by my testicles, but I was a hero to them now. I was the magnificent matador. I could do no wrong.

That night, I made wild, passionate love, but not to my society girlfriend. She was all over me, showering me with kisses, but I could not stand her, not after the way she had been yelling at me. I brushed her aside and grabbed one of her friends instead.

I was Antonio Quinn, conqueror of the bulls, and I would not take shit from anybody!

Voices

I AM HAUNTED BY GHOSTS.

Here, on this ride, I am startled by the slightest apparition, any sight or sound that alights where it does not belong. If it is not the kid, come to bait me with his agonizing reappraisal, it is something else. A bird flying too close overhead. A pebble kicked by my tires to the side of the road. A strange shadow at the corner of my eye. Each sound, each movement has something to tell me.

I believe in ghosts. (I truly do!) My argument is elementary: we have all been this way before, and we will soon pass this way again. I am not so brazen to think I have nothing to learn from those who have preceded me, or too humble to deliver what I know to those next in line.

I am haunted, yes, and I will do my share of haunting, soon.

The ghosts I believe in are real, although some are more real than others. There is Gable, back at the house, or Papa, waiting for my summons. And, even when I do not call on him, there is the boy.

And there are others. Once, in the hills outside Provence, I was paid a visit by a voice it took me some time to place. It was the summer of 1955, and I was cast to play the artist Paul Gauguin in a picture called *Lust for Life*, directed by Vincente Minnelli for MGM. I went for a walk one afternoon, as I was preparing to play one of my few scenes, and came upon a field of lilies. There, at my feet, my eyes were pulled to a small bottle of clear green glass. It was only about three inches long, and maybe an inch thick, with a narrow neck. It looked like something from an old-fashioned apothecary. I held it in my hand and was overcome by the simple beauty of it, and by the fact that I could stumble over such a splendid find in just this way.

Without thinking, I plucked a lily from the field, placed it in the bottle, and continued my walk into town. As I walked, I studied the glass, and the flower. I must have been looking with the eyes of a painter, because for a moment I lost all sense of where I was. I was swallowed up by this magnificent bottle, by this one small flower. There was nothing else in the world.

When I looked up, I was in the center of a village, and I suddenly felt foolish, gazing at this little vase I had made for myself. My first impulse was to set the object down on one of the tables at a sidewalk cafe, where someone might enjoy it more appropriately, but as I went to do so, a voice called me back. "Hey!" it said. "What the hell are you doing?"

I turned, but saw nothing, so I placed the bottle back on the table and continued on my way. Then the voice came again. "Don't do that," it warned. It was a booming voice—deep and throaty and very much alive.

This time I answered. "Why not?" I said.

"Because *I* would never do that."

"Oh, you wouldn't?"

"No, I would not."

If anyone was watching me, they must have thought I was out of my mind, because I was actually carrying on this conversation. "Tell me," I said, "who are you that I should care what you would do with this little flower?"

"Ah," the voice said back, "you know who I am."

And just then, I did. It was Gauguin, here to tell me that a true artist would walk through this town, lost in the beauty of the flower and the glass, unconcerned for the stares of the others. A true artist would give himself over to the moment. Let others think what they want. You are an artist. You are Paul Gauguin.

So I picked up the bottle and walked back to the set. I heeded the voice, but at the same time I dismissed it as some internal manifestation. I was always talking to myself, and I saw no reason that I could not play the part of Gauguin in one of these chats. There was logic in it, to me.

Two days later, I had an early call for an important scene with Kirk Douglas. I was Gauguin to his Vincent van Gogh. We were seated about twelve feet from each other, painting. To be precise, what we were doing was Hollywood's version of painting. Someone had gone to the trouble of sketching outlines on our canvases, and we were to fill them in for the camera.

As a painter myself, I could have managed just fine, and even Kirk had been practicing his technique, but this was the way they wanted it done. Kirk was to paint a bridge, and I was to paint a fence with a woman alongside it. The idea of the scene was to show the contrasting styles of the two men, and the relationship they shared through their painting, and when the director was satisfied with our rehearsals, he decided to go for a take.

Just then, I heard the voice again: "You're holding the brush wrong."

At first I thought it was Vincente, offering some stage direction, or perhaps it was Kirk, with an idea for my character. "You guys say something?" I asked, looking up from my canvas.

They shrugged.

"I'll be a sonofabitch!" I shouted, standing and kicking over the little stool I was sitting on. It was the same voice from the other day, and this time I thought I was going crazy. This time, there was no dismissing it, but I could not accept it either.

"Tony, what is it?" Minnelli asked. He could see I was upset.

"I can't tell you, Vincente," I said. "I'm ashamed." I was. I hated like hell to have these guys see me as some temperamental actor, given to emotional outbursts. By this time, Kirk Douglas had walked over, along with a few of the guys in the crew, to see what the fuss was about. I did not want to appear foolish to these hardworking people.

"Ashamed of what?" Minnelli asked.

"Jesus Christ," I said, "it's too fucking embarrassing." I was shaking, and sweating, and clearly shook up by . . . *something*. Even I was not sure what was going on. How the hell could I make someone else understand?

"Tony, look," Minnelli tried again, "we've got a picture to shoot here. If something's troubling you, then tell me what it is. Whatever it is, we'll figure it out."

He was calm, and genuinely concerned. I would tell

him, I decided, but I did not want the others to hear. Maybe he would not think I was a flake. Maybe he would understand. I put my arm around Minnelli and walked him off to the side.

"Shit, Vincente," I at last confided. "Gauguin is here. He's talking to me."

"He is?"

I nodded.

"And what is he telling you?"

"He's telling me I'm not holding the brush right."

"Ah." He nodded, and he seemed to consider this for quite a while. Then he looked at me and started to laugh. His laughter was joyous, infectious. What had been so strange and unsettling to me was something to celebrate to him. Oh, a ghost? Well, wonderful! Wonderful! He laughed again, louder, and soon the others were joining in.

"Tony's had a visit from our Mr. Gauguin!" Minnelli announced, and then he laughed some more. He turned to me and slapped me on the back. "So, where is he, Tony?" he said. "Where is your friend? Introduce me!"

To Minnelli, it was a miraculous thing, that the spirit of Paul Gauguin would visit the set of one of his pictures. It was not something to question, or deny. No, it was something to cherish, and nurture. He understood.

I thought I was out of my fucking mind, but Minnelli accepted it, and Gauguin was with me every moment of that picture. He won me my second Academy Award. I still hear from him, from time to time.

Quasimodo the Greek

IT TOOK AN UNEXPLAINED SKIN CONDITION—and an unlikely introduction to Nikos Kazantzakis—to redirect my life yet again.

I was in Paris, trying to outpace Lon Chaney and Charles Laughton in a remake of *The Hunchback of Notre Dame*, opposite Gina Lollobrigida as Esmeralda. I had never read the Victor Hugo novel on which the picture was based, so I tore into it during my transatlantic voyage to begin shooting. I was trying to discover what it was to play a monster like Quasimodo, how it felt to *be* a monster, but the book left me with more questions than answers.

I lay awake nights, brooding over the role, searching for some inspiration. One morning, I woke free of worry about the part. I could not explain it. It was as if Quasimodo had come to me during the night, fully realized. I could not wait to get to work, to see what I might make of it. Then I went to the mirror in my stateroom, to shave before breakfast, and saw that my face was horribly deformed. I did not feel sick, but I looked like death. It was the most incredible thing; nothing like it had ever happened to me before. My deliberate obsession with playing a monster had manifested itself on my body. To everyone else, it looked like a dreadful rash or facial condition, but I knew better.

At first, this was just a minor worry. I looked ghastly—my face swollen beyond recognition, and discolored to resemble a rotten apple—but I thought the worst that could happen is I would save the producers a few bucks on makeup. However, when I arrived on the set, the makeup people were terribly concerned. My condition changed drastically from one day to the next, and they would have a hard time achieving the continuity they needed to sustain the picture. There was nothing to do but suspend production and wait it out. Hopefully, the condition would disappear as quickly as it had surfaced.

In the meantime, the producers brought in specialist after specialist. I saw doctors from all over the world—Germany, Sweden, the United States. They tried strong acid solutions, X-ray treatments, medications that did nothing but burn my intestines. One clown even sandpapered my face, thinking this would help. For weeks, I lived like a pampered monster in the penthouse of the Plaza Athenée hotel, being visited by every reputable practitioner with a potential cure-all. After a while, even the disreputable ones were shown in. Anything was worth a shot. The producers were insured for such a thing, but they needed to get on with the picture. They could not keep the cast and crew waiting indefinitely.

Meanwhile, I passed the time in my penthouse, telling stories to a bevy of young models from the hotel across the way. The girls had heard I was in Paris and wanted to meet me, and I welcomed their company. I covered my face with a silk handkerchief and held sway, forgetting for the moment the monster I had become.

Soon, the producers decided they could wait no longer. While I sat grotesquely in my hotel suite, the part was being quietly shopped to every available actor in pictures. (I once heard that Marlon Brando was actively considered for the role.) But Gina Lollobrigida stood up on my behalf and refused to make the picture without me. Her kindness bought me another few weeks of convalescence, and I have never forgotten it. I used the time to find a cure for myself. These doctors the studio was bringing in did not know my face from their asses. Really, I looked terrible—all blisters and blotches and puffiness. In every other respect, I felt fine, but I was truly a sight. Each day, in front of the mirror, was a new adventure, and the experts were at a loss to explain it.

Finally, someone recommended an elderly doctor on a dark side street in an unfashionable part of Paris. The man was considered a quack, but what did I care? I was willing to try anything. When I went to his office for a consultation, I thought I was in the wrong place. It looked more like a used bookstore than a doctor's office. There were papers all over the floor, and old medicine bottles, and books stacked halfway to the ceiling.

I arrived wearing one of my handkerchiefs, to protect myself from the stares of passersby (and to protect them from me!), and I peeled it off to show the old man the damage.

"You are here to play Quasimodo?" he asked, examining my face under a big, cracked magnifying glass. I had told him the story over the telephone.

"Yes."

"And you look like a monster?"

"Yes."

He considered this a moment and started to laugh.

"What is so funny?" I wanted to know. My life was being ruined, and this quack was laughing.

"Have you ever heard of Kazantzakis?" the doctor asked.

I wondered what kind of acid that would be. "No," I replied. "What is it?"

"It's not an it," he said. "It's a he. Nikos Kazantzakis, he's a writer."

Now I knew for sure I was in the wrong place. Perhaps it *was* a used bookstore. The old man put down his magnifying glass and began searching among the piles of dusty books. He found the book he was looking for under a dirty sink. He slapped it against his pants, and the dust made him cough. He laughed again.

"Here," he said, handing me the book. It looked as if it had been stomped and pissed on. "Go home and read it."

"But what about my face?" I said.

"Ah," he said, "that's nothing. You wanted to know what it was like to be a monster. Now you know. Just go home and wash your face with mineral water, no soap, and sponge every now and then with spirit of camphor."

I reached into my pocket for some banknotes. I

wondered if the man was to be paid as a doctor or a book dealer.

He held up his hand. "No charge," he said.

"But what about the book?"

"The book is a gift. Someday you will give it to someone else."

When I got back to the hotel, I washed my face with bottled water and applied the stinging spirit of camphor. My face only seemed to get more inflamed. I got into bed and opened the book. *The Saviors of God*. It was all about the space between the conscious and subconscious, the world on top and the world on the bottom.

I did not go to sleep until I turned the last page. In Kazantzakis, I could recognize the great thinkers I used to study with Sylvia: Nietzsche, Dante, Buddha. And yet the man was entirely his own creation, a true original. I had never encountered anyone like him. It was 1956, the last year of Kazantzakis's life, and as I set the book down on my nightstand, it felt as if my own life was beginning once more.

I slept like a dead man, for twenty hours straight. When I woke, I saw that my face had started to clear. I looked ten years younger. I applied another treatment of bottled water and spirit of camphor, and called the studio to report my progress. In a few days, perhaps, I could return to work.

I never did follow the doctor's orders and pass the book on to someone else, but I like to think I went him one better. I called down to the concierge, and asked to be put through to the closest bookstore. I found a knowledgeable clerk on the other end of the line, and he recommended another Kazantzakis title and sent it up to my room. I got back into bed and tore into the book.

It was about a crazy old goat named Zorba, caught between the flesh and the spirit. It seemed to say that the true struggle of living was not freedom itself, but rather the *search* for freedom, that a man can only find happiness when he is in fact looking for happiness. It was, I thought, a beautiful but tragic message.

To this day, I still carry that stomped copy of *The Saviors of God*, scarred with my underlinings and margin notes. I also have that first copy of *Zorba the Greek*, similarly marked. I have yet to digest either book fully. I do not know that I ever will.

TEN

Truths and Dares

IN PICTURES, AFTER A WHILE, everything is connected. We Hollywood denizens were all caught in some otherworldly blender, whipped to resemble each other, to bounce off the same walls, to collide, particle against particle, for all time.

I collided with George Cukor again, years after our first encounter, and I did not know that I was happy to see him. But the man was to direct me in *Wild Is the Wind*, a picture I had contracted to make for Paramount, and there was no avoiding him. I figured we would just make the best of it.

The best of it, for Cukor and producer Hal Wallis, meant the hiring of Italian movie queen Anna Magnani to play my Italian sister-in-law, who comes to America after the death of her sister to assume the role of my wife. Here again, I did not welcome the connection, at least not at first. Rome was much like Hollywood. Magnani and I had a great many friends in common, from my travels with Fellini and Rossellini, but we had never worked together, and as uplifting as it might have been to watch her stroll the Via Veneto with her magnificent German shepherds, I did not know that I was anxious for her professional company. She was a fiery, tempestuous actress, but she was also a prima donna of the highest order. What did I need with that?

Anna Magnani was one of the most prepossessing stars

of her time, and she made her presence known the very
first day on the *Wild Is the Wind* set, on location in Carson
City, Nevada. The way she chose to do this was by not
showing. It was a Monday, and Cukor had called his principals for a week of rehearsals before shooting was to
begin. Apparently, the great Magnani could not be bothered. She stayed away until Friday, and announced herself
by slipping handwritten invitations under the doors of our
hotel rooms, summoning us to a pasta dinner later that
night at her rented villa.

There was not much else to do in Carson City, so we
all accepted the royal invitation. I arrived late. Cukor,
Tony Franciosa, Dolores Hart, and a few of the other
actors were already present, along with assorted members
of Magnani's entourage. Our hostess asked us all to sit
around in a large circle. There would be a parlor game
before dinner, she declared, and she laid out her goal.
"Since we will all be family in this picture," she began, "it
will be good to know one another intimately, don't you
think?"

A few of us nodded nervously.

The name of the game was Truth and Magnani was to
ask the first question. The only rule, she said, was that we
had to answer with complete honesty. Then we would go
around the room, taking turns, asking each other whatever we wanted to know.

I hated parlor games almost as much as parties, but I
was willing to play along. I would not let the great
Magnani intimidate me into backing down. What did she
have over me? And what did I have to hide from these
people? Besides, I thought, the truth was supposed to set
you free, right? Go ahead, truth, I mocked. Have at me.

Cukor must have felt he had something to hide
because he stood from the circle and made to leave. The
truth would not find him here. Magnani rolled her eyes,
and said something scurrilous about the director's bed-

room habits. The poor man floated out of the room like a
helium balloon the day after it had been filled.

With Cukor out of the way, Magnani turned to me to
start the game. "Tony," she said, her eyes bright with
trouble, "would you like to fok me?" She spoke with such
a thick, guttural accent that the ugly word sounded almost
cartoonish.

Ah, this was the type of game she had in mind. I
answered without pause: "No."

Magnani seemed startled at my response, and somewhat hurt, but she could tell from my demeanor that I was
telling the truth. I was only playing by the rules.

"Would you like to fok Dolores Hart?" she followed.

"Wait a minute," I protested. "I thought you said it's
just one question per customer. Those are the rules."

"I often make up the rules as I go along," she replied.
"Answer the question."

I was dreadfully embarrassed for poor Dolores Hart.
She was just nineteen, and stunning, but I did not want to
be the one to steal her innocence. (Jesus, would they *all*
look like virgins, from here on in?) "No," I said, being
only somewhat honest. In truth, I would have welcomed
the chance to know the girl on more intimate terms, but I
would not be the one to claim her cherry; for that, she
needed a man her own age.

Magnani seemed to enjoy my discomfort, and would
not let up. She turned to Dolores, to tighten the screws.
"How about you, dear?" she began. "Would you like to
fok Tony Quinn?"

"Yes," Dolores responded, without hesitation. She
flashed a demure look. I was extremely flattered, but
unable to act on it. I could never have touched her. She
was like one of my daughters. (Indeed, she would even be
playing my daughter in the picture!)

But Magnani would not stop. She let the poor girl's
response hang, and then turned to her secretary, a pretty

young woman in her early thirties. "Lydia," she said, "does your husband ever fok you in the ass?"

Now we were all embarrassed. Lydia swallowed her reply. I wanted to kill Magnani, but the bitch was not finished. She looked over to her hairdresser: "Carla, how many men have you foked?"

Carla looked older than my mother. She held up two fingers and gazed down at the floor.

Then it was Tony Franciosa's turn. "Antonio," Magnani tried, "would you like to fok me?"

Tony was a virile young man, and there was no denying that Magnani was a beautiful, passionate woman. It did not take him long to answer. "Yes," he said. "Absolutely."

"Okay," Magnani said. "Game's over." Apparently, now that she had the answer she was looking for, it was time to move on to something else.

The rest of the evening unfolded without incident, and the parlor game succeeded in ways our hostess could not have anticipated. The cast was so united in its dislike of Magnani that we all became great friends. I even found a bond with George Cukor, a man with whom I once thought I would never share anything more than a mutual disregard. Out of a melodramatic script, he managed to coax my third Academy Award–nominated performance (and my first in the lead actor category!), although I lost the Oscar to Alec Guinness, who was honored for his performance in *The Bridge on the River Kwai*. Magnani was also nominated, as best actress, so Cukor must have been doing something right.

Magnani was a world-class troublemaker, and she needled me all during the picture. She was such a constant vexation she nearly cajoled me into changing careers. One afternoon, after we had returned to the Paramount lot to finish the picture, she challenged me to walk in front of my father-in-law's table in the studio commissary. It was a curious trial. The woman thought little enough of me already; her opinion should not have mattered to me, but it did. And it should have been no big deal to coexist peacefully with Cecil B. De Mille, in his own backyard, but it was. Even after all these years, and all my successes of late, I still dreaded any public association with the man. His very existence had stamped my early career, and I had never lost the bitter jealousy of that time. I simply did not like the way I looked next to his legacy—or, in those days, the way his legacy looked next to my own.

Even in 1957, De Mille remained a commanding presence on the Paramount lot. He was in declining health, and not nearly as productive as he had only recently been. And yet he still had his own special table in the commissary, in the most prominent position, and he held forth like royalty. It was impossible for a newcomer to pass by De Mille's table without knowing who the great man was or what he represented. An invitation to dine with him was like receiving an audience with the King of England.

Of course, I was rarely asked to the head table, and I tended to avoid it when it came time for lunch. The commissary was huge—big enough to accommodate three thousand people—so it was easy to stay out of the way. That is, until Magnani came on the scene. She knew the long history of tension between me and my father-in-law; she knew what people used to say behind my back about my first Paramount contract; she knew precisely which buttons to push to get me going.

"Tony," she said, one afternoon at lunch, "you are not man enough to even walk in front of his table." She was simply baiting me, trying to get some reaction.

"Like hell," I shot back. "Name the time and place." The woman was out to emasculate me, and I could not let it stand.

"Here and now," she said. "Or is that not convenient for you?"

She had thrown down a challenge and I would rise to it, so I stood and strolled past De Mille's table like the big movie star I hoped someday to be. To many, I knew, I had already arrived at that distinction, but to De Mille, I feared I would always be a dark-skinned kid in a tattered loincloth. And a part of me could not help but see myself through the old man's eyes; until he accepted me in his world, I would never belong.

Magnani accompanied me on my little parade—probably to make sure I didn't sneak off into the kitchen—and relished my discomfort like it was her own doing, which indeed it was.

"Hello, Tony," De Mille said, as I sauntered by.

"Mr. De Mille," I acknowledged, ashamed that we were not on more familiar terms.

"Come," he said, gesturing to an empty chair beside him, "come and sit, there's room for both of you." He stood to greet Miss Magnani, and held out a chair for her. Really, he could not have been more solicitous, but in my head he was still the dispassionate bogeyman I had feared as a young man. I never trusted his kindness, or felt that it had anything to do with me.

"How's Tony in the picture?" he asked Miss Magnani.

I wondered why he did not ask my costar about her own performance, why he was always so concerned about mine. Was he afraid I would finally embarrass him, after all these years? Was this his secret hope?

"We'll know soon enough," Magnani replied, not exactly singing my praises.

"I've seen the rushes," my father-in-law said, "and you're both quite good."

Magnani gushed.

I smiled awkwardly, waiting for something to happen. I did not have to wait long. De Mille had a challenge of his own he wanted to put on the table. He turned to me. "Tony," he said, "I've just had lunch with Yul Brynner,

and he hasn't got the guts to direct a picture he's contracted for."

"Is that so?" I said, pretending interest.

"He's signed to play the lead, but I was hoping he
would also direct. He's wonderful with actors, you
know?"

"No," I managed. "I didn't."

"So I told him I have a son-in-law who's an actor,
who's made some pretty good pictures, and I'm sure he
has the guts to direct it."

I was not at all interested in directing a picture for my
father-in-law, but I wanted to hear what he had in mind.
"What's the picture?" I asked.

"It's a remake of *The Buccaneer*. Mr. Brynner thinks it'll
make a great musical."

I could not see the appeal of a pirate picture set to
music, but I was not one to let a challenge go unnoticed.

De Mille could see my uncertainty. "Of course, I don't
think it's a musical myself," he added, "but if Mr. Brynner
thinks it's a musical, we'll make it a musical. If it's not,
we'll just make another swashbuckler."

He was a very shrewd man, my father-in-law. He
knew that his failing health would not see him through
the rigors of directing another feature, and he knew he
could not attract an established director to a De Mille
production. He needed a first-time director to get the
picture made the way he wanted it, someone who lacked
the confidence to stand up to the great man's reputation.
And he knew that Yul Brynner and I were having our differences.

I had known Brynner since my days on the New York
stage, and found him to be one of the most pretentious
people in show business. He had a thing for brown rooms.
During every production, he had to have his dressing
room painted over in a deep, depressing brown, and I had
a constant image of him, sitting backstage, wallowing in a

room full of shit. He was such a drearily insufferable man that I sometimes thought they painted over his soul.

At the time, *The Buccaneer* was not the only project on Brynner's plate. He was riding high, after star turns in *The King and I* and De Mille's own *The Ten Commandments*, and was very much in demand. And it was not the only property I was considering, either. Despite our mutual disrespect, Brynner and I had jointly purchased the American rights to Akira Kurosawa's Japanese adventure classic, *Seven Samurai*, which had won the Oscar for best foreign film the year before *La Strada*. We both wanted to make Kurosawa's picture into a Western, and could not see the point in bidding each other up and inflating the price, so we became partners. As it turned out, I did not have the same scheming head for business as my new associate. In the months ahead, Brynner would dupe me from my share of the picture, and go on to make *The Magnificent Seven* without me. I never forgave him his trickery.

De Mille played me off Brynner like a maestro. "You're not gonna turn me down, too?" he asked. "Are you, Tony-my-boy?"

Tony-my-boy? Since when was I Tony-his-boy? "Jeez, Mr. De Mille," I stammered, "I don't know. I'm into another thing right now. I don't know about directing. I'm into a lot of other things."

"What the hell other things? You make pictures. This is a picture."

"But I've never directed before."

"So, you've never directed before. Everybody starts somewhere. You're not gonna say no to me too, are you? You're not gonna turn coward on me?"

Now, why did he have to go and put it in just these terms? "No, sir," I said, "I'm not a coward, but I do have to look at the script."

In Hollywood, asking to look at the script was like crying

uncle. De Mille knew he had me. "I'll have the script over at your office this afternoon," he said.

I shook the old man's hand and returned to my table with Magnani. "You are hooked, Antonio," she teased.

"We'll see. I'm not committed to anything just yet."

But underneath, I knew different.

I took the script home that night and was appalled. It was a silly, boring piece of fluff. I did not know what to do about it. I talked it over with Katherine, who was sometimes helpful in figuring her father—that is, when I could peel her from her religious tracts long enough to pay attention. I told her the story about the commissary. "He challenged me," I explained, "in front of all those people. There was nothing I could do."

"Oh, Tony," she dismissed, "don't be such a child. Do the picture if you want to do the picture, but don't do it because of a stupid little dare. Your whole life doesn't have to be a pissing contest, you know."

"I know," I said, but I was not so sure.

"How's the script?"

"The script is nothing."

"Will he give you a writer?"

"I'm sure he'll give me a writer."

"So get a writer. Tell him you'll do the picture if you can write a new script."

So that is what I did. De Mille authorized a rewrite. I hired Abby Mann, a talented young writer, and we set off in an entirely new direction, sticking only loosely to the popular version of Jean Lafitte's story. Abby did extensive research into pirate lore and legend. We wanted the picture to accurately reflect the fight for control of American shipping interests, the drama of the seas, the battle for New Orleans. We wanted the picture to look nothing like the overdone pirate adventures of Hollywood's past.

After a few weeks, Abby turned out a wonderful period script that resembled De Mille's in name only. (Happily,

there was no room for Yul Brynner to burst out in song!)
I took it to my father-in-law and placed it on his desk.
"Here's the script I want to do," I said.

He called me back into his office the next morning.
"Tony," he said. "I won't make that picture. I can't. It's
too dark, too political. Pirate pictures should not be political. It's not what people want to see. Pirate pictures
should be grand, sweeping entertainments, bigger than
life. They should be like a Western, on the seas."

"But cowboys like John Wayne never existed," I reasoned. "Cowboys like Gary Cooper never existed. And
pirates like Tyrone Power or Douglas Fairbanks never
existed."

"Damn right," De Mille said, with false pride, "but I
made them famous."

There was no talking the man down from his own
cliché, and it was clear to me that I would have to make
his picture or none at all.

In the end, I backed away from my position and into
De Mille's, although I never understood why. Perhaps it
had to do with all the great stars that I had already signed
to the picture during the rewrite: Chuck Heston, Claire
Bloom, Charles Boyer, Inger Stevens, E. G. Marshall,
Lorne Greene. Perhaps it had to do with Yul Brynner
already being committed to play the part of Jean Lafitte,
and me not wanting to be reduced in his eyes by resigning
from the picture at the last minute; Brynner had been too
chicken-shit to direct it, and I would be just chicken-shit
enough.

Perhaps it was that De Mille had awakened in me a
stewing desire to direct motion pictures, and now that I
was so close to production I could not step from momentum's way.

Most likely it was a combination of a host of factors,
but one thing was certain: if Anna Magnani had not
dragged me to the great man's table that afternoon, and

dared me to confront my father-in-law on his own turf, I would never have gotten myself into this mess.

Final Cut

I COULD NOT BE CECIL B. DE MILLE. I did not even try. The picture I wanted to make was not larger than life, but smaller, and far more intimate than anything De Mille had ever put on the screen. I wanted to direct a picture about Jean Lafitte, and his place in New Orleans society, while my father-in-law would have produced a romanticized epic, emphasizing sweep and scope over the human drama.

But (sour grapes aside) my version tested well when we screened the rough cut to audiences in Santa Barbara and Long Beach. It seemed people were just as tired of stock pirate corn as I was. Word filtered back to the studio that we had a hit. There was even an item in *Variety* reporting De Mille's pending triumph—he was, after all, the producer—and praising his new version of *The Buccaneer* as better than anything he had ever done.

This last was probably what set him off. De Mille was a very competitive man. In the years since his death, I have often wondered if the rivalry between us was played mostly in my head, but I believe it was reciprocated. I believe in his mind it was unacceptable for this Indian kid to step in and direct a successful picture, the first time out. I believe he felt it was a curse for me to receive any credit that was meant for him.

I believe that he had his own fixed notions about the picture he wanted to make and was only indulging me in mine in order to get the footage he needed for his. If I had any doubts, his actions took care of them. He pulled me aside after the results of our screenings were in. "So," he said, "whaddya think?"

"I think they liked it," I said.

"Yeah, well, I didn't." He was not unpleasant, but he was firm. Maybe the screening audiences liked it too much, or he took the response as a rejection of everything else he had ever done. Maybe he realized his time was passing him by. Whatever his reasons, he took the rough cut and disappeared into the editing room, to remake the picture in his own image. A few weeks later, he emerged with a Cecil B. De Mille production, in almost every regard.

He called me to his screening room for a showing. I sat for two hours, barely recognizing the picture I was watching. It was nothing like the picture I had shot. The cast was the same, naturally, and the dialogue, but the whole feeling was different. The pace I had carefully established was gone, replaced by frenetic jump cuts and wide shots. De Mille had even dropped some subordinate storylines and left the focus mainly on his bigger picture.

I did not like it at all. My intimate portrait had been reduced (inflated?) to a big, brawling epic, worthy perhaps of the De Mille name but not mine. When the lights went up I did not know what to say.

"So," I finally managed, "that's your version?"

"That's my version," De Mille announced. "My name's on it."

I walked away thinking, I might have known.

I thought back to some of the comments my director friends had offered when I took the job. Orson Welles warned that no director ever had the final cut, at least no director since Orson Welles. John Huston told me that he sometimes shot a picture so that it was cut-proof, producing only the footage that he needed and leaving nothing in the editing room for the producers to cut to. But I was not wise enough to heed Welles's caution or follow Huston's advice.

Eventually, I realized that all directors boast about how

well their pictures tested, about how much better their
version was than the final version, but this strikes me now
as useless self-indulgence. So De Mille painted over my
picture. It is no matter. The picture is what is up on the
screen. Nothing else exists. What proof do I have that my
cut was any good? And why do I still care?

At the time, of course, it was terribly important, to
each of us. De Mille walked away from the screening
room thinking he had won a great prize, when really all
that he had done was exercise his weight to his own end. I
walked away thinking I had been done a horrible injustice,
when really all that had happened was just business as
usual. Our strained relationship should not have had a
thing to do with it, but it did.

And I walked away thinking I was through with De
Mille—at last. We exchanged words a few days later, but
it was mostly a worthless discussion, filled with more than
twenty years' worth of venom and frustration. He was a
dying man, facing down his uppity son-in-law; I was a
misunderstood artist, beating back authority, trying to
break out on my own. The only victory I could claim was
that I would outlast him, and all he could claim was a last-
gasp failure.

Indeed, *The Buccaneer* was De Mille's last screen credit,
and this was our last confrontation, but it was not to be
our final scene. That would come a few months later, in
the small courtyard between his projection room and the
main house. His health had deteriorated. He was being
treated by an underhanded doctor who pumped him with
so many amphetamine concoctions that De Mille never
knew if he was up or down. He was prone to tremendous
mood swings. His energy came and went. It was sometimes difficult for him to talk. It was clear to everyone that
his time was short—to himself, most of all.

On this day, De Mille was dressed in his bathrobe and
slippers, and looking nothing like the man who once ruled

Hollywood from behind his powerful megaphone. There were two chairs set up, overlooking the property, and we sat down to say goodbye.

As we spoke, I was overcome by a warmth I had never felt for the man. I began to understand about him, to feel sorry for him, to forgive. We had run on different rails, I came to realize, on different clocks. The renaissance in motion pictures was lost on him. De Mille looked at the excitement of the Italian cinema, at pictures like *La Strada* and *The Bicycle Thief*, and could not understand what the fuss was about. It was too much for him to comprehend. I know he suffered terribly, wondering at the place he had made for himself, at the legacy he would leave. To him, I was a symbol of that change. My time was coming, his time had passed, and it was only in the crossing that we could stumble on a truce.

"We never really knew each other, Tony," he said, with a weak voice. Ever since my success in pictures, the old man had been rather tentative around me; now, in his illness, he seemed almost shy.

"No, sir, we didn't."

"I'm sorry."

"I'm sorry too," I said, and I was. It took saying it to recognize that I had needed a man like De Mille, a father figure, to guide me through some of the treacherous turns of career and manhood.

The world my own father left was no longer mine, and there was only so much his memory could teach me. I thought back to Papa's coat, the one that held me on the night that he died, and wondered how it would have looked on the shoulders of my father-in-law. No one could ever replace my father, but the job had long been open for someone to step in behind him, to offer comfort and counsel. And friendship.

Cecil B. De Mille—Mr. Hollywood, the one man to move the industry in which I had chosen to make my life—might have been that someone, but we were too pleased with ourselves and afraid of each other to ever attempt a relationship. And when we finally could see past our conceits and our fears, it was too late. All we could do was sit on his lawn for three hours, until twilight overcame us, making repairs.

Ride

IT IS A CONSTANT PUZZLE, this reminiscing. I am like the tides, here along this coast, drifting in and out of memory, cresting in the waves between past and present. Who knows what the hell will wash up on shore?

How I long to shut off one valve for the sake of the other! To take in this splendid scenery on its face! To wallow in my own history! Ah, but I must make up my fevered mind! Either I am out to lose myself in my surroundings, or I am out to discover the type of man I have been, the type I might still become. Take my pick. It is the two things, on top of each other, that leaves me reeling. It is like patting my stomach and rubbing my head, walking and chewing gum. I can do both at the same time, but why bother? One takes from the other and leaves me without any benefit.

Still, I press on. This business with De Mille has left me charged, invigorated. My legs are fresh, my heart racing. I can ride all day—all night, if I have to. Fatigue is for a lesser man, an older man. Me, I will go on forever. I will not end up like my father-in-law. I will do everything all at once. I will beat time into standing still. I will ride out my aches and pains. There will be no Young Turks to take me on, to strip me of what is mine. There will be no renaissance of which I am not a part. To hell with any kid who seeks to topple me from my perch!

A twin-engine plane buzzes overhead—principally to

dust the crops in one of the inland fields, but also to dust the cobwebs from my thinking—and the noise reminds me that De Mille and I lived in different times. Yes, it is easy for me to sit in judgment of the man, but where is my right? Who am I to moderate? I can never know how it was for him, or what was going on his head. I cannot even imagine. What do we know of what has come before us?

Here, in the hills outside Rome, I put the question in relevant terms. Is Julius Caesar history's despot or Shakespeare's martyr? Which picture is allowed to stand? Does the truth reside in the flesh or in the reflection? Or somewhere in between? And what about me? What will my children think when I am gone? My grandchildren? I like to believe they will know me, but of course they cannot. They will know about me, of that I am certain, but they will never see the things I have seen, or feel what I am feeling. There will always be a wall between us that the years cannot scale. They will never know what it was like to start from nothing, to sleep on a dirt floor, to relieve themselves in the woods, to stretch small change into enough money for food and clothes and rent. My very successes have forever obscured my children from my past.

I believe I knew my own father, but my father-in-law was an unattainable mystery. When Papa left, he was frozen in time. The world may have changed, but his perspective did not. And yet I never knew De Mille. He straddled three distinct eras—from silents, to talkies, to wide-screen extravaganzas—and he ruled Hollywood throughout all of them. My God, the man was absolutely revered in that town! He was everything, and yet I wonder how much he actually bent with the times, each time out. After all, he did not have to. The great man was powerful enough to make the times bend to him.

As a younger man, I thought De Mille pompous and superficial, but I have since tempered my view. What did he ever do to me? I was always welcome in his home. He was never the ogre I made him out to be in my head. He was, however, a dominant presence throughout my apprenticeship in pictures, so it was only natural for me to feel intimidated by him. I feared authority, and how it might rub off on me. Perhaps I even feared success, or at least the gilt-edged success as displayed by De Mille. Was my association with him an obstacle to my career? At one time, I was sure of it, but perhaps he was just a convenient excuse. Maybe I would have had to struggle through fifteen years of inferior parts, with him or without him. Maybe I just had to pay my dues, and I blamed him for the toll.

My own children do not know me. They know bits and pieces, each of them, but no one knows the whole story. I doubt they ever will. Why? Is it that I have kept from them some essential truth, the thread that ties my life together? Is it that I myself have yet to recognize the man I was in the man I have become?

Probably it is everything, all at once and on top of each other. Probably I will never let myself be known, even to my children; there is too much at stake for me to come completely clean. Probably they will always want to steer clear, to cut their own trail, to know me as I have shown myself and not as I might now wish to be known.

Probably this is not such a bad thing. In life, there are no rehearsals, no rewrites, no second takes. We shoot it once and print it.

Sir Larry and the Tramp

I FIRST MET LAURENCE OLIVIER at the Beverly Hills Hotel, shortly after the death of my father-in-law. It was yet another chance encounter that would refocus my career and rattle my tentative relationships.

We were lunching at separate tables, about a hundred feet apart. I was with my agent. He was with a group of people I did not recognize.

I noticed him first. He was a common-looking fellow, quite unextraordinary in his manner. Even from such a distance, I was alarmed at the smallness of his dimensions, the simple nature of the man. On stage, he acted like a giant—he had such tremendous command!—but here, eating lunch, he seemed altogether plain. I thought about walking over to his table, to introduce myself, but I was never good at that sort of thing. I was too self-conscious, too unsure of myself. Who was I to interrupt his meal?

At some point, Olivier spotted me and started crossing the room to my table. He had the most wonderful, rolling walk. It was almost stately. He walked like a man with a purpose. "You're Mr. Quinn," he said—asking? telling?—after he had rolled to my table.

"Yes." I stood to greet him.

"Wonderful to meet you," he said. "Just wonderful." He pumped my hand like I would give water. He told me how much he enjoyed *La Strada*, how he admired my work. He was effusive in his praise, and I was extremely flattered. As he spoke, he revealed a horribly low-rent British accent, which he managed to conceal on stage but which tumbled from him now like the most natural thing in the world. He spat out his words in rapid succession, like an excited boy. I was also struck by a strange obsession he appeared to have with his mouth. He was constantly licking his lips, sucking in his cheeks, flexing his jaw, almost like a nervous tic. I wondered if he had just eaten some bad grapefruit.

"You have such a peculiar sense of reality," he said to me, "quite peculiar, if you don't mind my saying."

"Not at all." I had no idea what he meant, but I did not mind his saying it.

"It's rather marvelous," he continued, "rather unlike

anything I've seen. I should love to be as real as you in my work. It has never come easily to me, you know. Perhaps I'll be lucky enough to work with you someday, and you can share with me some of that reality."

"That would be fine. It would be an honor."

"Really?" he remarked, as if I had just told him I was willing to lend him money. "Good to hear you say that. So good." He explained in a rambling sort of way that he had just been offered a play called *Becket*, by Jean Anouilh, and that he thought I was well-suited for the part of King Henry II. "Would you like to read it?" he asked, but then he did not wait for my answer. "It's the theater," he rambled, "and it's not a lot of money, I know, certainly nothing like pictures, but we could go halfsies. How is that? Partners on stage, partners off?"

"Wonderful," I said, "but let's not talk business. Let me read the play."

I read the play and thought it marvelous. I had not been planning a return to the stage, but I could not pass up the chance to work with Laurence Olivier, on Broadway. What actor could turn it down? There would be plenty of motion pictures. I signed on immediately. (Olivier was true to his word—we added his meager salary to my more meager one, and split the bundle right down the middle.)

Olivier was like a fighter in rehearsals. Back when I boxed, years earlier in East Los Angeles, my opponents sometimes came into my dressing room before the bout: Tony, they would sometimes say, listen, we're on tonight, four rounds, but I've just had my teeth fixed and do me a favor and stay away from the face; it's just a show for these assholes; we don't wanna get hurt. Then they would go out and kick the shit out of me. With Olivier it was the same. He had a way of romancing the other actors, and keeping us off-guard, but he fully intended to be on top. He was rather darling about it, but incredibly sly.

I noticed this most of all with his voice. I was still some-what tongue-tied on stage, frenum or no. I had difficulty enunciating and projecting. In pictures, this was never a problem, because the work was being done on such an intimate scale, but in the theater you needed to be enor-mous. I had to submit to all manner of vocal exercises, just to make myself heard. Olivier had no trouble at all with his voice. The man could pierce the still air of the theater with no strain at all—like Miles Davis on the trumpet!—and when I tried to keep up, he boomed even louder.

He sounded like thunder; I sounded like a belch.

I thought I would have to quit the play. One afternoon, I went to the director, Peter Glenville, and told him of my troubles. "I can't rehearse with him like that," I said. "He's testing me. I can't act on that level."

Glenville advised me to ride it out.

"But he has me screaming and yelling," I complained. "I'll have no voice!"

"To you, it's screaming and yelling," Glenville said. "To Larry, it's projecting. Let him test you in rehearsals. Save your voice for the audience."

So I did, and we opened *Becket* to good notices. The play was a demanding piece, and for most of us onstage the demands fell in keeping pace with Olivier. (The large cast featured Kit Culkin, Macauley's father and a boyhood friend of my son Duncan, as one of the heirs to King Henry's throne.) Much of the drama rested in the rela-tionship between my King Henry II and Olivier's prelate Thomas Becket, and Olivier got the better of me in our shared scenes. He was a relentless combatant, selling his performance at every opportunity. I kept up with him well enough, but I could not match his immense scale, his exaggerated rhythms.

Offstage, there was no fight to Olivier at all. As an actor, he was a tough little bastard, but as a man, he appeared utterly without guile, and almost desperate for

companionship. There was something pathetically
endearing about him, and rather sad. He was going
through a difficult period, he was quick to tell me. He was
in love with the British actress Joan Plowright, but their
careers kept them apart. And he was divorcing Vivien
Leigh, who had taken ill. He was terribly lonely, and terribly confused.

"If you don't mind, I'll lean on you, Tony," he said to
me one afternoon, early on in rehearsals. "I want us to be
friends. I want us to be very close friends."

And so, for the run of the play, I became Laurence
Olivier's very close friend. The poor man tailed me like a
puppy dog. Every day, he called to see what I was doing.
If I was going to a museum, to look at some paintings, he
accompanied me. If I went for a walk in the park after a
matinee, to clear my head, he went with me, to clear his.
At night, after the curtain, we went out to dinner
together. On our days off, he sometimes joined Katherine
and me and the children on a family outing.

"Tony," he would promise, "I'll just tag along. You
won't even notice me."

He was persistent company, but not unpleasant. He
had lived a hard-scrabble life, much like my own, and I
enjoyed listening to his stories. He had a way about him
that made me feel like the most important person in his
life—which, I suppose, I was, at that time.

Once, late in the run of the play, I was visited backstage by Jawaharlal Nehru. I had been asked by David
Lean to play Nehru in a picture he was producing on the
life of Mahatma Gandhi, and the prime minister wanted
to meet me. Lean's production never materialized (it was
Richard Attenborough who finally brought Gandhi's
remarkable life to the screen, in 1982), but this early
effort did yield a good story.

When Olivier learned that Nehru had been to see the
play, but had not been to see him, he threw a little fit.

"You?" he roared, bursting into my dressing room the next afternoon. "He came to see you?" He could not understand it. He took it as a great insult, that Nehru did not stop in to see him. Why on earth would a man like Nehru come to see a performance by an actor like Olivier and not pay a call backstage? my new pal wondered. They had met many times before, he insisted. He had thought they were friends.

Olivier calmed down somewhat when I told him about the Gandhi picture, but he still would not let it go. "What did he say about me?" he kept asking. "Surely he said something, Tony. What?"

"We didn't talk about you at all," I said. "He came to talk about the picture. David Lean set it up. We're meeting at his hotel on Sunday."

"Oh my God!" Olivier gasped. Then he started begging: "You're taking me with you, of course. Tell me you'll take me with you."

"Come on. I'm asked to a meeting by a head of state, in his hotel room. He wants to talk to me about his life, so I can play him in the picture. I can't very well call him and say I'm bringing my friend Larry."

"Well, why not?"

Ah, he was such an exasperating man! He kept at me all that afternoon, and into the next morning. Finally, I called Nehru and made the arrangements.

Olivier arrived at my apartment first thing Sunday morning. Katherine made him breakfast. He was bubbling with excitement. He cleaned his plate twice, and gulped three cups of coffee. Then we walked the few blocks to the Carlyle Hotel, where Nehru was staying. To be accurate, I walked and Olivier skipped. The man could not help himself. In the elevator up to Nehru's penthouse suite, Olivier started to do a little dance, and lapsed into the singsong meter of a small child. "I'm going to see Nehru," he sang. "I'm going to see Nehru."

"Jesus, Larry," I said, "cut it out." I worried that the elevator doors would open and there would be Nehru, waiting to greet us, struck dumb by the sight of Laurence Olivier singing and dancing like an idiot: "I'm going to see Nehru, I'm going to see Nehru."

Olivier bit his lip and put on his regular-guy face. He could do that, my friend. He had all these different faces, to front his many moods, and at my command he now played the somber intellectual. He moved from one to the next like he was changing masks.

We were met at the elevator by one of Nehru's aides, who informed us that the prime minister was finishing his breakfast and would be out shortly. "I'm terribly sorry for the delay, Mr. Quinn," the man said. "He's had a busy morning."

"What's he eating, yogurt?" Olivier asked.

The aide scowled at Olivier and disappeared into the next room.

I was terribly embarrassed. I turned to Olivier. "Jesus Christ, Larry," I railed, "what the fuck is that? 'Is he eating yogurt?'"

"He's from India, isn't he? Don't they eat yogurt?"

For all the class and erudition he managed to exude on stage, Olivier was one of the least refined people I had ever met. I came from poverty, from the lowest of the low, and even I knew how to behave in a situation like this. But Olivier was something else. He was a lower-class dolt, pretending at more, and the poor man could not fool anyone outside the beam of floodlights.

Still, I put up with Olivier because he was my friend. Actually, there was something rather amusing about him, in a pitiful sort of way. I had no trouble forgiving him his flights of idiocy.

When Nehru joined us, Olivier went after him. He was absolutely desperate for the man's attention, and went into what he must have thought was a virtuoso performance.

He dominated the room and began flitting about with such extravagantly broad gestures, I worried he might hurt himself. "We've met before," he said to Nehru. "Surely you remember."

Nehru tried to be polite. "I can't recall," he said. "Perhaps you can help me."

Olivier pretended to think about this, to search his brain for an appropriate time and place. "Aha!" he finally said, quite grandly. "It was at the Haymarket Theater, in London. You came to see me in *Romeo and Juliet*." Then he turned to enlist me in his charade. "My God, Tony," he boasted, "what a marvelous evening that was!"

Nehru watched Larry play out his story. "And when, exactly, was that date?" he finally asked.

Olivier made another grand show, fishing for the date. "I believe it was 1938," he announced at last, with conviction. "Yes, yes, I'm sure of it. The fall of 1938."

"That's curious," Nehru said, looking back and forth between Olivier and me. A thin smile appeared on his face. "I think perhaps you have the dates confused, Mr. Olivier, because at that time your people had me in jail."

Olivier turned ghost-white, while the rest of us tried not to smile.

My friendship with Laurence Olivier was the strangest thing. It took me a while to understand it, but I ultimately saw it as emblematic of most industry relationships. When you are making a picture, you see the same people over and over, for about two or three months. You enter each other's lives. You take on an inflated role. On location especially, there is a tendency for actors to become quite close, until the picture wraps and everyone moves on to the next thing. I am constantly duped into great friendships that last only the run of the shoot, and I have never gotten used to it.

With Olivier, the shift was transparent. After nearly a six-month run at the St. James Theater in New York, I decided to cast about for another picture, and accepted the title role in a Dino De Laurentiis production about the life of the biblical thief Barabbas. The picture was shooting in Verona, and I went to Olivier's dressing room to wish him well. He was staying on with the play (in fact, he would move into my part, while Arthur Kennedy was hired to play Becket), and was apparently put off by my leaving. That, or he was not one for goodbyes.

"Oh, yes, Anthony," he said, looking up from his tea. "Good of you to drop by." Suddenly I was Anthony to him, and not his great pal Tony. He seemed awkward, and uncomfortable, as if he wanted to be anywhere in the world but in that dressing room with me. "Well, good luck," he finally managed. "We'll see each other again, I'm sure."

And that was it. He shadowed me for six months, and now I no longer served a purpose. I was accustomed to this sort of thing, but I was still hurt by it. I had thought my relationship with Olivier ran deeper than convenience. He was a pesty fellow, but I had grown to love him, and the time we spent together.

We did not see each other for years, but for a few strained meetings. My occasional attempts to resurrect our friendship (when we were in London at the same time, or Los Angeles) were rebuffed. And yet when I was cast to play Pope Kiril I in *The Shoes of the Fisherman*, I could think of no better actor to play the pragmatic Russian premier (a part that was loosely modeled on Nikita Khrushchev) than my fair-weather companion. Olivier accepted without hesitation, and the friendship began anew. Indeed, as soon as he arrived on the set in Rome, it was like New York all over again: "Tony!" he exclaimed. "How are you, my dear? I've missed you!"

He reminded me of the drunken millionaire in *City Lights*, who passes a string of benders in the company of Charlie Chaplin's tramp, and pretends not to know him when he wakes up sober each morning. "Where's my pal?" "Who the fuck are you?"

Olivier was drunk with his profession, and perhaps he saw his colleagues as sobering reminders of his triumphs and his failures. Perhaps he thought that in order to grow as an actor he needed to move forward, in all things. Perhaps he was just a shy, nervous man, uncertain of his place when he was not practicing his craft.

Whatever it was, we resumed our great friendship for a few weeks, until he finished his scenes, whereupon we resumed our drifting apart. Once again, it was as if he did not know me. I was Anthony, or even Mr. Quinn on occasion.

The routine was repeated several years later, in Tunisia, when we were cast in Franco Zeffirelli's production of *Jesus of Nazareth*. Olivier had become a tired old man, but he lit up when he saw me: "Tony!" he cried. "My God! How wonderful!"

I tried to return his enthusiasm, but my heart was not in it. After so many stops and starts, I no longer trusted his friendship. I was married to Iolanda at the time, and she thought Olivier a phony. Perhaps he was just that, but as I weigh our relationship against the few friends I have managed to make, and hold, I wonder if it matters. After all, what is friendship but a coming together of like-minded souls? A safe haven from the cares and troubles that stalk us all?

Whether it lasts a moment or a lifetime, it is the same.

Dr. Feelgood

I DID NOT KNOW WHAT to make of the 1960s. It was such a permissive, anarchic time, so unlike anything that had preceded it and anything that has come since. I was no stranger to drink and drugs, and certainly no prude, but I was not at all prepared for the excessive attitudes of those times, for the wanton abuses of body and soul.

During the making of *The Buccaneer*, Yul Brynner sent my father-in-law to a doctor friend of his named Max Jacobson, a New York physician with a celebrity clientele and a reputation for miracles. He was known among his crowd as "Dr. Feelgood," and he was too good to be believed.

Dr. Feelgood was a big, barrel-chested man with dark hair and a sonorous voice. He spoke with a thick Viennese accent, almost like a caricature of Freud. There was an air about him of tremendous import. His specialty was a concoction made from methamphetamines and vitamins and monkey placenta, which he dispensed to his patients by injection. His nickname was well-chosen; his joy juice was known to cure all ills, and to leave his patients on top of the world. The Kennedys were said to be his most famous patients. Marilyn Monroe, Eddie Fisher, Alan Jay Lerner . . . you never knew whom you might meet in his waiting room. In time, I met them all.

It started with De Mille. He began seeing the doctor on Brynner's recommendation, and soon the old man reported feeling twenty years younger. We could all see the change. When De Mille's energy lagged, he would pick himself up with a shot of Dr. Feelgood's juice. He was hooked, and soon so was Katherine. She even started taking the children to see Dr. Feelgood. She thought Dr. Feelgood a great savant, and never questioned his practices. She never knew what he was pumping into her family. She tried to find out, but only in a halfhearted way. "You're feeling better, correct?" the doctor would say, whenever she asked. "Den zat is all you need to know."

After a while, I succumbed to Dr. Feelgood's black magic. I was having trouble with my voice, and feeling run down. All of those months trying to keep up with Olivier on stage were beginning to wear me out. I could make it through the performances well enough, but I had nothing left for the rest of the day. And I could not talk. I worried that one night I would step out on stage without any voice at all. I had to try something, so I went to the doctor's office on Seventy-second Street and told him my symptoms.

He filled a hypodermic and shot one of his cocktails into my hip. I did not know what hit me. I had the most fantastic rush. Almost immediately, I felt like I was lit from within. It started at my feet and climbed to the top of my head. Whatever it was, I thought it would take me to the moon.

"Dere, you sonofabitch," Dr. Feelgood said, as he put away his needle, "now you have ze voice." He was rude and charming. I thought he was wonderful. Among the theater community, he was a loosely held secret. Everyone knew him, but we never spoke his name.

I went out on stage that first night, high on Dr. Feelgood's juice, thinking I could do no wrong. My voice was stronger than ever, and I had energy to burn. If this was all it took, I thought, just a shot every once in a while to get me going, then I would be fine.

When I woke the next day, it was already dark. It was almost time to go back to the theater, and it seemed a good idea to stop by the doctor's office on the way, for another injection. And so it went. Soon, I was in love with Dr. Feelgood. Whenever I needed a jolt, he came running with his little black bag. One shot and I had a voice like Mario Lanza's. If I felt like painting, he gave me a special mix to help me paint. If I wanted to exercise, there was a different blend. Whatever his patients needed, whenever they needed it, Dr. Feelgood was happy to oblige. He boasted that he was the last doctor in New York to make house calls.

He cost me a fortune, but I did not notice the money. Between me and Katherine, he saw us Quinns several times a day, at about seventy-five bucks a shot. This arrangement went on for weeks. I became his best customer. It never occurred to me to question his methods. The man was a doctor, cloaked in authority; who was I to second-guess his successful treatment? Besides, I had never felt so good in my life. Of course, I had never felt so lousy as I did when I came down from these incredible highs, but I always knew the doctor could bring me out of it. I did not think I was addicted to anything but life itself.

Ah, I was such a fool. It took my own son, Duncan, to set me straight. He had never fallen under the doctor's spell. "Look at you, Pop," he said to me one day, when he was about fifteen. I had tumbled from bed at four o'clock in the afternoon. "Do you have any idea what the doctor's been giving you?"

I repeated the ingredients, as I knew them.

"It's speed, Pop," Duncan explained.

"It's medicine!" I shot back, defensive. "The man's a doctor. What are you trying to say?"

"I'm saying you're a drug addict, Pop."

And I was.

Quitting Dr. Feelgood was no easy thing. Katherine and the other children had no trouble, but I was truly addicted. He was such an evil man that he exploited my weakness. He started coming by the house, or the theater, to see how I was feeling, to keep his hold on me. He was cunning, and relentless. "I vill leave dese wit you," he would say, presenting me with a bag of needles. "You vill need dem."

I took the needles, but I never touched them and refused to pay for them. I refused to pay my other bills as well, thinking this might help. I owed the man thousands of dollars. Perhaps he would get the idea that I was no longer interested in his services and stay away.

But he kept at me. Finally, he showed up at my brownstone, on Seventieth Street, to collect his money. "Antonio," he said, "I have come about ze bill."

"I'm not paying you a fucking cent!" I screamed. "You're trying to kill me!"

We quarreled, and I started to push Dr. Feelgood toward the door. At the time, I owned the head of a famous Rodin sculpture, which I had on a stand in the front hall of our house. It was a priceless possession. As the doctor backed out the door, he grabbed the sculpture and ran with it down the steps to the street. I must say, he made an odd sight—a big man, dressed in a suit, running across Seventieth Street holding Rodin's head high above his own.

I chased after him. "My head!" I hollered. "Give me back my fucking head!"

A policeman stopped us on Lexington Avenue. He knew me, from the neighborhood. "What is it, Mr. Quinn?" he said, pinning Dr. Feelgood against a brick wall.

"This man is stealing my head."

The cop looked at the doctor, cowering by the wall like a hunchback, Rodin's head on his shoulders. "Does this belong to Mr. Quinn?" the cop asked.

"He owes me money," Dr. Feelgood said. "I took ze head because he owes me money."

The cop looked at the head and then back at me, trying to discover the likeness. "This is you, Mr. Quinn?" he asked.

"It's Rodin," I said, "but it's mine. He took it from my house."

I walked home with the sculpture, while the cop escorted the doctor in the other direction, and I remember thinking what a strange scene I had just played. And it was not finished. I had Rodin's head back, but I still did not have my own. The drugs continued to have a hold on me. On the night table beside my bed sat all of Dr. Feelgood's vials, and I went to my room to look at them. I stared them down, and vowed to beat them.

Three days later, I left for Verona. In all that time, I did not sleep. Either I was too afraid to come down from my last shot, or unable. The drugs coursed through me as if they did not want to leave. I took the vials with me on the boat to Europe, and set them up in my stateroom where I could stare at them some more. The others in my traveling party were up on deck, but I suddenly felt very tired. I told them I would see them all at dinner. I needed to be by myself, to lie down.

I went to my room thinking maybe I should take one last shot, to see me through the journey, but I decided against it. I would not take another shot as long as I lived. Even if it killed me. (At that moment, this seemed a real possibility.) I lay down on the bed as the boat pulled from the harbor and fell into a deep, dark sleep.

I slept for three days.

I woke to a bright sun, shining through my porthole. I thought I had slept the whole night through. I could not have known that I was waking to an entirely new world, that from here on in things would never be the same.

ELEVEN

Iolanda

I COULD BE A CAPRICIOUS BASTARD on a motion picture set. If I did not get what I wanted, when I wanted it, there was no telling what I might do. For all my grousing over temperamental creatures like Yul Brynner and Anna Magnani, I was no better. In some ways I was worse, and yet I indulged myself in this because it kept life interesting.

And why not? It was not in my character to acquiesce to a producer, even in matters of little consequence. Where was the sport in merely avoiding all friction, accepting what was given? The true measure of an actor's stature lay in his ability to make trouble. If they tolerated your tantrums, it meant you were a big star.

They tolerated mine, I made sure of it. I had a winner on the *Barabbas* set, and it was out of this nonsense that my future was spun. At issue was whether I was entitled to a dresser, someone to see me in and out of my costume changes and handle my wardrobe. What the hell did I need with a dresser? What did anyone need with a dresser? It had always seemed to me an unnecessary extravagance, and yet I was humiliated to learn that my costar and friend, the Italian matinee idol Vittorio Gassman, had a dresser at his disposal.

I learned this at an inopportune time, at least as far as Dino De Laurentiis and director Richard Fleischer were concerned. I was preparing to play a key confrontation with Jack Palance, in front of an arena crowded with extras. I was having some trouble with my robes, and needed an additional few minutes to meet my call. One of the production assistants suggested a dresser might be able to help. "Mr. Gassman's dresser is just finishing with him," he said innocently. "She can come in and dress you when she's through."

I fumed: "What? Mr. Gassman has a dresser and I don't? What the fuck is that?" At the time, the inequity struck me as intolerable—and just cause for a star turn.

"We weren't told you required a dresser," the boy very reasonably replied.

"What the hell. If Gassman's got a dresser, then I'll have a dresser. How the hell can I not have a dresser if he's got one?"

To this, the assistant had no reply. It was difficult to reason with a testy artist rattling off his demands. Actors are sometimes referred to on a motion picture set as "the talent"—as in, "The talent is causing some trouble"—and I always felt a certain condescension in the phrase. Here, I could tell, the poor boy was thinking of me in just these terms, and he looked at me as yet another in a string of petty annoyances sent to muddy his otherwise pleasant day.

Just then, I spotted a beautiful blond girl across the way, absentmindedly looking at the other actors' tunics. She moved with such grace and surety that I was drawn to her. (Or perhaps it was just that she pulled into my sight-lines with good timing.) I pointed in her direction. "That girl," I proclaimed, "she will dress me. Go and make the arrangements."

The assistant was in over his head, unable to help the temperamental talent or himself. "Mr. Quinn," he stammered. "I'm afraid I can do no such thing. She's one of the costume designers."

"I don't give a shit what she is," I bellowed. "She's gonna dress me!"

There were five thousand people milling about the arena, waiting to be put to work. They had been waiting all morning, and each minute was costing a fortune. Word of the delay traveled up the chain of command, and soon De Laurentiis himself was knocking on my door, wanting to know what the matter was. "What's going on?" he demanded. "Tony, it's eleven o'clock and we haven't done a shot!"

"Fuck you, Dino," I shouted, from the other side of the door. (I would not let him in.) "Who the hell do you think I am, offering me Gassman's dresser? I don't want his fucking hand-me-down. I want my own dresser. I've already picked her out."

"Tony," he pleaded, "they've told me about the girl. She can't dress you, she's a costume designer."

"She'll dress me, or I'm going home," I said. "You decide." Being a star meant you could sometimes get away with an ultimatum like this; it remained to be seen if this was one of those times.

De Laurentiis went to talk to the girl. She would not dress me. She wanted to do the work she was hired to do, and she wanted credit for it. The experience was one thing, she reasoned, but the credit would help her land her next job. He offered to give her a full designer's credit on the picture, and a salary bonus, if she would help him out, just this once.

Still, she could not decide. After about an hour, she came to see me. "Why do you want me to dress you?" she asked. "I don't understand." She did not speak English, and my Italian was lousy, so we settled on French.

"Because Gassman has a dresser and I don't," I explained. "What's to understand?"

The poor girl did not know what to make of my reasoning, and went to see her boss, the production designer, for advice.

"Well, my dear, what can you expect?" her boss said.

"Signor Quinn, he's a diva. He has chosen you. He is the diva so he gets what he wants. That's the way it is in pictures. Maybe it is not a bad thing, that he has chosen you. He has beautiful legs. It should not be such a chore to dress him."

The girl came back to see me. "I need a better reason to come and dress you," she said. "So Signor Gassman has a dresser and you do not? What concern is that of mine? I am a costume designer, not a dresser."

"You are absolutely right," I agreed, not wanting to put the girl through any more anguish than I already had. I figured a little civility might help my case. "I have put you in a terrible position, and for that I am sorry. I did not know what to do. But now I'm in so deep, they'll eat me up alive if I give in. Please, you must help me. I'll pay you anything you want."

The girl finally agreed. She would not accept my money, but took the job, she said, for the good of the picture. Her name was Iolanda Addolori, and she was lovely. She was from Venice, and her familiarity with the region was an immediate benefit to me and my family. She introduced us to wonderful restaurants, and occupied Katherine and the children with grand adventures while I worked.

It was nothing to dress me, but Iolanda devoted herself to even the most mundane aspects of my existence. She even started driving me to work each morning, when I balked at the drivers the studio provided. Most of those ambitious young actors just wanted to talk, and show you how much they knew, but Iolanda was all sweetness and serenity. With her it was all right to say nothing, or to vent, or to talk of something other than motion pictures. We barely spoke the same language, and yet we had no trouble communicating. Soon, it got to where I did not even have to speak to make myself understood.

I believe even Katherine sensed what was about to pass

between Iolanda and me, and in her own way gave sanction. Midway through the *Barabbas* shoot, she retreated with the children to a gathering of her Moral Rearmament fanatics in Switzerland, and all but left me in Iolanda's hands. "That girl will take care of you," she said, upon her abrupt leave-taking. "Everything you need, she can give you."

It was as if she had found me a stand-in.

Inevitably, Iolanda and I grew close. There was no fighting it. Whether it was fate or Katherine that brought us together, I could not be certain, but our passion sprang in full flower, almost of its own will. At first, I did not think our affair any different than relationships begun with dozens of other women, but what did I know? After nearly twenty-five years in an empty marriage, it was sometimes difficult to distinguish among my many diversions.

But Iolanda had no trouble with the contrast, and I was grateful. She had a striking head of long blond hair, which she wore up in the style of the day. I was wild about her hair, and everything else in the package. There was a fire in Iolanda's soul I had never seen in a woman. There was also a facile mind with which I might match wits and test my mettle. She was, and remains, an exceptionally smart lady. She could see the situation between me and Katherine. She had heard the talk about me on the set. She probably knew more of my affairs than even I could recall. And yet she did not care about my past.

She felt that she could change me.

Who was I to question her judgment? I had already consigned myself to her care in most other matters. Why not let her take charge of what mattered most? All I knew was that she was a fantastic beauty, who doted on me day and night. How could I help but fall in love?

Ride

TO BE LOVED IS THE TRIUMPH OF LIVING.

It is a simple truth, but it is everything, and I am reminded of it this late afternoon as I make my second pass through the streets of Anzio. I have been loved a thousand times, and still I am wanting. Does this leave me a triumphant success, or a colossal failure?

Always, there was someone or something to muck it up and send me reeling. Mama, Dona Sabina, Sylvia, Katherine, Mama Borgia, Maureen, Suzan, Irene, Iolanda . . . The list runs deeper, but these are the heavy hitters. These are the ones who have set me up for my greatest fall.

Just yesterday, here in Anzio, I lunched with Iolanda at a small restaurant across the harbor. I was in a completely different frame of mind. There was no box from Katherine to weigh on my soul, no dreadful reminders that my time was running out, no drags on the better part of my conscience. Anything was possible.

I was out on my bicycle, as ever, and Iolanda drove down to meet me in the car. It was a typical arrangement. In the mornings, half in sleep, she would ask in what direction I was headed, and we would plan somewhere to meet for lunch. For me, it broke up the ride nicely, to have a meal to look forward to; for Iolanda, with our three boys grown and out of the house, it nicely broke up her days. "Besides," she once explained, "it is not good for you to ride so long, without eating"—as if I could not manage without her.

I arrived a few moments ahead of schedule. I sat by the window, facing the street. The waiter placed a glass of the house wine on the table in front of me. I sipped in silence, enjoying the respite and the scenery. Then I looked up and noticed Iolanda outside. The sight of her filled me with a strange happiness. I watched her cross the street and thought she had the most indolent walk in the world. It is rather marvelous, I noted, the way she perambulates through life by lifting her feet just a sixteenth of an inch off the ground. Sometimes she does not even achieve that, and her walk gives off a shuffling sound.

She shuffled inside and made for our table. I waited for her smile.

"Che c'hai?" she asked suspiciously.

"Nothing," I said.

She handed me a bag: a change of clothes. (One of her peccadillos is that she will not sit down to table with a husband in sweat-stained clothes.) "Ha successo qualche cosa?" she asked.

"No, everything is fine. I had a good ride."

"Sei stanco?"

"No, I'm not tired."

I went to the bathroom to remove my plastic jacket and soggy sweatshirt. I promised myself as I washed my face and combed my hair that we would have a pleasant lunch. Lately, our talks had circled around only some maintenance problem at the house, or my continuing infidelities, or one of the boys. It would be nice to talk about something else for a change.

It would be nice to see her smile. For years, I have tried to teach Iolanda to smile, but she thinks it an American affectation. She has a complicated philosophy about American women and their dental work, believing that smiling is not a sign of happiness but of prosperity, that people who smile all the time are phony. If you have nice teeth, according to custom, you are to show them off. She thinks Americans are smile-crazy. "They are always smiling on television," she says, "whether they are selling toothpaste, used cars, or toilet paper." All of this smiling is what is wrong with America, and part of the reason she chooses to live here.

When I got back to the table, she was not smiling, still. That is my Iolanda, I thought. Chin up and proud and defiant. God forbid she should show the world her soft edges. At home, alone, she has another personality. When we are alone, at times, she becomes an animated creature; she dances when she talks, shakes like lemon jelly when she laughs. She does not do these things often, not anymore.

Still, among all of the women I have known in my life, Iolanda is the one to whom I can show the worst side of myself and be accepted. With Iolanda, early on, I did not have to weigh my words. I could rut and grunt in bed without care. When I was sick, she could tend to me. She could reach across the table and clean with her fingernail a bit of lettuce stuck between my teeth and leave me grateful rather than embarrassed. My old friend Jimmy Cagney once said about his own wife, with great love and admiration, "She could take a hell of a punch." Well, my wife could take life's punches with the best of them. And she could smile like a Venetian goddess, when she was so inclined. I reached across the table and took her hand, to coax her along. There, at last. It was hardly a full-wattage American smile, but it would do.

I remember the moment now like it was a lifetime ago. That fucking box has made all the difference. What I could accept yesterday is suddenly unacceptable, what I did not notice is now everywhere apparent. To live out my days with an inhibited woman like Iolanda seems an unbearable sentence. Her reluctant smile is just a symptom.

As I ride, I notice dozens of women cut just like my wife—firm in their resolve, devoted to their men, uncompromising in their ways. It is a condition of this region, and I suppose it has served our marriage well. Yes, Iolanda's constancy has seen us through a great deal. It is one of her strongest qualities, and yet it is the one that drives me away. Italians are very close to Mexicans in that they will do everything to outlast you. Italian women are like this most of all: they stay with their men, and die with their men, no matter what. The feminist movement never quite reached into Italy, and where it did it was misinterpreted. Italian women simply started wearing jeans and thought they were free, but they were the same. They will always be the same.

It is a wonderful quality, Iolanda's constancy, but it is also frightening, and suffocating. And I worry it is no longer for me. Today I believe that a woman must be able to change with the times, with her man, that a woman married to an actor must change more than most. He changes, and so must she, but Iolanda is unmovable. To deny change is to go against nature.

I flash back to my friend Lee Thompson, one of the few men I have known who was not afraid of change. He never did the same thing twice. He was called in to direct *The Guns of Navarone*, for Columbia, after two others had tried and failed. He was a tiny man who carried a large sketchpad, and refused to read the script. I had never heard of anything like it. His direction consisted of one arbitrary decision after another: Gregory Peck would smoke a pipe; I would grab a knife and look menacing; David Niven would tinker with the dynamite. Irene Papas, Anthony Quayle, James Darren . . . Thompson had a tossed-off piece of business for each of us. He never read a scene until he had to shoot it, and approached each shot on a whim.

And yet the cumulative effect was astonishing. Lee Thompson made a marvelous picture, but how? Perhaps his inventiveness lay in defying convention, in rejecting the accepted methods of motion picture making and establishing his own. Perhaps it was in his very formlessness that he found the one form he could sustain, and nurture, the one form that could, in turn, sustain and nurture him. Perhaps he was just a lucky Englishman who pulled a good picture out of his ass.

Art is like that, I think. Life is like that only sometimes, but lately I have begun to think that the one I am living is not like that at all.

I pedal faster, trying to bust the barriers I imagine Iolanda has placed before me. I needed her permanence once, but now I need to rid myself of all stasis, and right away. I can never be as free as a man like Lee Thompson, but I will die underneath Iolanda's oppressive routine. It is not her fault, but my own. I will die loving her, but that is not enough. I wonder if perhaps it is not time to shed my skin once again, to cast off the ties to my ancient life and start in on another.

I wonder if I am too old to change.

Auda Abu Tayi

IOLANDA SIGNED ON as my personal assistant, with a liberal job description. Katherine seemed to approve of the arrangement; in fact, it was she who suggested it; when she was through communing with her God and her cohorts in the Swiss Alps, she returned to the States with the children, leaving me to fend for myself, reminding me that I would be fine with the Italian girl to look after me.

Naturally, Iolanda was paid for her time, but she gave of herself freely. Her first order of business, after *Barabbas*, was to accompany me to the Jordan desert, where I had been handed a part in one of the grandest spectacles yet committed to the screen.

The sojourn was brokered by Mike Frankovitch, an old friend who oversaw all British-based production for Columbia Pictures. Mike and I had known each other since our boyhoods in the same district of East Los Angeles (he was a star Lincoln Park athlete and standout football player at UCLA, and later an accomplished sportscaster), and had resumed our friendship once we found ourselves plying the same trade. He called to offer me the part in a picture for David Lean, chronicling the life of British adventurer T. E. Lawrence, and his crossing of the Nefad Desert into Arabia.

"How much?" I asked. Too often, this was the first question out of my mouth when I was considering a picture.

He mentioned a scandalously low salary, but tried to inflate it by listing the actors who had already committed to the project: Peter O'Toole, Alec Guinness, Jose Ferrer, Omar Sharif.

"You mean to tell me Alec Guinness is working for that kind of money?" I wondered. I could not get past the salary.

"Well, no," Mike said, "but your part is only for four weeks."

"I don't care if it's four days. I can't afford to work for so little. I'll get killed."

"What'll it take? We'd love to see you in this role."

At this point, I still had no idea what part I was to play, or what was involved. All I knew was that it was work, and possibly an adventure. "Four hundred thousand dollars," I said.

My old friend choked on the figure. "But Tony," he pleaded, "they'll never go for it."

"Then they'll never go for it. You asked what it would take and that's what it would take."

He called the next day to tell me that Lean and producer Sam Spiegel had accepted my terms, and I set off for the Middle East before they could change their minds. Katherine had no desire to uproot the children to join me for a month in the desert, so Iolanda graciously agreed to make the trip with me. I hated to travel alone, especially to such out-of-the-way locations, and Iolanda knew she was doing me a great kindness. In our brief time together, she had all but abandoned her career as a costume designer and devoted herself to our relationship. I did not think there was a future in it for her, but she was convinced otherwise.

Before I was officially hired for the part of Auda Abu Tayi, I had to meet with David Lean for his final approval. It was a formality, but the producers were paying me a lot of money, and I wanted them to think it was well spent.

Lean was already on location, in the middle of the desert shooting the picture, so I went to see him in costume. I stopped at the production headquarters and had Iolanda outfit me in the appropriate robes. Next I visited the makeup tent, and showed the artists there a picture of Auda Abu Tayi. An hour later, I emerged with Abu Tayi's beard and famous hooked nose, looking to all the world like the man himself.

I drove with Iolanda in a jeep to a dune a few miles away. We stopped about one thousand feet from a dramatic cliff, on the other side of which I knew I would find Lean, shooting the day's scene. I ditched the jeep where it would not be spotted. I wanted to make a grand entrance, appearing out of the sands on foot.

I had not counted on the locals. Up ahead, beneath the overhang of the cliff, sat four or five hundred Arabs, escaping the midday sun. They were huddled together like sheep. They spotted me on the horizon, and began to chant: Abu Tayi, Abu Tayi, Abu Tayi. To them, I was Auda Abu Tayi, come to lead them out of the hot sun, as if from a mirage. They fell in line behind me, and followed me to the other side, where I had been told I would find the crew. As I walked, the Arabs continued with their chant, churning it into a raving song. Their voices lifted me, and carried me straight to the set, to where Lean was consulting with Peter O'Toole.

I was told that the Arabs made quite a commotion, which I could see, and that I made quite an entrance, which I could not.

Lean looked up from what he was doing and asked one of his assistants about the ruckus.

"It's just the Arabs, sir," the assistant replied. "They're chanting for Abu Tayi."

"And who the hell is that, at the head of the line?" Lean wondered.

"I don't know. I guess it must be Abu Tayi."

"Well," Lean said. "Screw Anthony Quinn. Let's hire that guy instead."

Swimming with the Chicken Fish

THE MAKING OF *Lawrence of Arabia* was one calamity after another. In the end, David Lean produced a memorable picture (winner of seven Academy Awards), but who knew we would ever get there?

The worst of it came at the front end. Iolanda and I were lodged (in separate quarters) in a sprawling tent city the studio had set up for cast and crew, and shuttled to our far-flung locations each morning by propeller plane. It was a treacherous commute. One morning, we almost did not make it. The pilot forgot to engage his landing gear and we had to put down on a wadi—the dry bed of a stream, where the sands had been soaked through and hardened enough to normally accommodate a small plane.

As we made our approach, we heard a terrible siren inside the cabin. Something was wrong. I looked out the window and saw the endless stretches of sand coming up at us, at great speed. It was clear we were about to crash. Poor Iolanda thought she would die in my arms, and for a moment I worried if I was up to the responsibility. Then I realized I was probably the only person on that plane who understood what was about to happen. There were about fifty of us on board, but it was a mostly British cast and crew, and I was the only one impolite enough to raise my voice.

(I believe what I said was, "Oh, shit!" but others on board have since recalled that it was, "Oh, fuck!" or perhaps even, "Jesus Fucking Christ!")

As the ground reached up to claim us, I thought what a pleasure it was to die with the English. They were all quite proper in their panic, and wonderfully behaved: Oh, yes, I believe we're crashing; how odd, darling, don't you think? If the situation was any less grave, it might have been hilarious; at the time, it was only mildly amusing. To die like this! With these people!

We plummeted into the sands, nose down, and the plane kept hurtling forward. I grabbed Iolanda and dragged her to the floor in front of our seats. I looked up and could see the windows covered with sand. From inside the cabin, crouched on the floor, it felt as if we were completely submerged in a dune of our own making. If the crash did not kill us, we would surely be buried alive.

It was a moment accelerated and frozen, both. The crash seemed to happen at a too-fast speed, but at the same time everything was in slow motion. It was a strange sensation, to operate on such separate planes, but at the time I found it useful, even comforting. How reassuring it was to learn that even in dire straits I am capable of rushing ahead and pulling back, at the same time. I supposed this was a good thing to know.

Finally, the plane came to a stop. I felt around for Iolanda's hand and took it in mine. She was all right. Everyone was all right, but for a few cuts and bruises. We stumbled from the murky darkness of the plane and into the harsh sunlight. It was barely six o'clock in the morning, and already the sun had baked hot on the sands. I held Iolanda close, and looked around at the damage. The fuselage was ripped open, and mostly submerged. We had to climb up to get out. The proper Englishmen were flitting about as if on holiday, searching for their bags and their papers, worrying over their next spot of tea.

"A frightful thing, that," I heard one of them say. "Wonderful no one's hurt," another remarked. "On with the show, shall we?"

I wanted to shake the bloody lot of them and scream.

The historical backdrop to our location shooting was the ongoing tension between Jordan and Israel. It was a difficult time to be living in that part of the world, on contested territory. At our various locations, I could sometimes see the Palestinians, looking on at our strange doings from the other side of mesh fencing. Compared to our pampered existence, they lived like dogs, and the juxtaposition was at times too much to be believed.

I have often wondered how it was that Sam Spiegel, an observant Jew, was able to make all our arrangements in such hostile territory. I wondered how he justified it to himself and to Jordanian officials. Sam was a fantastic character and a lifelong friend. I had known him for years. I used to see him late at night, waiting at the public tennis courts behind the Goldwyn studios, desperate to get into a game. For some reason, he never had a quarter to turn on the lights, so he sat hoping to round out a threesome for a game of doubles. It was heartbreaking, in its way. Sam had produced some wonderful pictures by this point—*The African Queen, The Bridge on the River Kwai*— but still he was left to hustle a game on the public tennis courts.

During the production of *Lawrence of Arabia*, Sam made great friends with Jordan's King Hussein. I suppose he had to, in order to get the picture made. He attended a string of royal cocktail parties. I never went, and my not going was sometimes a shame to the production. Still, I was curious about the goings-on at these state affairs, and Sam brought back the most marvelous stories. Once, he

asked Hussein what occasion they happened to be celebrating. Hussein responded in terms he thought Spiegel
might understand. "It's like the Jewish Yom Kippur," he
said.

Sam thought about this, and could not make sense of
it. "But Yom Kippur is a solemn holiday, a time for reflection," he said. "Here, everyone is dancing."

"Well," Hussein replied. "We do things a bit differently around here. I hope you don't mind."

Every now and then, Hussein came out to our set, to
take in the proceedings. He was, I was told, something of
a film buff. One afternoon, during a break, he walked over
to introduce himself. There had been a party the night
before. He knew who I was, from my pictures, and I knew
who he was, from his.

"Mr. Quinn," he said, "we were sorry you could not
join us last night. Were you not feeling well?"

"No, Your Highness," I replied. "I consider myself a
friend to Israel, and did not think it proper for me to
attend."

"I understand," Hussein said, and from his tone it
appeared that he did. He struck me as an affable, articulate man, and quite pleasant company.

My position seemed a small thing to me at the time,
but it turned out I made an impression. Years later, when
I lived next door to Yassir Arafat in a hotel in Tripoli, I
discovered the Palestinian leader had heard of my stand.
"You are a principled man," he said to me, in the elevator
up to our rooms.

"I try to be," I averred. "But that business, back in the
desert, that was nothing."

With a wave of his hand, he indicated that such gestures were more significant than I knew.

I had never liked Arafat, and resented his behavior on
the world stage. To carry a gun onto the floor of the
United Nations seemed to me the foolish act of an arrogant

man. And yet I understood his cause. The Palestinians were like the Mexicans of Southern California. They were not Mexicans or Americans, Arabs or Jews. They were not anything. I hated the way those people were treated and could not begrudge Arafat his fight, even if I could not abide his tactics.

Beyond Hussein's cocktail parties, there was not much in the way of amusement. For a time, a favorite pastime was to visit the local tailor in Aqaba, just outside our tent city. It cost nothing to have a suit made—about ten dollars—and I passed several afternoons with Peter O'Toole and Omar Sharif, being fitted for suits. It was something to do. I had about thirty suits made, during the shoot, and I gave them all away.

Across the Gulf of Aqaba was the Israeli town of Eilat, and we spent many nights looking through field glasses at the activity there. Aqaba was like a ghost town, but Eilat was alive, especially at night. We sat on the beach and marveled at the lights. We were so bored, we looked at anything. It was like television to us. The Arabs used to joke about the clever Jews across the way, hiding behind their cardboard cut-out of a town, and staging their frolic to drive the rest of us mad. Who knows? Maybe they were, but it did keep us amused.

The other thing to do was swim in the Red Sea. This was a deceptive idyll. The water was filled with an amazing variety of fish. My favorite were the chicken fish, which swam about looking just like wet chickens, with feathers and everything. But they were a deadly curiosity—the chicken fish could kill you with their sting. Once the locals were kind enough to point this out, I left the swimming to the others. I preferred to take my poison only from familiar enemies.

Most of our troubles on and around the set had to do with David Lean's exacting nature as a director. He was an endearing man, who cherished the good company of like-hearted souls, but he could be a demanding artist. He had a strange way of giving his actors a voice in his direction, while making them pay for it. Nobody questioned Lean, even though he claimed to encourage the input.

It took just the slightest rebuke for me to learn why. Early on, I made the mistake of challenging a piece of staging Lean had orchestrated, involving hundreds of horses and camels and extras. In the scene, Peter O'Toole's Lawrence was to inform Auda Abu Tayi of his plans to attack Aqaba, and Abu Tayi was to endorse the plan without hesitation. I played the scene as directed, but my mind was someplace else.

"Excuse me, everybody," Lean said. (He rarely said, "Cut!"—just "Excuse me.") He took me aside. "What's wrong?" he asked. "You're not playing the scene."

"I know, David," I said. "I know, it's just that it feels wrong to me."

"What do you mean, it feels wrong?"

"Well, the army is mine, and here comes this young imbecile, telling me what to do. Who the fuck is he to tell me what to do? I can't just attack Aqaba, without thinking about it, on his say-so. The way it's written, it's like he's just suggested we go out for ice cream, but it's not just ice cream. I could lose my whole fucking army. I could lose everything. My God, I'm a mercenary. I have to know what I'm getting out of it."

Lean considered this a moment. "And what do you propose to do about it?" he asked.

I told him that what I thought we should do was send my character off behind a rock, to contemplate Lawrence's plan and formulate a plan of his own.

"I like it, Tony," Lean said, after a moment. "I see what you mean." Unfortunately, he also said that this new bit required him to move all the horses and camels and extras, so that he might frame an appropriate rock in the scene, and that it would take at least until four o'clock in the afternoon to reset the shot. It was then just ten o'clock in the morning.

"Forget about it, David." I shrugged, when I learned what the small change would cost. "Let's just go ahead and do it your way."

"No, Tony," he calmly insisted. "I want to do it your way."

So we sat around the entire day, waiting for the crew to set up the shot. I felt like an absolute shit, making these people wait like this. I wished I had kept my mouth shut.

Finally, just as the sun was about to disappear over the horizon, the shot was ready. We only had one try at the scene, before losing the light. If I flubbed my lines, or O'Toole flubbed his, the whole day would have been lost. I did not need this kind of pressure.

O'Toole hit his marks and I hit mine, and everyone claimed to be thrilled with the new scene, but I sensed that all of this was besides the point.

I raced over to Lean, who was climbing into his jeep, anxious to return to his quarters. "Jesus, David," I said. "I'm terribly sorry. I almost cost you the whole day. You're a wonderful director. I should never have questioned your instincts."

"Nonsense, Tony," he said. "I am not that insecure."

I thought that was a marvelous line, coming from an artist of his stature. David Lean may not have been that insecure, but almost every other director I had ever worked with would have shied from such self-deprecation. Lean's priority was to the picture, and not to his ego. He was a perfectionist, to just this side of a fault. Often, his attention to detail threatened the picture. Several months into the shoot, he invited me to a meeting with Sam Spiegel in the dining room of the one hotel in town. The production was famously over schedule and over budget. My pro-rated salary, at one hundred thousand dollars per week, was a small windfall to me but a drain on Columbia

Pictures, and yet it was the least of the studio's worries. Now, it appeared, the director was having trouble with the script.

Iolanda joined the three of us for lunch, and Lean took control of the meeting. Always, the director carried himself in grand manner—his speech was impeccable, and the way he held his cigarette (upside down) was divine!—which might have softened the blow of what he had to say. "Sam," he delicately explained, "I may have a bit of a disappointment for you. I've been studying the script and I find that the second half is not up to the first. I'm afraid I'll have to get with Bolt in England to see if we might strengthen it a bit."

(Robert Bolt, the screenwriter, had estimated that the rewrite would take up to ten weeks.)

"Ten weeks!" Sam huffed. He was not nearly as refined as Lean. "It'll cost me a damn fortune!" Then he started to twitch, and dropped his head into his soup. Literally.

With supreme gentility, Lean looked to Iolanda and said, "Darling, would you please see that Sam recovers?" Then he left.

When Sam came to, he had to be restrained. Also literally. "Where is that fucking Lean?" he wailed. "I'll kill him!"

Sam was already outraged at the delays, and now to have to pull up stakes for ten weeks was a disaster. All of the actors were under contract, and we would have to be paid during the down time. I had no idea what the others were earning, but my own math left me with enough to finance my own picture.

In the end, Sam Spiegel saved the picture with a brilliant scheme. It would have broken him to keep the actors on the payroll, so he finagled jobs for us in other pictures during the hiatus. He knew that most actors would rather work than sit idle, and that we could not very well double-bill for our time. I did not know how he managed it, but the timing worked out, all around. He arranged a picture for Alec Guinness, a picture for Peter O'Toole, a picture for Joe Ferrer.

For me, he arranged one of my best roles.

Therefore I Am

THE PART SAM SPIEGEL found for me was as the broken-down fighter Mountain Rivera, in the feature adaptation of Rod Serling's *Playhouse 90* television classic "Requiem for a Heavyweight," opposite Jackie Gleason, Mickey Rooney, and Julie Harris.

It was a juicy role, and it yielded what I have come to regard as one of my better performances, although at first I worried I could only deliver a hackneyed job. I struggled to strip my portrayal of the meat-handed boxing cliches found in most fight pictures, and instead present a portrait of a beaten man with nowhere to turn, but my initial efforts were unsuccessful.

All during rehearsals, I reworked my characterization, trying to get it right. One day I played him as a tough lout, the next as a sweet has-been. No one seemed to notice my flailing, or to mind it. Director Ralph Nelson, who had also directed the television play, was busy with some of the complicated staging. Gleason and Rooney were busy with their own characterizations. And producer David Susskind was busy trying to keep everything from falling apart.

The day before I was to shoot my first scene, I still had not settled on how to play the role. I had some ideas, but nothing felt right. Finally, I was doing some last-minute work on a boxing sequence with one of our fight coordinators, Abie Bain, when I discovered my voice, just across the ring. Abie Bain had been a great light-heavyweight. He might have been a champion, but he never played with the mob and so never reached the top. He spoke in a weathered rasp, like a man who had been kicked in the throat a thousand times too many. "Tony," he wheezed, when we were finishing up for the night, "sweetie, whatsa matta?" He was eerily soft-spoken; there was power in his voice, but also pain and uncertainty and tenderness.

There, I thought. This was just what I had been looking for. Abie Bain, like it or not, would add the finishing touch to my portrayal of Mountain Rivera. I grabbed the old fighter and took him out to dinner, to try to soak up what I could of his inflection, and then stayed up all night trying to perfect my delivery.

The next morning, I was ready. I was scheduled to do a scene with Julie Harris, who played an employment officer out to help Rivera find a job. It was not the opening scene of the script, but it was just as important. Always, the first shot of a picture is the point of no return for an actor. Whatever voice I used here, I would have to sustain the rest of the way.

Miss Harris looked at me like I was crazy. She must have heard my raspy voice and thought I had a nervous laryngitis. This was nothing like we had played it in rehearsal. Still, she held up her end, and we played the take all the way through. When we finished, Ralph Nelson stepped onto the set and began retching. He was not the most subtle director in the world, I would learn, or the gentlest personality. When he did not like something, he went to elaborate lengths to show it. Here, it sounded like he was vomiting. I gathered that this was not a good thing.

"What's the matter, Ralph?" I said. "Something you ate?"

"Something you said," he replied. "Matter of fact, it's everything you said. Where the hell did you come up with that voice?"

"It's Abie," I explained. "That's the way he talks.

That's the way I decided to go with my character. I thought it sounded run-down and beat-up, a real fighter's voice."

"Yeah, well it sounds like shit," the director said. "I can't shoot a picture with you sounding like that. You're in almost every scene!"

Susskind, Gleason, and Rooney were on the set for the big first shot, and I looked to them for support. Gleason turned away; he would not be pulled into the debate. Rooney nodded his head in approval, but only Susskind voiced his enthusiasm. "You surprised the hell out of me, Tony," he said, "but I like it."

Unfortunately, Ralph Nelson did not, and it turned out Gleason was not thrilled about it either. Susskind put it to a test. He gave us the rest of the morning off, and asked the principals to reconvene after lunch, to look at the rushes. Then we would decide what to do about my voice.

It was a democratic solution, and I admired Susskind for standing up to his director. Too many producers are afraid to upset the touchy artists in their employ, and this was especially so during the early 1960s, but Susskind was a reasonable man who respected reason in others. Now it just fell to him to exact some of it from his rigid director.

Susskind had the film sent down to the lab, and called us back to the screening room just after noon. I hated looking at myself on screen, and looking at dailies through the eyes of my colleagues was particularly discomfiting. I never knew whether to watch the picture, or the players in the screening room. On this day, I sought out Mickey Rooney, and watched him watch the scene. He was the best actor of all of us, and I figured his reaction would tell. When he began to applaud, at the end of the scene, I felt sure the work had made my case.

Susskind stood and turned to the director. "All right, then, what do you think?" he asked.

"I don't know," Nelson said. "I still don't like it. I just don't know."

"Well you better fucking know," Susskind yelled, "because we're back on the set in an hour, and if you don't know I'll have Tony Quinn direct the picture."

There was a terrible silence. Nelson squirmed in his seat. "Well," he finally said, "I guess I'll just have to get used to it."

The victory only led to another battle. It might have been a battle of wits, but I could not be sure. Gleason cornered me outside the screening room. My sudden shift in character seemed to have him worried, now that it had been forced on the director. "I've got my eye on you, Anthony Quinn," he warned. "Don't fuck around with me." The man was a bigger star than I was, at least in his own mind, and he set this out like it mattered.

"I wasn't planning on it," I replied. "Just worry about your part and I'll worry about mine."

"Not good enough," he said. "I didn't like the way you talked to Ralph on the set this morning, and when I don't like something I can't concentrate on the picture."

"What's wrong with the way I talked to Ralph?"

"You said 'I think' too much."

"And you, when you're doing your television show, you never have an opinion about something?"

"Yeah, but I only have one or two a day. You, all day long, you've got so many 'I thinks' they're coming out your ass!"

I had never heard one actor tell another to keep his opinions to himself. It went against everything I believed about the craft. I thought actors were supposed to support each other. I thought Gleason was kidding. He was a strange man, and known for his unpredictable behavior behind the scenes; I thought maybe this was his idea of a joke; that, or he was just a controlling bastard.

Whatever it was, he kept at it. "You heard me," he

continued. "You talk to the director, the director tells you one thing, and you say, 'But, I think.' All morning long, you think, you think, you think. I want you to keep your 'I thinks' to yourself."

Next, Gleason went to Susskind and demanded that I only be allowed three "I thinks" per day. Susskind also thought Gleason was kidding and played along. Who could be serious about something like this?

Gleason kept a running tally of my opinions. Every time I said "I think," he bellowed in protest. He flashed that big, bug-eyed, cheeks-puffed look that made his Ralph Kramden character an American icon, except he also appeared to give off steam. If I reached my third violation of the day, he stormed off. Sometimes, Susskind had to be called in to mediate, or to wheedle Gleason back to work. Things went on in this way for eight weeks. It was laughable, but it would not go away, and if it began as a joke, it quickly turned into something else.

I pushed Gleason's buttons at every turn. The slightest thing would set him off. Usually, it was nothing at all. Once, we did a scene with Mickey Rooney that nearly drove Gleason mad. Mickey and I were to play gin rummy in the background, while Jackie was to make a telephone call. Each time Jackie picked up the phone, I did a little business to distract him. Either I shuffled the cards with too much flourish, or made a funny face, or spoke in something more than a stage whisper. The poor man was so frustrated, he looked like he might explode.

We went through a half-dozen takes, but Gleason kept tripping over his lines. With his fuse nearly spent, he turned to the director for an assist. "Ralph," he complained, "Quinn's chewing an apple on my scene. You're gonna just sit there and let him get away with it?"

(To chew an apple on another actor's scene was to steal his spotlight.)

"I've been here the whole time," Nelson said, not

knowing what to make of the nonsense. He had an insight to match his subtlety. "I haven't seen a goddamn thing. What's he doing that's so terrible?"

Gleason could not say, at first. "He's thinking," he managed. "Tell the bastard not to think so much."

Either he was completely serious, or a better actor than his work had shown.

Mickey Rooney and I sat back at our table, giggling like schoolboys.

Nelson did not appreciate our tittering. "Tony," he interrupted, "what's he talking about?"

I chose my words carefully: "I think what Jackie's upset about is that I think too much. At least that's what I think."

"That's three right there!" Gleason roared, and disappeared to his dressing room.

Tchin-Tchin

I JOINED KATHERINE and the children in our brownstone on Seventieth Street for another run at the Broadway stage, and a last run at our marriage. It was October 1962. My wife and I barely spoke. I felt I had lost her—to God, and to the previous men in her life. She felt she had lost me—to my work, and to a streak of lunatic jealousy that would not go away. We lived a life of propriety, just. There was nothing between us but our children, but they were reason enough to press on.

The tug and pull of a child is an overwhelming connection, and I would soon feel it from an ocean away, to another woman. Iolanda was back in Italy, pregnant with my child, hoping that I would return and build a life with her and the baby. I could not deny my own flesh, and yet I could not break from my family. I did not know what to do, and I struggled through rehearsals, trying to concentrate on the play while hoping that my life would take care of itself. I could be a lazy coward when it came to responsibility, and found the smallest reasons to set the most difficult decisions aside.

The play was not the answer I might have hoped. It was, however, a distraction. It was an American production of the French drama *Tchin-Tchin*, about a man and woman who take up with each other after discovering their spouses were having an affair. (The title came from an Italian expression for "Cheers!" or "Bottoms up!") The subtext struck me as too much like my own situation, but the real complication arose between me and my costar, the British actress Margaret Leighton.

In truth, it was a delightful complication. We fell for each other on the first day of rehearsals. Maggie was a terrific woman, and a classic beauty, with a proper manner that belied her true nature. She could belch and curse like a sailor, and still come off looking like a lady. She was great fun, and I enjoyed her company immensely. Our amusement spilled over onto the stage. I played my part with a mustache one night, and with a Brooklyn accent the next. I mixed it up, every time out. People came back to see the play four or five times, never knowing what to expect. It kept Maggie on her toes, and laughing, and it kept me from dwelling on my brewing domestic crises.

The play was a great success. We went on to packed houses for six months, and I juggled my three relationships for the entire time. Maggie knew the full story, but Iolanda and Katherine knew only of each other. I was honest with Maggie because I felt most comfortable with her, and because she would have seen the truth without my confession. She was a smart lady, and an absolutely effortless actress and great comedienne, but I was drawn to her worldliness, her sophistication. I loved her, I felt, like a man.

For a time, I thought we were fated to be together. She

came to the house one evening, for an innocent dinner with Katherine and the children, and revealed what might have been my destiny. I had recently purchased an unsigned self-portrait of Gauguin from a dealer in London, and it was on display in our living room. I had no doubts of its authenticity, but did not have the documents to support it.

Maggie looked at the masterpiece and screamed: "My painting! Oh my God, Tony, how on earth did it end up here?"

I told her the story of my acquiring it, and she told me how she had been forced to part with it in an ugly divorce proceeding. The papers I needed to support its authenticity were in her desk drawer at home, and she offered to send them to me on her return to England.

We took the coincidence as a sign, and over the next months conspired to be together after the run of the play. She wanted to marry me, and I thought it was not such a bad idea. I thought she could make me happy.

And then I thought about Iolanda, and the baby. Jesus Christ, I was so confused! I was in such a cloud that for a few weeks I even began a fourth relationship, with a young American star who came to visit me backstage. She had seen the play, she said, and decided she had to be with me, that very night, and I could find no reason—not Katherine, not Iolanda, not Maggie—to deny her my company. I had admired this actress for years, and could not resist her enormous sensuality. Still, I did not want to be found guilty of such exponential duplicity (even I had my limits!), so I searched for an appropriate place for us to be alone. We could not go to her place, or mine. She was too precious for us to use my dressing room at the theater. We could not go to a hotel, where our comings and goings might arouse suspicion.

What we could do, we thought, was hire a limousine, to squire us about Manhattan and turn our lovemaking into a moveable feast. This we did, and we must have made a scandalous picture, me and my eager star, our asses pressed recklessly against the tinted windows as we toured New York City. We kept at it, over several afternoons and evenings (and through all five boroughs!). It was a wild affair, but at the same time a deeply tormented one. At least, for me, that is how it was. There we were, fucking in the middle of Central Park, or stopped at a traffic light, and my head was everywhere but inside that limousine. How could I even consider making love to another woman, I sometimes wondered, while Iolanda was pregnant with my child? How could I make a life with someone else? How could I rationalize leaving Katherine for Maggie, but not for Iolanda? And how could I tell my children I was building a new family, with a woman other than their mother? What the hell was I doing?

I told myself I had no choice, that a man longs to go where he has never been—especially to well-known cul de sacs.

The European tabloids found scandal in my uncertainty, and I fed the headlines. They never learned of my distinctly American affair on wheels, but they found out about Iolanda soon enough, and when they did, I stepped forward. I could not let a child of mine enter this world without my name. I did not care what people thought. I had lived a life of not belonging. My father had too. The next generation would feel a part of something even if it killed me.

I did not know what to say to Katherine, and so I said nothing. She already knew about my various affairs, and suspected many others. What would it accomplish to tell her about Maggie? Or to involve her in the news about the baby? She would find out eventually, if these were things she was meant to know. I told her I had accepted a picture in Rome, and would be leaving New York shortly. It was just for a few weeks, I said, so there was no reason to uproot the children from school. It was best for them to go on with their lives without interruption, without me. She did not ask questions, or challenge my decision. That was how things were between us. We each moved to our own cadence. What was best for us was left unsaid.

And so I made arrangements to leave *Tchin-Tchin* and join Iolanda in Rome. I still had not decided what to do about the women in my life, but I had no doubts about the baby, or my being there. I would be a father to the child, and everything would have to fall from that.

David Merrick, the producer of the play, was disinclined to put on an understudy in my absence, thinking it would hurt ticket sales. "Either you stay or you go, Tony," he said. "You can't have it both ways."

I knew Maggie would never continue in the play with another actor, so I consulted her on the move. As it turned out, she was eager to leave *Tchin-Tchin*, even if she was not too happy about my plans for the baby. Still, she was determined to follow me to Europe, to see if we might find a future there.

(Merrick hired Jack Klugman and Arlene Francis to replace us in the lead roles, and *Tchin-Tchin* closed in less than a month.)

A few nights before my final curtain, I was visited backstage by Irene Papas and a kinetic young Greek director named Michael Cacoyannis. They had something important to discuss with me, Irene said. She had heard I was leaving for Europe, and wanted to speak to me before I left. I could not imagine anything more important than the dilemmas I was already weighing, and tried to put them off. I did not wish to hear about Irene's career, or her love life, not after what we had been to each other, and I had no desire to clue her in on my own travails. I did not need her condemnation, on top of everything else.

"Tony, please," she persisted. "It's rather urgent." She looked to her friend in what I took to be a conspiratorial way. He seemed to tell her to keep after me, whatever it took.

I agreed to join them for a drink later that evening, at the Plaza Hotel, and as we sat through our small talk I felt Cacoyannis eyeing me with great suspicion. He had a disarmingly clinical way about him, I would come to learn. "What's the matter with you?" he finally asked, as if he had known me for ten years and not ten minutes.

I resented the question, particularly in front of Irene, whom I had always wanted to impress. I hardly knew this man. Who was he to ask after my life? Just that morning, Katherine had calmly suggested I commit myself to a mental institution, and in my agony I was beginning to think this an acceptable solution. What did I need with the condemnation of strangers?

"Nothing's wrong," I said. "What did you want to talk to me about?"

Cacoyannis looked at Irene. He appeared to have done an about-face, and now wanted her to forget the subject, but I saw her shake her head. She seemed to have a great deal of influence on him.

After a long hesitation, he spoke. "Have you ever read *Zorba the Greek*?"

"Yes."

"Would you like to do it next year?"

"Okay."

"There's not much of a budget, but I'm willing to make you my partner."

"Fine."

Just like that, we cemented a deal of a lifetime. I was a drowning man, and Kazantzakis's story was like a raft. It had saved me once, and I thought it might save me again. I wanted to hug Cacoyannis, and thank him for offering me the part, but I was afraid to tilt the machinery. I wanted to hug Irene too, but that was out of the question. I left the Plaza for a bookstore I knew on Fifty-seventh

Street that stayed open late. I bought up everything I could find by Kazantzakis, including a fresh copy of *Zorba the Greek*. Then I checked into a hotel and stayed up all night reading it. By dawn, I knew my life would change. Zorba had already started to take over.

Ride

FRANCESCO QUINN was born on March 22, 1963. He had my name and my father's. He would be all right. The Italian papers screamed: "Antonio E Vero?" But the American press gave scant notice.

Katherine too paid us little mind. We talked around my relationship with Iolanda, and the baby, but it did not take us anywhere. Nothing changed between us. Nothing could dent Katherine's faith. She had expected as much, or as little. We went on as before.

I consider Frankie's birth as I head through the flats of the Pontine Valley, for Aprilia. It was the moment of my transformation, the turn in the road that has brought me to this place. I loved this child like a gift. If he was to be my third act, I would give him all my energy, all my attention. I would reinvent myself, for him.

I loved my other children, but I knew Frankie would be different, or that I would be different because of Frankie. I was petrified that I would not live up to the moment, but I did not back away from it. He was baptized at the Basilica of St. Peter in Rome, and I spent the day in silent prayer, hoping that my young son would somehow answer the turmoil inside me.

Of course, he could not—not yet!—but he could prepare me for his brother, Daniele Antonio, born the following year, and the two boys together told me it was time to shed my skin once more. They gave me the strength to finally leave Katherine. We divorced in Juarez, Mexico, in

January 1965, more than twenty-seven years after our doomed wedding night. It took just a few months for us to come together, and a lifetime to tear ourselves apart, and it took a return trip to the scene of my childhood to acknowledge our irreconcilable differences.

Iolanda and I were married the following year, while she was pregnant with our third son, Lorenzo Alexander. The decision to marry was instinctive, finally. Margaret Leighton was still in and out of the picture, in London, and there were other entanglements to confound me, but Iolanda was the right move, the next move. She was where I belonged. Our boys were where I belonged. Italy was where I belonged. We had bought a villa for Francesco in Cecchina di Roma, on the street that now bears my name, and started in on another life. We added to the house as we grew. I dreamed of a home for all my children, for all time.

God, it was wonderful, going through these motions, with my Italian family. Iolanda hated the idea of moving away from Rome (to her, it was the center of the universe), but she grew accustomed to a life in the countryside. She was an outstanding wife and mother—loving, attentive, comforting. She was everything I had never let Katherine be (probably everything I had never wanted Katherine to be), and our home pulsed with the aches and elations of childhood, and wonder. I was fifty years old, but I was a young man, all over again.

This ride is about my Italian children, as much as it is about anything else. These hills are more theirs than mine. They were born here. They are a part of this region. Me, I am passing on their ticket, looking through their eyes. Just this morning, on the downhill ride from Velletri, I was reminded of Danny's coming of age. It was a moment laced with my own failure. It was in the hills of Cori, to the southeast. We were on a family outing, looking for an out-of-the-way restaurant that had been recommended by one of the townspeople. Larry and Frankie were talking. They were trying to remember the road, so they could return to it on their motorcycles. They were mapping a great adventure. They turned to Danny, to include him in their plans.

"I don't have a motorcycle," Danny said. He was about fifteen, rail-thin and worried at his own frailty. He tired easily, and tended to more sedentary pursuits. He was the least rambunctious of all my children.

"You can come on your bicycle," his older brother Frankie said. "We'll go slow."

"No. I'll just hold you up."

"Why don't you have a bike?" Larry wondered.

"Pop won't buy me one."

I had been listening in, from the front seat. "What do you mean, I won't buy you one?" I shot back. "You never told me you wanted a bike. You want a bike, you have to prove to me you're man enough to have a bike. Your brothers climb mountains with me. You never want to climb, or to walk, or do anything."

"You go too fast for me," he said.

"Ah," I dismissed, thinking like my own father. "You can keep up if you want to keep up." I pulled to the side of the road, just beneath a firebreak cut into the hillside. "Tell you what," I said to Danny. "You run up that path, to the top of the hill, and we'll drive around to meet you. If you make it to the top, without stopping to rest, I'll get you any motorbike you want." It was about two or three kilometers, up a fairly steep pitch.

"You mean it?"

"I mean it. I don't care if you walk, but don't stop."

We shook hands on it, and I could read the determination in his eyes. His brothers got out of the car to run alongside and cheer Danny on, but he did not need their encouragement. He was the first one up the hill, and we were all overjoyed—Iolanda too, although she hated those motorcycles. The next day, we went out and bought Danny a top-of-the-line model. Frankie had dozens of motorcycle magazines, and the boys stayed up all night, weighing which one to buy. I wound up spending more than seven thousand dollars, but I did not care.

Iolanda was right to fear those machines, because that very motorcycle nearly cost Danny his life, just one year later. He was almost killed here, on this same stretch of road, outside Campo-verde. The accident was my failure, for it was I who encouraged Danny's adventurous spirit. (And I was the one who bought him the goddamn motorcycle!) One afternoon, on slick roads, he spun out and tore all the skin from his body. It was a miracle he survived. No one was home to take the call from the hospital, and the agony of that moment, for me, was knowing that the boy was alone all that time. It was bad enough that Iolanda blamed me for the accident (she blames me still), but I blamed myself for good reason: I was not there to beat back the pain and make my son whole; I was the one who put him on that bike; I was the man he was trying to be.

Danny is now the strongest and most athletic of my Italian children, but he will never be as conventional. He is most like me, I have come to realize. He was born while I was playing Zorba, and I used to think the old goat had passed through me and come to live inside Danny. Surely, such a thing is possible. A fine madness like Zorba's cannot be expected to follow any laws but its own.

I am lost in thoughts about my boys, not paying attention to the road, and I am startled from my wanderings by a speeding truck. There is almost no shoulder on the Via Anziate, and the backwash sends me to the dirt at the side of the road. It leaves me laughing, and on my ass. I stand, and dust the gravel from my clothes, thinking it could have been worse, reminding myself to concentrate on what I am doing.

I walk for a kilometer, not wanting to resume riding just yet. Perhaps I do not wish to refasten my thoughts, and the walking frees me momentarily from having to do so. I breathe deeply, and notice that the sea air of Anzio has given way to the evil-smelling marshes of the valley. I have come upon wine country, I am late to realize, surrounded by acres of fields topped with plastic, where fertilizer and soil mix to leave the air with a sick medicinal odor. There is no explaining this smell, but there is no denying it either. The wines of Aprilia are born from volcanic soil—part sand, part clay, and part volcanic matter. Indeed, the most famous wines of Latium are those known by the generic name of di Castelli—the Castles— and all are tinged with the tamed madness of the volcanic hills south of Rome. Perhaps what I am smelling is ancient sulfur, rising from the ashes of dormant volcanoes to reclaim this region.

It was an adjustment, moving here, and it was best seen through the wine. Wine was the national beverage of Italy. It was basic, just as tortillas were to Mexico, rice to China, potatoes to Ireland. In America, those who drank wine were suspect; in Italy, those who did not were questionable. Here a man who is afraid of wine is afraid of the truth.

I wonder if the distinction lies in the wine or the people. The California wines are lacking, but in what? The vines are fine, the earth is healthy, and the wine is good, but there is no joy in it, no life. The picking season in California is painful, and surely the wine reflects the discontent of the workers. I know this, from experience on both ends. Winemaking cannot be industrialized. Even in France and Italy, money-grubbing vintners have tried to copy the assembly-line operations of Ford and Fiat, but their juice is missing something essential and gets by on name only.

It starts to rain. I reach into my pack for my shell. I do

not have far to ride, but I do not want to catch cold. It is late in the day, and the road is cluttered with huge trucks, tractors, and horse-drawn wagons. It is not a good time for an old man to be out on a bicycle, to be treading on such uncertain ground.

In the fields, the grape pickers are racing to fill their baskets. Most of this region lives for the grape crop, and the heavy rains are always a great loss to the "contadini," who sell to the big combines but skim the best grapes for their homemade wines. Years before, when we first bought our own vineyard in the Alban hills, the grape-picking week, or *vendemmia*, had been a festive period. Men, women, and children dressed in heavy clothes and thick rubber boots, and tromped out into the fields, singing as they worked.

I tried to schedule my pictures so that I would be home for the festival, and looked on with pride when my wine reached the lips of a friend or stranger. Each man relished the wine produced by his small patch of land. In the local trattorias, we would shrug deprecatingly at the wine we were served. Rivals would boast that in their wine it was possible to taste the sun itself.

But today, as I gaze into the fields, I see the "vendemia" has changed. The pickers no longer sing as they work. Perhaps it is the rain, I hope, but I realize the changes run deeper than the weather. All of Italy is in for a makeover. There is a new government, yet again. Taxes are suffocating everyone. There are constant strikes, and political bombings. Kidnappings no longer make the front pages. Everywhere I turn, there is congestion, and smog. This quiet road has become unpassable. For Iolanda, the countryside to which we retreated is now Rome itself.

Why did I choose to live here? Because in Italy everything seems a miracle, always. Because in Italy there is no place to hide. Because after thousands of years of invasions, wars, empire builders, kings, popes, dictators, the

Italians remain a cynical people who cannot help but reject their own cynicism. They love life, with or without cause. Even in anger, an Italian softens before a plate of spaghetti. My adopted countrymen taste life. They drink it. They live by divine spirit and shun divine logic. They know that shrewdness is far more important than intelligence, that it has kept them from the Huns, the Moors, the Greeks, the Austrians, the Germans, the French, and the Americans. They have survived their own oppressors.

How can I live anywhere else? I look to the fields at my right and watch the workers defy the elements. They must pick the grape before the downpour starts so that the rich life-juice does not become soggy with rainwater. They must persevere. They must beat all.

TWELVE

The Full Catastrophe

MY AGREEMENT WITH Michael Cacoyannis and United Artists offered me a one-third interest in *Zorba the Greek*, and a modest living salary during production. The entire picture was budgeted at four hundred thousand dollars, to be shot over a five-week period in Crete. It was, we all thought, a rare opportunity to do good work, on a tight schedule, with wonderful material.

Our first real dilemma came in casting. Alan Bates quickly signed on as Basil, the British writer who inherits a local mine and falls under Zorba's intoxicating influence, and Irene Papas agreed to play the unapproachable widow who becomes the object of Basil's affection.

For the part of Madame Hortense, the aging French matron who ran the town's one small hotel, we looked initially to Simone Signoret, the great French actress. Cacoyannis and I went to Paris to offer Simone the part. She loved the book, and the script, but was reluctant to accept the picture. "I don't think I can do it," she said. "I don't think it's in me."

"I think you'll be fantastic, Simone," I said. "I think it'll be one of the greatest characterizations of your career."

"We can rehearse," Cacoyannis offered. "If anything's uncomfortable, we can work it out in rehearsals."

"Oh, I don't like to rehearse," she said. She looked to me. "Tony, I know you are that kind of actor, but I am not. I like to play a part spontaneously."

"That's fine," I said. I would have said anything, to get her to do the picture. The studio was anxious to see a star of her caliber in the role.

Cacoyannis looked at the ceiling, because rehearsals were terribly important to his way of working. But if Simone Signoret did not want to rehearse, she would not rehearse. Like me, he just wanted to see her name on a contract.

Finally, Simone agreed to take the part, at what for her was a small salary, and she joined us in Crete a few weeks later, to begin production.

Well, Cacoyannis had a devilish mind. He decided to start Simone on her most difficult scene, where Hortense was to dance and make a fool of herself in front of Basil and Zorba one evening, over dinner. Most directors would allow an uncertain performer to ease into her part with a lesser passage, but not Michael. He pushed Simone into her characterization right away. She was extremely tentative in preparing to do the scene. She looked marvelous—the makeup technicians had aged her beautifully—but at the same time uncomfortable, and as she started to play the scene, it was apparent her performance was not yet where it needed to be. Madame Hortense was to prattle on in an expository way about the great admirals who used to be her lovers, but Simone was not ridiculous enough, not pathetic enough in her portrayal. Michael kept after her, trying to get it right.

We started shooting at eight o'clock in the evening, and by midnight, when we broke for lunch, the scene had not moved anywhere. As the night wore on, Simone became even more unsure of herself, and for the first time I became concerned. It was getting late, and we were all tired. I did not think to worry for the picture itself—Simone would be fine, eventually—but we could not afford to waste a whole night's shooting.

Then, during a pause between takes, I looked over and

saw Simone, on the floor, crying. She was weeping deadly, deadly tears. I motioned Cacoyannis to join me, and we walked over to see what was wrong.

"Forgive me," Simone said, up from her weeping, "but I can't. I can't do this part. I should never have taken it. I just can't do it."

"But you can," Michael said. "I've seen you act. You can do this part."

"My God, Simone," I tried, "you'll be wonderful. You can do anything. It's just the first day of shooting. We'll shoot around you till you're ready."

"No," Simone said, "no, I can't kid myself. I know it's going to make a lot of trouble, and I'm terribly sorry, but I just can't do the picture."

"Why not?" I said. I could not understand it. "Do you think it's terrible?"

"No, Tony. I think it's wonderful. But Hortense is an old woman, and I've got a young husband. I cannot let him see me like this."

She left for Paris the next day, leaving us with no one to play a pivotal role. We immediately got on the phone to every actress who was remotely right for the part. I called Barbara Stanwyck, Ann Sothern, Tallulah Bankhead, Stella Adler. Cacoyannis worked through his own list. Everyone said she loved the script, but they all needed time to prepare for the role, and to get their affairs in order before joining us in Greece. We did not have such a luxury. We needed someone on the set in just a few days, if possible. We could not sit idle, with a crew of over seventy-five people, not on a four-hundred-thousand-dollar budget.

After several days of this frustration, Cacoyannis came up with a possible solution. "There's a wonderful actress I know," he said, "she's in Paris right now, she's just finished a play, and I think she'd make a fantastic Hortense."

"Fine," I said. "Who is it?"

"Lila Kedrova."

I had never heard of Lila Kedrova. "Michael, I'm sorry," I said, "but how in the hell do we sell Lila Kedrova to the studio? She's no Stanwyck. She's no Stella Adler."

"No, but she'll be wonderful. We'll find a way to finance the picture, if the studio doesn't want her. I'll sell my house if I have to."

And so we traded one problem for another. Kedrova agreed to do the part, on our moment's notice; United Artists executives voiced their disinterest; and we set off in search of another studio to back the picture. My first call was to my old boss, Darryl F. Zanuck, at 20th Century–Fox.

"Mr. Zanuck," I said, "I'm in trouble. I need some money."

"Jesus, Tony, you in trouble with a broad?"

"No, it's not a broad this time, it's a picture."

"What? A picture? Ah, shit." His laugh told me he would have much preferred if it was a broad.

I told him the situation with United Artists, and Lila Kedrova. I told him that Cacoyannis and I were to share two-thirds of the picture, and that the remaining third would go to the studio. I told him we needed $750,000. I upped the figure to compensate for the casting delay, and to provide a cushion against any future snags.

"You believe in it, Tony?" he asked.

"I think it could be the best picture I've ever done. It's a story about life, and how to live."

"I don't know why," Zanuck said, "but I believe you. When do you want the money?"

"Tomorrow."

"It'll be there."

And it was. He never even asked to see a script. He just sent his son-in-law over with the money, and we were back in business.

The moment I saw Lila Kedrova, made up to look like a foolish French coquette, I knew we had a hit on our hands. And I knew we had found our Madame Hortense. Kedrova was perfect, and I could no longer imagine anyone else in the role, not even Simone Signoret. Kedrova played her first scene brilliantly, with just the right shades of ridiculousness and pathos. She wound up winning the Academy Award, as best supporting actress.

Indeed, *Zorba* was nominated for six Oscars that year, including best picture. I received my second best actor nomination, but was outdone in the final tally by Rex Harrison, for his signature role in *My Fair Lady*. To his credit, Harrison came up to me at the gala reception following the awards ceremony and placed the statue on the table in front of me. "We made a twenty-million-dollar picture," he said. "You made a seven-hundred-and-fifty-thousand-dollar picture. You should have won."

It was a grand gesture, but a gesture just the same. Harrison took the statue with him and continued on his rounds.

Too Damn Bad

THE SEA AIR FINALLY leaves my nostrils, on the road through Campo di Carne, toward Aprilia. I have come to dread the sea—not in the way of a man who has something to fear, but in the manner of one who will not be made to look foolish. It is a peculiar distinction—vainglorious perhaps—but it is with me, here, as I ride.

Somewhere in my middle age, I decided that I hated to wade into the surf. It was a sudden realization, magnified by circumstance. Only children and grandparents stuck close to the shore. Up until then, I had been terrified of the deep ocean waters, but I would not be thought childish or feeble. I was a strong enough swimmer, but I did not trust the waves, or the undertow. I imagined all sorts of sea monsters swimming underneath, ready to pull me down. And yet I willed myself out beyond the whitecaps, stroke after stroke, far enough so that no one might mistake me for an old man, close enough in so that I might swim back in one piece, finding the balance between fooling myself and fooling everyone else.

Always, the ocean leaves me on the defensive, trying too hard. And yet I cannot ignore its siren pull. I was even sucked into purchasing a fantastic yacht—a 135-footer!—which I anchored for a time back at Anzio. The boat was discovered by my stand-in, a man who had shadowed me over several dozen pictures. There is often a funny relationship between an actor and his longtime stand-in; at least there was between me and mine. Over the years, this man became my alter-ego, my parasite. It was not unlike a bad marriage. One day, I looked up and saw that he was behaving like me, telling me what to do, helping me to spend my money. I began to resent the hell out of it, but still, I did nothing. It was easier to keep him around than to find someone new, to adjust to my resentments than to build whole new ones, and here again the bad marriage analogy is apt.

I was preparing to leave for the *Zorba* shoot in Crete, when my stand-in came to me with his exciting news about the yacht. Specifically, I was finishing up a 20th Century–Fox picture with Ingrid Bergman called *The Visit*, which I coproduced, during the shooting of which I fell momentarily in love with my sublime costar—and, curiously, met her gorgeous daughter. Ingrid and I had known each other for years, but (as too often happened) it took the cocoon of a motion picture set to bring us together. It was Ingrid who taught me that you can tell an actress she is a lousy cook and she will forgive you; you can tell her she is lousy in bed and she will explain it away; but God forgive you if you question her acting. I did not question the gift of her company, however, even as I questioned myself for returning her affection. Iolanda was pregnant with our second child, and I had not yet separated from Katherine, and my entanglements were enough to choke me.

And I tied myself up in still another knot. I had just purchased a bright red Maserati—my first toy!—and drove out to the set of *The Visit* to show it off. I asked Ingrid to join me for lunch, and a drive up into the hills, but she preferred to rest before her next scene. I did not mind. I would enjoy the afternoon on my own, tooling around in my new car, getting the feel of it.

As I walked over to the Maserati, I was pulled back by a woman's voice. "My God," I heard, "whose car is that?"

I turned to find Pia Lindstrom, Ingrid's stunning young daughter. "It's mine," I said. "Do you like it?"

"Do I like it? It's marvelous."

I smiled. She giggled. She was always giggling, I was soon to learn, even in her sleep.

"Do you drive it?" Pia asked.

"Well, I just bought it, and I'm not very well acquainted with it, but I'm learning. I've just asked your mother to join me for a drive, but she wants to rest. Would you like to come?"

Pia nodded, and giggled, and disappeared to find her mother. A few moments later, we were speeding off, bound for adventure—and, inevitably, for each other, thus beginning a rather complicated relationship, laced with a strange mother-daughter competition. Pia was constantly asking about her mother—did she do this? oh, and what about this?—but the bounds of propriety kept me from responding. (Ah, to hell with decorum! Proper or not, there is no way to answer such questions!)

Years later, when I took up with Ingrid again on the set of *A Walk in the Spring Rain*, the mother reheated the rivalry. I did not think much of it at the time, only that it was an unusual thing. And it was.

Here again, I digress. My stand-in had read about the yacht in a magazine and made some inquiries. It was being offered at a distress sale price. It was, he said, a rare find, a prized vessel in the wrong hands. The owner had declared bankruptcy, and needed to make a quick sale. The boat was a drain on his already meager funds, and not too many buyers could afford such a luxury.

I would later learn this jinx for myself, when I tried to unload the boat after it had begun to drain me. It got to where I gave serious thought to sinking the damn thing out at sea. My lawyer advised against it, but I was tempted. I did not care about the insurance money, but I could not see spending tens of thousands to put the boat in dry-dock, or to dispose of it properly, even after factoring in the various tax advantages of such a move. In the end, I found someone to take it off my hands for ten thousand dollars—leaving me with an out-of-pocket loss of close to a quarter-million!—and yet I was thrilled to be out from under.

But I do not want to get too far ahead of the story. At the time, the boat was probably worth about a half-million dollars, if you could find a buyer, but the hidden cost was in maintaining it. According to my stand-in, we could grab the boat for about one hundred thousand dollars—not bad, I thought, not knowing of the upkeep.

My man fancied himself an old sailor, and wanted to oversee the purchase. I had no idea there would even be a purchase, but he pushed hard for it. I finally agreed to send him to Spain, with his wife (he called her "Matey"), to inspect the boat. What the hell did I care? I was a big star, making big pictures. I thought a boat would be a marvelous plaything. I had it all figured out. I would toil in the hot sun on the *Zorba* set and retire at night to my great yacht on the Mediterranean. When I wrapped the picture, I would sail back to the harbor at Anzio and bicycle home, up into the hills—a true Italian playboy. It sounded heavenly.

My stand-in returned with his report about a week

later. "My God, what a boat!" he said. "You must have this boat. Think of the adventures!" He told me the price, but what he did not tell was that it took a five-man crew to keep the boat running, and that these guys liked their beefsteaks for dinner, and the best wine, and everything. (He recommended that we keep the same crew, because they already knew the boat—and because they had probably greased his palm for the recommendation.)

The boat he described was like a palace, with elaborate bedroom suites and marble bathrooms and a formal dining room. He brought back pictures, but said that they did not do the vessel justice.

"I can live on it, right?" I asked. Everything else, at the time, was detail.

"Absolutely."

I cut the check without thinking about it, and left for Greece about a week later. The plan was for the crew to join up with me in Crete in another week to ten days. Then I would live on the boat for the rest of the picture.

The boat was named *Ke Karai*, which in Spanish meant "What Lousy Fortune," or "Too Damn Bad." It should have tipped me to the trouble ahead. Every day, I received another telegram from my captain, describing some further delay. They had engine trouble just outside Barcelona. They hit a storm in Tangier, and took in water. They busted a propeller in Tunisia. Each mishap meant a week of repairs, and a week of hotel bills and high living. When these louts finally pulled into port, they had run up almost forty thousand dollars in expenses—at the time, an outrageous amount! We were three months into the shoot, and living in a place called Xania. There were no hotels in town. I was staying in a tiny house with the minister of culture. (The house was quite brazenly divided by a phantom flight of stairs, running up into the wall!) My captain and his crew were all tan and happy. For them, it had been a grand vacation; for me, a maddening misadventure.

I was keeping company on Crete with Pia Lindstrom, whom I had cast as Zorba's first wife. Her character was eventually cut from the picture, but we shot some marvelous scenes together. In one, a wedding scene, we slogged through a pile of watermelons, and bathed ourselves in the joyous juice. Pia looked summery, full of life, translucent. It was a rich, celebratory moment, and we could not keep ourselves from laughing. As much as any of the footage that made it into the final cut of the picture, that wedding scene showed Zorba's true spirit, and zest for living. When we shot it, I was reminded of my Uncle Cleofus, whose infectious passion touched our ramshackle home all those years ago.

Almost twenty years later, when I returned to the role of Zorba on the Broadway stage, I received word at the theater of an interview the publicist had arranged at one of the local television stations. I went down to the studio at the appointed time, only to learn that my old friend Pia would be asking me the questions. She was working as an arts and entertainment reporter for WNBC-TV. I had known this, but did not make the connection until just then. I took one look at Pia, and she took one look at me, and we both started laughing. We could not help ourselves. We giggled all through the interview. People must have thought we were out of our minds, and in a way we were. We were back slogging through those watermelons, lost in laughter and celebration.

Still, whenever we see each other, we laugh.

Now, back to the story. There was only another week or two on the *Zorba* shoot, and the mishaps continued. I broke my foot on the next to last day of filming—falling from a fifteen-foot platform into a rock quarry. There were no doctors in Xania to set the foot properly, so the studio made plans for me to see an orthopedist in Athens, and suspended shooting until my return.

We traveled to Athens on my yacht: me, Pia, the ship's

captain and his wife, my good friend Sam Shaw, and a British writer who was working with me on a script. I hired three new hands, to replace the five bums who had sailed down with the boat. We made a motley crew.

It was to be my maiden voyage—an evening cruise to Athens, a half-day in port to see the doctor, and a half-day back—only I should have changed the name of the boat before we left. We hit a raging storm, an hour out at sea. We were sitting down to dinner in the formal dining room. The generator went out. The boat began to sway, back and forth. Soon, the rocking motion was so violent that a number of us became sick. The darkness and our various stages of drunkenness did not help. The giant waves swatted us about like Ping-Pong balls. At one point, my writer friend went up on deck to throw up. (How very civil, those Brits, even in dire extremis!) We did not see him for the rest of the evening.

Then, in a fit of sobriety, it occurred to me that the poor man might have been heaved into the wild sea. I crawled above-decks, not wanting to put weight on my bad foot, and not knowing how in hell to find my crutch in the crazy darkness of the galley. I would find the writer, or I would not, but I could not be certain what I would do in either case. He was not on deck when I reached it, but that could have meant anything. The hard rains had subsided, but the winds remained heavy. Again and again, the surf slammed against the hull of the ship and sprayed me with enough force to knock me down—that is, if I had not been down on my knees, crawling, already.

My mind raced. After three months playing Alexis Zorba, I was no longer myself. Lately, I looked at the world through slightly maniacal eyes, and now—in the middle of a great storm and a great drunk—I was more Zorba than me. I tried to process the situation, but I could not touch its importance. In my stupor, I thought my British friend would turn up somewhere, soon enough. I could not think how he might manage this, only that he would. Then I thought he might have tipped over the railing, but I did not think there was anything to do about this. Then I thought perhaps he had retired to his suite.

Then I thought of something else. I spotted the captain's wife, across the deck. She was standing, head back, drinking in the storm. She was soaked through. It looked as if she had been out here a long time. I crawled over to her, still mindful of my foot. She was a captivating sight: defiant, and strangely beautiful. I had never seen her in just this way. She leaned down, to see if I was all right. (Perhaps my crawling startled her.) I pulled her toward me and put my mouth on hers. I could not control myself, and she returned my embrace with an equal fire. She tasted of salt and sweat. Soon, we were all over each other, and rolling about the deck like wet tumbleweeds. It was a marvelous, heedless fuck—made resonant by the fiery surf, and by the presence of her husband and my lover just below us.

I told myself that Zorba made me do it. I grabbed at life, as he would; this woman, at this moment, was what I could reach. When it was over, I had forgotten about the writer, and the storm, and the others down in the dining room. I had forgotten about everything. I was Alexis Zorba, filled with life.

The next morning, we could not get the writer to come out of his room. By dumb luck, he had not been spilled overboard, but he would not face the rest of us. We took turns banging on his door, to rouse him.

"Jesus!" I yelled, when my turn came, "what the hell is the matter with you?"

Finally, he cracked the door and motioned me inside. "I can't come out," he said, quite proper. "I seem to have lost my teeth."

"Your teeth? Where the hell did you lose your teeth? They must be around here somewhere."

"That's just it. I'm afraid they won't turn up. Last night, up at the railing, they came out with everything else."

"You vomited your teeth?"

"Dentures, actually," he confirmed.

I looked at the writer's thin, rubbery lips and started to laugh. It was a big laugh—mine and Zorba's—and it filled the sleeping quarters like the thunder from the night before. It seemed to me about the funniest thing I had ever heard. "Ke karai," I said, winding down but laughing still. "Ke fucking karai."

Four days later, we returned to Crete to finish the picture. There was one scene left. Naturally, Michael Cacoyannis did not work in a linear fashion—we played all the scenes at the mines, and then all the scenes at the hut on the beach—but it fell that the final shot of the finished picture was also the last scene on our shooting schedule.

The doctor had not set my foot in a cast, because I was supposed to do a dance in the final scene, on the beach with Alan Bates. Instead, he wrapped me with tape and bandages, thinking that I could remove the wrap at the last possible moment and replace it as soon as we were through. The dance required me to jump and hop, but I could not jump and hop on my broken foot—certainly not with the zest of a passionate Greek like Alexis Zorba.

Cacoyannis was more worried about the scene than my foot, and I could not blame him. He had already kept the crew waiting several days, and did not want to lose any more time or money. "How are we going to do the dance?" he said, when he saw how badly I was injured.

"Don't worry, Michael," I assured him. "Set up the shot, and I will dance. Play the music and you will see."

And I danced. I could not lift my foot and set it down— the pain was unendurable!—but I found that I could drag it along without too much discomfort, so I invented a dance with an unusual sliding-dragging step. I held out my arms, in a traditional Greek stance, and shuffled along the sands. Soon, Alan Bates picked up on the move, and the two of us were lifted by the music and the sea, taken arm in arm to a spiritual place, out of the ordinary and far away. We were born-again Greeks, joyously celebrating life. We had no idea what we were doing, but it felt right, and good. (It goddamn better have felt right, and good, because it was all I could manage on that fucking foot!)

"What the hell was that?" Cacoyannis asked, after the first take.

"Why?" I said. "What's wrong with it?"

"Nothing. Nothing's wrong with it. It's wonderful. What dance is that?"

I thought for a beat before answering. I could not tell all these people I had made it up. Maybe they would change their minds about it, if they did not think it authentic. "It's a Sirtaki," I said, pulling the name from the sea air. I had no idea what it meant, but it sounded Greek.

"A Sirtaki?" Cacoyannis asked, wanting to get it right.

"A Sirtaki."

"Where in hell did you learn that?"

"It's traditional," I lied. "One of the villagers taught it to me."

The director was skeptical, but he did not challenge me further. He did not have to. Instead, he smiled. "Traditional, huh?" he said.

I nodded. What the hell was the difference? It was all Greek to me.

Ride

WHAT A FINE ARC I HAVE MADE! I reach the antique square of Aprilia and map my course in my head. It has been, like life, a meandering loop—filled with hills and valleys, roads not taken, points of departure.

Then I get to thinking. It occurs to me that I am littered here, along this path. Yes, there is rich history beneath my wheels, but the richest of all, I see now, is the history I have lived for myself. To hell with the ancient Roman Empire, to hell with Goths and Visigoths. These hills are about what I have made them, what they have made in me. They are my legacy, and I am theirs. We are hopelessly, endlessly connected, as surely as a man is tied to his children. We are what is left of each other.

Ah, my children. Perhaps it all comes down to them. After all, in the end, what else is there? I think, once more, of Christopher, snatched from my world and into his own, living his life on a separate plane I can only imagine. I think of Christina, the sister he never knew, off somewhere between stops and starts. She married a guy I never liked, divorced, and moved to Seattle to open her own business. She tells me she is doing well, and is as happy as can be, considering. I do not know what she means by this. She also tells me I scare off all the men who show an interest in her, even the ones I never meet. I do not know what she means by this either.

I think of Catalina, in Arizona, married to a decent man. We are close, at last. They have three sweet children. Like her mother, Cati has zealously devoted her life to the Moral Rearmament movement. Her husband shares her views, and neither thinks much of mine. She was once asked to comment on our relationship, and responded in kind. "I push for the moral rearmament of the world," she said, "and my father pushes for our moral disarmament." So there.

I think of Duncan. I do not know where he gets his bluster. Perhaps from me. His fears he gets from his mother. The poor boy is frightened of everything. He is fighting the whole world, constantly. He is outmanned and outarmed, but he does not give a shit. He lives thinking he will one day subdue this immense animal to its knees. Even I am cast in his struggle. I am, alternately, friend and enemy, and while I am among the opposing forces, his willfulness grows. "Nothing will bring me down!" he shouts. "Not even my old man!"

I think of Valentina, my wandering soul. The sadness of Vally's life is that she has yet to find something to believe in, someone to believe in her. She is an actress— or, at least, she means to be. My friends in Los Angeles tell me she has one of the most gripping stage personas of any performer they have ever seen, but she has yet to leap into her craft. She is always studying, studying, study- ing—the perennial student, unable to kick life into gear. I wonder if she is afraid. Strike that: I am sure she is afraid, but of what?

I think of Frankie. He is most like my father. I smile at all the family tree he lugs within him: Mexican, Irish, Indian, Italian. He is my chameleon, at home in all worlds. In the States, he looks and sounds like an American kid. In Italy, he is Roman or Venetian, depend- ing on his mood, or his needs. In Mexico, he struts like he was raised in a barrio. He has strength and authority. When his mother and I used to argue, he could stop us with a single word: "Basta!"

I think of Danny, my inquiring child, grown to an inquiring man. I have often felt that the answer a child gets to his first question limits, and determines, what his next questions shall be. With Danny, the questions keep coming, no matter my response, alighting on his head as if from the sky. Somewhere inside him, there will always be a crazy old Greek, but he is no caricature. He is a big- hearted, big-visioned man, unlucky in marriage but hop- ing for the best. He means to follow his father's path, acting in pictures, but I worry I have not left him a wide enough trail.

I think of Larry, the true artist of the crop. He is gifted in the hands, and sees the world from a marvelous place.

He is not like his brothers. He understands me most of all. He knows what it means to create, to taste life, to give life in return. And, years from now, he will give me the greatest gift of all: a grandson named Christopher. He will know what it means to me. He was never truly gone, my Christopher, and now, in my old age, he will come back to me, and it will take Larry for me to feel I am worth coming back to.

I think of Sean, my child with a German woman whom I will not name. The mother and I parted over what I took to be a deceit. She called me five months later, with the news that she was pregnant. I never knew why she waited so long. She wanted to have an abortion, but I would not allow it. Katherine listened in on the extension and supported my decision. "Tony is responsible for that child," she told the woman. "He will pay for everything." I took one look at Sean and knew he was mine. I gave him my name. He lives in Paris now. I put him through college, but I do not know what his dreams are. Maybe someday he will tell me.

I think of Alex, Sean's brother, the wonderful product of a biological accident with the same German woman. The mother came to visit me with Sean, in Johannesburg, and stayed in my hotel room. We ended up in bed together. For a long time, I would not acknowledge Alex as my own. How could this woman be so sure, after only one night together? She told me herself she was involved with other men. But I could not punish the son for the sins of the mother. What if he was my child? I flew Alex out to California for a visit, and a blood test. Now we are playing catch-up. He is a delightful young man—shy, and giving, and ready to bloom. I regret the lost time. Of all my sons, I sometimes think he could love me the way I loved my father.

I think of my French son with the biblical name, whose identity his mother wishes to protect. We speak on the phone, and exchange letters, but we have yet to meet. This is as his mother wants, and I must respect her wishes, even if it kills me inside. How can a man not know his own son? How can a boy—a young man already—not know his own father? Soon, I pray, we will come together and erase the time lost.

And I think, comically, of my old friend Ruth Warrick, the veteran soap opera actress. We were together for a brief time, during the making of *China Sky* for RKO in 1945, and at the end of our relationship, she had me pegged. Years later, she offered the following comment to a reporter: "Anthony Quinn, in the middle of a love affair with me, once said he wanted to fuck all of the women in the world, and impregnate all of them. I never knew he'd get this far!"

And neither did I, but I truly believe that all my children were sent for a purpose. It is up to me, now, to determine what it is.

I push ahead. My route has finally taken shape, around and about—a touchstone tour!—and these last kilometers are what cyclists and long-distance runners call the home stretch. I have made it this far. The rest should not be too bad, even underneath these thoughts of my children. I try to place their snapshots alongside my prevailing concerns. What do my children know of me, as a man? What pieces of myself have I shown? As a boy, my father was a great mystery to me, and it was not until I became a parent myself that I understood about him. Now, though, I believe I know him fully, mysteries and all. Have I given my children the same ammunition? What will they know of me when I am gone? It is difficult to lump them all together, because I have vastly different relationships with each, but I must consider them in sum. I must filter the man I have been through their shared view. I must see myself as I have let myself be seen.

My, but that is a lousy bargain! That is not like me at all.

Art

I SEE THE WORLD THROUGH MY FINGERTIPS. Through them, the brushes and pencils and chisels run straight to my soul. It is a connection I have known since I was a small boy, sketching Douglas Fairbanks, Ramon Novarro, Pola Negri, or Rudolph Valentino on a crude pad while my father worked. I had a flair for drawing, but it did not end there. To touch, to see, to feel . . . for me, it is all the same.

I do not know when, precisely, I turned to the canvas for my release. Or to stone, or clay. As an actor—reaching fifty, then sixty, then seventy—I worried my artistic muscles would start to atrophy. I stopped winning the girls in my pictures and started winning whole countries. Eventually, there was nothing to win but the part itself, and the simple satisfaction of the craft. I worked new muscles instead of old, and I could see the day when there would be nothing left of me.

It is a miserable thing, for an actor, this business of growing old. I put it off long enough. Perhaps it was more than a putting off. Or less. What I have done, really, is displace the process. I determined that motion pictures could not age me if I supplanted them with something else. And so I started painting again. I toted paints and brushes to my various location shoots, to fill the long, unproductive hours between scenes. Soon, I began sculpting as well, and on my breaks hiked among the dunes or the hills, foraging for stones and scraps of wood, looking to bring the inanimate to life, to transform the mundane into a thing of beauty.

Sometimes, the beauty lay waiting. On Crete, for example, during the making of *Zorba the Greek*, I hunted among dozens of buried cities, collecting fragments of pottery, a small sculpted head, a carved walking stick. I filled boxes and boxes with my finds, and sailed with them on my boat back to Italy like a conquering archaeologist. Most times, though, the beauty lay beyond the find—the trapped forms within a slab of marble, the lines inside a fine piece of wood.

Picasso once said that it takes two men to be a painter: one to paint, and the other with a hammer to tell you when to stop. He also said that time is the best sculptor, and that the wonderful surprises in his painting were in his mistakes. If all of this is so, then I suppose I am more at ease as a sculptor than as a painter. I always know when a stone is finished, but never a painting. And I always leave room for erosion and space in my work. But I must be more careful as an actor than as a painter. An actor's mistakes cannot be ignored, or embellished. As an actor, I must get on with it.

I have shown my work all over the world—with exhibitions in such cities as Honolulu, Vienna, Zurich, Paris, New York, Beverly Hills, Buenos Aires, and Mexico City—but I sometimes feel my only talent is perseverance, a good eye, and an open mind. I know what looks good, what feels right. I do not have a discernible style. Some days I paint like an Indian, some days I paint like a Mexican, some days like an African. I steal from everybody. Picasso, Modigliani, da Vinci . . . they all stole from other masters, from other cultures. There is a saying: a big talent steals, a small talent borrows. I steal, but only from the best.

There is no message to my art, except to keep at it. I am just trying to be. In this, I am no different than anyone else.

When I first moved to these hills, one of my great friends was the noted Italian sculptor Giacomo Manzu. He lived and worked in Ardea, not far from my home. He was always glad to see me on my bicycle. One day, he asked if I would sit for a sculpture. I was thrilled.

Manzu was known for his renderings of Papa Giovanni—Pope John XXIII. The man simply adored Papa Giovanni, and his portraits of him shone in the most spectacular way. In Manzu's gifted hands, the pope looked as if he was lit from within. Manzu's work seemed to glow, from the inside. I had never seen anything like it. He also did some magnificent carvings in black African wood, but his translucent Papa Giovannis made his reputation.

Of course I would sit for Manzu. It was an honor. He took me up to his studio and sat me on a stool. He had everything laid out the way he wanted it. He talked distractedly as he worked the clay. He had a funny habit of wetting his fingers with his tongue, as if turning the pages of a magazine. After a while, his tongue became so thickly coated with wet clay, he could not keep up his end of the distracted conversation. The poor man nearly gagged. I knew each session was over when he had to rinse out his mouth.

After a half-dozen sessions, spread over several weeks, Manzu called me to his studio to see the finished product, which he had placed under wraps. I was terribly excited. He pulled off the cloth with great flair. I looked at the sculpture suspiciously. I have since made several busts of myself, but this was the first time I had seen my own face cast in bronze. It had a lifeless quality about it. I was not sure what to make of it. I wondered why my cheeks did not radiate as Papa Giovanni's. Perhaps I was not close enough to God to give off the same glow.

Still, I was moved by the likeness, and touched by my friend's generous gift. "I'm crazy about it!" I said, drawing on reserves of enthusiasm. I could not thank him enough.

I took the sculpture home and set it down in the garden. Then I called Iolanda out to see our new treasure.

"What is that?" she said, eyeing the bronze.

"It's me."

She looked at the piece again. "No," she said. "It's Gregory Peck."

"No, Iolanda. I've been sitting for Giacomo Manzu. It's supposed to be me."

"I don't care who you've been sitting for, Antonio. That looks just like Gregory Peck."

I stepped back a few paces and tried to look at the piece anew. I studied it from every angle. Goddamn it, Iolanda was right. It did look like Gregory Peck. But I told myself this was not important. What counted was Manzu's generosity, his dedication—the effort of the climb!—his resolve to find my form in a lump of clay, and his refusal to give up when it did not reveal itself.

What counted was that he took the time at all.

Politics

I HAVE LONG BELIEVED that the ways we live are misdirected. We do not know what we want, or what we need, or how to go about claiming either. Our entire Western civilization has veered off course, and I suspect the problem. The starting point is all wrong—what Saroyan called "the foundation"—and we cannot help but go awry. From birth, we are sent to discover for ourselves what no one can teach us.

Consider: our schools are antiquated cinderblock monuments to passive learning; our cities stand as dry, suffocating reminders of our own despair; our workplaces turn on antiseptic, harshly lit assembly lines; and our houses of worship are but soulless reflections of our empty lives. We are not meant to live in boxes, to think in categories, to pray in straight lines, and yet we expect to thrive under the weight of our own sameness, our own routines.

We have become a civilization of limp convictions, and we must all share in the blame. I need look no further than myself. I recognize the failings of man—they are my own!—but I do not do a damn thing about them. Perhaps there is nothing I can do, but I do not even try. Indeed, I look the other way. I go along with the accepted precepts. I honor our system of government, even as I question it. I go along with the notion of our monetary exchange, but I am not sure that I do. I pretend to be a good Christian, but I am not. I long to be a good father and husband, but I do not know how.

Moses himself would not cut it in today's world. From those Ten Commandments we now have a thousand derivatives, countless nerve ends through which we might measure our doubts and pains. We do not know how to live because we have lost what it means to be alive.

The problem starts at the bottom but flows from the top. We invest our leaders—prophets, politicians, star athletes with shoe contracts—with the power to certify our existence, as if we have lost the ability to form our own opinions, to distinguish between right and wrong. As an actor, I have talked about leading through the parts I choose to play, of setting examples through the work, although ultimately this is a lot of crap. The parts I choose are a reflection only of the parts I am offered, and not of any grand message. And yet, somehow, I have managed a kind of leadership—in my acting and my painting, both. This I regard as a good thing, a redemptive thing, but I realize it is just a happy accident. It is in spite of me as much as it is because of me. All art carries with it the power to transform, no matter the artist. Who are we to question the gifts we are given? Who are we to question the artist himself?

Nothing surprises an artist, actors especially. We must remain open to everything, because in our work anything is possible. We hate being human, being earth-bound. We live in such protracted fantasy that we come to disregard our own lives, and the lives of others. They are nothing to us. We live and we die, like everyone else, but we resent it, deeply. In the end, in our work, we can only succeed in creating the essence of life. Life itself remains elusive, just as it seems beyond the reach of man.

How can this be? I believe it all comes down to leadership—or, at least, it has to do with it in an elemental way. We are desperate for guidance, for sublime intervention, and yet our designated leaders are suspect. We build up our celebrities and relish their downfalls. We regard royalty as an accident of birth, dictatorship as an accident of wealth and weaponry, and elected office as an accident of deceit. We have stripped the American presidency of all dignity and purpose. Even the papacy has been diluted.

I have never been a political animal, but others have seen in me the potential for leadership. I did not share their lofty opinion of my abilities, but I listened to what they had to say. (Why the hell not?) Once, not long after the release of *Viva, Zapata!*, I was visited by a group of Mexicans anxious for my help in overthrowing the Mexican government. We were introduced by a man I knew and admired. These people understood about my Mexican childhood, about my parents fighting in the revolution, about the pictures I had made, and felt sure that I was the man to lead them in their cause.

"Will you come down and talk to our people?" their leader asked.

"What about?" I wondered.

"We just want to talk to you and see how you feel, see if you might help us."

I knew enough about Mexican politics to know that it was a one-party country, and that this did not please me, so I agreed to drive down to Tijuana that night to learn more. I had nothing better to do. When we arrived, I was led from one car to another. The driver headed up into the hills. We drove for another three, four hours. I was beginning to wonder if I had been foolish to accompany them.

Finally, just before dawn, we pulled into a remote camp. There were guards all around. We were herded into a kind of clearing, where freshly cut trees served as benches. I stepped from the thicket into a crowd of about two thousand bandoleros. When I was introduced, the men burst into applause. I said a few words in greeting and then stepped aside. It was the strangest scene. I did not know what was expected—and I had not been expecting this.

Next, the host led me to a tent, beyond the clearing, to meet with the organizers. Everyone was crowded around a large table. "We are planning a revolution," he said, "and you are the man to lead us."

My first thought was not for me but for their fight. "You have no chance," I implored. "The Americans will put you down."

"They can't put us down if we are armed."

"What armed? You'll need millions of dollars."

Someone placed a box of American currency on the table. There looked to be a few hundred thousand dollars, in assorted denominations. "Money we have," one of the organizers said. "What we don't have is a voice." Then he looked to me. "You can be our voice."

I thought they were crazy, and that I had been crazy for coming. "I am not your man," I said. "My Spanish is no longer what it was. I don't think I can express myself well enough to help you."

"But you were a preacher once," one of them said. "You can talk to people."

"Yes, I can talk to people, but I don't know whether I can lead them. There's a difference."

"There is no difference. In any language, it is the same."

I promised to think about it, but I knew it was folly. These people needed real guidance, not some imported figure from Hollywood. They were desperate, but I could not help them any more than they could help themselves.

I returned home that morning, and found myself rejecting the notion before I could embrace it. I thought about it, for a few days, but never as seriously as I had in those first moments, in that tent beyond the clearing. The more I removed myself from that scene, the less real it seemed. Soon, the idea that I could lead this band of men to overthrow the Mexican government was laughable, preposterous, and I doubted myself for believing otherwise.

I never learned what happened to the leaders of this effort, or to the bandoleros, but that is not surprising. Back then, there were revolutions hatched in the Mexican hillside almost every day. The group might have disbanded the moment I pulled away, but what counted was that I had been asked to dance at the bullfight, to lead the same battle that had once excited my father. Secretly, I was thrilled. I would have been a very rich man—the money they laid out before me was astounding!—but the money was not the appeal. I turned them down knowing that somebody, somewhere felt that I belonged.

Many years later, during Ronald Reagan's term as governor, I was approached by a respected group of Mexican Democrats and asked to consider a run at California's highest office. I had been active in Screen Actors Guild politics, opposite Reagan, but I had never contemplated a political career. I understood Los Angeles politics, but the business of state government was beyond me. Still, I figured if Ronald Reagan could meet the call, perhaps I should at least consider the overture. In the SAG offices, it was never felt that Reagan would amount to much of a statesman. Bill Holden was always seen as the more skilled politician. There were even some who spoke of Holden as being "presidential timber," but I never heard Reagan discussed in those terms.

And so, with my friend Jose Herrera acting as delegate to the California Democratic Party, I went on an exploratory tour of the state, to see if there might be support for my candidacy. He had scouts lined up throughout California, arranging informal meetings with disaffected voters and malcontents. We visited with a group of militant Mexicans known as the Brown Berets, up in Northern California; I met these people in seedy back rooms, with their guns and bayonets and hateful looks. I met with warring gang leaders in our inner cities, and welfare mothers scrabbling to keep their children safe on the streets of Watts. I met with blacks, Filipinos, Italians, Jews, Greeks, American Indians, Chinese, Japanese . . . just about every minority group the organizers could find.

Surprisingly, these people identified with me, and my supporters started to feel I might give Reagan a run for his office. I would have thought a viable candidate needed something more to build on than a varied acting career, but perhaps the fact that I had played all these different minorities in pictures was enough. In me, these working-class people saw themselves, someone who might look out for their interests, someone who had suffered what they were suffering.

Before long, my supporters took our loose, exploratory efforts to the next level. I still had not decided to give up acting and go into politics, but I remained open to it. This was no small thing. It was a luxurious time for me as an actor—I was working steadily, in big-budget pictures—but I could have walked away from it, for the right reasons. I knew my best years in pictures were behind me.

I started meeting with minority congressmen throughout the state, and with various women's organizations and political action groups, and found that I had something to contribute to the dialogue. One of my big concerns at the time was education: the state university system was in disarray, and urban public schools were crumbling under the weight of busing and overcrowding. I began to believe the bullshit party officials were spreading on my behalf, that I could actually do some good for the working man, that I even stood a chance.

I called on my friend Cesar Chavez, to see if he might set me straight. I had known Chavez since the 1940s, before his rise to prominence. He was a wonderful man, who cared deeply about the rights of the California fruit pickers, but a reluctant leader. He was never comfortable with the symbol he had become. In the beginning, all he wanted was to preserve the jobs and wages of his friends and neighbors. I trusted his instincts, and knew that he was probably the only man in a position to accurately assess my prospects.

Chavez invited me up to see him at his house in Tahachapee, and I went not knowing if he would endorse my candidacy or talk me down from it. I myself did not know which I was hoping for. He lived near a prison, up in the hills. It was, oddly, a peaceful place. When I arrived, he greeted me warmly, and got right to it. "I understand you've been going up and down California," he said, "and the people like you very much."

"I've gotten a lot of support."

"Yes, I know, but what for? Why does a man like you, a true artist, wish to be governor?"

"Because I've been asked." I laughed, knowing there was more truth to this than my joke allowed. "Because I think I could do some good for the people, for the working-class people especially."

He put his hands on my shoulders and looked into my eyes. "Listen to me, Tony," he said. "Politics is not for you. It's a dirty game. It's about making deals. You're a man of principle. You're not a man to make deals. But do this and you'll be making deals every day. You'll bend your principles, and then you'll bend them a little more, and one day you'll be flat on your ass and know that you can't get back up."

"But these people are desperate for someone to lead them," I argued.

"It'll ruin you, Tony," he said.

Perhaps Chavez was right. Perhaps politics would have ruined me. Perhaps the whole rotten business would have left me flat on my ass, unable to right myself. Or, maybe, I might have done some good. I might have been a leader to California's struggling poor, a symbol. I might have quelled some of the seething hatreds that still threaten that entire region. I might have meant something.

I will never know.

Ride

I HAVE LIVED A JOYOUS LIFE, but I am not a joyous man. I consider this as I approach the straightaway of Via Anziate, and wonder at the distinction. I suppose the two are only loosely connected. The joys in my long life have flowed from success, the sorrows from my own uncertainty. Success is an ephemeral thing. If it has made me happy, it has never been for very long. Below the high, always, was the nagging reality that I was built on a cheat.

There is no denying it, not now, not after all these years. Who the hell am I kidding? I have been a cheat in my work, and in my life. Why? I cannot say. Perhaps it has been that in simply longing to lead an army of men in the ultimate Mexican revolution—my father's revolution!—I have excused myself from actually doing the job. Perhaps it has been that by sidling up against lesser challenges I have not had to rise to the big ones.

Most likely it has been that in order not to face the truth, I surrounded myself with toadies and lesser mortals, to remind myself how wonderful I was. Nothing, no one could nourish the deep hunger within me, but at least they could numb some of the pains.

So why am I here, still? What has made me go on living? If my life has been a lie, then what has kept me from putting that bullet through my head? Well, I have an idea. I believe it has to do with a vague sort of balance, a complex of tensions. My life has been rather like this ride, and it remains so. I have taken each hill as if it were my last, turned each corner as if there might be some secret around the bend. I did whatever came next. Eat. Laugh. Work. Bury my father. Work. Eat. Pick the kids up at school. Answer the phone. Learn my lines. Fuck. Paint. Laugh, again. Cry.

There is always something new. There has to be. And if you keep at it, you put enough kilometers between yourself and your troubles that you no longer make the connection. The gaps grow wider with each moment. One hill leads to the next, and you must take them well: the momentum from one will lead you up another. You run from what ails you, what haunts you, and press on. We must keep moving, always. Otherwise the balance would be upset, the tension would break.

And what, for me, has been the steepest hill of all? Love. It is no contest. Where there is nothing but the nearness and the hopelessness of clasping a naked body in your arms, the pain of hunger beneath everything, the dreamless sleep after orgasm. This last is like death, a fleeting pause between the desired and the feared. Indeed, what is death but the longed-for sleep? What are we afraid of but the terror of the unknown? That is the meat of it. We billboard our fears, but these are not the ones that do us in. What gets to us are the unspoken fears of childhood, the private anguish of a man without tether, the fear of the high dive.

And then there is the arch fear: the fear of being afraid. There is no escaping it—not even if you slip into your lowest gear and pedal as fast as you can. That fear sits throned in my heart. It fills the road before me, blocking my path. It hovers over me like a black cloud. There is no way around, over, under, or through it. There is no end to it but the end itself.

THIRTEEN

Ride

MY LEGS FEEL AS IF they belong to someone else. Perhaps they do. The bone of my spine, bruised by the hard bicycle seat, leaves me standing as I ride. (I wonder what shades of black and blue my cheeks have taken on!) My palms have been rubbed to calluses against the tape of the handlebars; there is no grip to my grip; I could not lift a bucket of water to put out my own fire.

I labor through the quaint congestion of Aprilia, past the automobile dealerships on the side of the road, and consider the dishonor in trading my Kline mountain bike for a shiny new sports car. Think of it!—I could put an end to my misery with one swipe of a credit card. Where is the shame in an old man aborting such a long ride? Who would know the difference?

But the shame, for me, would be everywhere, and never-ending. I would know the difference. I might as well shoot myself in the head.

The road pitches uphill, only slightly, and I am forced off the bicycle yet again. Shit! There is a shame in this as well, but I tell myself it is not that great. The ride has left me reducing my failures to inconveniences, or inflating them to nothing at all. I make little deals with myself, to set things right. I cannot manage even the smallest climb, and so I settle on walking. Somehow, I have decided that failure, on this ride, has to do only with stopping. Walking, I can accommodate, as long as I maintain some momentum.

I have all but given up, but I do not despair. I am in denial. It is a phrase I have pirated from too many shrinks, over too many years, but a condition I have always known. In denial, I think of my friend Joe DiMaggio. I used to watch him play, in Oakland, California. We were kids together. He and his brothers were big stars. If you cared about baseball—growing up in that part of the country, at that time—you cared about the DiMaggio brothers. Joe was like no other athlete I had ever seen. If there was ever a man with a shot to outrun time, it was him. He moved with such effortless grace, I thought he would never grow old.

He told me a famous story, one night over dinner. The Yankees were playing a meaningless game, against Detroit, toward the end of the 1951 season. Joe had a bone spur in his right foot, and was unable to move without pain. Stengel had him out in left field, where he would have to cover less ground, and Joe said he spent half the game hoping no one would hit a ball to him. He worried that he would not be able to run or—worse—that he could not lean back, push off his right foot, and make a respectable throw to the infield. The Yankees were up by a run, late in the game, with the Tigers threatening to score: runners on first and second, two outs.

The great ones can tell where a ball is headed from the crack of the bat, and Joe heard the ball coming before he saw it. He knew it would be over his head, and positioned himself to play the carom. In the second it took to accomplish this, he thought about his foot, and his throw. It would not have mattered to any but a few fans if the runner on first came around to score. The Yankees had clinched the pennant; the Tigers were well back in the standings; the players were all anxious to go home.

But it mattered to Joe. He could not make a throw with nothing on it, with the game on the line. Baseball was about winning. His life was about winning. Nothing was more important. So he reached back, pushed off his bad right foot, and let fly with everything he had, knowing that it would probably be the last meaningful throw of his career. The doctors had told him that the bone could not support his full weight, that he should not be playing at all, but the warnings fell away at the thought of losing the game.

Joe threw the runner out at home, and sent the game into extra innings, but the essence of that moment, for a man like Joe DiMaggio, was that he gave himself entirely to it. There are many who think that throw cost Joe his career—he never played another season—but he could not live his life any way but all out, all the time.

I see him now—in restaurants, in New York—and people no longer recognize him. This makes me sad, although Joe does not seem to mind. If he does, he does not let on. He has aged gracefully—but he has aged, there is no denying it. To generations of New Yorkers, he is Mr. Coffee, or a savings bank spokesman, but to me he will always be the young man who rocked back on his bad right foot and risked everything, just to beat a lousy base runner. To me, he will always be an inspiration, and a gentle reminder that there is no profit in pulling back, in saving your best shot for another day, in playing it safe.

"Nice story," I hear. "I'm all broken up." It is the kid in me, here to rattle me from the safety of my musings, to taunt me back onto the bicycle.

"What do you want?" I ask.

"From you, old man? I don't want anything from you. That's just the problem. There's nothing left to you."

I know he is full of shit, and I will not let him get to me. "You want the truth," I say. (I have him figured out.) "You want me to say what it is that's been gnawing at us, all these years."

"Is that so?"

"Damn right, it's so. And I'll tell you something else. I'm not gonna give you the satisfaction."

He smiles like a devil. "Suit yourself," he says, and disappears behind a neat row of sparkling Ferraris.

(Jesus, these car dealerships are all over the place!)

"Fuck you!" I shout after the boy. He cannot hear me, so I shout it again, louder. I do not need to be reminded of my own failings. I know I am no DiMaggio. I too have played in pain. I have played to win. And yet, here I am, trying to salvage a draw. At this point, that is all I can hope for, but it is my own doing. At every turn, I have taken the easy way around—with Katherine and Iolanda, with Suzan and Maggie and all the others. I tried to win with my own children, to mislead them from my own cowardice. Even in my work, lately, I take the downhill roads. One *Zorba* buys me a dozen rotten pictures. In the studio, now, it is the same. I paint for myself, but also for money. I used to find the sculpture in a piece of stone, but these days it finds me.

The boy is right to badger me, but I am free to think for myself, to focus dead ahead, to rewrite my history so that it does not drive me mad. I will the boy away, to never return. To hell with him. To hell with everyone. To hell with me.

I keep walking, pushing the bicycle. To my left, in the portico to a family-style restaurant, is the headless statue of a Roman empress, a bird on its shoulders. The statue is a cheap imitation, of the sort found in porticoes of most family-style restaurants, but I am pulled to the space where the head had been, to the bird. Once, on those stone shoulders, there must have been an extraordinary testament to young Roman beauty. Now the face of the girl is gone, and the bird gives the body a strange kind of life. The statue sings and lives once more.

I climb back on the bicycle and continue pedaling, thinking there is hope for all of us who have turned to stone.

Harlem

THE CAMPAGNA IS SWARMING with prostitutes. The girl to my right is nothing special. I have seen her before. She roams this piece of Via Anziate, outside Aprilia, as if it were her own. The two girls this morning had some soft edges to them; this girl is all angles, all business.

Still, when I pass, her dark, angelic features manage a shudder throughout my tired body. She is Moroccan, I can tell, and I glide by thinking of the terrible ways her people are treated here. The treatment is not undeserved, at least not by extension. The Moroccans raped this region, and the Italians have never forgotten it. Her people are tolerated, but not trusted.

Her face takes me back over twenty years, to the mean streets of New York's Upper West Side. Here, on a cobblestone street, against the backdrop of green hills and open sky, she is a stunning black princess, anxious to bestow her gifts on any stranger who would have her. In Harlem, the same face is desperate and worn. It is the face of a thousand hookers, working for a meal, or a fix, or a place to sleep. I know those faces too, but they do not belong here.

Once again, I am returned to Harlem. It is an unfortunate link, but it is so. Specifically, I am reminded of the girls I hired as extras in a picture I shot there called *Across 110th Street*. I played a crooked cop, caught trying to serve the public interest and a Mafia-backed numbers racket. I was also executive producer of the picture, and it was in this role that I came to hire these girls, and to learn some of the brutal ways of the city streets.

The picture had a story underneath it, and a sucker-punch line. The story first. I took the job because I thought the script offered a gritty, realistic look at early 1970s life in the urban ghetto, and because I did not think it would get made without me. Once I signed on, I wanted to do it right, so I hired a handful of the biggest black actors in movies at that time: Bill Cosby. Sidney Poitier. Harry Belafonte. Sammy Davis Jr. These guys, I felt sure, would bring people into the theaters, and the world would finally see what the city was like north of Ninety-sixth Street.

Bill Cosby was my friend, and I was anxious to work with him. I had known him for years. We used to sneak into football games together, at the Los Angeles Coliseum. We could have bought tickets, or requested passes through the Rams' offices, but Cosby thought it was more fun to hop the gates. I was always frantic about it. I worried we would be caught, but he told me I was being ridiculous. "What are they gonna do to us, Tony?" he always asked.

I never had an answer, so I played along. The trick, Cosby said, was to look like you belonged, so we marched ourselves around like VIPs. We went down to the field, and joked with the players on the sidelines. We waved to the crowd, and signed autographs. No one ever challenged us, or asked us to leave, and I believe the thrill of those afternoons, for Bill Cosby, was in our getting away with something. The game itself was secondary. In this, he was like a troublemaking kid—and so was I.

But we were not meant to work together on this pass. Our production was shaken off course by forces we could not predict or control. This was a time of great unrest in New York City, a time when the Black Panthers and other militant groups controlled the black community. And it was not just the gang leaders. All the black racketeers and neighborhood thugs had their own opinions. They objected to our casting of these big Hollywood stars. They said Cosby and the others did not know these streets, could not play these scenes. Who knows, maybe they were right, but we would not have listened to them if we were not made to.

We listened because we needed the community leaders and local numbers guys on our side. They ran that part of town, and it would have been nothing for them to shut us down. If they did not want our trucks shooting on their streets, then our trucks would not make it down their streets. We were already in for a hard time. We did not want to make things worse.

And so we wound up casting a powerful young actor named Yaphet Kotto to play my partner, the good cop role that was to have gone to Sidney Poitier. We signed a gangly kid named Antonio Fargas to play Sammy Davis's small-time hoodlum, and a strong character actor named Paul Benjamin to be the leader of the black gang, the part that was intended for Harry Belafonte. It turned out to be an exceptional cast, and quite a few of these actors went on to long, distinguished careers, but at the time, I was furious at being denied the chance to work with all these superstars. How dare these thugs tell me who I could hire for one my pictures! It was an outrage, but one that I swallowed to get the picture done.

As it happened, casting was the least of our worries. We had a devil of a time with our location shots. The entire picture was shot on location, even the interiors, and the local gangs were constantly harassing us. It was not enough to muscle us from Sidney Poitier, probably the greatest black actor in pictures at that time. No, these guys also wanted to muscle us from their turf, from their action. To them, it was their show.

We paid out all kinds of money, to grease our way into their neighborhoods. After a while, these under-the-table payments put us dangerously over budget, and United Artists was set to pull the plug. I was terribly upset. We needed about one million dollars to complete the picture, which was a lot. Today, one million here or there is nothing. Back then, it was everything.

Now, the sucker punch. During this time, I had struck

up an unconventional friendship with Frank Costello, the notorious Mafia boss. Guys in my line of work were always attractive to guys like Frank, and I had developed a fondness for a lot of these mob characters. Plus, we had our respect for Mama Borgia in common, and knew a lot of the same people. We took to meeting for breakfast each morning, at Rumpelmayer's, and it was Frank who really broke ground for us on this picture. He got us into Harlem, opened some doors for us, but even his reach extended only so far. We were still being blackmailed by the small-timers, who threatened to choke the streets to keep our trucks out of town.

One morning, I told Frank about our money troubles. "United Artists is going to pull the picture," I said.

"Over money?" he asked. Frank was a sweet man, but money did not mean the same thing to him as it did to other people.

"Sure, over money. What else?"

"How much?"

"About a million."

"Oh, that's nothing." He was loose and easy, and I was infuriated at the way we were being screwed out of the picture.

"What the hell do you mean, it's nothing?" I barked back. "I can't shoot without it."

"What the hell, Tony. I'll give it to you. Just calm down and enjoy your breakfast."

How do you like that?—a legendary figure like Frank Costello was perfectly willing to hand me a million dollars, just because he did not want to see me so upset. I knew it would not be as simple as that, but I was still touched by the gesture. "I can't take your money, Frank," I said.

"Why not?"

I told him it would not look right, taking a check from him and mingling it with studio funds. I told him that sort of thing was not done.

"What check?" he said. "I'll give you cash."

"What am I gonna say? They'll ask where I got the money."

"For Christ's sake, don't tell them anything. Just put it in the bank and finish the picture."

I smiled at his largesse. "If I do that," I said, "then you'll have a big piece of the picture."

"Fine," he said. "Good. Make me a millionaire." He laughed.

But I could not take Frank Costello's money, even if it troubled me to turn him down. "What if I can't pay you back?" I said. "The studio won't let me sign for anything."

"No contracts, Tony. We shake hands."

"Ah, good," I said, as if this made me feel better. "But still, supposing I can't pay you back. What then?"

"Well then, my friend," he said, a wide smile filling his face like a sunrise, "then you send me back the hand."

He laughed again, but below the punch line a part of me felt duped, a little. I was taken in by my friend's show of generosity, and for a moment I had let my guard down to accept his kindness on its face. With me, Frank Costello was a lovely man, and I adored him, but I should have known there would be a price for his benevolence. I should have seen it coming.

We got our million dollars someplace else. We finished the picture. I kept my hand. I never got to work with Cosby or Poitier. The picture was tolerated by critics. And here I am, twenty years removed from those unsettled times, obliged to remember it all at the sight of this hardened black angel. The faces flash back in an instant, and then fade.

"Buon giorno, bellezza!" I call out, as I pedal past.

The girl looks up and blows a perfunctory kiss. I blow one back, and then I smile, remembering.

A Fat Mexican

JESUS, WHAT A MISERABLE DECADE, the 1970s. The effort in my legs is the effort of those years, back to claim me. I could not buy a decent picture. I could not get a woman to look at me. I could not even face myself. In the mirror one morning I could see what I had become: a weathered cartoon, desperate to reclaim what was once his, cast by the fates to leave his best work behind him.

It hit me unaware. I had worked steadily since *Zorba*, and in some memorable pictures: *A High Wind in Jamaica*, with James Coburn; *The 25th Hour*, with Virna Lisi; *Guns for San Sebastian*, with Charles Bronson; *The Secret of Santa Vittoria*, with Anna Magnani (produced and directed by the gifted Stanley Kramer); *A Dream of Kings*, with Irene Papas (directed by my good friend Danny Mann). But the parts dried up as I approached my sixtieth birthday, loosely coinciding with my growing disinclination to pursue them. Indeed, I could not see the point in playing old men on screen when I rejected the role for myself.

Too, I worried that I had lost a step in my acting, that my time had passed. It happened to Barrymore, and De Mille, and now it was happening to me. Others must have sensed it, because the few scripts I saw were mostly silly distractions. Even my own agent did not believe in me, and these guys believed in anything for their ten percent. Once, he tried to convince me to take a supporting role in a picture, after an offer to play the lead had been withdrawn. I refused to settle for the smaller part.

"Face it, Tony," he said, in making his case. "These days, you're nothing but a fat Mexican."

The man had represented me for thirty years. In better days, he had called me "Tiger," but he finally showed himself and what he thought of me. I swallowed hard and took the lesser role. It was better than nothing.

I worked only in fits and starts, only when I needed the money, or the distraction. I spent most of my days in my Italian retreat, with Iolanda and our three boys, thinking about what was no longer mine: youth, vitality, hope, presence. These had come and gone for me, and I did not think I would ever replace them.

I was faithful to Iolanda by default. I was terrified of approaching another woman, struck vain by my gray hairs and sagging muscles. The bags under my eyes were like satchels. Who the hell would want anything to do with me? Oh, there were the usual star-fuckers and sycophants, but no one who had anything to offer, no one who wanted anything more from me than my name. I was prepared to shrivel up and die.

Until Dominique—my redemption! Dominique Sanda was an alluring French movie queen, cast to play my daughter-in-law in an Italian picture called *The Inheritance*, directed by Mauro Bolignini. She was a brilliant young actress and a fine beauty. I was terribly nervous about meeting her. It was 1975, and just about the worst period in my life. It had been a long time between pictures, and a long time between loves. I had lost a great deal of money in a string of bad investments, and saw no easy way to earn it back. I could not land an important picture if my life depended on it—and I believed, at last, that it did.

Finally, I was offered this part of an elderly man, who becomes involved with his son's wife, and I was embarrassed to have to take it. It was not a very big part, and the producers offered me a nothing salary, but it was all I had. And they would not even give me the part outright! I had to go and meet Miss Sanda, to win her approval. It struck me as an immense indignity, to have to audition like this, but Dominique Sanda was a big star at that time, and my star had fallen.

I was sweating when I went up to see her. I hated what

I had become. I had been having trouble with my teeth, and worried Miss Sanda would smell the rot in my mouth and refuse me the part, but she set me at ease right away. She stood to greet me, and hurried into my arms. Then she gave me the most wonderful kiss. I was petrified she would pull back in disgust, but she lingered well beyond my worry. Then she tenderly wiped her gloss from my lips with her fingertips. "Signor Quinn," she said, in a delicious voice, "I have loved you forever. I have always wanted to work with you. We will be wonderful together."

It was, without question, the most welcoming embrace I had ever received, and it did not end there. Dominique Sanda brought me back to life with that one long kiss, and so began a rejuvenating relationship. We were together throughout the shoot, and well after we wrapped the picture. She visited me on location in the Middle East, on the set of an Iranian picture called *Caravans*. I visited her in Paris. She was endlessly interesting, absorbed in art and literature and world affairs. She had the most remarkable white skin. She was a tonic, sent to jump-start my passion for life and love and work. She loved me as I was, and not as what she wanted me to be.

It is a blessing, to be loved just enough, by just the right woman, at just the right time. And, thus blessed, I moved into the next phase of my life with renewed confidence. I was a snake once more, shedding my skin, trying on my new guises. I would be an old man, if that was next on my list, if it was not too late.

I would have it all. Again.

It took no time to accept my new persona, but playing old men on screen was a tough adjustment. For some months, I fought it. Most actors do, and few recognize it for what it is. I invented whole new categories of reasons not to work: Rome in the winter was too dreary; Hollywood in the summer was too hot; New York year round was too oppressive. I did not like the script, or the director, or one of my projected costars. The combinations were never right. Indeed, just after *The Inheritance*, I turned down what would become one of my most identifiable roles. I was asked by Lee Thompson, who had directed me so haphazardly in *The Guns of Navarone*, to play the part of billionaire shipping magnate Aristotle Onassis in *The Greek Tycoon*, opposite Jacqueline Bisset.

It was a part meant for no one else, but I resisted. I told myself it was unseemly, to play a picture based on the life of someone I knew. During the Kennedy administration, I had been on friendly terms with the president and first lady. Through his brother-in-law, Peter Lawford, the president developed a taste for Hollywood doings, and I fit right in. I campaigned for Jack Kennedy, and sent him my rambling, recorded diatribes, on reel-to-reel tapes, to which he would occasionally respond. It was a coldly intimate correspondence, but a correspondence just the same, and I cherished the thought that I might have had something to contribute to the national dialogue.

Over the years, I kept in contact with Jacqueline Kennedy, through the New York social circle. After her marriage to Onassis, we often found ourselves at various gatherings of prominent Greeks, in the States and abroad. After all, *Zorba* had cast me as the most prominent Greek in pictures, and she was now married to the most prominent Greek in fact, and it was only natural that our paths cross from time to time.

I went up to see her, to discuss the picture. I did not need her permission, but I did not want to go against her wishes. She served cucumber sandwiches. We talked about the turns our lives had taken. It was all rather dainty, and refined. Then, sweetly, she asked me not to play the part of Onassis. "They'll do the picture with or without you," she said, "but with you they'll have so much more credibility."

I was touched that she had placed her feelings in just these terms, and agreed to back away from the project. Now, of course, I realize that I was looking for any excuse not to have to play a monstrous old bastard who would claim an American icon for himself. The studio moguls had offered me a million dollars, at a time when I was desperate for money, but I turned them down. I would not age gracefully, even at these prices. And now that Jacqueline Onassis herself had asked me to decline the part, I could blame my inactivity on her.

Some weeks later, I was in the south of France, lunching with Iolanda and Simone Signoret, when Jackie walked into the restaurant. It was the strangest coincidence, but I never believed in coincidences. Iolanda noticed her from across the room. "There's your girlfriend," she said. Poor Iolanda was always suspicious, about everyone.

I turned to see which woman had roused my wife's jealousy, and was surprised to see the former first lady. I stood to greet her, but she walked brusquely past our table. It was as if I was not there. Perhaps, for her, I was not. Perhaps she did not expect to see me, there in the south of France, at that time. I could understand this. Many people stood as Jacqueline Onassis passed their tables. It must have been a fact of her life. I myself had learned to look past the well-meaning glances and glad-handing of strangers, in order to concentrate on my own business, so I could only speculate on what it was like to move about in her world, the focus of such constant attention.

Iolanda took it as a slight. "For that, you are turning down a million dollars?" she said, incredulous.

"What?" I wondered. "What did she do that's so terrible?"

"She looked right through you. She did not even smile."

"She's a busy woman. It's a crowded place. Probably she didn't even see me."

Iolanda looked at Simone Signoret and shrugged. "He is a foolish man, my husband," she said. "He is so concerned with appearances, with doing the right thing, he does not recognize when he has been snubbed."

I had not been ashamed for myself, but Iolanda's wrath became my own. It was as if she was challenging me, daring me to take the part despite my better judgment, despite my word. It was not the decent thing to do, but she made me feel it was the only thing to do. Plus, the coincidental timing was too much to ignore. I took it as a sign.

I excused myself from the table and went to a telephone. I woke up my agent, back in Los Angeles. "Tell them I'll take the part," I said.

"What part?" He was disoriented, and half-asleep. There was a time when there were so many offers outstanding he could not have known what I was calling about, but this time no other viable parts were on the table. How could he not have known? It had only been a few weeks since Lee Thompson's call.

"Onassis," I said.

"You'll play Onassis?"

"Of course, I'll play Onassis. Who the hell else could play Onassis?"

And so it was settled. I would play the fat Greek, Iolanda would save face on my behalf, and Jacqueline Onassis would never talk to me again.

Tripoli

IT TOOK THE FAITH OF 750 million Muslims to restore my faith in myself.

Just as my Italian sojourn helped to restart my career more than twenty years earlier, so my Middle Eastern period saw me through these recent stumbles, and returned me to firm financial ground.

I owed my comeback to a crazy Arab director named
Moustapha Akkad. He called me to Lebanon to play the
lead in *Mohammed, Messenger of God*, launching a prof-
itable working relationship. The picture itself was a gar-
bled retelling of the life of the Muslim leader, with epic
touches borrowed from Cecil B. De Mille. It did virtually
no business in the States (where it was released as *The
Message*), outside of a few urban areas with significant
Muslim populations, but the wide international release
made me a star in the Arab world.

It also made a tremendous amount of money for
Moustapha Akkad and me, and we looked to repeat the
winning combination. Even as we wrapped on
Mohammed, we tried to get started on our next project. At
the time, Akkad had the backing of Muammar al-Qaddafi,
and was anxious to develop another property to spark the
interest of the Libyan government. He was willing to give
me a cut of our next picture, if I could help him develop a
viable idea. I had heard that Qaddafi held a fanatical interest in Omar Mukhtar, the guerrilla leader who had suc-
cessfully forestalled Mussolini's advances into Libya.
Mukhtar was a wonderful historical character—an elderly
teacher who was called on by his people to defend them in
battle. He could not ride a horse or shoot a rifle, but he
was Libya's hope. For me, he stood as an ideal role: he
was the right age, out to prove that it was never too late to
teach an old dog new tricks.

The problem with Mukhtar's story was that
Moustapha Akkad had no sense of history. He had no idea
who Omar Mukhtar was, or what he meant to the Libyan
people. I had to give him a crash education, in order that
he might make his pitch to Qaddafi. And yet for all his
failings as a student of history, Akkad was a shrewd busi-
nessman, and a keen student of human behavior. He had
the idea to appeal to Qaddafi's national pride, and
arranged for me to be photographed as Mukhtar, using

archival materials as a guide. He hired the best makeup men and costumers he could find, and when the pictures were ready he went to see Qaddafi. He brought with him a pile of history books, and maps of the countryside, with my pictures stuffed inside.

Akkad baited Qaddafi with a number of decoy projects, saving the Mukhtar pitch for last. Then, in the middle of his presentation, he "accidentally" dropped his pile of books, leaving the loose photographs spread on the floor in full view.

"What's this?" Qaddafi wondered, picking up several of the shots.

"Oh, that's nothing," Akkad said, gathering up his things. "These are just some pictures of one of your generals, from a long time ago. I believe there's a museum here, in his honor."

"Omar Mukhtar. Yes, he is one of my heroes. But where did you get these pictures? I have a collection, from all over the world, and I've never seen these."

"These I got from England," Akkad lied. "I have an idea for a picture I want to do. These are to help me in my research."

"A picture about Omar Mukhtar? Tell me, you are planning a picture about him?" The Libyan leader was very excited.

"I've been thinking about it."

"I will back it," Qaddafi declared. "Make a list of what you need and I will see that you get it."

And so we were in business. Akkad cut us a wonderful deal. He told Qaddafi he wanted to shoot in the desert, but worried there was no place to house the cast and crew on location, so he factored into his budget construction costs for an instant village—with bungalows, tennis courts, swimming pools, and every conceivable luxury. With Qaddafi's money, he built a first-class facility, out in the middle of nowhere, and then sold it back to the

Libyan government for tens of millions. It was a brilliant scam.

The making of *Lion of the Desert*, the story of Omar Mukhtar, was a protracted ordeal, with some amusing distractions. For much of the months-long shoot, we were headquartered in Tripoli, at the Beach Hotel. Yassir Arafat, the Palestinian Liberation Organization leader, lived in the suite next door, and we shared an elevator from time to time, or a walk down the hall to our rooms. It was during these chance meetings that I came to know the reach of my pro-Israeli stand back in Jordan, on the set of *Lawrence of Arabia*, all those years ago. Arafat knew who I was and what I stood for.

After a while, we greeted each other on a first-name basis. Arafat never invited me to his room, and we rarely exchanged anything more than pleasantries, but I found him to be an extremely intelligent, likable man. And funny. The man was always laughing, and quick with a joke, and I used to marvel at my fortune, to be swapping one-liners with one of the most enigmatic leaders on the world stage, my neighbor.

At the time, in Tripoli, there was a sizable American colony of resident businessmen and long-term tourists, and several of the local establishments catered to various Western interests. One of the biggest interests, inevitably, was alcohol. Hard liquor was forbidden in the Western hotels, but as far as I could determine, the Libyan government secretly imported whiskey for the German and American workers out in their desert oil fields, correctly thinking that the men would not work without their booze. Whether Libyan officials were directly responsible for these shipments was never made clear, but they certainly looked the other way from the wide distribution.

There was also an underground network of bootleggers and back-door operators, who made themselves known to hotel guests. Legitimate Arab shopkeepers even sold the equipment necessary to set up small bathroom distilleries.

I had no stomach for the homemade mash, and started asking after one of the more prominent bootleggers. After all those weeks out in the desert, and long hours on the set, I was anxious for a real drink.

Late one night, at the agreed time, there was a knock on my door. On the other side, I expected to find a seedy little man with whiskey bottles stitched into his too-large overcoat. Instead, I got an eyeful. There to greet me was an absolutely gorgeous blond girl, probably in her late twenties. She was decidedly American, and so completely sure of herself, I thought she might step inside without an invitation.

"I understand you wanted to see me, Mr. Quinn," she said.

My first thought, I am ashamed to admit, was that she was one of the high-ticket hookers working the Western hotels. It never occurred to me that she was my bootlegger. There was nothing to do but play along and see where things went. I asked her in.

She sat down and crossed her long legs. "I can provide you with whatever you need," she said. Her double-entendre was plain.

"Meaning?"

"Meaning you tell me, and I will have it delivered."

"You're the bootlegger?" I asked, making sure.

"You were expecting someone else?"

"No," I stammered, "it's just that I did not expect to find someone like you in that line of work."

She explained that her father worked out in the oil fields, and that she supplied him with homemade and imported varieties from her many contacts. What she had left over she sold to Western tourists and interlopers like myself. It was a successful enterprise. "The stuff I make is just as good as the regular bottles," she insisted. "Guaranteed."

I told her I preferred the regular bottles, just the same. She set me up for the next few days and promised to return. When she did, we struck up a conversation. We talked and drank well into the night. We were together for the next several months. Her name was Sandy, from Texas. She was the funniest, most spirited girl. She was not afraid of anyone, or anything. She introduced me to her family, and to her favorite local haunts. We had some marvelous adventures together. With Iolanda back in Italy, she was quite pleasant company.

Sandy tooled around the desert like it was her back-yard, and what was remarkable was the way the Arabs left her alone. It was hard to miss what she was up to, but she was held to a different standard than the local women. Even in Tripoli, I guessed, a girl looking like Sandy could get away with a lot. The other remarkable thing was that she never gave me a break on her prices. She shared what we had, when we were at her place, but she charged me top dollar for my own stores.

In the end, Qaddafi got his money's worth on the picture, despite the shrewd dealings of Moustapha Akkad. *Lion of the Desert*, with supporting turns by Oliver Reed, Irene Papas, Rod Steiger, and John Gielgud, went on to become one of the biggest Arab pictures of all time. It remains so. To this day, I am stopped by more people who know me as Omar Mukhtar than as any other character. In the States, of course, this reception is somewhat diluted, but audiences abroad will take me for Mukhtar quicker than Alexis Zorba, or Eufemio Zapata, or Zampano the strongman.

It has been a gift, this warm embrace from the Arab people. Once again, I lifted myself into the next phase of my career quite by accident: I would play old men on screen, but with a purpose, and if I could not get the girl in the story, I could at least claim her behind the scenes.

Under these terms, I could live with myself for the next while.

Ride

IT IS GETTING LATE. It is not quite twilight, but the sky has taken on the pale yellow of approaching sunset. In another hour or two, the hills of Rome will be dotted with footlights and floodlights. I will step into my garden and look out at the horizon as if at a forest of Christmas trees. If the night is clear, the bright lights of Rome will fill the northwest sky with a halo of portent and purpose. I will sip at a glass of wine made from my own grapes and be humbled by the view.

But I am not there yet. First I must loop through Ariccia and into Albano, hard by the Lago di Castelo. Up ahead, I can make out the parapets of Castel Gandolfo, the pope's storied summer palace. His Holiness is a fine neighbor, but I could do without some of the Vatican guards. I am reminded of a story. Once, on a walk around the lake, I was stopped by a half-dozen burly men, on patrol. The pope was out for a stroll of his own, they said, and they needed to clear the area.

I accepted the need for security, but I was in a mischievous temper. These men all knew who I was. Indeed, *The Shoes of the Fisherman*, in which I played a fictional Russian priest who rises from political exile to become Pope Kiril I, was said to be required viewing on Vatican VCRs. I felt I was as entitled to saunter around Lago di Castelo as any man—as any pope.

I grabbed the biggest and burliest guard by the sleeve. If I was anyone else, he would surely have drawn his weapon, but he knew I was not dangerous or crazy. "You tell your pope," I said, playing at menacing, "that I was pope long before he was, and that I will walk around this lake any time I choose!"

Then I broke from my menacing and started to laugh. The big guard joined in, and soon we were all laughing. That is how it is, here on the outskirts of Rome, where the pontiff walks the same path as the rest of us. It is difficult for an outsider to understand, this papal proximity, but it is impossible for the locals to ignore. We live in the pope's shadow. Castel Gandolfo, even vacant, stands in judgment of us all.

The vendors rimming the lake are boarding up their carts for the night. They have been out since first light, servicing the whims of cyclists, tourists, commuters . . . perhaps even popes. Everything is for sale here—canned soda, Porcini mushrooms, baskets, newspapers, light bulbs—but there is nothing I need. Besides, I am on the flats now, pumping hard. There is no reason to stop, and every reason not to. I have found my second wind. (Or is it my third?) My legs, suddenly, are the legs of a young man. The aches of this afternoon have congealed into a new determination, a new strength. I just might ride forever.

But of course I cannot. This last-gasp adrenaline rush is a delusion, I know. It would be nice to avoid the realities of my life, to steer away from Katherine's diabolical packing crate, to put off any confrontations with Iolanda or my children, to keep pedaling into my own sunset. And yet if I have learned anything on this ride it is that there is no safety in living, that in the end about all we can hope for are the balls to face the truth.

It occurs to me that there are only two dominant tragedies in life: the mistakes a man makes, and the steady passage of time. But everyone makes mistakes and everyone grows old, so where does that leave me? Perhaps the crux is that the older I get, the less willing I am to be lulled and mellowed by the past. Perhaps it is that the less I have had, the less I will become.

I sometimes think that my life is one long script, and as I spin my last kilometers toward Vigna S. Antonio, I can foreshadow my own ending. Most of my days have been spent racing past similar stage sets. I was always on some lot or other, acting out my lines, listening to directions hurled by my conscience. There has been an interminable quality surrounding every part of the progression, but now that the action is nearly over, I see that everything has moved with remarkable celerity. The time between childhood and old age was swift, the intermissions were confusing.

I am not a calm man. I am not a tolerant man. I never learned the patience to take the good with the bad, or that I even had to accept them both. I have known a great many less talented people who have made a success of living, and yet I continue to struggle. Why? What is it about me that makes my life so damn hard? Well, now that it is perhaps too late, I believe I have the reason. I have been too concerned with other matters to fully live for myself, too busy with illusion to fret over reality.

Yes, that is it. It must be.

I believe a man writes the story of his life not in order to remember, but in order to forget. It is a literary purging, and I see it through to cleanse myself of my ancient demons and emerge fully formed, on a blank page. I am too wizened to give a shit about how I have evolved, only that I have. What the hell does it matter what went into me as long as I know what I am? I am Anthony Quinn— son, brother, fruit picker, student, lover, actor, husband, father, sculptor, painter, arrogant bastard. I am Mexican, Irish, Indian, American, Italian, Greek, Spanish, Chinese, Eskimo, Muslim. I am all these things, and more. And less.

But what am I most of all? Well, at my core, I suppose

I am an artist. That has been my beginning and it will be my end. The drive to create has defined me, and left me with no time to work free of the agonies facing other men. A true artist must conquer or be destroyed, create or die, move or be caught in the crush. In a man's work there are not only the seeds of life but also the seeds of death. The power of creation that sustains us will also destroy us, like a leprosy, if we leave it to rot in our vitals.

Know thyself, the philosopher said. It is sound advice, in any language, but hard to follow. I honestly tried to know myself—again and again—but I kept changing. There was always something new to throw into the mix, something old to discard. I was never the same man from one day to the next, which is perhaps why I am desperate to know the man I have become, finally. This is it. I have lived a flurry of images, but I will go out in freeze frame.

I reach the mouth of Vigna S. Antonio and lean into it. This is the last stop of all, the place to shout for joy or cry unashamed, the final deposit for my few accomplishments and great bag of failures.

Home.

This morning, on the climb, the debilitating hill from my house to the main road nearly sent me to my feet in fatigue, but now, on the way down, it is like a chute. I quit pedaling and kick my legs into a V. I am a child again, sliding on a giant roller coaster, free of trouble and despair. It is a moment of sweet victory, and triumph, and yet is also an elaborate distraction.

At the bottom of the hill, I will face the truth. I will lift the bicycle onto its hook in the shed and walk across the garden to the house. I will go out to the garage, back to the house, back to the garage. I will sip from my own wine and gather my resolve. I will circle Katherine's neatly packed box of mementos and finally crack into it. I will cut my finger on the corrugated cardboard. I will sift through my past. I will look at old pictures, and study old notes. I will remember about the eggs, about the stinking canal, about the dirt floor. I will smell my father's coat, and feel its warmth. I will see myself as a boy and justify what I have become. (With my luck, the kid will turn up himself, to argue his own case!) I will look on the faces of my father, and Dona Sabina, locked in their own freeze frames, and see what they have to tell me. I will think of Christopher. I will be reminded, in the margins of my books, of Sylvia and Katherine and all the women I could not claim as my virgin, all the virgins I could not claim as my woman. I will reconsider my wistful musings, set to paper for that years-ago writing class, to stack what I have lived against what I had thought. . . .

"How I'd Live" (1935)

HERE, AT THE TOP OF THE BOX, flattened between the hard covers of one of my diaries, are the handwritten pages I scribbled for Selma Thorpe's writing class, in Los Angeles, all those years ago.

I start to read, and between the lines I am met by a strange reality:

"I'd wake at six, before light, and step outside into the cold morning air. I'd walk and walk, finally reaching to the top of the highest hill. Below, in the valley, I'd see the lights in the kitchens and imagine the women turning fat, sizzling bacon in their frying pans. Children would be getting ready for school, men for work. Cars would not start. I'd hear the cursing of the men over the whir-wha-whauhauhauha of the engines. I'd see the city up and running.

"Then, I'd race down the hill, singing, feeling good and healthy. I'd return home soaked through, the perspiration like soft, warm oil all over my body. I'd take a warm bath, and steal another few hours of sleep.

"The doorbell would wake me, at about ten. It would be well known among my friends that I breakfasted late, and that all were welcome to join me. On this morning, I would be joined by a singer, an actor, a doctor, a prize-fighter, an artist, a scientist and a few other guys interested mainly in breakfast and only secondarily in conversation. There would be a lot of talk, and laughter, and coffee all around.

"At noon, the others would leave as my painting teacher arrived. We would go to my workshop—a spacious studio, with a grand fireplace to one side. The floor of the studio would be of wide ship's planking, washed daily to leave the room smelling of damp wood and turpentine. The entire north side of the slanting roof would be of glass. We would work on my canvas for about an hour, and then retire to discuss the history of art. I'd know more than most—not just the obvious names that the fakes at the galleries are always eulogizing, but the forgotten ones, the brave visionaries who started new schools and were then surpassed by their pupils: Diriano, Van Meeker, and Giotto, another lost Mexican.

"My daughters would come, to tell me my lesson was through. With the instructor gone, I'd kiss my girls twenty-seven times each, praying to God that nothing would ever happen to them. We'd laugh and play for about an hour.

"Later, I'd retire to my office upstairs with my secretary. There I'd sign huge checks to my favorite charities. There would also be a check or two for some worthy individuals: a Mexican girl who wants to be a lawyer to help her brother in San Quentin, a childhood friend whose family garment business has hit a snag. People would come to me with their troubles, and I'd do what I could.

"Then, the director of the picture I'd be scheduled to start shortly would come upstairs to go over his working script. He'd listen to my every suggestion, and agree wholeheartedly. He could not be a very good friend of mine.

"Before dinner, I'd be visited by an authority on military affairs. He'd sit outside the bathroom as I washed and dressed for dinner, barking the latest news from Russia, Tunisia and all battle fronts. I'd know what he meant when he spoke of the left flank, the rear guard, this division and that. I'd know what was going on in the world.

"Downstairs, people would be gathering for dinner. Drinks would be served—only the finest wines and liquors. The discussion would be enthusiastic and well-attended. Over in the corner, there would be a frightened little man, working facts and figures in his pocket notebook: my scientist friend, developing a new drug that would eliminate the need for eight hours sleep. 'It will make you sleep twice as hard, for four hours,' he'd explain, when I'd ask after his latest calculations. Later, the same scientist would be huddled with a Russian chess master, needing my help to escape certain defeat.

"The dinner conversation would be politics, religion, history, literature, sports, theater, ballet . . . subjects I'd know as well as I'd know myself. Between courses, there would be dancing, and singing, and bawdy jokes. Maybe Rachmaninoff would sit down at the piano and throw off a concerto or two.

"At midnight, before dessert, I'd slip out the back unnoticed, determined to break things off with a woman who was hopelessly in love with me. The poor thing. I'd retreat to some Main Street dive. There would be a girl from a nearby striptease show sitting at the bar. After a few drinks, she'd invite me to her one-room apartment, on a bleak street in the center of Los Angeles. The room would be a horrible mustard color. The hot and cold water pipes would be in plain view, in one corner. She would tell me she wrote poetry, and read to me in a nasal voice. Everything about her would be beautiful and sad. I would not sleep with her. I would kiss her eyes and leave.

"Back home once more, I'd go to my desk and write. I'd write the story of the striptease girl with the nasal voice who read poetry. I'd write and think and write. If I knew a doctor, I'd probably call him over to give me a shot, so that I might get up the next day and do a little more.

"Then I'd go to bed and be afraid—for my children, for my wife, for myself."

APRIL 3, 1995

Now

I SET THIS TO PAPER, now, a different man than when I toured these hills just a few years ago. The transformation was a long time in coming, but immediate on arrival: one moment I was choking, the next I was breathing deep and full.

Now I am back at it, and fighting. My baby daughter, Antonia, has made all the difference. She is my small miracle, sent to release me from the furrows, to sustain me. My God, what a precious child! A brilliant treasure! She has my eyes, I am told, and my spirit. I cannot see the one, but I am cowed by the other. My Antonia is stubborn and bending, trusting and suspicious, tough as bricks and soft as down. She is resolute. She is whatever she needs to be to survive, and to drag me with her into the next century. She is every child I ever had, every woman I ever loved, every picture I ever made. She is my past, present, and future. We are the stuff of each other.

Here I am, now, counting on a child to save my life, to propel me forward. Just a few seasons ago—in the hills, on my bicycle—my future was in my legs, and in my stubborn pride. Today, everything I am is riding on Antonia. I sometimes think she was born unto me to loose the rust from my soul, and I pray she is up to it.

We do not have all the time in the world, but we have all the time we need. There will be hundreds of days like the day just before. We were on the beach in Santa

Monica. I had spent the morning at the studio, shooting a picture. We passed the afternoon in the sand and in the ocean. Antonia, not yet two years old, had no fear of the waves. It was the most remarkable thing. She looked so small against the big ocean, but she stood to meet it. She raced down the slope of wet sand to the surf and jumped into the water like it was nothing at all. She had her own strange momentum, her own purpose. I chased after her, and zipped her up into my arms before the big breakers could knock her down. She laughed and laughed. We picnicked on the beach—wine and bread, some fruit, and Cheerios for the baby—and then we went back home for a nap. I could not sleep. I did not need sleep. Lately, I have the energy of a man half my age. To nap, now, would be to miss something. I lay on the bed and watched my baby. In sleep, her crinkled-up face awakened my protective instincts: there was only me to keep the world away. I took out a pad and began to sketch. There was no way to hold the moment except to let it pass through my hands. Soon, the rustling of paper roused Antonia, and she picked up a pencil and made to join me. She held the pencil as I had taught her to hold a brush—pinched loosely among her tiny fingers—and her lines were steady and sure. (She is an artist, already!) She reached for her paints and moved across the room to the canvas. Always, she loves the heavy film of paint between her fingers, and she clapped her hands and splattered herself with red and blue and yellow. She had me doing the same, and before long there was paint all over our clothes, and in our hair, and in the space between nails and fingertips that can only be reached with luck and scouring.

I think back on that afternoon as the sum of our time together. This is what I have become, now. This is what matters.

God, I hate the way I must count such moments! But at my age, everything must be measured. This is the tragedy of our time on this earth, and it sets me reeling. I think of all the great days I will not be here to share with Antonia, of all the things I will never have a chance to teach her. Will she know happiness? True love? Consequence? Will she know me? I think of the mess I will leave behind. I think of the inventions I will not discover, the questions I will not answer, the wonders I will not taste, the grandchildren I will never cradle.

But that is not all. I think also of the pictures left to paint, the people left to meet, the characters left to play, the books left unread. I think how all the stories of my life will turn out, and know that I will be left hanging. Ah, yes. This is what it comes down to, now. Finally. I think of myself, and my leaving. There is no avoiding death, not anymore. I have ridden around it, on my bicycle, but it will catch me eventually. There will be no bullet through my head, and no gentler suicides, but it is coming. I know this now.

I am here for the duration, and yet when my time is called I wish to go out in style. There will be no pine box sunk six feet under ground, no urn to be placed on a mantel and forgotten. No. I have thought this through. There will be my dozen children, carrying me up a hill in Chihuahua and leaving me to rot in the hot sun. I can picture the scene, transposed over the fertile ground of my youth. (I have the specific hill mapped for my executors.) I will be laid to rest at the top of the rise, a feast for the vultures. My children will go back to the rest of their lives, and the birds will peck at what is left of me. They will lift me up, piecemeal, and defecate me out all over the countryside, returning me to the earth from which I had sprung, leaving me forever a part of all Mexico.

And the dance goes on.

INDEX

ELVIS AARON PRESLEY:
Revelations from the Memphis Mafia
ALANNA NASH with BILLY SMITH, MARTY LACKER, and LAMAR FIKE

Billy Smith, Elvis's cousin and the person he reputedly loved most after his own mother; Marty Lacker, Elvis's best man and the foreman of the famed Memphis Mafia; and Lamar Fike, part of Elvis's touring crew. Together, these men present the most candid portrait of Elvis ever on record.

Intimate gossip, close-up gems, and stunning allegations . . . An essential addition to the Presley library. *Entertainment Weekly*

GOLDEN GIRL:
The Story of Jessica Savitch
ALANNA NASH

The real-life tragedy that inspired the hit movie *Up Close and Personal* starring Robert Redford and Michelle Pfeiffer.

Compelling . . . makes you feel you are inside [Savitch's] brain. *Glamour*